Krishna in History, Thought, and Culture

Krishna in History, Thought, and Culture

An Encyclopedia of the Hindu Lord of Many Names

LAVANYA VEMSANI

ABC-CLIO™

An Imprint of ABC-CLIO, LLC
Santa Barbara, California • Denver, Colorado

Library of Congress Cataloging-in-Publication Data

Names: Vemsani, Lavanya, author.
Title: Krishna in history, thought, and culture : an encyclopedia of the
    Hindu lord of many names / Lavanya Vemsani.
Description: Santa Barbara : ABC-CLIO, 2016. | Includes bibliographical
    references and index.
Identifiers: LCCN 2015047019 | ISBN 9781610692106 (alk. paper) |
    ISBN 9781610692113 (ebook)
Subjects: LCSH: Krishna (Hindu deity)—Encyclopedias.
Classification: LCC BL1220 .V45 2016 | DDC 294.5/2113—dc23
    LC record available at http://lccn.loc.gov/2015047019

ISBN: 978-1-61069-210-6
EISBN: 978-1-61069-211-3

20 19 18 17 16   1 2 3 4 5

This book is also available on the World Wide Web as an eBook.
Visit www.abc-clio.com for details.

ABC-CLIO
An Imprint of ABC-CLIO, LLC

ABC-CLIO, LLC
130 Cremona Drive, P.O. Box 1911
Santa Barbara, California 93116-1911

This book is printed on acid-free paper ∞
Manufactured in the United States of America

Contents

Alphabetical List of Entries

Topical List of Entries

Preface

Krishna is a pervasive phenomenon in Hindu religion, and his influence extends beyond religion into all spheres of life. Literature, art, architecture, theology, philosophy, and meditation surrounding the divine persona of Krishna occupy a major place in Hinduism. As a result, Krishna is a major force in the history of Hinduism. *Krishna in History, Thought, and Culture*, brings disparate information on Krishna together in an easy-to-read, accessible form to anyone interested in learning about Krishna in particular and Hinduism in general. The encyclopedia covers textual sources, historical practice, philosophical traditions, devotional practices, classical theological scholarship, and the artistic and creative expression of Krishna from the earliest available reference (Vedic, 1300 BCE) to the present day, in an accessible style primarily suited to high school to undergraduate students as well as a general readership interested in the area of world religions. It covers India as well as places where major Krishna religious centers and temples are established worldwide. It gives as much importance to classical Indian sources as to the folk and worldwide literature on Krishna. It supplements reading materials for higher education, but will be useful for those seeking authentic information from all walks of life related to Krishna.

Organization and How to Use This Encyclopedia

Krishna in History, Thought, and Culture is composed of nearly 195 entries, ranging in length from 300 to 3,000 words. The encyclopedia is organized in an easy-to-use alphabetical format. Cross-references at the end of each entry alert the reader to other related entries. Each entry is also supplemented by a scholarly list of further readings not only to provide sources, but also to inform the reader about additional readings on the subject. The encyclopedia also contains topical lists of entries to assist researchers within a particular area in locating related material. Survey or overview articles are listed with other relevant entries given under appropriate headings. Blind entries have been created to accommodate references that may use different terms. Readers will notice that most entries contain words of Sanskrit and other Indian languages such as Braj Bhasha, Gujarati, Telugu, Tamil, and so on. However, I have not used any diacritics for any of the words, since there is no agreed-upon use of diacritics across all Indian languages, which may cause some confusion, although the usage of diacritics for Sanskrit is fairly standardized. Therefore for all the non-English words, I have used the most common English spellings encountered in general Indian and scholarly usage. Double a (aa) is used to indicate a long vowel in the case of names, such as Vaasudeva to differentiate it from Vasudeva.

Acknowledgments

I am grateful to the publishing staff at ABC-CLIO, especially my editors, George Butler and Anthony Chiffolo, who encouraged me to embark on this task and supported me in its timely completion. I would like to take this opportunity to thank my mentor, Dr. Paul Younger, who has always provided me immense support. I am greatly indebted to my friend R. L. Mohl, Interpretive Specialist, Hopewell Mound Museum, Ohio, who supported me through his many animated discussions, especially on Christianity and Krishna, as well as for his keen reading of earlier drafts of the manuscript. I would also like to thank my friends Brian Richards, Shawnee State University, and the staff of the Shawnee State University's library, and my colleagues in the department of Social Sciences for their friendship and support. Last but not least, I would like to thank my husband, Venkata Ramana Vemsani, and my son, Aashish S. Vemsani, for their unwavering support and love.

Introduction

In Krishna come together the history, theology, arts, culture, and devotional practice of Hinduism. Not merely a historical hero of ancient India, Krishna is also the representation of the living presence of the supreme God in Vraja. In Krishna temples across India and the world, associated with his incarnation, Krishna is lovingly roused in the mornings, bathed, fed, given rest in the evenings, and daily offered devotions by way of chanting, music, dance, and theater performances.

Geographically the association of Krishna with Vraja is indelible; the places connected with Krishna's life are mostly located on the Ganga-Yamuna *doab* (fertile plains between the Ganga [also sometimes referred to as Ganges] and Yamuna Rivers). However, the most important places (*tirthas*), such as Prabhasa and Dvaraka, are located on the now extinct Saraswathi River and its tributaries. Hence, Krishna's life connects to the tri-river (*triveni*) complex of the three holy rivers Ganga, Yamuna, and Saraswathi, the nucleus of which is located at the confluence of the three rivers, epitomized as the *Triveni Sangam*, forming the most important sacred geography of India, consisting of its heartland.

While the geographical location of Krishna's life had been precise, the determination of a time period for Krishna has not been as straightforward, and has been the subject of intense discussion and debate. Chronological approaches differ in placing the life of Krishna variously between 3000 BCE to 1500 BCE. The early date of 3000 BCE was established on the basis of astronomical calculations based on the precise data mentioned for the times of birth and death of Krishna in the *puranas*, while the date of 1500 is based on archaeological dating of the *Mahabharata* based on material identification from archaeological excavations. While numerous concepts such as bhakti, karma, *atma*, and so on are widely noted in the early *Vedas* (dated between 4000 and 1800 BCE), references to Krishna are scarce, but authentic. Therefore, historically Krishna tradition and practice can be divided into four phases to facilitate clear understanding: Phase 1, Beginnings and Early Vedic Krishna; Phase 2, Legendary and Classical Traditions of Krishna; Phase 3, Mystical and Passionate Devotional Traditions of Krishna; Phase 4, Creative and Passionate Devotional Traditions of Krishna.

1. The Beginnings and Early Vedic Krishna

Krishna's life has been the subject of numerous Hindu texts, in a variety of styles and languages. There are also comparative studies on Krishna in relation to other religious traditions, including Christianity, Buddhism, and Jainism. Unique types of texts continue to be produced, as the study of Krishna and earlier sources is undertaken not only in the Krishna theological centers of India and devotional centers, but in the academic departments of universities in India and the West.

Early textual references to Krishna are available in Vedic texts but only provide scant evidence: however, they provide typical information on Krishna and devotional traditions of Krishna (see the entry **Historical Krishna**). The earliest reference to Krishna in the *Rigveda* (1.22.164) mentions the cowherd who never stumbles, and another verse in the *Rigveda* (8.96.13) also mentions Krishna who is like a black drop. Although there are numerous other early references to Krishna in the Vedic texts such as the *Rigveda,* the reference in the *Chadogya Upanishad* (III.17.6), dated between 900 and 800 BCE, contains the clearest evidence, stating the name Krishna Devakiputra. It not only mentions Krishna, but also mentions that he is the son of Devaki. Even though the other early evidence from the early Vedic sources is ruled out as ambiguous by some scholars, the evidence of the *Chandogya Upanishad* establishes unequivocally that traditions of Krishna were well established by the turn of the first millennium BCE. Other later Vedic texts such as *Satapathabrahmana* and *Aitareya Aranyaka* (600 BCE) mention Krishna of the Vrishni clan.

Numerous nonreligious texts, such as grammar texts and historical texts, also provide early evidence of Krishna. Yaska's *Nirukta,* an etymological dictionary datable to 600 BCE, mentions the *syamantaka* jewel in the possession of Akrura. Panini's *Ashtadhyayi* (500 BCE), a grammar text, mentions Vaasudeva Krishna and his contemporaries Kaurava and Arjuna. Patanjali's text, the *Mahabhashya* (400 BCE), mentions musical group performances (*samsadi*) in the temple of Krishna, which brings forward not only the evidence for the existence of temples for Krishna, but also establishes the fact that music and performance traditions were associated with Krishna at such early dates. Megasthenes's account of India, the *Indica,* includes descriptions of the supreme God of Mathura, Heraklese, whose name was derived from Harikuleya (Harivamsa—lineage of Hari), meaning Krishna, born in the lineage of Hari.

The *Mahabharata,* including the text *Bhagavadgita* and its appendix, *Harivamsa,* provides the complete legend of Krishna and his devotional worship. Numerous inscriptions also provide early evidence of devotional traditions of Krishna before the beginning of the first millennium. Hindu sources note that its central text, the *Bhagavadgita,* was revealed by Krishna to Arjuna in a quick rendering while the armies were arrayed on the battlefield of Kurukshetra.

2. Legendary and Classical Traditions of Krishna (300 BCE–600 CE)

Though his life fits a pattern seen in the lives of prophets and saints, the legend of Krishna does not fit modern notions of biography. His life is seen as the play (*lila*) of the divine. Krishna is presented as human, yet the events of his life are touched with the miraculous. Thoroughly human and thoroughly divine, Krishna performs such superhuman feats as the raising of the dead. The search for Krishna is the joy and fulfillment of life in the numerous bhakti traditions of India.

Krishna brought the dead to life; for example, he brought his teacher Sandipani's son from Yama, brought his foster father Nanda from the world of Yama, and brought the divine Parijata plant from the world of Indra to the Earth. It is a common tendency for the biographies of prophets and divine persons to be embellished with miraculous details, and when the legends are thousands of years old, biography and mythology become one.

However, the dates posited by the *Mahabharata*, *Harivamsa*, *Vishnupurana*, and *Bhagavatapurana*, including the other *puranas*, put the birth of Krishna in 3227 BCE (see **Biography of Krishna**) and the death of Krishna in 3102 BCE. The Bharata war, in which Krishna participated at the age of ninety (see **Mahabharata**), took place in the year 3138 BCE. Krishna's death is recorded as having happened in the year 3102 BCE, which is also the beginning of the *Kali* age, as the *Dvapara* age ended with the death of Krishna (see **Cosmogony; Death of Krishna**). Krishna's birth, childhood, young adult life, education, and adult life are extensively described in the *puranas*.

The divinity of Krishna is apparent in his legend, even before his birth as it is narrated in the classical texts. It was revealed to Kamsa that the eighth child of his sister Devaki would bring an end to him, thus an end to his tyrannical rule. For this reason Kamsa subsequently imprisoned Devaki and Vasudeva when Krishna was born. As soon as Krishna was born he revealed his true form as Vishnu to his birth-parents, Devaki and Vasudeva. Subsequent events reveal how he showed the universe in his mouth to Yashoda, his adopted-mother, as if in play. His divine form is gradually revealed in almost all the events recorded in the mythology of Krishna.

The most central divine-human relation appears in the *raasalila* episodes of the Krishna legend. These events obliterate the distance between the divine and the human, as gender norms no longer apply. The world of Krishna's childhood in Brindavan, known often as Gokula, is in fact the divine world of Krishna, Goloka, according to the *Harivamsa*, the *Vishnupurana,* and the *Bhagavatapurana*. Although this fact is clearly noted in the major *puranas* narrating the legend of Krishna, art and performance traditions represent it only later. His message was clear from the outset, his followers understood it, and the simple folk of the cowherd village (Govraja), the cowherd maidens, were his first followers, who enjoyed the divine through their passionate devotion. The message came as a play that the most naïve of the crowd understood first, while the most esoteric message comes later in the form of the *Bhagavadgita*. It was this multifold nature of the message, and multiple approaches, that found ready followers. His followers include philosophical thinkers such as Uddhava and naïve village folk such as the *Gopis* and *Gopas*, as well as action heroes such as Arjuna. Meditation is as much a way to realize Krishna as the song and dance of the *Gopis* or the selfless actions of Arjuna.

The *Song Divine*, the *Bhagavadgita*, is the message of Krishna, which was directly imparted to Arjuna at the beginning of the Bharata war, while both the Kaurava and Pandava armies were arrayed on the battlefield of Kurukshetra (see **Bhagavadgita, Mahabharata**). It was directly watched by and imparted only to Arjuna, to whom the *Bhagavan* Krishna had provided *divyacakshus* (divine eyes/vision).

However, it was also indirectly watched by Sanjaya as he narrated what was happening on the battlefield of Kurukshetra to the blind king Dhritarashra (see **Bhagavadgita, Bhagavan, Mahabharata**). It was Sanjaya's recorded speech that brought the *Bhagavadgita* to Hindu laypersons, as part of the *Mahabharata* narration. Krishna's life is represented theologically as *lila* (divine play), narrations of which are preserved in several Hindu scriptures, including the *Mahabharata,* the *Harivamsa,* and the *puranas.* The stories of the life of Krishna are represented in literature, arts, and culture. They show that the simple life lived by the *Gopis* of Brindavan leads to salvation as much as the lives of the most knowledgeable yogis. The simple acts of life, when performed with detachment, without any intent of personal gain or loss, bring one closer to the divine and therefore salvation. Krishna is seen as the giver of joys, the fulfiller of wishes (see **Mathura**). The *Bhagavadgita,* the *Song of the God,* is the central scripture of Hinduism, which describes human life as opposed to the universal divine. The *Bhagavadgita* teaches the most esoteric scriptures of Hinduism, such as *samkhya,* yoga, bhakti, and *advaita,* in the simplest and most accessible style, which is one of the reasons for its universal appeal. During his life Krishna had a large number of followers who took part in his divine play and derived joy, but there were also a number of rivals that tried to belittle Krishna, and some even plotted to kill or oppose Krishna till their deaths (see **Jarasandha, Kalayavana, Kamsa, Narakasura**). However, the most interesting aspect of Krishna cosmology is that those who hate Krishna obtain salvation, as do those who love and follow Krishna. While his life illustrates the yoga of the simple life, the *Bhagavadgita* illustrates the yoga of detached action, ultimately putting multiple ways of religious practice such as yoga, *samkhya,* *karmayoga,* and bhakti on equal footing.

Krishna's life ended in an unexpected way (see **Death of Krishna**). It is narrated in the *Mahabharata* that after several Yadavas died in a skirmish that broke out in which they hit each other with *eraka* grass, Krishna and Balarama proceeded alone toward Prabhasa Tirtha (see **Prabhasa**). As Krishna sat under a tree in yogic posture, a Bhil archer, Jara, passing by while hunting, shot him in the big toe, mistaking it for the ear of a deer. The wound was fatal, so Krishna sent a message to fetch Arjuna, to whom he delegated the responsibility for the women and children of Dvaraka that were left as orphans after his death (see **Death of Krishna**).

The death of Krishna not only marks the end of his life, but the end of an era (*Dvaparayuga*), the end of his clan (annihilation of the Yadavas), and the end of his empire with his capital submerged under the sea. Krishna is considered the last and full incarnation of Vishnu, although there is hope for a future incarnation of Krishna among some sections of his followers.

Although the life of Krishna is mostly placed in the northern and northwestern regions of India, as recollected in the *Mahabharata* and the *puranas,* his stories spread throughout the length and breadth of India, though only scant references remain. From 300 BCE onward, references to him in Tamil *Sangam* literature, as well as by Greek writers such as Megasthenes and in inscriptions dating from 100 BCE, not only from northern India, but southern India, indicate the complex ways in which Krishna influenced religious practice in India. Accounts of Krishna produced between 600 BCE to 600 CE, therefore, placed the background of Krishna theology in India, which later evolved into a full-fledged, all-encompassing aspect of Hinduism.

3. Mystical and Passionate Devotional Traditions of Krishna (600 CE–1200 CE)

Evidence of the devotional traditions of Krishna is noticed from 400 BCE. As time progresses more evidence becomes available in the form of literature, art, philosophy, and religious practice. Although references to bhakti are encountered in the *Vedas* (*Rigveda* 8.27.11) and Upanishads (*Svetasvatara Upanishad* 3.5, 4.11, 6.21; *Katha Upanishad* 2.20, 23), most popular bhakti traditions are noted among the devotional traditions of Krishna. *Alvar* saints (600–900 CE) of the Srivaishnava devotional tradition are praised as the harbingers of *Virahabhakti*.

Around this time (600–900 CE), numerous saints of southern India known as the *alvars* began singing hymns through their revelations, thus gathering communities of followers based on the central bhakti worship to connect with Krishna as the central deity. This passionate worship then led to a number of faith communities being established across India, based on the bhakti practice. Unlike the ascetic practice of yoga, the bhakti practice is accessible to everyone, even householders. Several saints (*sants*) and their communities of followers (*satsangs*) became a notable phenomenon of Krishna worship from 1200 CE to 2000 CE. Although Krishna worship includes householders, both men and women equally, monasticism and monastic life is a common feature of the Krishna devotional traditions and often served as the backbone of faith communities for gatherings and offering of prayers during all the three phases of history noted above. The most preferred method of devoting oneself completely to Krishna is without any familial or worldly bonds. Several male and female ascetics are thus featured prominently in each phase of Krishna in history. Notable saints are often ascetics, although sometimes householders are also recognized as saints. Most ascetics practice moderation in their devotion, but it is also known that sometimes their ascetic practices are taken to extremes.

4. Creative and Passionate Devotional Traditions of Krishna (1200–2000)

From the twelfth century onward Krishna is not confined to temples and textual compositions, but is found in all cultural forms through the development of passionate expressions of bhakti (see **Bhakti**; *Gaudiya* **Vaishnavism**; **Madhva** *Sampradaya*; **Sants**; **Srivaishnavism**; **Vallabha Tradition**; **Yoga and Krishna**). Devotion to Krishna is now expressed in new ways such as in art, dance, and music (see **Music and Krishna; Painting and Krishna; Temples of Krishna in India**) as well as in textual compositions. Numerous regional performing arts styles of India owe their origin to Krishna devotion (see *Ankiya Nat*; *Bhagavatamela*; *Jatra*; *Kirtana*; *Kuchipudi*; *Manipuri* **Dance**; *Samaj Gayan*). Although these styles include intense devotion to Krishna in his physical form, such devotion far surpasses his human existence (see **Brindavan; Cosmogony; Cosmology;** *Kirtana*; **Mandala; Mantra;** *Samaj Gayan*).

Numerous other traditions of bhakti are encountered from the twelfth century onward: the Vallabha tradition (*Pushtimarga*) is based on *Vastalya* bhakti; the Haridasi, Caitanya, and Radhavallabha traditions are based on *Madhurya* bhakti. Individual practice, as well as practice of the numerous devotional traditions, resulted in a repository of artistic, literary, and cultural expressions. Therefore, Krishna's influence is felt in numerous fields in art, literature, and architecture.

Texts of faith followed, such as commentaries, glosses, translations, interpretations, both in literary as well as other performance and artistic media, created by followers of Krishna (see **Alvars**; **Bhagavatapurana**; **Bhagavatas**). The divinity of Krishna is always expressed by these texts, and the variety of epithets used to refer to Krishna indicates his significance in Hinduism. As a deity Krishna is most commonly referred to as *Bhagavan*, Vaasudeva, *Purnavatara*, *Vyuha*, Vishnu, *avatara*, and Jagannatha. Each of these terms later acquired theological significance, and the conviction that Krishna is the only god to provide *moksha* from the samsara, whom the followers can please by total devotion, gained numerous followers, resulting in all these epithets turning into nomenclature for the faith communities, such as Bhagavatas, Pancaratrikas (based on the theology of *vyuhas*), and Vaishnavas (based on the theology of *avatara*).

Even though the followers of Krishna increased, each devotional community functioned as an independent institution rather than being allied to a central organization. Vaishnavism mainly grew among the populace without much support from the top. The kings or ministers proclaimed their faith periodically, which resulted in the construction of numerous large temples with substantial endowments.

However, sometimes the wealth of the temples was the cause of persecution, as beginning in the twelfth century some kings attempted to monopolize the riches of the temples. Persecutions were not commonly known or recorded prior to 1200 CE, although incidents such as attacks on and destruction of temples and beheading of the followers have been recorded periodically.

Although over the thousands of years several royal families came to be associated with Krishna, it is mainly through the contributions of the common people living the simple life that most rituals and religious practices of Krishna were developed. Depicting Krishna is considered a service (*seva*), so depictions of Krishna in painting, poetry, sculpture, and other art forms are abundant and continue to multiply. Mythological texts place Krishna's life in the Braj region in Mathura, Vraja, and Brindavan, yet Krishna's influence is much more widespread. Over a thousand years creative traditions based on the Krishna legend exploded: Krishna is prevalent in literature, art, and architecture. There is little historical data, but Krishna is known through numerous later creations in art, literature, and architecture. Literary and artistic creations in Sanskrit and regional languages abound across India. Although the mythological and philosophical tracts continued to underlie the developments from 1000 CE onward, a clear path in the way of expressions of emotion (bhakti) as a way of devotion dominated popular religious practice. Of the numerous devotional movements, foremost is that of the *alvars* of southern India, followed by several saints in other parts of India, such as Mira Bai,

Kabir, Namdev, Vallabha, and Ramanuja (see *Alvars*; **Bhakti**; **Mirabai**; **Namdev**; **Ramanuja**; *Sants*; **Vallabha**). Expressions of passionate devotion toward Krishna took various forms in dance, theater, music, painting, and poetry, which was the most common.

Since the nineteenth century, Hinduism has entered academia; while the *Vedas* and early religions of India attracted initial academic interest, Hinduism and its popular practice gained attention gradually. Krishna, recognized as one of the main deities of Hinduism, received immense attention, followed by scrutiny and academic curiosity. Historical studies based in archaeology, inscriptions, numismatics, and other early evidence began dominating the field, and the traditional doctrines and classical texts were analyzed with a sense of mystique as well as doubt. Prior to this academic interest, only people of faith had written about their faith and religion to other people of their faith, which had limited circulation. Academic study of Krishna has truly broadened the horizons leading to comparative, analytical, and theological studies.

This book aims to shed light on the life of Krishna, as well as examine the influence of Krishna on art, architecture, literature, geography, philosophy, and religion. For numerous people Krishna is the divine being, and the quest for realization of Krishna (bhakti) forms a lifelong mission. The search for Krishna is the joy and the fulfillment of life in the numerous bhakti traditions of India. It is hoped that this book will help in this quest by providing information on an extensive range of subjects as discrete as art, literature, religion, and philosophy.

As such, this book has several aims: to shed light on the life of Krishna; to examine the influence of Krishna on art, architecture, literature, geography, philosophy, and religion; and to assist both those who seek academic understandings and those who wish to walk more personally with Krishna.

A

ADVAITA

Advaita (nondualism) is a central Vedic concept adopted by theistic Hindu traditions and referred to as *advaita* Vedanta. *Advaita* Vedanta is the first attempt to reconcile popular theistic Hinduism with the central philosophical concepts of the *Vedas*. Devotional Hinduism, especially Vaishnavism, is greatly beholden to *advaita* Vedanta. The *Vedas* contain esoteric religious philosophy accessible only to the religious specialists of Hinduism, while *advaita* Vedanta is available to all the practitioners of popular theistic Hinduism. Almost all the theistic schools of India derive their philosophical understanding from *advaita*, except for some of the theistic traditions that are aligned with *advaita* Vedanta, which holds an exactly contrarian viewpoint. Vedic *advaita* (nondualism, also known as monism) philosophy is closely bound to Krishna in the *Bhagavatapurana* and the *Bhagavadgita*. Therefore *advaita* Vedanta could rightly be described as the most influential formative principal associated with the theistic devotional traditions of Hinduism.

The *Vedantasutras* (also known as *Brahmasutras*) attributed to Badarayana, along with the Upanishads and the *Bhagavadgita,* form the three main source texts of *advaita* Vedanta. The *Brahmasutras* comprise the quintessence of Vedanta in fifty-five couplets divided into four sections. The first section establishes the supremacy of Brahma as the ultimate reality, based on numerous selections from the Upanishads. The second section counters the opposite views on Brahma as the supreme reality, utilizing selections from the Upanishads. The third section prescribes directions for achieving ultimate knowledge (*brahmajnana*) of Brahma, the universal soul. The fourth section describes the results of achieving such supreme knowledge of Brahma. The *Brahmasutras* could rightly be termed the bridge between the *Vedas* and popular theistic Hinduism. Two of the most common theistic schools of Hinduism, *advaita* and *dvaita*, base their philosophical conventions on the *Brahmasutras*, thereby influencing popular Hinduism in numerous ways. While early theological and philosophical explorations of *advaita* are attributed to Sankara, its true theological and philosophical application and widespread practice is only seen in Krishna bhakti traditions. Jnanadev, *Varkari sant* of Maharashtra, translated the *Bhagavadgita* into Marathi, interpreting it in the light of *advaita* philosophy, which is the mainstay of the bhakti tradition of Maharashtra. There are numerous philosophical and theological traditions derived from *advaita* Vedanta such as *suddhadvaita* (pure monism) and *visishtadvaita* (qualified monism), which form the foundational philosophy of several Krishna bhakti traditions. While *visishtadvaita* is the most important philosophy of the Ramanuja school of Vaishnavism (Srivaishnava tradition, Swaminarayan tradition, etc.), it also served as the basis for

---

Brahmasutras

The *Brahmasutras,* with the *Vedas,* form the basic philosophical nexus of the bhakti traditions of India. The text of the *Brahmasutras* is a compendium of Vedic concepts composed by Badarayana (100 CE), drawing from the celebrated Upanishads (*Chandogya, Brihadaranyaka, Katha, Taittiriya, Kaushitaki, Mundaka,* and *Prasna*). Although the text of the *Brahmasutras* is one of the *Prasthanatrayi* (three source texts), it is extensively quoted in theological and philosophical texts of the Vedanta religion, hence directly linking the tradition to the *Vedas.* The *Brahmasutras* contain the essence of Vedanta in fifty-five couplets divided into four sections. The first section establishes the supremacy of Brahma as the ultimate reality, based on numerous selections from the *Upanishads.* The second section counters the opposite views on Brahma as the supreme reality, utilizing selections from the Upanishads. The third section prescribes directions for achieving ultimate knowledge (*brahmajnana*) of Brahma, the universal soul. The fourth section describes the results of achieving such supreme knowledge of Brahma. The *Brahmasutras* could rightly be termed the bridge between the *Vedas* and popular theistic Hinduism. Two of the most common theistic schools of Hinduism, *advaita* and *dvaita*, base their philosophical conventions on the *Brahmasutras,* thereby influencing popular Hinduism in numerous ways.

---

the Vishnuswami, Caitanya, Madhva, and Vallabha traditions. A further exposition of *visishtadvaita* known as *suddhadvaita* forms the most important philosophical background of the Vallabha tradition. Hence *advaita* could be understood as the most influential philosophical theology of Hinduism. Anthropologists and ethnographers who study the modern-day practice of Hinduism without paying close attention to the philosophical basis afforded by *advaita* Vedanta for the popular practice of Hinduism may miss these historical links, and may understand Hinduism merely as a disparate practice of devotees toward numerous personal deities. *Advaita* may help in the understanding of the unique structure behind these seemingly disjointed practices of worshipping various personal deities with utmost devotion in popular Hindu practice.

Advaita has its roots in the meditative and contemplative traditions of the Upanishads. Even though the Upanishads do not refer to *advaita* by name, references to *advaita* could be gleaned from the Upanishads in sayings such as "*tat tvam asi*" (*Chandogya Upanishad* 6.10.3), meaning "you are that," which is in conformity with the *advaita* convention that the Brahma (universal soul), and the *atma* (individual soul) are one. This understanding insinuates that Brahma and the creation are one, not two. Sankara's statement, "*Brahma satym . . . Jagam midhya*" (Brahma is the only reality . . . Creation is an illusion) echoes this perception that everything that is created in this world is not true reality, except for the soul, which is ultimately destined to join the Brahma. According to this conviction creation emanates from Brahma and returns to Brahma, hence it has a temporary existence, and therefore the only true goal of existence is Brahma, the ultimate reality.

Advaita philosophy profoundly influenced theistic Hinduism as noted by its centrality in a number of bhakti practices prevalent in Hinduism since the turn of the first millennium. Although *advaita* is a philosophical tradition based on Vedanta, its widespread application is prominent in devotional practice and popular Hinduism.

See also: Bhakti; Caitanya; *Dvaita;* Madhva; Ramanuja; Srivaishnavism; Vallabha

Further Reading

Anderson, J. 2012. "An Investigation of *Moksha* in the *Advaita Vedanta* of Shankara and Gaudapada." *Asian Philosophy* 22 (3): 275–287.

Dalal, N. 2009. "Contemplative Practice and Textual Agency in *Advaita Vedanta*." *Method & Theory in the Study of Religion* 21 (1): 15–27.

Nicholson, A. J. 2007. "Reconciling Dualism and Non-Dualism: Three Arguments in Vijnanabhiksu's *Bhedabheda Vedanta*." *Journal of Indian Philosophy* 35 (4): 371–403.

Ram-Prasad, Ch. 2002. *Advaita Epistemology and Metaphysics: An Outline of Indian Non-Realism*. London: Routledge.

Raveh, D. 2008. "*Ayam aham asmiti*: Self-Consciousness and Identity in the Eighth Chapter of the *Chandogya Upanisad* vs. Sankara's *bhasya*." *Journal of Indian Philosophy* 36 (2): 319–333.

AKRURA

Akrura is described in multiple roles: as the greatest devotee of Vishnu, a *Bhagavata* (devotee of *Bhagavan*), a close relative of Krishna, and a councillor of Kamsa, the king of Mathura. The name Akrura is derived from the Sanskrit word *krura* (evil, cruel), joined by the negative prefix represented by *a*, thus giving the meaning of nonevil or noncruel. True to his name, he was known as a very gentle person among the clan of Vrishnis, the clan of Krishna. Krishna and Balarama gave Akrura the *nijarupa darsana* (vision of true form) resting in the divine world *Vaikuntha* (heaven of Vishnu).

Kamsa was aware of the virtuous reputation Akrura held among the Yadavas, and especially the Vrishni family to which Krishna belonged. Hence, hiding his true intentions, Kamsa sent Akrura on a mission to visit Braj, where a number of Kamsa's deputies had not only failed to kill Krishna, but they themselves were miraculously killed. Kamsa requested that Akrura visit Braj as his envoy to invite Krishna and Balarama to Mathura to participate in a wrestling match during the bow festival. Akrura, not suspecting any foul play, duly reached Braj and dispatched the royal invitation to Krishna and Balarama to participate in the wrestling match in Mathura. Krishna and Balarama left for Mathura, taking leave of their family and friends who were overcome with grief on their leaving. On their way to Mathura they stopped at a lake for a short rest. Akrura went to the lake to perform ritual ablutions, taking a dip in the waters. As Akrura took a dip in the lake and uttered the *aghamarshana* mantras, he had a vision of *Vaikuntha* in which Krishna and Balarama appeared as Vishnu and Sesha. Akrura's vision portrayed Vishnu sitting on the lap of the thousand-headed divine serpent Sesha surrounded by numerous other deities. Akrura was bewildered, and he came out of the lake to check on

Krishna and Balarama. He saw them sitting on the chariot. He took a dip in the lake again and found the previous vision of *Vaikuntha* again with Krishna and Balarama appearing as Vishnu and Sesha. This second vision convinced Akrura, who quickly realized the true nature of Krishna and Balarama. However, he completed his rituals at the lake and paid homage to Krishna and Balarama, continuing the journey quietly toward Mathura. Akrura was persuaded that a cosmic event would unfold in Mathura, acknowledging the divine portents of his vision. This place of Akrura's divine vision is marked by Akrur *ghat*, a lake in Brindavan. It is one of the sacred

Akrura drives Krishna and Balarama to Mathura, which marks Krishna's departure from Vraj. Watercolor illustration of *Bhagavata Purana (Ancient Stories of the Lord)* text, ca. 1730. (Los Angeles County Museum of Art)

tirthas visited by devotees and pilgrims undertaking the Braj *parikrama*. Near this lake is a temple containing Krishna, Balarama, and Akrura, reminiscent of the vision of Akrura. After the death of Kamsa, Akrura remained a trusted general of Krishna and continued to serve him. Krishna trusted him immensely, so he appointed Akrura as the guardian of the *syamantaka* gem, which produced a set amount of gold each day. Akrura took good care of the gem, as well as the wealth produced from it, continuing to support the prosperity and welfare of the Yadavas.

See also: Balarama; *Bhagavan*; Braj *Parikrama*; Brindavan; *Gopas* and *Gopis*; Kamsa; Mathura; Vishnu; Vrishnis

Bhagavata Mantra

The *Bhagavatapurana* describes Akrura as meditating on the *bhagavata* mantra, which resulted in his obtaining the view (*darsan*) of the lord in his original form (*nijarupa*). Although the *Bhagavatapurana* describes other instances in which Krishna gave his *darsan* to a number of his devotees, Akrura's experience is unique. Akrura's *darsan* of Krishna differs in its emphasis on his ritual oblations accompanied by the mantra. The central place of the mantra in devotion to *Bhagavan* Krishna is obvious in its descriptions.

Further Reading

Couture, A. 1986. "Akrura et la *Bhagavata* selon le *Harivamsa*." *Studies in Religion* 15 (2): 221–232.

Vemsani, L. 2006. *Hindu and Jain Mythology of Balarama*. Kingston, Canada; Lewiston, NY: Edwin Mellen.

ALVARS

Alvars (Vaishnava saints of South India) are crucial in establishing Krishna as the central deity of Vaishnavism in South India by establishing Krishna as the full incarnation (*purnavatara*) of Vishnu (see *avatara*), and also for popularizing the emotional worship (bhakti) of a personal deity in the form of self-surrender (*prapatti*). *Alvar* is a Tamil word meaning "one who is immersed," indicating a person's emotional immersion in devotion toward the personal deity, but not a physical immersion such as in water. Established Vaishnava tradition records twelve *alvars* as the founders of the Srivaishnava tradition: Poigaialvar, Peyalvar, Tirumalisalvar, Kulasekhara, Tondaradipodialvar, Tiruppanalvar, Bhuthatalvar, Periyalvar, Andal, Tirumangai, Nammalavar, and Madhurakavialvar. The *alvars* came from diverse social backgrounds: some were of the Brahman caste; Tiruppanalvar is said to have been a *pancamam* (fifth caste/outcaste); Kulasekhara *alvar* was a Kshatriya, belonging to a royal family; while Andal was a woman. Although the Srivaishnava tradition considers the *alvars* to have lived around 3000 BCE, historical dating places these Vaishnava saints between 600 and 900 CE. *Alvars* play an important role in the Hindu religion for their diversity, contributions to devotional practice, and bringing religious philosophy to the masses through their poetical compositions in the medium of common language. Twenty-five compositions by *alvars* are collected in *Nalayira Divya Prabandham*, a Tamil title that simply means "sacred collection of four thousand verses." Poems of the *Divya Prabandham* are considered to be revealed texts similar to the *Vedas*, although their composition is attributed to

---

Virahabhakti

Virahabhakti (devotion of anxiety in separation) is the devotion of pining for Lord Krishna. Initially, *virahabhakti* is expressed as the complete devotion of the *Gopi* maidens after Krishna left Brindavan as described in the *Bhagavatapurana*. Since the sixth century *Virahabhakti* has been the most common mode of the bhakti practice of devotional traditions, popularized in the *alvar* poetical devotional traditions. *Araiyar Sevai*, a theater festival held each year for ten days during January–February at the temple of Sri Muddu Tirunarayan Swami in the village of Selvamudaiyan Pattai (Jalladampet) and in other temples on different occasions, provides an aesthetic expression of the *virahabhakti* of the *alvars*, their longing for union with the soul of Krishna, which sometimes may take the expression of a lonely, desperate, lovelorn woman's longing to unite with her lover.

the *alvars,* unlike the *Vedas,* most of which are anonymous compilations that are not ascribed to human authors. However, poems of the *Divya Prabandham* are particularly significant for two reasons: first, because they contain the esoteric meaning of the Upanishads, and second, because they are composed in Tamil, not in Sanskrit, the language of Hinduism. These two features meant a phenomenal change in how the divine was approached by various sections of the society. While the earlier texts composed in Sanskrit could only be recited by men of upper caste (often only of the Brahman caste), the poems of *Divya Prabandham* could be recited by anyone, including women, thus laying the foundation for bhakti, personal devotion to the divine. This inspired several bhakti traditions, including those of Caitanya, Vallabha, Surdas, and so on, and popularized the bhakti tradition as one of the foremost modes of approaching the divine. *Alvars* are regarded as Vaishnava saints within Hinduism, although the Srivaishnava community regards *alvars* as founder-saints of their tradition, worshipping them at home and at temples. The *Divya Prabandham,* the central text of Srivaishnavas, is recited along with Veda mantras in temples and homes, and it is also a part of marriage ceremonies. In the Srivaishnava tradition faith is more important than one's social status, such as caste or gender, in approaching the divine. Early hagiographic literature on the *alvars* was late, and available sources barely date to the late twelfth to fifteenth centuries, although the collection of *Nalayira Divya Prabandham* was composed earlier and popularly acknowledged since the eleventh century, while textual commentary on some of the *Divya Prabandham* poems was likewise written around the eleventh century. The first of the most renowned early hagiographies is from *Manipravala* (Gems and Corals) literature known as *Guruparampara Prabhavam* (The Splendor of the Succession of Teachers). The next most well-known text, known as *Divyasuricarita* (The Narrative of the Divine Beings), is attributed to Garuda Vahana Pandita and is written in Sanskrit. The *Alvarkal Vaipavam,* written in Tamil by Vativalkiay Nampi Tacar, contains the biographies of the *alvars,* as well as summaries of their poems. *Periyatirumuti Ataivu* contains brief biographical details of the *alvars.*

Alvars are the true harbingers of the bhakti tradition, which serves as the major framework for popular religious practice in modern Hinduism. Although only scant information is available about their lives, *alvars* are nevertheless revered in numerous temple festivals of South India.

See also: Andal; *Mutatalvars*; Nammalvar and Madhurakavialvar; Periyalvar; Ranganatha; Srirangam Temple; Srivaishnavism; Tirupathi; Venkatesvara

Further Reading

Ayyangar, S. K., ed. 1975. *Arayirappati Guruparamparaprabhavam.* Tiruchirapalli.
Champakalaxmi, R. 1981. *Vaishnava Iconography in the Tamil Country.* New Delhi: Orient Longman.
Cutler, N. 1987. *Songs of Experience: The Poetics of Tamil Devotion.* Bloomington: Indiana University Press.
Hardy, F. 2001. *Viraha-bhakti: The Early History of Krishna Devotion in South India.* Delhi: Oxford University Press.

Narayanan, V. 1994. *The Vernacular Veda: Revelation, Recitation, and Ritual*. Columbia: South Carolina University Press.

Varadacari, K. C. 1966. *Alvars of South India*. Bombay: Bharatiya Vidyabhavan.

ANDAL

Andal is the only female saint among the twelve *alvars* (Vaishnava saints of south India). "Garland" is the signature of Andal (she who rules); she is also known as Goda (Kotai in Tamil, indicating her long black hair). Bhakti is sometimes equated with making garlands for the god, such as "weaving garlands" in Tamil bhakti tradition, which indicates the central place the passionate devotion of Andal holds in Indian bhakti tradition, and in particular, the Srivaishnava tradition of south India. If her service represents the intense feelings of bhakti (devotion), then she herself is the embodiment of the *Gopis* (cowherd maidens) or the primary devotees of Krishna, with whom the tradition of emotional bhakti originated. In this tradition of the *Gopis'* whole-hearted devotion, Andal is not only an individual, but also a personified representation of the emotions of the devotees of Krishna. Thus Andal evokes awe and inspiration combined with passionate emotions in followers of Krishna. For those devotees (especially those devotees in south India) reading her *pasuralu* during daily prayers in *Dhanurmasam* (*Margali* in Tamil), which occurs during the winter months of December and January in temples across India, she is one with them, expressing passionate emotion to the lord Vishnu (Krishna).

Andal composed fifteen poems, organized in two titles. Andal's first composition is a single poem of thirty stanzas known as *Tiruppavai*, and her second composition is a set of fourteen sequential poems known as *Nacciyar Tirumoli*. Both are read in Vishnu temples in south India as part of festivals and daily rituals, and especially during *Dhanurmasam*. Andal has reserved a special place for herself in the hearts and minds of Krishna devotees, not only through her devotion to Krishna (Vishnu), but also because in historical India, she is the only woman to have been chosen by the Lord to be united with him in life, through marriage. These two

Culture and Media

Andal's legend is well known beyond Tamilnadu in all the states across India. *Pavai Nonbu* is undertaken during the month of *Margali* (Dhanurmasam), during which recitation of Andal's *Tiruppavai* and discussions on the text of *Tiruppavai* are held in temples across India and abroad in reverence to Andal.

Several TV shows and dance-dramas are performed each year about Andal's life. The first movie on Andal, released in 1949, was produced in Tamil, with TV shows that followed on National Television of India. Andal is still the beloved goddess of young women, and her shrines are found all across India; shrines dedicated to her are also found in American Hindu temples in Pittsburgh, Lanham, and so on.

Andal, the foremost female saint of India. Copper alloy sculpture, ca. 14th century. (Los Angeles County Museum of Art)

events, that is, Andal's passionate love for Krishna and her final union with Krishna (through her marriage to Sriranganatha in Srivilliputtur), thus dominate the hagiographic literature about her life. Several biographies about her life have been known since the twelfth century. The most well-known version of Andal's life in Telugu appeared as early as the fifteenth century: *Amuktamalyada,* written by Krishnadevaraya (1471–1529), emperor of Vijayanagara. *Amuktamalyada* is not, in the strict sense, merely a translation, but a free adaptation of the famous legend of Andal in Telugu, into which Krishnadevaraya has introduced a number of philosophical and theological elements, in addition to a number of cultural facts particular to the Telugu region during the late fifteenth century. Although in the *Amuktamalyada* Andal lived in Srivilliputtur, true to her legend, she is described like a typical Telugu princess, and several cultural features of Andhra Pradesh are added to the legend.

Although Andal lived in the ninth century, legend places her life in the ninety-eighth year of the *Kaliyuga* (about 3000 BCE), which would make her birth occur only a century after the death of Krishna (3102 BCE). At least two scholarly English translations of Andal's Tamil works exist. There are numerous scholarly articles and several books as well as several dance dramas and children's versions of Andal's story.

See also: Alvars; Brindavan; *Gopas* and *Gopis*; Radha; Ramanuja; Ranganatha; Srilaxmi; Srirangam Temple; Srivaishnavism

Further Reading

Dehejia, V. 1990. *Andal and Her Path of Love*. Albany: SUNY Press.

Hudson, D. 1980. "Bathing in Krishna: A Study in Vaishnava Hindu Theology." *Harvard Theological Review* 73 (3/4): 539–566.

Hudson, D. 1996. "Andal's Desire." In *Vaishnavi: Women and the Worship of Krishna*, edited by Steven J. Rosen, 171–211. New Delhi: Motilal Banarsidass.

Hudson, D. 2010. "Andal Alvar: A Developing Hagiography." In *Krishna's Mandala: Bhagavata Religion and Beyond*, edited by J. S. Hawley, 175–209. New Delhi: Oxford University Press.

Jaganathachariar, C. 1982. *The Tiruppavai of Sri Andal: Textual, Literary, and Critical Study.* Madras: Arulmigu Parthasarathy Swami Devasthanam.

Narayanan, V. 1999. "Brimming with *Bhakti*, Embodiments of Shakti." In *Feminism and World Religions*, edited by Arvind Sharma and Katherine Young, 25–77. Albany: SUNY Press.

Narayanan, V. 2007. "Weaving Garlands in Tamil." In *Krishna: A Sourcebook*, edited by Edwin F. Bryant. New York: Oxford University Press.

ANIMAL PROTECTION AND VEGETARIANISM

Devotees of Krishna in particular and Vaishnavas in general play an active role in animal protection and promoting a vegetarian lifestyle. Krishna is always depicted with cows and as a deity preferring a vegetarian diet. *Gopashtami* is the festival of the cattle, celebrated during the month of *Kartik* (October–November). During *Gopashtami* the cows and other domestic animals are washed, decorated, and hand fed with food specially cooked for them. *Gopashtami* is celebrated to mark the special occasion of the day Krishna began grazing the cows as a cowherd. Vaishnava devotional groups support cows and maintain cow shelters (*Gosalas*). The Bishnois are a Vaishnava group in northwestern India who are strict vegetarians and live by twenty-nine rules, two of which pertain to animal and tree protection: "Have pity on all animals and love them," and "Do not cut green trees, protect the environment." Devotional traditions of Krishna such as Srivaishnavism, *Pushtimarga* (Vallabha tradition), Caitanya Vaishnavism, and ISKCON (International Society for Krishna Consciousness) strongly support vegetarianism and expect all adherents to follow a vegetarian lifestyle. The Vaishnava groups of the Braj region maintain several forests in Govardhan and the Mathura region along the pilgrimage route of the Braj *parikrama* (circumambulation). The pilgrimage path is marked by twelve major forests or groves, twenty-four small groves, and numerous ponds and lakes, all of which could have succumbed to commercial interests, mining activities,

Gosalas

Krishna is most commonly depicted with cows. His relationship to cows is part of his life as a cowherd. Hence, Krishna devotional traditions support vegetarianism and cow protection. *Gosalas* (cow shelters) are maintained by the Krishna temples and devotees in almost all the major cities across India. Sick, old, and abandoned cows are provided shelter and care in the *gosalas*.

Hindu devotees offer prayers to a cow during *Gopashtami*, also known as *Goshtashtami*, in Hyderabad, India. On this day cows are given a bath, decorated with colorful clothes and offered special food. (Mahesh Kumar A./AP Photo)

industry, and commercial exploitation, if the devotional groups were not actively engaged with their protection. Numerous forests have been destroyed in the last fifty years. By fostering a lifestyle that promotes animal welfare and conservation of nature, Krishna devotees have made a positive contribution. According to the devotional traditions of Krishna, the lives of humans and animals are combined in samsara (the cycle of birth and death); they have a joint existence and a joint fate, sharing karma. Hence it is essential to religious practices to consider the ecology when humans and other life forms exist as a single, shared, and interconnected reality.

See also: Braj *Parikrama*; Brindavan; Forests of Krishna; Mathura; Nandgaon; Twelve Forests of Braj

Further Reading

Chapple, C. K. 1993. *Nonviolence to Animals, Earth, and Self in Asian Traditions.* Albany: SUNY Press.

Framarin, C. G. 2011. "The Value of Nature in Indian (Hindu) Traditions." *Religious Studies* 47 (3): 285–300.

Jain, P. 2011. *Dharma and Ecology of the Hindu Communities*. Surry: Ashgate.
Lodrick, D. O. 1981. *Sacred Cows, Sacred Places: The Origin and Survival of Animal Homes in India*. Berkeley: University of California Press.

ANIRUDDHA

Aniruddha is a grandson of Krishna, son of Pradyumna and Prabhavathi. Aniruddha is also a *vyuha* incarnation, one of the major forms of the four *vyuhas* revered as the primary descending divine forms of the ultimate divine Vishnu, according to the *Pancaratra* system of philosophy. Aniruddha is described in a significant role in the *Bhagavatapurana* as one of the central figures of the Vrishni heroes (also known as the *Pancaviras* (five heroes): Krishna, Balarama, Pradyuma, Aniruddha and Samba), while he is also influential in the philosophical sphere as one of the *vyuhas*. The marriage of Aniruddha leads to an inadvertent war with the demon Bana, the eldest son of Bali, a demon, vanquished by Vishnu during one of his previous incarnations as Vamana *avatara* (dwarf incarnation). The war between the Yadavas and the armies of Bana, father of Usha, ensues without the express knowledge of or involvement from Aniruddha. It so happened that Aniruddha had been envisioned in a dream by Usha (daughter of Bana), who fell in love with him instantly, even though she became pensive as she did not know any details about him, let alone have any hope of meeting her dream paramour. However, her close friend, Chitralekha, knew magical arts with which she could view anyone remotely, and she could also transport anyone from remote locations without their knowledge. Through this method they launched a search, and finally Usha identified Aniruddha as her paramour. Chitralekha subsequently transported Aniruddha to Usha's palace, while he was still asleep. Upon waking up in Usha's palace, a surprised Aniruddha found Usha, fell in love with her immediately, and stayed in her palace. Happily living in the palace of Usha, Aniruddha even forgot to contact his family and provide information to them about his residence away from home. It took some time for his father, Pradyumna, and his grandfather, Krishna, to notice that Aniruddha was missing. When Krishna and the Yadavas found out that

Parikshit and Janamejaya: Narrative Beginnings

Parikshit and Janamejaya, son and grandson of Aniruddha respectively, are connected with the popular retelling of the *Bhagavatapurana* and the *Mahabharata*. Indeed, the current versions of the *Bhagavatapurana* and the *Mahabharata* are traced to these retellings. When Parikshit was cursed to die within a week from a snakebite, he arranged to listen to a narration of the *Bhagavatapurana*. This upset his son Janamejaya immensely, so he planned to exterminate all the snakes by conducting *sarpasatra* (sacrifice of snakes). Janamejaya arranged for the first narration of the *Mahabharata* at the *sarpasatra*. These narrations remain in the memory, according to the tradition.

Aniruddha was living in Bana's palace, they laid siege to the kingdom, thinking that Bana had orchestrated the kidnapping of Aniruddha, imprisoning him in the palace. Battle escalated so much that Shiva finally intervened on the side of Bana and negotiated a ceasefire between Krishna and Bana, which ended the war. Both sides agreed to the marriage of Usha and Aniruddha, and Krishna returned to Dvaraka with the bride and groom, after attending a happy wedding ceremony on the invitation of Banasura in Sonitapura.

See also: Avatara; Dvaraka; Mathura; *Pancaratra*; Pradyumna; *Vyuhas*

Further Reading

Bryant, E. 2003. *Krishna: The Beautiful Legend of God (Srimad Bhagavatapurana Book X)*, 264–271. London: Penguin Books.
Iyengar, S. A. 1956. *Aniruddha Samhita*. Mysore. eBook: Archive.org.

ANKIYA NAT

Ankiya Nat (also known as *Sattriya*), a single-act theatrical style created by Sankaradeva, is a crucial element of Assamese Vaishnavism centered on devotion to Krishna. It has assumed such an important part of Krishna devotion that it has become a necessary part of the training of *sattradhikara. Sattradhikara* are well versed in composing and organizing this type of religious theater. *Ankiya Nat* is performed in the late evenings in the *namghar* in the *satra*, and performances may continue into the wee hours of the morning. Subjects of *Ankiya Nat* plays address religious themes, directed by a *sutradhara* who also doubles as the narrator of the play. *Ankiya Nat* is usually performed by amateur *bhaktas* for the devotional audiences of the *satra*. In addition to the actors, a *sutradhara*, and musicians (sometimes a full orchestra), this mixed form of musical theater also features large effigies to represent the characters of demons in the epics and the *purana* stories being depicted. Sometimes the effigies may exceed fifteen feet in length, requiring a number of people to manipulate their movements during the play. The effigies are

---

Symbol of Assamese Culture

The *Ankiya Nat* was selected as part of the world's Intangible Cultural Heritage (ICH) by the Asia Pacific Cultural Center (APCC) of UNESCO (United Nations Educational, Scientific, and Cultural Organization). It is said that Sankaradeva (1449–1549), who composed seven *Ankiya Nats,* was the founder of the style; only six are currently available. Out of these six *Ankiya Nats*, five are based on stories of Krishna: *Kaliya Daman, Patni-Prasad, Kaliya-Gopal, Rukminiharan,* and *Parijatharan.* The *Ankiya Nat* still remains close to its original form, even after five hundred years and after numerous political and economic changes in Assam. One of the ingenious features of the *Ankiya Nat* is its use of paper masks that are sometimes as tall as fifteen feet high. These masks commonly represent demons or other animal characters.

made of bamboo covered with papier-mâché masks representing the demons appropriate to the play. Effigies of minor characters and animals could also be constructed, in small or large sizes as the play requires. Effigies can also be used to create special effects for mythological beings. A particular style of ritual drumming is usually performed in the beginning at the gateway of lights (*agni-gada*) specially arranged for the occasion on the opposite side of the *namghar*. It is followed by the *sutradhara* reciting a relevant verse from the play being staged, and it concludes with a song. Then Krishna makes an entrance with dance accompanied by song and music, proceeding to the *manikuta* in the *namghar*. Firecrackers may sometimes mark Krishna's entrance. The actual play commences after these introductory performances. As the play continues, the *sutradhara* remains on the stage directing the music and the actors, as well as giving commentary to the audience when necessary. *Ankiya Nat* plays are also performed outside of the *satra* in nonreligious public theaters as a symbol of traditional Assamese culture. There may be minor adjustments when they are performed in a theater as opposed to the spiritual settings of the *namghar*. However, the content of the particular *Ankiya Nat* being staged is never changed. In this respect, the *Ankiya Nat* style has avoided the fate of the *Jatra* form of theater of Bengal, which was completely transformed by adopting it for secular theater. *Ankiya Nat* developed in the Krishna devotional traditions of Assam employing the regional arts and language as its mainstay. Consequently, even though the *Ankiya Nat* plays are spiritual in nature, they epitomize the popular culture of Assam.

See also: Jatra; Performing Arts and Krishna; Sankaradeva; *Satra*

Further Reading

Barua, B. Kumar. 1954. *Ankiya Nat: A Collection of Sixteen Assamese Dramas of Sankaradeva, Madhavadeva, & Gopal Ata*. Guahati: Government of Assam, Department of Historical and Antiquarian Studies.
Sarma, S. 1985. *Madhavadeva*. New Delhi: Sahitya Akademi.

ARATI

An *arati*, also spelled *arti* or *harati*, is a symbolic offering of a devotee's self to the deity by involving the participant's five senses through light, sound, touch, smell, and vision. Every service of *arati* includes elements to invoke the five senses of the participants. *Arati* is an important service performed by the devotee or through the mediation of a priest. *Arati* involves showing lighted camphor along with the offerings of food, garlands, and so on to the deity in the morning, afternoon, evening, and at night. During the performance of *arati*, lighted camphor or a lighted lamp of ghee (clarified butter) is waved in front of the deity, music is played, *arati* songs are sung, a conch is blown, and bells are rung. In the temple the *arati* service is more formal and elaborate than that which a devotee might perform at home. Each *arati* involves a different dressing pattern, adornments, and presentation of the deity to the devotees. Krishna temples closely follow this pattern of services with their own minor variations according to local traditions and practice. However, most Krishna temples dedicated to devotional traditions such as Srivaishnavism, Caitanya Vaishnavism, and the Vallabha tradition follow an eight-period (*ashta-kala*) *arati* closely corresponding to Krishna's Vraja-*lila* as follows:

1. *Mangala Arati*: This is offered at 4 a.m. As the deities are waking up, they are offered various items to begin their day.
2. *Sringara Arati*: Deities are ready for the day. A snack is offered with *arati*.
3. *Rajabhoga Arati*: Deities are offered a midday meal and prepared for their afternoon nap.
4. *Utthapana Arati*: Deities are awakened from their nap and offered a snack.
5. *Sandhya Arati* (Twilight *Arati*): Deities return home at the end of an active day.
6. *Vyalubhoga Arati*: Deities are offered *arati* and the evening meal.
7. *Sayan Arati*: The last offering of the day; this service may involve *jhoola seva* (swing). The deities are supposed to take a rest, and they are left alone after this service.
8. *Raasalila*: Deities are at rest, but they are expected to sneak out and enjoy *Raasalila* or *vahyali* (a walk in the moonlit night). No formal *arati* is performed for this last period, but devotees are encouraged to continue their personal meditation and singing of *bhajans* (devotional lyrics).

The names of the *aratis*, their timing, and the rituals offered with each *arati* period may differ from temple to temple; however, the preceding list shows the most common practice. *Arati* is an important part of devotional practice in which the direct involvement of the devotee precludes every other aspect of the ritual, and the spiritual involvement of the devotee is an essential part of the ritual, transforming the performance of mundane activities and imparting deep meaning to the ritual.

See also: Bhakti; Caitanya Vaishnavism; *Lila*; *Raganuraga*; Srivaishnavism; Vallabha Tradition

Further Reading

Fuller, C. J. 1992. *Camphor Flame: Popular Hinduism and Society in India*. Princeton: Princeton University Press.
McHugh, J. 2014. "From Precious to Polluting: Tracing the History of Camphor in Hinduism." *Material Religion* 10 (1): 30–53.

ARJUNA

Arjuna, the middle Pandava (son of Pandu), is a close associate of Krishna. Their intimacy was so absolute that Krishna summoned Arjuna when his death was imminent, and Krishna also became Arjuna's charioteer during the Bharata war, disregarding his own reputation. A number of crucial events link their lives meticulously together. Krishna was always present during all the major events in Arjuna's life. The most important of all events was the Bharata war on the battlefield of Kurukshetra, at the beginning of which, to dispel Arjuna's *vishadayoga* (yoga of dejection), Krishna gave him *divyacakshus* (divine eyes) and imparted divine knowledge to him through the *Bhagavadgita*. Arjuna and Krishna are depicted as a *Naranarayana* pair in the *puranas,* and their image is depicted in the Vishnu

Krishna and Arjuna in a chariot in Rishikesh, India. A sculptural representation of the most important event in the life of Arjuna, this image depicts when Krishna imparted wisdom to Arjuna at the beginning of the great war of the Bharatas, the *Mahabharata Yuddham*. (Bhairav/ Dreamstime.com)

Ayudhapuja

Arjuna's bow is known as Gandivam and his arrow is known as Angelika. Arjuna is recognized as the best archer and is depicted as a master of weapons in the *Mahabharata*. Legend has it that the Pandavas hid their weapons in a *shami* tree (*Prosopis cineraria*) while assuming their disguises to complete their exile incognito for a year. At the end of the year they removed their weapons and offered their reverence to the tree for safeguarding their weapons. The day before *Dassera* is known as the day of *ayudhapuja* (obeisance to the weapons), which was considered the day when Arjuna removed his weapons from the tree. In modern India, people do not commonly buy or worship weapons; therefore their place is taken by utilitarian equipment such as vehicles and any appliances made of base metals such as refrigerators, stoves, and vacuum cleaners, which are often bought for the occasion. Another important tradition during *Dassera* associated with the *shami* tree, known as *Jammi chettu* in Telugu, is exchanging its leaves with friends and family as a sign of good luck. For this reason the *Jammi chettu* tree was selected as the state tree of the newly formed state of Telangana.

temple in Deogarh (325–450 CE). In this pairing, Arjuna is Nara, the human counterpart of Narayana (Vishnu), who is represented by Krishna in his earthly *avatara*. The *Naranarayana* form of Vishnu is one of the central forms of worship in the Swaminarayan tradition. The following is a brief review of the *Mahabharata* narrative, which depicts Krishna and Arjuna as close compatriots.

Khandava Forest

Khandava *dahana* (burning the Khandava forest) is the foundation of the beginning of the independent Pandava state. When the Pandavas staked their claim to a share of the Kuru Empire, and the Kauravas gave the Pandavas only a patch of wild forest on the outskirts of the Kuru kingdom to establish their state, Krishna helped Arjuna clear the forest by burning it down. Subsequently, the Pandavas built a great capital there called Indraprastha. Therefore, it is clear that Krishna advised the Pandavas to obtain their share of the kingdom and supported them in establishing their own independent state.

Arjuna and Subhadra's Marriage

Krishna orchestrated the marriage of Arjuna to his sister Subhadra while Arjuna was in his year of pilgrimage to atone for his breach of the marriage contract that he entered with his brothers and their common wife Draupadi. Arjuna arrived in Dvaraka as a mendicant sage during this yearlong pilgrimage visiting sacred sites in India. Krishna promptly appointed Subhadra to serve the sage, whose true identity was known only to Krishna. The two fell in love with each other and married even though their elder brother Balarama had other plans for the marriage of Subhadra.

Sashirekha and Abhimanyu's Marriage

Several years later Krishna repeated the same type of astute marriage plan. He arranged for the marriage of Sashirekha (daughter of Balarama) and Abhimanyu, the son of Subhadra (sister of Krishna) and Arjuna. Sashirekha also has another name; she is called Vatsala. Balarama, the elder brother of Krishna, fixed Sashirekha's marriage with Lakshmana, the son of Duryodhana. Krishna invited his sister Subhadra home along with her son Abhimanyu, while the preparations for Sashirekha's marriage were underway. Sashirekha and Abhimanyu fell in love as soon as they met, and they eloped, cancelling the wedding of Sashirekha with Lakshmana, Duryodhana's son. While this incident embarassed Balarama, it enraged Duryodhana. However, the familial bonds of Krishna and Arjuna were strengthened because of the weddings of Subhadra and Sashirekha.

Bharata War

This episode demonstrates the soul connection of Arjuna and Krishna. Both Duryodhana and Arjuna visited Krishna to seek his support when it was clear that the Bharata war was imminent following Duryodhana's refusal to return the Pandava kingdom to them after their return from a fourteen-year-long exile. This exile included a year of incognito residence in a neighbor's kingdom, which had been imposed on them because of a dice game staged by Duryodhana as a ruse to drive the Pandavas out of their kingdom. To enlist support for the Bharata war, both cousins, Duryodhana and Arjuna, simultaneously reached Krishna while he was resting. Arjuna decided to sit by the side of Krishna's feet, and Duryodhana chose to sit near Krishna's head, waiting for Krishna to awaken. As Krishna opened his eyes, he first noticed Arjuna sitting at his feet, and then he also noticed Duryodhana sitting near his head. Considering their appeal for support in the imminent war, Krishna assented to providing support to both of them. He left the choice to Arjuna and Duryodhana by pitching himself on one side as a noncombatant supporter, and his well-trained fighting army on the other side. Krishna indicated that since he had noticed Arjuna first, he should be allowed the opportunity to make his choice first. Arjuna then chose Krishna nonchalantly, leaving the army to be taken by Duryodhana, which made Duryodhana immensely glad. This episode is seen as an indication of the human being's connection to the divine (the *Naranarayana* bond), since Arjuna chose Krishna, a single person who would not even fight in the war, leaving aside a well-trained army of Yadavas, which would fight in the war.

Arjuna is the most important associate of Krishna. The divinity of Krishna and the divine message is revealed in multiple ways through his associates. While the *Gopis* envisioned it in the *Raasalila*, Arjuna envisioned it in the *Bhagavadgita*, Uddhava received it in the *Uddhavagita*, and Sridama received it in the immense grace in the form of wealth. Arjuna as a representative of quintessential human ties to the worldly duty (dharma) of action is depicted as connecting to Krishna in action, receiving the message of *karmayoga* (yoga of action) as an important mode of connecting with the divine. Therefore, Arjuna performs an important role in the cosmological revelation of the ultimate divine and the goal of human life.

See also: Avatara; Balarama; *Bhagavadgita*; Draupadi; *Lila*; Subhadra: Krishna's Sister

Further Reading

Chandramouli, A. 2013. *Arjuna: Saga of a Warrior-Prince*. New Delhi: Platinum Press.
Hiltebeitel, A. 1988. *Cult of Draupadi*. Chicago: University of Chicago Press.
Katz, C. R. 1989. *Arjuna in Mahabharatha: Where Krishna Is, There Is Victory*. Columbia: University of South Carolina Press.

ASHTACHAP

Ashtachap designates the eight devotional poets of Braj, associated with *Pushtimarga*, who were nominated by Vitthalnath, son of Vallabha, to sing their lyrics in the temple directly to Krishna. *Ashta* is a Sanskrit term denoting the number eight, while *Ashtachap* means "eight seals" after their signature lines that were generally included in their poems indicating their individual compositions. Four of them, Surdas, Paramanandadas, Kumbhandas, and Krishnadas, were disciples of Vallabha, while Cahurbhujdas, Nandadas, Chitswami, and Govindswami were disciples of Vitthalnath. Number eight (*ashta*) is significant in the devotional traditions of Krishna in general, while it is especially significant in the Vallabha tradition with which these eight poets (*Ashtachap*) are associated. Most importantly, Vitthal-nath instituted eight *Gaddis* to succeed him in carrying on the Vallabha tradition; there are also numerous other significant *ashtas* (eights) associated with this tradition such as the eight-period worship (*ashtayam seva*) and eight friends (*ashta-sakhis*) of Radha. Although it is not clear by whom or when the term *asthachap* was coined to refer to the eight musicians, its first use could be attributed to Vitthalnath in the *Vartha* literature of the Vallabha tradition.

The most famous singers among the *ashtachap* are Surdas, Nandadas, and Para-manandadas. Surdas's legend is the most famous and celebrated of all the eight poets, and his connections outside of the Vallabha tradition are notable as well. Surdas is said to have instructed Abul Fazle, the famous singer in the court of the Mughal emperor, and is said to have sung in the court of the Mughal emperor himself. Legend also has it that Kumbhandas had been invited to the Mughal court, but he did not enjoy singing there or staying away from his favorite deity, Srinathji. Its founder, Vallabha, initiated Nandadas, whose dedicated service to Srinathji and the Vallabha tradition was noted with praise in the later *Varta* literature. Krishna-das was a close contemporary and associate of Surdas, who was also initiated by Vallabha. Not much is known about Krishnadas's life other than his service and devotional singing in the Vallabha tradition. However, Krishnadas's death is mentioned in the *Varta* literature, which noted that he died when he accidentally fell into a well. Chitswami was a local *Chaube (Chaturvedi)* Brahman from Puchchari, who was noted for his unconventional ways before joining the Vallabha tradition. Chitswami was said to have been one of the delinquent *Chaubes* sitting on the stairs of Vishramghat mocking the visiting devotees with playful banter. Krishnadas was a *Kunbi Patel* from Gujarath, who was appointed manager of the Srinathji temple in Govardhan. A number of events are recorded about his disputes within the Vallabha tradition and his excesses as manager of the Srinathji temple. Krishnadas was also known to have banned Vitthalnath from the Srinathji temple over a dispute about a wealthy female devotee who was allowed by Krishnadas to have a special *darshan* during the offering of *Mahabhog* to Srinathji. Krishnadas was also known to have played a crucial role in excluding *gosvamis* (followers of Caitanya Vaishnavism) from the services of Srinathji. Krishnadas is said to have been responsible for the fire that burned down the huts of *gosvamis* of the Caitanya tradition near Radhakund, and eventually a compromise was negotiated between the Vallabha and Caitanya followers of Krishna. Eventually an image of Madanmohan was given to the *gosvamis*, but their role in the Srinathji temple was eliminated gradually.

See also: Brindavan; Govardhan; *Haritray*; Jayadeva; Jiva *Gosvami*; Kumbhandas Gorva; Mathura; Rupa *Gosvami*; Six *Gosvamis*; Surdas; Vallabha Tradition; Vitthalnath

Further Reading

Hawley, J. S. 1983. *Krishna, the Butter Thief.* Princeton: Princeton University Press.
Hawley, J. S. 2005. *Three Bhakti Voices: Mirabai, Surdas, and Kabir in Their Time and Ours.* New Delhi: Oxford University Press.

ASTHANA

Asthana is a tradition commonly associated with the *Pushtimarga* (way of divine grace) tradition. *Asthana* is a Sanskrit word meaning court, as in the word *rajasthana,* meaning king's court. Services to Krishna in this tradition are organized so that they closely resemble Krishna's adopted father's court in Brindavan, where Krishna was reared as a child. *Sevas* (services) performed in the temple are customized to please a child, closely resembling the loving, nurturing care of a mother (*vastalya bhava*). The services replicate the loving bond of Krishna and his adopted mother Yashoda in Vraja. Temples are commonly referred to as *Devasthana*, which can be translated as God's court. Similarly, the *Pushtimarga* tradition refers to temples as *haveli*, a term for palace. Therefore, it is only natural that *asthana* refers to God's court in the *haveli*. According to the *Pushtimarga* tradition, all the services are voluntary, and the employees of the temple are referred to as *sevaks*, meaning servants.

See also: Goloka; Govardhan; *Haveli Sangit*; Nandagopa; Srinathji *Haveli* Nathdvara; Vallabha; Vallabha Tradition; Vitthalnath; Yashoda

Further Reading

Haberman, D. 1988. *Acting as a Way of Salvation.* New York: Oxford University Press.
Wulff, D. M. 1984. *Drama as a Mode of Religious Realization.* Chico, CA: Scholars Press.

AVATARA

The Sanskrit word *avatara* simply means incarnation, although it has acquired a special theological connotation in Hinduism. The concept of *avatara* is associated primarily with Vishnu, even though its fluid use in describing the descent of any divinity to the earthly realm has become common since the turn of the first millennium. Vishnu, as part of the holy trinity (Brahma, Vishnu, and Shiva) of Hinduism, is the primary god responsible for the maintenance of the balance between good and evil on earth. Hence, Vishnu is born on earth any time the balance between good and evil is disturbed. The Vedic Vishnu signifies *vish*, to spread. In fact, Vishnu's fifth *avatara,* Vamana, illustrates this in demonstrating the spread of Vishnu spanning the earth, the sky, and the underworld. Therefore, conceptually Vishnu, even though staying in his divine world, maintains his constant presence on earth with one foot firmly on the earth, according to the theology of Hinduism. Vishnu's weapon, *Sudarsanachakra* (wheel), and his associates such as his mount Garuda and serpent-bed Sesha are also known to have incarnated along with him during his numerous incarnations in this world.

Numerous types of *avataras* came to be associated with Vishnu. Classical Hinduism presents ten *avataras* of Vishnu (*dasavataras*): Mastya (fish), Kurma (tortoise), Varaha (boar), Vamana (dwarf), Narasimha (man-lion), Parasurama (Rama with axe), Rama, Krishna, Buddha, and Kalki. The Buddha, the ninth *avatara,* is the founder of Buddhism, while Kalki is a future *avatara,* expected to incarnate right before the end of creation (*kalpanta*). Sometimes the Jain *tirthankara* Mahavira is listed as the tenth *avatara,* while Kalki is eliminated from the list. The eighth *avatara* of Vishnu, Krishna, is the most important *avatara* of Hinduism. Krishna is denoted variously as *purnavatara* (full incarnation), *lilavatara* (incarnation in play), and finally as the Supreme God from whom Vishnu takes his form, in a reversal of roles. According to this final theological concept, Krishna is an *avatara* and the Supreme Lord at the same time. Followers of Krishna, such as Vallabha and Caitanya, are designated as *avataras* of Krishna. Krishna as an *avatara* manifestation illustrates several aspects that came to be associated with the theological concept of *avatara* within Hinduism.

The *amsavatara* is another theological concept of incarnation, one that is more flexible than the concept of *avatara*. *Amsavatara* is considered the partial incarnation of Vishnu. Several minor personalities—followers or companions of the central avatara of Vishnu—can be identified with Vishnu simultaneously through this concept. Some minor *avataras* such as Hayagriva (horse incarnation) are not part of the *dasavatara* list, but they could be identified with Vishnu as *amsavatara*.

Purnavatara (full *avatara*) is a term used to equate Vishnu and Krishna in south Indian Vaishnavism, especially the Srivaishnava tradition, which is also the central philosophy of later devotional traditions noticed in northern India. The names Krishna and Vishnu are utilized simultaneously to refer to the Supreme God in devotional Vaishnavism. Numerous *alvar* poems name Vishnu; however, their narrative references allegorically indicate Krishna as the central god being addressed. The Maharashtrian *Varkari* tradition names its central god Vitthala (Vishnu), although the central deity is in fact Krishna, worshipped along with his wife Rukmini as seen in the *Varkari* tradition's central temple of pilgrimage (*vari*) in Pandarpur.

The *arcavatara* is the central deity of worship (*arca/arcana*), also regarded as the incarnation of Krishna (although referred to as Vishnu) in several temples across India. Sri Ranganatha of the Srirangam temple is regarded as a worshipful incarnation (*arcavatara*) of Krishna. Srinathji worshipped in the Vallabha tradition's temples is considered a manifestation of Krishna himself in the form of Srinathji in Braj. Alternatively, the central deity of a temple could also be described as *Kaliyuga Pratyaksha Daivam* (Revealed God of *Kaliyuga*) to indicate that the image in the temple itself is the revealed form of Krishna, which can be noticed in the temples of Tirupathi, Guruvayur, and several others across India.

The *lilavatara* is the *avatara* of Vishnu in play, a term that is routinely used to describe the Krishna *avatara*. Krishna's incarnation is understood to be a part of the divine play (*lila*). Krishna is presented as an actor playing on the stage of Brindavan.

Less frequent is the concept of *gunavatara*, which refers to the gods as manifestations of certain qualities of nature (*satva, rajas, tamas*). For example, Vishnu is referred to as a manifestation of *satva* at the beginning of creation, while Brahma and Shiva are considered the manifestations of *rajas* and *tamas* respectively.

The *vyuhavatara* is a combination of two concepts, *vyuha* and *avatara*. *Vyuha* is another concept used with Krishna in the *puranas* and the *Mahabharata*, but with a very different view of the divine manifestation. As a *vyuha*, Vaasudeva (Krishna) is the second manifestation following Samkarsana, unlike the *avataras* where Krishna is the primary *avatara* manifestation, almost equaling Vishnu in importance.

Avatara is a central concept most commonly used and expressed in the devotional traditions of Krishna. As such *avatara* is the most important concept in Vaishnavism. Several teachers of philosophical systems as well as Vaishnava *gurus/ acaryas* are also identified with Krishna, but only as partial incarnations. This is *avataravatara*, an incarnation from an incarnation. Caitanya is considered an incarnation of Krishna, while Vallabha is considered an incarnation of the mouth of Krishna. However, this is not a new phenomenon. Kapila, the founder of Samkhya, had been identified with Vishnu previously. In fact, in the *Bhagavadgita*, Krishna identifies several beings, trees, animals, and so on as identical to himself.

Avatara is a concept frequently used in relation to Vishnu, although its use extends beyond the standard list of *dasavataras* (ten incarnations) and includes several other modes of incarnation. *Avatara* as a concept cannot be narrowly defined, but is typical of Vishnu, emblematic of his involvement with creation as a maintainer of balance between good and evil on Earth. As Krishna is equated with Vishnu, several concepts of *avatara* (*vyuha, arcavatara, avataravatara, amsavatara,* and *lilavatara*) are noted in relation to Krishna; so also the names of Vishnu, which are used to designate Vishnu, are simultaneously used to refer to Krishna.

See also: Bhagavan; Caturvyuhas; Krishna; Narayana; *Purusha;* Vishnu

Further Reading

Biardeau, M. 1994. *Etudes de Mythologie Hindoue II: Bhakti et Avatara.* Paris: Ecole de Paris.

Couture, A. 2001. "From Visnu's Deeds to Visnu's Play, or Observations on the Word *Avatara* as a Designation for the Manifestations of Visnu." *Journal of Indian Philosophy* 29 (3): 313–326.

Jacobson, K. A. 2008. *Kapila: Founder of Samkhya and Avatara of Vishnu* (*with a translation of Kapilasuri Samvada*). New Delhi: Oxford University Press.

Narayanan, V. 1985. "*Arcavatara*: On Earth as He Is in Heaven." In *Gods of Flesh, Gods of Stone,* edited by J. P. Waghorne and N. Cutler, 53–66. New York: SUNY Press.

Parrinder, E. G. 1997. *Avatar and Incarnation: The Divine in Human Form in the World's Religions.* Oxford: One World.

Sheridan, D. P. 1984. "Sacramentality of Kishna-*Avatara* in *Bhagavata-Purana*." *Journal of Dharma* 9 (3): 230–245.

Vekathanam, M. 1988. "Mystery, Myth, History, the Dimensions of Spirituality in the Context of *Avatara*." *Journal of Dharma* 13 (3): 204–216.

BALARAMA

Balarama is the elder brother of Krishna, and also an *amsavatara* of Vishnu. Variously, he is also identified as an *avatara* of Sesha, which characterizes his mythology, popular worship, and rituals; and he is also identified as the first *vyuha,* Samkarsana, among the four *vyuhas* (*caturvyuhas*). Balarama as the foremost *vyuha,* Samkarsana, is known as the harbinger of knowledge. Balarama's birth is narrated as a miraculous event in the *puranas.* Devaki conceived Balarama in prison, but the goddess Nidra transferred him as an embryo during the seventh month of Devaki's pregnancy to Rohini, another wife of Vasudeva. As a result, Balarama was born to Rohini in Vraja, where Krishna was transferred after his birth to be raised by his adopted parents Yashoda and Nanda. Balarama was a constant companion of Krishna in all the events of his life that took place in Vraja, Brindavan, and Dvaraka. During their childhood in Vraja, Balarama was always with Krishna: they stole butter, chased calves, or played in the cow pens. During their young adult life in Mathura, Balarama and Krishna participated in numerous significant events together: a wrestling match in Mathura, education with the sage Sandipani, battles with Jarasandha and Kalayavana. It was only during their adult life as rulers of Vraja and Dvaraka, respectively, that Balarama and Krishna found their separate paths. Major incidents in the life of Balarama indicate his authority on primal knowledge. The true nature of the divine is revealed with the intervention of Balarama during the numerous events narrated in the *Bhagavatapurana.* The first incident of this nature unfolded when Balarama complained to Krishna's mother Yashoda that Krishna had eaten dirt. Yashoda promptly made Krishna open his mouth, revealing a vision of the universe (brahmanda) in his mouth, thus allowing her to understand Krishna's true nature. Krishna then used his divine *lila* to cloud her mind, which

---

Luk Luk Dauji

Luk Luk Dauji can be translated as "peeping elder brother," a name given to Balarama, Krishna's elder brother. Dauji was said to secretly look at the *Raasalila* in Brindavan, hence the name *Luk Luk Dauji* was given to him. An alternative explanation states that from inside his temple near Govind Kund, Dauji looks at the *Chappanbhog* (fifty-four varieties of food) cooked for Krishna in the *Pushtimarga* tradition's kitchen located opposite to the temple, hence giving him the name *Luk Luk Dauji.*

Krishna killing King Kamsa, and Balarama slaying a wrestler called Chanura. Watercolor, ca. 1630, Rajasthan, India. (Los Angeles County Museum of Art)

made her forget what she had seen in his mouth and act like his usual doting mother. This is the first incident of the role of Balarama as the harbinger of true knowledge. In other events Balarama imparted appropriate knowledge to others. Another aspect of his divine nature as the protector of resources is revealed in the *purana* texts in which he vanquished numerous demons such as Dhenuka, Pralamba, and Dvivida, restoring groves, forests, and farms to the people of Vraja. Balarama also changed the course of the river Yamuna in Vraja, bringing its water to the center of Vraja. Balarama imparted wisdom to Rukmi, brother of Rukmini, when Rukmi chased them during the wedding of Rukmini and Krishna. Balarama was married to Rohini, who is depicted as the goddess of drink. She is also described as older and larger than Balarama.

Although Balarama was like Krishna's alter ego and supported him in all his efforts, there are a few instances when Balarama opposed Krishna. Balarama was performing a pilgrimage during the Bharata war, thus missing it, but he returned in time to watch the last wrestling match between Duryodhana and Bhima. Balarama opposed Bhima, who was obliged to hit Duryodhana on the thighs with a mace, as Duryodhana's body was made invincible as steel by the touch of his mother, Gandhari, due to her special boon, except for his thighs, which were covered by his shorts and remained untouched by her. Balarama also proposed to conduct his daughter Sashirekha's marriage with Duryodhana's son, Lakshmana Kumara, but Krishna finally managed to get Sashirekha married to Abhimanyu, son of Arjuna and their sister Subhadra. The deaths of Balarama and Krishna happened at about the same time, but Balarama's death differs significantly from that of the other Yadavas' and also from Krishna's. He is not subject to fate (karma) as they are. While the Yadavas were immersed in their fight, Balarama could see the signs of the end of the age (*Dvaparayuga*); he withdrew and sat in meditation on the sandy beach of the ocean. Balarama's divine form, Sesha, emerged from his mouth, left the Earth and joined other serpents waiting for him in the *nagaloka*, the world of serpents. Noting Balarama's exit from the world, Krishna left the coast of Prabhas and entered the forest. While sitting in meditation under a tree in the forest, Krishna lost his life due to an arrow shot by the hunter Jara.

Six major temples of Balarama are mentioned in the pilgrimage texts of Mathura: Unchagaon, Aring, Ram Ghat (Shergarh), Baldeo, Nari, and Talvan. Of these, Baldeo (Dauji) is the oldest and most popular. Balarama is the *kul-devata* (clan deity) for *Ahivasi Gaur* Brahmans, who officiate as priests in a number of Balarama temples in the Mathura region. The priests of the Baldeo temple also belong to the *ahivasi* community, but they have adopted the Vallabha tradition, although they function independently and follow their own traditional ritual practices. The main icon of Balarama in Baldeo was tested by the Department of Archaeology and Museums in Mathura, which confirmed that it is one of the oldest images of Balarama, belonging to the Kushan period (200 BCE), based on the inscriptions on the back of the icon. The Baldeo temple also hosts an image of Balarama's wife Revati, which might belong to a later period. Revati's image is smaller than Balarama's image and is placed in a corner of the temple opposite Balarama. The current temple and its practices were initiated by Gokulnath, fourth son of Vitthalnath, who discovered the image of Balarama when informed by two cowherds that cows were letting milk fall on a stone in his village. Gokulnath had the stone extracted and consecrated in the local temple. It is now housed in a new large temple, which stands by the old abandoned temple. Balarama is also the patron deity of the royal house of Datiya. Many Bundelas also revere Balarama and have their customary life cycle rites, such as ear piercing (*karnavedha*), first head shaving (*siromundan*), and so on, conducted in Baldeo.

Balarama is also an important deity in Jainism. He is depicted as the ninth *Baladeva*, a series of associate divinities of Jain *Tirthankaras*. Jain canonical literature portrays Balarama and Krishna as the cousins of Neminatha, the twenty-second *Tirthankara*. Hence, the life story of Balarama and Krishna is narrated along with the life story of *Tirthankara* Neminatha. Images of Balarama and Krishna are also depicted in Jain temples flanking Neminatha on his two sides, although in a smaller size than the images of Neminatha. Jain narratives of Balarama preserve unique elements of his life story, such as his mother's dream visions and a series of past lives leading up to his birth as Balarama. Balarama is projected in a positive light, unlike Krishna, and depicted as the purveyor of dharma. According to the Jain tradition mothers of *salakapurushas* (distinguished beings) envision typical dream sequences indicating the birth of each individual divinity. Hence, Balarama's mother Rohini saw four dreams indicative of the impending birth of a *Baladeva*, a series of associate gods of *Tirthankaras*. Significant elements commonly associated with the birth of Balarama in the Hindu story are missing, such as the embryo transfer from Devaki to Rohini, which was accomplished by the goddess Nidra. In the Jain stories, Balarama is the protector, teacher, counselor, and companion of Krishna. He trains and accompanies Krishna to the wrestling match in Mathura, and also helps Krishna in the wars with Jarasandha. However, Jain stories typically avoid descriptions of Balarama's association with violent wars. Hence his battles with Pralamba, Dvivida, and Dhenuka are missing, while his role in the battles with Jarasandha is minimal. Balarama is depicted as an upholder of Jain dharma, including nonviolence, and as a protector of Krishna in the Jain texts.

Balarama is an important associate deity of Krishna in Hindu and Jain traditions. Some elements of the stories in the Hindu and Jain traditions may differ, but both traditions assign Balarama an important role as the protector of the child Krishna and as supporter of the dharma.

See also: Avatara; Braj *Parikrama*; Childhood of Krishna in Brindavan; Jarasandha; Kalayavana; Revathi; Subhadra: Krishna's Sister; Vitthalnath; *Vyuhas*; Yashoda

Further Reading

Bigger, A. 2004. *Balarama im Mahabharata*. Frankfurt am Main: ZDMG.
Joshi, N. P. 1979. *Iconography of Balarama*. New Delhi: Abhinav Publications.
Sanford, W. 2005. "Holi through Dauji's Eyes: Alternative Views of Krishna and Balarama in Dauji." In *Alternative Krishnas*, edited by B. Guy. Albany: SUNY Press.
Vemsani, L. 2006. *Hindu and Jain Mythology of Balarama*. New York: Edwin Mellen.

BAREDI

Baredi is a style of dance-drama said to have originated with Krishna and commonly performed by cowherds of the Bundelkhand region of central India. *Baredi* are mostly dance performances performed during the fourteen days beginning with *Dipavali* (also known as *Diwali*—Festival of Lights) during the month of *Kartika* in the Hindu calendar. The *Baredi* performances closely resemble cowherd cultural life and are commonly associated with the Yadava community of Bundelkhand in Madhya Pradesh. Themes that are usually presented include events of Krishna's life, such as Govardhan worship, *Mahabharata*, *Kaliyadamana*, and so on. Elaborate costumes, stage props, animal masks, and a variety of musical instruments are used in the performances. *Baredi* performances take place in open temple compounds on *Diwali*, but the dance is subsequently performed in the front yards of the households of the village for the remaining fortnight after *Diwali*. Today, the performers of *Baredi* are cowherd folk of the region, known as Yadavas or *ahirs* in Madhya Pradesh.

See also: Diwali; Performing Arts and Krishna

Further Reading

Shah, S., and A. Manohar. 1996. *Tribal Arts and Crafts of Madhya Pradesh: Living Traditions of India*. Ahmedabad: Vanya Prakashan.

BARSANA

Barsana is the town of Radha, the beloved *Gopi*, also considered the soul of Krishna. Although she was born in Rawal, she spent her childhood years in Barsana. Etymological explanations of the name of the town connect it to the name Vrishabhanu-pura, deriving it from the name of Radha's father, Vrishabhanu. The mountains next to the village are called Brahmaparvata and Vishnuparvata, or they are also called Varasanugiri and Brihatsanu. The popular tales of the town explain that the dark hill is Vishnuparvata, while the lighter one is Brahmaparvata. *Mahatmya* texts

Lathmar Holi

Barsana celebrates *Holi* in a typical style popularly known as *Lathmar Holi*, since it involves the use of sticks (*lath* or *lathi* in Hindi). Legend has it that this tradition started with Radha and her *Gopi* friends who hit Krishna and his *Gopa* friends with sticks on the occasion of *Holi*. In continuation of this tradition, the women of Barsana hit visiting men from Nandgaon with bamboo sticks as part of the *Holi* celebrations.

mention how Vajranabha repopulated Barsana in an ancient period and established temples, although its modern revival could only be dated to the sixteenth century based on the evidence of existing temples, which is also supported by other datable sources. Rup Ram, supported by local rulers Suraj Mall and Jawahar Singh, constructed the temple of Lariliji on the hill, and other facilities such as stairs, a marketplace, gardens, and several other buildings. However, the temples of Barsana were looted and faced destruction in the early eighteenth century during the reign of the Mughal ruler Aurangzeb.

Barsana is one of the important places of pilgrimage, which can be completed either in one day or three days. For the three-day pilgrimage, the circumambulation begins with a visit to the temple of Svaminiji (Lariliji), followed by visiting the Gendokhar tank, which is also known as a *tirtha*, referred to as Bhanutirtha, and also as Bhanusarovara after the name of Vrishabhanu, Radha's father. Temples of Caturbhuja (Nimbarka tradition) and Brajeshwar Mahadev are located near the tank. Numerous other tanks frequented by pilgrims here are Ravarikund, Pavarikund, Tilakkund, Mohinikund, Lalitakund, and Dohanikund. On the second day, pilgrims visit the Ashtasakhi (eight friends of Radha) temple and Piri Pokhar. Numerous other temples in the vicinity of the Ashtasakhi temple, including the temples of Vrishabhanu, Sakshi Gopal, and Dauji (Balarama), are also generally visited by pilgrims. On the third day pilgrims visit Sankari Khori to watch *Danlila*, which is enacted by actors. The performances, called *burhi lila*, include *Danlila*, in which Krishna taunts Radha and finally accepts favors. *Holi* and *Radhashtami* (birthday of Radha) are the most important festivals held in Barsana. *Holi* as it is played in Barsana is called *lathmar holi* (hitting with sticks *holi*) because of its unique style of celebration. Since Krishna is the son-in-law of Brihatsanu, the men of Nandgaon, the village of Krishna, are treated as sons-in-law of Barsana, the village of Radha. Therefore, on the day of *Holi* men of Nandgaon visit Barsana and are welcomed with color and sticks by the women of Barsana. The celebration is enacted in perfect good humor by both sides, the men of Nandgaon and the women of Barsana. The celebration of *Holi* is one of the most widely attended festivals of Barsana. Visitors from other parts of India as well as international devotees of Krishna attend the celebration, taking part in it as participants and spectators. Barsana, the birthplace of Radha, enchants pilgrims and devotees with performances of events from the life of Radha and Krishna, as well as unique celebrations of festivals such as the birth of Radha and *Holi*.

See also: Holi; Radha; *Radhashtami*

Further Reading

Growse, F. S. Reprint 1993. *Mathura: A District Memoir.* New Delhi: Asian Educational Services.

Knapp, S. 2010. *Spiritual India Handbook.* Delhi: Jaico.

BHAGAVADGITA

The *Bhagavadgita* is the most important text of Hinduism. Its centrality is indicative of how important Krishna's influence is in Hinduism. It is a compendium of Hindu philosophical concepts including but not limited to Hindu cosmology, cosmogony, yoga, *samkhya*, bhakti, karma, and the concept of god itself. Hence, the *Bhagavadgita* has been interpreted and reinterpreted continuously numerous times since its first composition before 500 BCE. Composed in simple language as part of the *Mahabharata*, the *Bhagavadgita* contains the esoteric essence of Hinduism, only comprehensible in the context of Hinduism and based on a deep understanding of its philosophical concepts. Hence several earlier Hindu gurus (teachers) have warned against hasty, individual reading of the *Bhagavadgita*. Inclusion of the *Bhagavadgita* in the *Mahabharata* had been understood by some modern scholars as a later addition completed before 200 BCE when the *Mahabharata* acquired its final form. However, lacking evidence for the existence of an independent text of the *Bhagavadgita* in any Indian tradition independent of the *Mahabharata* tradition, this assumption is at best questionable. In the West the *Bhagavadgita* has been compared to the Bible, as a holy text. Similar to the *Vedas*, the *Bhagavadgita* represents the revealed word of the God in Hinduism.

The *Bhagavadgita* as a text occurs as a dialogue (*samvada*—conversation) at a crucial juncture on the battlefield of Kurukshetra. As Arjuna peers at the opposing army, consisting of his cousins and other relatives led by his own grandfather, he feels completely dejected and gets ready to put down his arms. Krishna stops Arjuna from giving up his arms, and there on the battlefield of Kurukshetra, not heard or seen by anyone else, Krishna instructs Arjuna, instruction that comes to us as the *Bhagavadgita*. However, the transcript of the *Bhagavadgita* comes from Sanjaya (who was given the divine gift of the ability to see things from afar).

Bhagavadgita in the Media

Although it is not uncommon to include verses from the *Bhagavadgita* in films, a full-length feature film based on the *Bhagavadgita* was produced in 1993, and it also won the Golden Lotus award for best film in the National Film Awards presented by the government of India each year. In the twentieth century the *Bhagavadgita* has also been adopted for popular media series such as TV, anime, and theater. Several cartoon films of the *Bhagavadgita*, as well as audio renditions of the *Bhagavadgita* in Sanskrit followed by commentaries in regional languages of India are also common.

Sanjaya sits ready to narrate to Dhritarashtra, the blind king, as the war transpires on the battlefield of Kurukshetra. The *Bhagavadgita* is embedded in *Bhishmaparva*, the sixth book of the *Mahabharata*, between chapters 23 and 40, consisting of eighteen chapters with about seven hundred verses. Colophons within the text of the *Bhagavadgita* refer to it as an Upanishad, aligning itself closely to the revealed tradition of Hinduism, the *Vedas*. The *Bhagavadgita* stands in close comparison to the *Vedas* as a revealed word of the God, since the *Bhagavadgita* was revealed by the God (*Bhagavan*) and was heard from a distance by Sanjaya. Throughout the text, in addition to the voices of Krishna and Arjuna, one also hears the voice of Sanjaya as a supporting narrative.

Chapter 1 of the *Bhagavadgita* is devoted to Krishna urging Arjuna to adhere to the *kshatriyadharma* and fulfil his duty. Arjuna's dilemma in chapter 1 reflects both the inner and outer conflicts of an individual: the outer struggle of war in which his cousins have arrayed their armies on opposite sides, and the inner struggle of over-coming the grief facing the family as a result of the war. Chapter 2 begins with Arjuna requesting Krishna to help him resolve the dilemma between *kuladharma* (duty to family) and *kshatriyadharma* (duty of the warrior), which he had already noted in chapter 1. Krishna addresses Arjuna's concerns, his grief at the impending loss of family, and his duty as a Kshatriya. Krishna's explanation includes performing actions as a yogi, akin to the *samkhya* and yoga philosophy. Desire and attachment are seen as the root cause of the problem of Arjuna's dejection. Chapter 3 continues with how one must direct one's soul to perfect detached actions, thereby detaching the soul from the consequences of such actions. Chapter 4 elaborates on perfecting the detached action (*karmayoga*). Chapter 4, however, also includes notable aspects of other yogas such as *sanyasa* (renunciation), which forbid any attachments. The *Bhagavadgita* says that the *karmayogi* is a renouncer in the sense that he is not attached to the fruits of his action, while a *sanyasi,* by abstaining from action, is allowing others to perform action by his withdrawal. Hence the *Bhagavadgita* notes the *karmayogi* as the only truly detached yogi. Chapters 5 and 6 continue the explanations of yoga as a path leading to liberation from the cycle of rebirth. Chapter 5 demonstrates why a *karmayogi* might be released from the samsara (cycle of life) even though he continues to perform action. Chapter 6 continues with an exposition of such an evolved soul (*atma*) and its recognition of identity with Brahma (the universal soul). It is in chapters 7–12 of the *Bhagavadgita* that the core concepts of devotion are explained by Krishna. Bhakti (devotion or devotional service) is also a variety of yoga called bhakti yoga, which places Krishna as the central deity. Krishna's *visvarupa* (universal form) is revealed in chapter 11, leading Sanjaya to remark that the radiance of the Lord (*bhagavan*) is equal to the radiance of a "thousand suns shining with radiance simultaneously." Chapter 12 also includes praises of the different forms of the Lord, such as *visvarupa* (universal form) and *ugra* (terrifying form) as *kala* (time). Chapters 12–18 continue to expound on the topics of samsara, yoga, and the divine with deeper perspectives, without a repetition of concepts, and provides a clear understanding of the destiny of human life.

The *Bhagavadgita* is interpreted as a text on yoga for its exposition on a number of yogas, and also due to the fact that several colophons at the end of the chapters also mention yoga, such as *Arjuna Vishada* yoga in chapter 1. Yoga is not conceived as an isolated action in the *Bhagavadgita*. The variety of yogas described in the *Bhagavadgita,* such as *karmayoga, bhaktiyoga,* and *jnanayoga,* in addition to the *samkhyayoga,* make it clear that yoga is a holistic activity involving the mind, body, and detached soul of the devotee, in addition to service to the deity, but not withdrawal from society and family. The *Bhagavadgita* is unique in not supporting *sanyasa* (renunciation) as the best or the only way to escape samsara, and considers a *sanyasi* (renouncer) an escapist at best. The *Bhagavadgita* offers several alternatives to *sanyasa,* promising escape from samsara while fully engaged with one's everyday activities, through devotion, and through complete detachment from the fruits of one's actions. In other words, the *Bhagavadgita* sympathizes with the struggles of the householder (*grihasta*) and proposes an alternative solution without suggesting the drastic measure of leaving loved ones for the purpose of spiritual attainment.

Bhakti is established on an equal status with other yogas, and several chapters of the *Bhagavadgita* specifically address the issue of bhakti. The *Bhagavadgita* makes it clear that bhakti is not passive but active. Bhakti through an active practice should produce qualities like clarity of mind, detachment from desire, happiness within the soul, and more. There are no requirements for bhakti, and very simple worship accompanied by self-surrender with complete dedication will suffice, according to the *Bhagavadgita,* which may be accomplished by offerings such as a flower, a fruit, or a little bit of water.

The *Bhagavadgita* was read only by *pandits* (learned wise men) and priests in its original language, Sanskrit. Common people, not well versed in Sanskrit, might only have heard Bhagavadgita commentaries explained in various languages at temples or mathas. Translation of the *Bhagavadgita* into regional languages in India only began after the twelfth century. English and Western translations appear even later, in the early eighteen hundreds, only after the colonization of India.

The *Jnanesvari,* also known as the *Bhavarthadipika* or the *Jnanadevi,* is *sant* Jnanadev's Marathi rendering of the *Bhagavadgita,* which is the first treatment of the *Bhagavadgita* in a regional language. Since Jnanadev does not name the text, it came to be referred to after his name by Ekanath and Namdev as the *Jnanadevi,* or as the *Bhavarthasandarbha* by some others for its exposition of the meaning of the *Bhagavadgita.* Jnanadev mentions that he completed this work in the town of Nevasa on the banks of the river Godavari. A colophon in the text indicates the completion of the text in the year 1290, refers to the book as *tika* (commentary) rather than translation, and mentions the name of the scribe as Saccidananda. Although some scholars dispute the date, it has been commonly agreed upon among the Marathi scholars that the *Jnanesvari* had been composed by the turn of 1300 CE. Rather than a strict commentary, the text is a creative commentary and explanation of central concepts of the *Bhagavadgita* in easily understandable Marathi. Although the *Jnanesvari* is divided into eighteen chapters similar to the *Bhagavadgita,* it is twelve times as long, containing around nine thousand verses. The *Jnanesvari* is composed in *ovi*-style poetry, which contains simple four-lined stanzas. The first three lines become longer with each line and end in similar or similar-sounding syllables, while the fourth line is shorter and does not rhyme with the others. The fourth line provides a contrast to the first three lines and provides a break. This style of poetry, especially in Jnanadev's composition, is rhythmical and set to meter, thus lending itself easily to singing or reading aloud. Scholars have attempted to connect the *Jnanesvari* to commentaries of Sankara, Ramanuja, and Abhinavagupta. Although the *Jnanesvari* betrays the influence of *advaita*, it can only be attributed to the *Varkari* context of Jnanadev, rather than any external influence. However, it should be noted that translation of the *Bhagavadgita* into regional languages of India such as Telugu, Tamil, and Bengali was also completed by the fifteenth century. While high-quality illustrated manuscripts of the *Bhagavadgita* were produced in Rajasthan, Gujarath, and Karnataka, translations only appear there in the seventeenth century. The first English translation of the *Bhagavadgita,* by Charles Wilkins, was published in 1785; the first French translation appeared in 1787, and a German translation followed in 1801. Several translations and commentaries have appeared in almost all Indian languages and several world languages. In fact, several bibliographies have attempted to compile the available data on translations and commentaries on the *Bhagavadgita,* such as the *Bhagavadgitanuvada* by Callewaert and Hemaraj in 1983. Several new translations and commentaries on the *Bhagavadgita* have been published since then, and it continues to be translated into other languages of the world, including tribal dialects.

The *Bhagavadgita* achieved a strange prominence in the 1950s when physicist Robert Oppenheimer recited, "Death have I become . . . ," a verse from the *Bhagavadgita* (Ch.11.32), in describing the first atomic explosion he witnessed. It also achieved prominence in India among nationalist leaders such as M. K. Gandhi, B. G. Tilak, and V. Bhave during the early twentieth century, with each of them producing his own *Bhagavadgita* commentary.

The name *Gita* has come to refer exclusively to the *Bhagavadgita* as a central text of Hinduism, although several other *Gitas* such as *Devigita, Shivagita,* and so on are known in Hinduism. The *Bhagavadgita* is one of the most commented-on texts in the world. In fact, the *Mahabharata* includes its own commentary of the *Gita* known as *Anugita.* The *Gita* is also revered with the *Gitamahatmya* verses, which is a unique tradition in itself within Hinduism. *Gitamahatmya* is included in several *puranas* such as *Padmapurana* as a conversation between Shiva and his wife Parvati. The *Bhagavadgita* also has been adopted for TV and film in the twentieth century. A Sanskrit film produced in 1993, *Bhagavadgita,* won the Golden Lotus award for best film at the National Film Awards presented by the government of India each year. Several cartoon films of the *Bhagavadgita* as well as audio renditions of the *Bhagavadgita* in Sanskrit followed by commentaries in regional languages are also well known in India.

See also: Arjuna; *Avatara*; Bhakti; *Mahabharata*; Pandavas; Sanjaya; *Visvarupa*; Yoga and Krishna

Further Reading

Adluri, V. 2010. "The *Bhagavadgita*: Doctrines and Contexts." *History of Religions* 50 (1): 102–107.

Dorter, K. 2012. "A Dialectical Reading of the *Bhagavadgita.*" *Asian Philosophy* 22 (4): 307–326.

Jacobsen, K. A. 1996. "'Bhagavadgita', Ecosophy-T, and Deep Ecology." *Inquiry—an Interdisciplinary Journal of Philosophy* 39 (2): 219–238.

Kasimow, H. 1983. "The Jewish Tradition and the *Bhagavadgita*." *Journal of Dharma* 8 (3): 296–310.

Minnema, L. 2008. "The Complex Nature of Religious Sacrifice in the *Mahabharata*, in the *Bhagavadgita*: A Cross-cultural Comparison between Indian and Western Theories of Religious Sacrifice." *Neue Zeitschrift Fur Systematische Theologie Und Religionsphilosophie* 50 (3–4): 196–215.

Nelson, L. 1988. "Madhusudana-Sarasvati on the Hidden Meaning of the *Bhagavadgita*—*Bhakti* for the *Advaitin* Renunciate." *Journal of South Asian Literature* 23 (2): 73–89.

Nicolas, A. T. D. 1979. "Problem of the Self-Body in the *Bhagavadgita*—Problem of Meaning." *Philosophy East & West* 29 (2): 159–175.

Sharpe, E. J. 1988. "Western Images of the *Bhagavadgita*, 1885–1985." *Journal of South Asian Literature* 23 (2): 47–57.

Sreekumar, S. 2012. "An Analysis of Consequentialism and Deontology in the Normative Ethics of the *Bhagavadgita*." *Journal of Indian Philosophy* 40 (3): 277–315. www.bhagavadgita.us/summary-of-the-bhagavad-gita/

White, D. 1971. "Human Perfection in *Bhagavadgita*." *Philosophy East & West* 21 (1): 43–53.

Young, K. K.1988. "Ramanuja on *Bhagavadgita* 4.11, the Issue of *Arcavatara*." *Journal of South Asian Literature* 23 (2): 90–110.

BHAGAVAN

Bhagavan is a term used as a synonym for Krishna to refer to him as the ultimate Supreme God. Although it is used to denote the ultimate lord, etymologically, *bhagavan* has been interpreted variously by modern scholars and defined theologically, being attributed with rich philosophical meaning by Vaishnava *acaryas*, Sanskrit grammarians, and linguists. *Bhagavan* is a Sanskrit word meaning one who possesses *bhaga*, a noun used in ancient India to indicate concepts such as prosperity, dignity, distinction, excellence, majesty, power, and beauty. All these epithets were used to describe the divine in Hinduism in ancient India. The most common meaning of *bhaga* is illustrious or radiant. Light representing divinity, Krishna, is identified as *bhagavan*: most lustrous, hence radiant. While other *puranas* present

---

Bhagavata Mantra

Akrura stopped at the lake in Brindavan, while taking Krishna and Balarama to Mathura, and worshipped *Bhagavan* Vishnu with *Aghamarshana* mantras (*Bhagavatapurana* 10.38.39) and *Bhagavata* mantras (*Harivamsa* 69–70). As soon as he took a dip in the lake he perceived a vision of Krishna and Balarama appearing as Vishnu and Sesha under the lake. Akrura is considered the first Bhagavata (follower of *Bhagavan*) since he received the vision of *nijarupa* (original forms) of Krishna and Balarama due to his devotion.

Krishna as an *avatara* of Vishnu, the *Bhagavatapurana* presents Vishnu as derived from Krishna. Krishna is held supreme, equal to Vishnu, if not greater. Who came first, Krishna or Vishnu, remains a matter of speculation among the major Vaishnava traditions of India. However, persistent use of the term *bhagavan* indicates the supremacy of Krishna as the major deity of Vaishnavism as far back as 200 BCE, based on the reference of the Besnagar inscription by Greek ambassador Heliodorus mentioning himself as a *Bhagavata* (follower of *Bhagavan*). *Bhagavan* as a term must have been in use to refer to Krishna and his followers as *Bhagavatas* at least a couple of centuries before 200 BCE for it to be used as a well-known epithet to refer to the followers of Krishna. Even though the texts *Bhagavadgita* and *Bhagavatapurana* are dated

Krishna is the last and full incarnation of Vishnu, the *Bhagavan*. Radha with Krishna represents the blissful state of the supreme soul. (tunart/iStockphoto.com)

later than 600 BCE, this inscriptional evidence provides strong support for the existence of the worship of Krishna as *Bhagavan* by that period.

Krishna is referred to as *Bhagavan* frequently. In fact, the texts of the Krishna legend are known as the *Bhagavatapurana*, and the discourse of Krishna, the central text of Hinduism, is known as the *Bhagavadgita*, a derivative title based on the divine name *Bhagavan*. Therefore, etymologically *bhagavan* is derived from the Sanskrit root *bhaga* meaning burning, flaming, radiant, lustrous, and so on. It was mistakenly interpreted by modern scholars as a derivative of other Sanskrit roots such as *bhaaga* or *bhaaj,* meaning divide or share. However, this second root contains a long vowel, *aa,* on the first syllable, which constitutes a misreading of the first syllable in the word *bhagavan*, which is always written with a short vowel. As *Bhagavan* the god is understood to be the light of the world, or the one that provides light to the world. Followers of *Bhagavan* were known by the name *Bhagavatas* in ancient India and noted as followers of Krishna. *Bhagavan* is a conceptual representation of Krishna as the luminous light of the world. Krishna's birth is symbolically narrated as the rise of light and the awakening of the world. Krishna is born at midnight and transferred to Vraja, from where Nidra (sleep) is brought to Mathura. Krishna's appearance in Vraja marks the end of Nidra (sleep) and night. However, Nidra was killed by Kamsa, assuming her to be the eighth child of Devaki. Hence the name *Bhagavan* as Krishna and as luminous lord of the world was used before the turn of the first millennium.

See also: Bhagavadgita; Bhagavatapurana; Bhagavatas; Historical Krishna

Further Reading

Vemsani, L. 2006. *Hindu and Jain Mythology of Balarama.* New York: Edwin Mellen.

BHAGAVATAMELA

Bhagavatamela is an open-air theater form in which groups of artists perform mythical stories of the *puranas.* Although *Bhagavatamelas* were once performed in the temple precincts, they are now performed in the open grounds of the villages, although the subjects of the plays are still derived from the *puranas. Bhagavatapurana*, Book 10, or Krishna's epic story, is traditionally presented by theater troupes in a song and dance theater performance for devotees in Andhra Pradesh, Tamilnadu, and Karnataka. A number of other *purana* stories are also performed. Modernization of the theater form currently includes additional topics, but still remains allied to religious themes. *Krishnattam* (Kerala), *Kala* (Karnataka), and *Kuchipudi* (Andhra Pradesh) are other highly stylized dance-drama performances of the Krishna stories in particular regional styles.

Melattur

Melattur, located in the Tanjavur district of Tamilnadu, is known for its annual performing arts festival celebrated over a week during the *Narasimhajayanti* festival (February–March). The festival includes dance and drama shows, which are based mainly on subjects from the *Bhagavatapurana*, although other subjects are not uncommon. Melattur has been home to a number of artist families since the tenth century. Beginning with the Chola Empire successive states supported and sponsored the artistic and literary activities of Melattur by settling artists there. A number of dance, music, and theater programs and competitions are held in Melattur each year.

See also: Krishnattam; Kuchipudi

Further Reading

Jones, C. 1993. "Bhagavatamela Natakam, a Traditional Dance Drama Form." *Journal of Asian Studies* 22 (2): 193–200.

Terada, Y. 2008. "Temple Music Traditions in Hindu South India: *Periya Melam* and Its Performance and Practice." *Asian Music* 39 (2): 108–151.

BHAGAVATAPURANA

The *Bhagavatapurana* is one of the eighteen *mahapuranas* of Hinduism; it contains the narration of the complete life of Krishna in his earthly realm as well as his connection to the other world as Supreme Lord. The *Bhagavatapurana* is a Vaishnava *purana* (accepting Vishnu as Supreme God) that narrates the stories of several incarnations (*avataras*), as well as Vaishnava philosophy. The *Bhagavatapurana* consists of twelve *skandas* (books) divided into 335 chapters with about 18,000 verses. The tenth book of the *Bhagavatarpurana* contains the legend of Krishna. It is the largest book of the *Bhagavatapurana*, containing about 4,000 verses, and forms about a quarter of the book. Although its dating has been contentious among modern scholars, there is general agreement that its earlier portions could be dated to 400 CE, while its later portions could be dated as late as 1000 CE. However, it has been known in its present form for more than a thousand years at least. The *Bhagavatapurana* contains a lively narrative of Krishna's childhood in Vraja and Brindavan, his adult life in Dvaraka, and finally his death at Prabhasa. Krishna's childhood in Vraja and Brindavan forms the center of several devotional traditions such as Vallabha, Nimbarka, and so on. Images depicting Krishna's childhood in Vraja or depicting Krishna with Radha in Brindavan are the most favorite ritual images of Krishna used in temples as well as in the homes of devotees for individual worship. Episodes of the legend of Krishna from his childhood and young adult life in Vraja and Brindavan were the subject of numerous painting traditions, sculptures, dances, dramas, poetical works, and *kavyas* (literary texts) in the past, and they still remain popular subjects of artistic expression. The Krishna legend is the most popular subject of artistic imagination in India.

The *Bhagavatapurana*, as the name suggests, is the story of the *Bhagavan*, the god, identified with Krishna. Hence, the text presents Krishna as the supreme deity, sometimes even surpassing Vishnu, almost suggesting that it is the god Vishnu that may have emerged from Krishna, not the other way round, as could be seen in the other major texts including the *Mahabharata,* the *Harivamsa,* and the

---

Bhagavatapurana as Prasthana

The *Bhagavatapurana* is considered the supreme *purana,* almost equated with the supreme God, Krishna/Vishnu himself. Devotional traditions (*sampradayas*) centered on Krishna such as the Vallabha tradition incorporate the *Bhagavatapurana* as one of the source texts (*prasthana*) in addition to the three texts (*prastanatrayi*), the Upanishads, the *Brahmasutras,* and the *Bhagavadgita.* The *Bhagavatapurana* presents itself as the sun, arisen after Krishna departed to his abode (I.3.45), and another *purana* verse in *Padmapurana* states that *Bhagavata* is the Lord himself in this world (*Padmapurana* VI.193.20). Therefore *Bhagavatapurana* is the literary incarnation (*vangmayavatara*) of God. Jiva Gosvami's book *Bhagavatasandarbha* addresses the *Bhagavatapurana,* attempting the analysis of its theological and cosmological premises.

Vishnupurana. The first nine books of the *Bhagavatapurana* narrate the stories of the *avataras* of Vishnu, leading up to the legend of Krishna in book ten. The first nine books form a prologue, which establishes the superiority of the *Bhagavan*, narrated in full in the tenth book. An underlying theme of the first nine books is also the teaching of *bhaktiyoga* (the path of devotion) through the depiction of stories of several *bhaktas* such as Prahlada, Gajendra, Ajamila, and Bali. Interestingly, in the *Bhagavatapurana* it is not a sole male *bhakta*, but several female *bhaktas* (*Gopis*) that are presented as the ultimate model of devotion to Krishna. The *Bhagavatapurana* also unequivocally established the supremacy of Krishna over all other manifestations of Vishnu (*Bhagavatapurana* I.3.28) in saying that "Krishna is the *Bhagavan* himself," while all the previous incarnations were either *amsas* (partial incarnation) or *kalas* (secondary/similar but not the same). The term *lila* is attached to the life of Krishna in Vraja and Brindavan. The *Bhagavatapurana* includes the complete theology of Vaishnavism, while philosophically it also presents its major practices: yoga, *samkhya,* and bhakti.

A unique feature of the *Bhagavatapurana* is its central focus on narrating the divine pastimes (*lila*) of Krishna. The *Bhagavatapurana* legend of Krishna as narrated in the tenth book could be divided into two sections. The first section, chapters 1 to 49, contains the stories of Krishna's birth, childhood, and young adult life, ending with Krishna traveling to Mathura on Kamsa's invitation to participate in a wrestling match, which finally culminated in the killing of Kamsa and the freeing of Krishna's parents from prison. The second section, chapters 50 to 90, contains the stories of Krishna's adult life in Dvaraka and his major role in the *Mahabharata.*

As the best known, most commonly read, as well as most widely performed legend of Krishna, the *Bhagavatapurana* acquired a special place in the minds and hearts of Hindus, especially Vaishnava devotees. The *Bhagavatapurana* has been translated into numerous regional languages of India as well as into many other world languages.

See also: Bhagavadgita; *Bhagavan; Bhagavatas*; Braj *Parikrama*; Brindavan; *Gopas* and *Gopis; Harivamsa; Lila*; Mathura

Further Reading

Brown, C. M. 1983. "The Origin and Transmission of the 2 'Bhagavata Puranas,' the Vaisnava 'Bhagavata Purana' and the 'Devi-Bhagavata Purana'—A Canonical and Theological Dilemma." *Journal of the American Academy of Religion* 51 (4): 551–567.

Coleman, T. 2010. "*Viraha-Bhakti* and *Stridharma*: Re-Reading the Story of Krisna and the Gopis in the *Harivamsa* and the *Bhagavata Purana.*" *Journal of the American Oriental Society* 130 (3): 385–412.

Matchett, F. 1986. "The Taming of Kaliya—A Comparison of the *Harivamsa, Visnu-Purana,* and *Bhagavata-Purana* Versions." *Religion* 16 (2): 115–133.

Sheridan, D. P. 1984. "Sacramentality of Krishna-*avatara* in *Bhagavata-Purana.*" *Journal of Dharma* 9 (3): 230–245.

Sheridan, D. P. 1989. "Maternal Affection for a Divine Son, a Spirituality of the *Bhagavata-Purana.*" *Horizons* 16 (1): 65–78.

Theodor, I. 2007. "The *Parinama* Aesthetics as Underlying the '*Bhagavata Purana*'." *Asian Philosophy* 17 (2): 109–125.

BHAGAVATAS

The word *Bhagavatas* designates devotees of *Bhagavan* (radiant, luminous). Krishna is most frequently referred to as *Bhagavan* by at least 300 BCE, although this term is not used exclusively to describe Krishna.

Early evidence of the *Bhagavata* tradition comes from northwest and central India (Rajastan, Maharashtra, and Madhya Pradesh) in the form of short stone inscriptions commemorating temple construction. The most familiar inscription is the Garuda Pillar inscription of Besnagar (Madhya Pradesh) dated to 200 BCE. It states that the inscription is issued by *Bhagavata* Heliodorus, a Greek ambassador of Taxila, to commemorate the establishment of a Garuda Pillar in honor of Vaasudeva (Krishna). Another inscription obtained from the same place and temple says that a king named Bhagavata established a Garuda Pillar in front of the Bhagavant temple to mark his twelfth regal year. The next inscription comes from Ghosundi, near Nagari (Rajasthan). This inscription records that the *Bhagavata* king Sarvatata built Narayana a *vatika* (enclosure for Narayana) for the gods Samkarsana and Vaasudeva. This can be a place of worship for *Bhagavatas*. It is also notable that the king refers to himself as Bhagavata while referring to the god as Narayana. Association of the names, Bhagavan and Narayana, with Vishnu and Vaasudeva (Krishna) is already established by the references in *Satapatha Brahmana*. Hence these early inscriptions might help us understand that the deities Bhagavan and Narayana could be identified with Krishna. Another inscription from Pratapgarh from the Chittorgarh district of Rajasthan (not far from Besnagar) dated to 200 BCE mentions that *Saca Bhagavata* erected a pillar. The Nanaghat cave inscription (Maharashtra) of the Satavahana queen Nayanika dated to 100 BCE begins with the invocation to Samkarsana and Vaasudeva, identified with Balarama and Krishna respectively. These inscriptions range over 100 years before the turn of the first millennium and span a large geographical area, at least one-third of the area of modern India. Considering the fact that any such evidence for most of the deities in this early period is lacking, the inscriptions, almost four in number, which are more than 2,300 years old and come from an extensive geographical area, may indicate a significant following and devotion for Krishna. Several punch-marked coins as well as an Indo-Greek coin of King Agathocles depict Krishna and Balarama, which may also indicate the popular devotion for Krishna. This evidence supports an early devotional tradition centered on Krishna known as the *Bhagavata* tradition, which existed in northern and central India during the second half of the first millennium BCE.

Textual evidence about the *Bhagavatas* appears in the *Bhagavadgita*, the *Mahabharata* (especially the *Narayaniya parva*), and the *Harivamsa*. The *Bhagavadgita* is the most extensive text on *Bhagavata* dharma, and Krishna explicitly states that those who worship him certainly reach him (*Bhagavadgita* 9.25). The *Harivamsa* explicitly mentions the term *Bhagavatas* as worshippers of Bhagavan. The *Harivamsa* mentions that Akrura meditates on Ananta (also known as Balarama or Samkarsana), with *Bhagavata* mantras to please the great god of the *Bhagavatas* (*Harivamsa* 69.70). This verse indirectly indicates the prayers to the great god of the

Bhagavatas through prayers to Ananta (Sesha), who is the serpent bed of Vishnu. The vision Akrura experienced following his prayers depicts the serpent Sesha on whose lap Vishnu was sitting. It could be assumed that by the time of the composition of the *Harivamsa,* the theological unity of Bhagavan, Krishna, and Vishnu might have been completely established. In the *Bhagavatapurana* version of the story, Akrura meditates with *aghamarshana* mantras (*Maha Narayana Upanishad* of the *Rigveda*) and finds a vision of Vishnu sitting on the lap of the serpent Sesha. Akrura first sees Krishna and Balarama in his chariot, then meditates and finds them under the lake in their divine forms (as Sesha and Vishnu). He is taken aback; he comes back and sees Krishna and Balarama sitting on the chariot. He dives into the lake and sees Krishna and Balarama as the serpent Sesha and Vishnu. The *Harivamsa* is presenting the great god of the *Bhagavatas,* Bhagavan, Narayan, Krishna, and Vishnu, as one and the same in the visions that Akrura saw in the lake. Together the *Bhagavadgita,* the *Mahabharata,* and the *Harivamsa* represent the prevalent practices of devotion to the *Bhagavan* between 300 BCE and 300 CE. From 400 CE onward the frequency of occurrences of the term *Bhagavata, Paramabhagavata,* in the inscriptions and texts increases considerably, which indicates the continued popularity of the *Bhagavata* tradition. Varahamihira's (380–412 CE) *Brihatsamhita* mentions the proper ways *Bhagavatas* should follow to construct temples and install the icon of their *Bhagavan* according to their specific ritual rules. Varahamihira's mention of the term *Bhagavatas* and also his description of temple construction is significant and establishes that the tradition may have gained notable status by that time. *Bhagavata* is mentioned fairly frequently in Vaishnava texts from the seventh century onward. *Bhagavatas* and Vaishnavas came to be used as synonyms during the early phase, while the occurrence of Vaishnavas as a common designation increased gradually. However, several regional traditions under the name *Bhagavatas* still flourished in India. Sankara (800 CE) mentions the *Bhagavatas* in his *Brahmasutra Bhashya* and identifies them as *Pancaratrasiddhanta* (*Brahmasutra Bhashya* 2.2.42–45). He attributes to them the worship of *Caturvyuhas,* including their five phases (*pancakalas*) of worship. Srivaishnavas of South India are also identified with *Bhagavatas* by the eleventh century CE. The designation of *Bhagavata* continues to be applied to devotees of Vishnu, who follow *Pancaratra* and *Vaikhanasa samhitas.* Evidence of the *Bhagavatas* has also been found outside India in Southeast Asia since the mid-seventh century. Several inscriptions from ancient temples including Prasat Komnap and Prasat Kok Po in Cambodia mention *Bhagavatas.* The *Bhagavata* tradition continues to the modern day. Even though its connection to the ancient *Bhagavata* tradition is not known, there is no dispute that a group of devotees of Vishnu under the name of *Bhagavatas* were present in ancient India, and a similar devotional tradition was also practiced in Southeast Asia. The historical association of the *Bhagavatas* with *Pancaratra, Vaikhanasa samhitas,* and meditative rituals is also clearly established, and they have close ties with Srivaishnavas. There are also other *Bhagavatas* in south India. The *Bhagavatas* of Karnataka are *smartas* associated with the Madhva tradition, while the *Bhagavatas* of Andhra Pradesh perform *Bhagavatamela* (a Vaishnava tradition of dance-drama), are followers of Ramanuja, and narrate the stories of *Bhagavata* known as *Harikatha.*

In conclusion, it could be said that *Bhagavata sampradaya* is one of the oldest Vaishnava traditions devoted to *Bhagavan* Krishna, centered on *Pancaratra* worship. The term *Bhagavata* seems to have been used as an alternative name for Vaishnavas in some regions, while in certain other regions it was practiced as an independent tradition (*sampradaya*). Aside from whether Bhagavatism exists as a tradition in modern India, or if it became part of *advaita* traditions such as Srivaishnavism, the *Bhagavata* tradition makes it clear that a group of devotees of Krishna were known for their distinct practice and recognized as an independent *sampradaya* in ancient India.

See also: Aniruddha; Balarama; *Bhagavan*; *Caturvyuhas*; *Pancaratra*; Pradyumna; Srivaishnavism

Further Reading

Carman, J., and V. Narayanan. 1989. *The Tamil Veda: Pillan's Interpretation of the Tiruvaymoli.* Chicago: University of Chicago Press.

Couture, A. 1986. "Akrura et la Tradition Bhagavata selon le Harivamsa." *Studies in Religion/ Sciences Religiuses* 15 (2): 221–232.

Farquhar, J. N. 1967. *An Outline of the Religious Literature of India.* Delhi: Motilal Banarsidas.

Kielhorn, F. 1908. "Bhagavat, Tatrabhavat, and Devanampriya." *Journal of the Royal Asiatic Society*: 502–508.

Narasimhacary, M. 1998. *Contributions of Yamunacarya to Visistadvaita.* Hyderabad: Sri Jayalakshmi Publications.

BHAKTI

Bhakti is the most commonly practiced way of god realization in Hinduism. Krishna equates bhakti with the other eminent paths of self-realization such as yoga and *samkhya* (knowledge) in the *Bhagavadgita* and the *Bhagavatapurana*. In fact, Krishna declares that it is the best method of self-realization available to humanity, as it does not require one's complete withdrawal from worldly activities (one's dharma); other modes of practice, such as *sanyasa* (renunciation), require renouncing one's family and householder life as a precursor to seeking self-realization. Etymologically *bhakti* is a compound of two Sanskrit words, *bhaga* (radiant, luminous) and *ti* (participate)—sharing or participation, in this case devotion or devotional feeling, *bhakti bhava* toward *bhaga* or *bhagavan*.

Bhava (emotion), *rasa* (essence), and *prema* (love) are commonly used in the expression of bhakti toward Krishna; although these words are also used in secular expressions, they are imbued with a special meaning in terms of devotion. Bhakti is understood as *bhava* when invoked in a person and a *rasa* when expressed by a person. For example, *vastalyabhava* (emotions of affection) or *sevakabhava* (emotions of a servant) are experienced when cultivated in the mind of a devotee through constant meditation and participation in the services. Once the *bhava* is cultivated in a devotee's mind, it is expressed in poems, lyrics, or service, as a *rasa*, and may help other devotees follow him or her. Bhakti is a complex term explained in numerous ways by language specialists, religious practitioners, theorists of

---

Bhaktisandarbha

Jiva *Gosvami* (1513–1598), one of the Six *Gosvamis* of Brindavan, was crucial in the revival of the theological background of bhakti. Jiva *Gosvami's* book *Bhaktisandarbha*, along with his uncle Rupa *Gosvami's* (1489–1564) book *Bhaktirasamritasindhu,* form the most important texts of the Caitanya Vaishnava tradition in particular and bhakti traditions in general. The *Bhaktisandarbha* describes the nine types of devotional service and their practice for attainment of divine union with Krishna.

---

theater, and drama. Bhakti has become a difficult concept to understand as more and more definitions and theoretical visions have been proposed from literature, practice, and art.

Bhakti is explained as derived from *bhaga* (god), related to *Bhagavan*, but it was also mistakenly explained as a derivative of the Sanskrit word root *bhaj* (partake, or divide) and sometimes confused with the Sanskrit word root *bhoj* (to eat, enjoy). It would seem that it should have been derived from a noun rather than a verb as defined earlier. *Bhag*, as a common noun, denotes something that is burning or bright; when *ti* is added, *bhagti* or *bhakti* denotes an action noun meaning that which is burning or flaming. This may be a closer meaning to describe the feeling of emotion in the mind of a follower of the god.

It seems obvious at least in the case of Krishna *bhaktas* to imagine that the word *Bhagavan* must have shaped the term *bhakta* as a follower of *Bhagavan*, and may have contributed to the immense popularity of this word, bhakti, as part of *bhakti-yoga,* its central spiritual practice denoting spiritual union with Krishna. In modern India this word is used in a variety of contexts to refer to a person's passionate connection or service to a religion or deity.

Nine types of bhakti services are encountered in the texts; however, no strict rules describe how one may conduct the services. The nine types of bhakti are *sravana* (listening), *kirtana* (singing or recitation), *smarana* (remembering), *padasevana* (serving the feet of the deity), *arcana* (worshipping), *vandana* (saluting or showing reverence), *dasya* (serve or service), *sakhya* (friendship), and *atmanivedana* (surrendering oneself). As one undertakes any of these types of bhakti, one experiences its emotional and spiritual attitudes, which are expressed as *bhavas* (attitudes of moods) such as *santa* (peaceful), *dasya* (attitude of a servant), *sakhya* (feeling of friendship), *vatsalya* (motherly affection), *madhura/madhurya* (a woman's sweet love toward her lover). *Madhurya bhava* is sometimes replaced by *sringara bhava* in several Krishna bhakti traditions, which may sometimes verge on the feelings of romantic love. Jayadeva's lyrical text *Gitagovinda* is an example of such approximation of *madhurya* by *sringara*. Numerous varieties of bhakti practices can be noticed within Krishna bhakti, while the most important are the *virahabhakti* of the Srivaishnava tradition and the *raganuraga bhakti* of the Caitanya Vaishnava tradition.

Bhakti as a devotional worship of one's favorite deity (*istha devata*) is ubiquitous in India. The ancient religions of India, Hinduism, Buddhism, and Jainism, use it frequently.

Aside from the spiritual context, bhakti is also traditionally linked to the theory of Indian performing arts as noted in Bharata's text on aesthetics, the *Natyasastra*.

However, bhakti as passionate attachment also finds widespread current usage in modern India when it is applied to nonreligious issues such as, for example, *deshabhakti* (devotion to country) as a designation for patriotism. Its traditional usage in personal contexts such as *pitribhakti* (devotion to father), *matribhakti* (devotion to mother), or *gurubhakti* (devotion to teacher) are also encountered in classical texts such as the *puranas* and the epics of India.

Sociologically, bhakti brings forward egalitarian practices among the devotees, excluding no one on the basis of gender, class, or caste from participation in the devotional services. Hence several female bhakti saints, as well as lower caste saints are commonly found in the bhakti traditions of India. Andal (an *alvar*) of the south Indian bhakti tradition (Srivaishnavism), Mirabai (north India), Janabai, and Bahina Bai (Maharashtra) are all well-known female bhakti saints; Chokamela (*Varkari* tradition) and Ravidas (Madhva tradition) are bhakti saints from low-caste origins. The *Gopis* in the *Bhagavatapurana* are considered the supreme *bhaktas* of Krishna and serve as models to the later bhakti traditions. Hence, several activities described in connection with the *Gopis* such as singing, dancing, and recitation (*kirtana*) became part of the devotional practice of bhakti. Such devotional practice makes achieving union with the deity accessible to common householder men and women as noted in the *Gopis* of the *Bhagavatapurana*. The *Bhagavatapurana* notes that Krishna has encouraged the *Gopis* to return to their families to serve and fulfill their duties as householders, while they are simultaneously submerged in Krishna bhakti.

Although erotic sentiment and expressions of *prema bhava*, *sringara rasa*, *madhurya bhava*, and *madhurya rasa* are accepted as the expression of devotees' emotional experience, devotional traditions such as Caitanya Vaishnavism, the Haridasi tradition, and the Radhavallabha tradition regulate and contain the eroticism through an intellectual system of practice. The expression of such sentiments has never translated into physical practice, except in the case of tantric devotional schools, such as the *Sahajiyas*, which mix the *bhava* and *rasa* concepts with tantric sexual practices.

See also: Alvars; Caitanya; *Gitagovinda*; *Lila*; Radhavallabha Tradition; Srivaishnavism; Vallabha Tradition; *Varkari* Tradition

Further Reading

Bhaduri, N. P. 1988. "*Bhakti* (Devotion) as an Aesthetic Sentiment." *Journal of Indian Philosophy* 16 (4): 377–410.

Biernacki, L. 2013. "Interpreting Devotion: The Poetry and Legacy of a Female Bhakti Saint of India." *International Journal of Hindu Studies* 17 (1): 112–114.

Burchett, P. 2009. "*Bhakti* Rhetoric in the Hagiography of 'Untouchable' Saints: Discerning *Bhakti*'s Ambivalence on Caste and Brahminhood." *International Journal of Hindu Studies* 13 (2): 115–141.

Chackalackal, S. 2004. "Modern Saints of *Bhakti* Tradition." *Journal of Dharma* 29 (3): 273–278.

Cort, J. E. 2002, "*Bhakti* in the Early Jain Tradition: An Understanding of Devotional Religion in South Asia." *History of Religion* 42: 48–76.

DeNapoli, A. E. 2009. "By the Sweetness of the Tongue: Duty, Destiny, and Devotion in the Oral Life Narratives of Female *Sadhus* in Rajasthan." *Asian Ethnology* 68 (1): 81–109.

Hardy, F. 2001. *Viraha-bhakti: The Early History of Krishna Devotion in South India.*

Kannath, S. 2004. "Mystical Consciousness as Culmination of Bhakti in Tagore." *Journal of Dharma* 29 (3): 371–385.

Moran, A. 2013. "Toward a History of Devotional Vaishnavism in the West Himalayas: Kullu and the Ramanandis, c. 1500–1800." *Indian Economic and Social History Review* 50 (1): 1–25.

Narayanan, V. 1994. *The Vernacular Veda: Revelation, Recitation, and Ritual.* Columbia: University of South Carolina Press.

Nelson, L. E. 2004. "The Ontology of Bhakti: Devotion as Paramapurusartha in *Gaudiya* Vaisnavism and Madhusudana Sarasvati." *Journal of Indian Philosophy* 32 (4): 345–392.

Pechilis, K. 1999. *The Embodiment of Bhakti.* New York: SUNY.

Pechilis, K. 2009. "Experiencing the Mango Festival as a Ritual Dramatization of Hagiography." *Method & Theory in the Study of Religion* 21 (1): 50–65.

BHAKTI MOVEMENT

The Bhakti movement is a name given to a religious phenomenon in India that developed from 300 CE onward, gathering clear momentum between 900 CE and 1600 CE across India. Bhakti influenced almost all aspects of culture and thought: arts, languages, philosophy, and a quite sweeping shift in spiritual and religious organization and ritual life. Numerous Vaishnava traditions have a pioneering role in this cultural phenomenon that channeled the spirituality of the common people of India through artistic expression. *Advaita Vedanta* (Sankaracarya), *Catuh Vaishnava sampradayas* (the Four Vaishnava Traditions: Ramanuja, Madhva, Nimbarka, Vishnuswami), and the Nath *sampradaya* (*Varkari* tradition) are the founding movements of this tradition that influenced later popular bhakti traditions. Through the Bhakti movement, religion and spiritual experience that were once confined to temples, practitioners of esoteric yoga, and Vedic rituals were gradually adapted to regional languages, popular practices of music and dance such as *kirtan,* and *samaj gayan* along with pilgrimage as the mainstay of religious practice, with devotion to a personal deity whether worshipped in a *nirguna* (without attributes) or *saguna* (with attributes) form. Almost all of these Bhakti movements focus on devotion to Krishna. Another important feature of the Bhakti movement is recognizing the love of the deity, igniting a passionate devotion within the devotee. Almost all the bhakti traditions prescribe strict rules for the personal diet and behavior of their disciples. The four abstentions commonly associated with Vaishnava bhakti center on devotion to Krishna and abstaining from alcohol and other intoxicants including tobacco, meat consumption, illicit sex, and gambling.

See also: Advaita; Bhagavatapurana; Bhagavatas; Bhakti; Caitanya Vaishnavism; Madhva; Nimbarka Tradition; Ramanuja; *Sants; Varkari* Tradition

Further Reading

Lutze, L. 1977. "*Bhakti* Lyric Poetry as Modern Literature." *Indo Asia* 19 (4): 378–385.

Pinch, V. 2003. "*Bhakti* and the British Empire." *Past & Present* (179): 159–196.

Williams, R. B. 1998. "Training Religious Specialists for a Transnational Hinduism: A Swaminarayan *Sadhu* Training Center (Tracing the Growth and Development of the Modern Global Devotional Movement within the *Bhakti* Sect)." *Journal of the American Academy of Religion* 66 (4): 841–862.

BHAKTIVEDANTA SWAMI PRABHUPADA

Bhaktivedanta Swami Prabhupada, also referred to as Prabhupada or Bhaktivedanta Swami, is an Indian guru of Vaishnavism credited with bringing Vedanta Hindu missionary activity to the United States in the fall of 1965 along with his translations of major Hindu texts including the *Bhagavadgita* and the *Bhagavatapurana*. Prabhupada is a disciple of Swami Bhakti Siddhanta Saraswati. Prabhupada's guru and his guru's father, Kedarnath Datta Bhaktivinoda, are gurus in the Caitanya Vaishnava tradition, also known as *Gaudiya* Vaishnavism. Prabhupada's devotional movement is centered on Krishna devotion (bhakti), which is reflected in the name of the movement in the United States: International Society of Krishna Consciousness (ISKCON), also known as "Hare Krishnas" after the frequent and public chanting of "Hare Krishna" by its followers.

Born as Abhay Charan De in Calcutta on September 1, 1896, he was raised in an upper-class family and was educated and lived in Calcutta until his retirement in 1950. In 1950, taking *vanaprastha* (retirement from social and economic obligations), he moved to Brindavan and dedicated himself completely to religious contemplation and writing. Abhay Charan De accepted *sanyasa* from Bhakti Prajnan Keshava at Keshavaji *Gaudiya Math* in Mathura, taking the new name Bhaktivedanta Swami. Bhakti Prajnan Keshava gave the title "Bhaktivedanta" to everyone who accepted *sanyasa* from him, and Swami was Abhay Charan De's *sanyasa* name, although he is popularly referred to as Srila Prabhupada. Prabhupada renewed his writing efforts after assuming his *sanyasa diksha*. He arrived in New York in 1965 and managed to establish ISKCON there by the summer of 1966, opening ISKCON in San Francisco and Montreal by 1967. Soon ISKCON centers multiplied in the United States and quickly spread through Europe, beginning with Germany and England. ISKCON Press was established in 1969 in Boston to publish translations of Bhaktivedanta Swami and *Back to Godhead* magazine, which was later shifted to Los Angeles and renamed Bhaktivedanta Book Trust (BBT). Soon translations of his original English publications appeared in Spanish, German, French and a number of other world languages. Bhaktivedanta Swami returned to India with a group of his disciples in 1970, settling there and establishing temples in Bombay, Vrindavan, Hyderabad, and an international headquarters of ISKCON in Mayapura, West Bengal. He passed away in Vrindavan on November 14, 1977.

Bhaktivedanta Swami was a prolific writer, working every night until 1 a.m. He planned a sixty-volume translation of the *Bhagavatapurana*, of which he completed thirty-one volumes before his passing. The first volume was published in India (*Srimad Bhagavatam*, Vrindavan, Delhi: League of Devotees). Prabhupada had translated the tenth *Bhagavatapurana* book containing the legend of Krishna as a separate book (*Krishna, The Supreme Personality of Godhead*, Boston: ISKCON Press, 1970). Several other books containing his speeches were published during these years. He also translated a seventeen-volume publication on *Chaitanya Charitamrita* by Krishnadas Kaviraja, and *Bhaktirasamritasindhu* by Rupa *Gosvami* as *The Nectar of Devotion: The Complete Science of Bhaktiyoga*. He also completed several other works of importance for Hinduism such as *Isopanishad* and *Upadesamrita* by Rupa *Gosvami*. Bhaktivedanta Swami was a most successful guru in that he attracted a large following of non-Indians while staying firmly grounded in the traditions of *Gaudiya* Vaishnavism, especially those emphasized by his own guru, Kedarnath Datta Bhaktivinoda.

See also: Bhagavadgita; *Bhagavatapurana*; Brindavan; Caitanya; *Gaudiya* Vaishnavism; ISKCON; Mathura; Puri Temple

Further Reading

Berg, T. V., and F. Kniss. 2008. "ISKCON and Immigrants: The Rise, Decline, and Rise Again of a New Religious Movement." *Sociological Quarterly* 49 (1): 79–104.

Shukavak, D. N. 1999. *Hindu Encounter with Modernity: Kedarnatha Datta Bhaktivinoda, Vaishnava Theologian*. Los Angeles: Sri Press.

BHIMA

Bhima, the second Pandava and a close cousin of Krishna, is the second son of Pandu and Kunthi through the Wind God, Vayu, and he inherited Vayu's strength and speed. Bhima is known for his voracious appetite, which gave him the

---

Vrikodara

Bhima is known as Vrikodara (Wolf Belly) for his voracious appetite. A story of Bhima's appetite matching that of monsters was described in the *Mahabharata*. The villagers of Ekacakrapura, where the Pandavas were hiding, entered into a pact with the demon Bakasura to stop the monster's uncontrollable daily harassment and began sending him food. One day it was the turn of the host family of the Pandavas to send food to the monster. Bhima was deputed to accomplish the task in place of the hostess's son and was sent to the forest with a cartload of rice and other food. However, Bhima finished the cartload of food by the time he reached the forest and then killed the hungry monster.

Vrishaketu and Bhima fighting Yavanatha, scene from the *Story of Babhruvahana* folio from the illustrated copy of the *Mahabharata* (*Great War of the Bharatas*) dated to 1850 from Paithan, Maharashtra, India. (Los Angeles County Museum of Art)

nickname Vrikodara (Wolf Belly). Bhima's life story described in the *Mahabharata* and the other *puranas* includes a number of tales of his incredible strength. He helped Krishna vanquish Jarasandha, one of Krishna's sworn enemies. Krishna, Arjuna, and Bhima reached Girivraja, the city of Jarasandha, under the guise of Brahmans. Jarasandha received them, thought they might be Kshatriyas dressed as Brahmans, and wondered if he had seen them somewhere earlier. However, assuming them to be visiting Brahmans, Jarasandha served them and said he would offer anything they might desire. Krishna declared that they were not Brahmans, but Kshatriyas. He introduced them, said that they desired to have one-to-one combat, and offered to fight with anyone Jarasandha chose. Ruling out Krishna as cowardly for previously withdrawing from the battlefield and Arjuna as younger and weak, Jarasandha said he would fight with his equal in strength, Bhima. A terrible wrestling match ensued between Bhima and Jarasandha that lasted for seven days and nights without an end in sight. While still continuing to fight Jarasandha, Bhima glanced toward Krishna seeking advice on how Jarasandha could be vanquished. In response, Krishna symbolically indicated a plan by splitting a twig and throwing the pieces crosswise, not side-by-side. Understanding Krishna's strategy, Bhima immediately took hold of Jarasandha's legs and split him open lengthwise. He threw both sections of the body crosswise, so the body parts did not fuse together. Thus Jarasandha died. Krishna then met the 20,800 kings imprisoned by Jarasandha. He gave them the vision of his four-armed form (*caturbhuja bhagavan*) with his typical adornment and received their homage. Krishna freed all the imprisoned kings and informed them that they were all free to return to their kingdoms. Krishna returned with gifts to the Pandava capital, Indraprastha, along with Arjuna and Bhima, where Dharma was preparing to hold the sacrifice of *Rajasuya*, performed by the greatest kings of the earth.

Bhima's life story described in the *Mahabharata* and the other *puranas* includes a number of tales of his incredible strength. Krishna was aware of his strength and knew that only Bhima could vanquish Jarasandha. Thus Krishna took Bhima to meet Jarasandha, who had defeated the Yadavas eighteen times previously. In the cosmological events of Yadava history, Bhima performed a significant role by killing Jarasandha, which brought peace to the Yadava state.

See also: Arjuna; Draupadi; Jarasandha; Kamsa; Pandavas

Further Reading
Picard, B. 1968. *Story of the Pandavas*. New York: Dobson Books.

BILVAMANGALA SVAMI, LILASUKA (1100)

Although Bilvamangala is one of the most popular *acaryas* of the Krishna devotional tradition, very scant details of his life are known. Bilvamangala's biography is narrated in Nabhadasa's hagiographical text, the *Bhaktamala* (1600); Gadadasa's text, the *Vallabhasampradayakuladipika*; and also the *Vallabhadigvijaya* of Jadunath Maharaj.

Bilvamangala Svami, also known as Lilasuka, composed two of the important texts on Krishna, the *Krishnakarnamrita* and the *Balagopalastuti*. Scholars also contend whether Bilvamangala Lilasuka and Krishna Lilasuka are the names of a single person or if they were two different persons. A consensus has emerged among scholars in the last fifty years that Bilvamangala Lilasuka is a mendicant (*parivrajaka*) Vaishnava poet of the eleventh century, while Krishna Lilasuka is a grammarian of the fourteenth century who admired and quoted poems of Bilvamangala Lilasuka widely in his works, the *Purushakara* and the *Sricihnakavya*. Bilvamangala is noted as an influential poet whose work impressed Caitanya, founder of Caitanya Vaishnavism. It is said that Caitanya liked listening to the poems of Bilvamangala when he was in his devotional ecstasy. Not much is known about Bilvamangala's early life, although some later references connect him to Kerala. Bilvamangala traveled widely across India, especially south India. Legends of Bilvamangala note that he was attracted to a prostitute called Cintamani, wasting his money, time, and energy on meeting her, while focusing on little else. Nabhadas's hagiographical text on the lives of Vaishnava *acaryas* states that Bilvamangala pricked his eyes with thorns and needles in order to control his desire for Cintamani. Popular theatrical versions of this story, a play by the name of *Cintamani*, were notorious in Andhra Pradesh and Bengal. Modern revised version of this play in the nineteenth century earned acclaim from theater connoisseurs as well as criticism from nationalist reformers in Andhra Pradesh. However, Cintamani is also

Krishnakarnamrita

The *Krishnakarnamrita* is an anthology of about three hundred devotional poems composed by Bilvamangala Lilasuka. The text of the book is organized into three sections containing about a hundred poems each called *sataka*. While Rupa *Gosvami* accepted only the first *sataka* as authentic, most of the extant manuscripts contain three hundred and more poems. The Bengali manuscript obtained by Caitanya during his southern Indian tour only contained the first hundred poems (*sataka*). This version containing the first hundred poems continues to remain the standard authoritative text of the Caitanya Vaishnava tradition.

Almost all the poems of the *Krishnakarnamrita* are hymns (*stotras*) dedicated to the pastimes of Krishna in Brindavan. The verses express all the *rasas* and *bhavas* associated with bhakti. Adoration expressed by the associates of Krishna as mother (*vastalya*), friend (*sakhi/sakha*), lover (*sringara*), partner (*madhurya*), and servant (*seva*) form the subject of the poems, although *madhurya rasa* dominates the composition as most of the poems express the soul's irresistible desire to be united with the ultimate reality represented by Krishna.

considered Bilvamangala's first guru, since she later urged Bilvamangala to dedicate himself to the grace of the god Krishna to find permanent joy and enjoyment. Bilvamangala lived his final days in Brindavan and composed the *Krishnakarnamrita* about the lovely pastimes of Krishna in Brindavan. *Krishnakarnamrita* contains about 300 verses, written in a simple style expressing emotion. It is said that Krishna himself would visit to listen to the poems of poet-saint Bilvamangala, who was also blind. It is also said that his poems were most popular in devotional circles, and copies of his poems circulated widely. Vernacular poets were inspired by Bilvamangala's poetry in the treatment of subject matter. The subject of Krishna's love for Radha becomes central to several texts following Bilvamangala's presentation of Radha and Krishna. Vaishnavism also has another blind poet-saint of the sixteenth century, called Surdas, another devotee of Krishna, whose poetry is also said to have brought Krishna to listen to him sing. Even though separated by a gap of hundreds of years, Bilvamangala's and Surdas's life stories appear analogous for their biographical details and theological conventions.

Bilvamangala's *samadhi* (memorial) is on Gopinatha Bazar in Vrindavan. Bilvamangala is connected with *madhuryabhava* as described in his book, the *Krishnakarnamrita*, and known for worshipping Radha as a way to accomplish unity with Krishna. Hence, devotees visit his *samadhi* to pay reverence to his memory and the unique devotional tradition he established.

See also: Bhagavatapurana; Braj *Parikrama*; Brindavan; Caitanya; *Lila*; Mathura; Radha

Further Reading

Rosen, S. "Blind Visionaries: The Twin Lives of Bilvamangala Thakura and Surdas." *Agni and Ecstacy: Collected Essays of Steven Rosen.* UK: Arktos Media.

Wilson, F. 1975. *The Love of Krishna: The Krishnakarnamrita of Lilasuka Bilvamangala*. Philadelphia: University of Pennsylvania Press.

BIOGRAPHY OF KRISHNA

Legends of Krishna provide the dates of his birth and death fairly uniformly across the *puranas* and the epics of Hinduism, as well as Jainism. According to these traditional sources Krishna lived around 3000 BCE. Historically 3000 BCE. marks the high point of an ancient civilization in northwestern India between the Indus and Narmada river valleys in Maharashtra (currently referred to variously as the Sindhu-Saraswathi civilization or Indus valley civilization). During its greatest phase it also began spreading toward eastern India into the fertile Ganga River valley between 3500 and 1500 BCE. This civilization began to decline in the Indus valley due to climatic changes from 2000 BCE. onward, finally losing its distinct features by 1000 BCE. However, this civilization continued to grow and flourish between the Ganga and Yamuna river valleys, acquiring regional variations gradually. It is difficult to know the historical life and circumstances from this period, since most of the cities were lost to floods, and the cities were abandoned due to rivers changing course because of earthquakes and other geological changes in the Himalayas. The classical life stories of Krishna mention such calamities at the beginning of the *Kali* age (3102 BCE), beginning with the drowning of Krishna's city, Dvaraka. However, it is hard to corroborate archaeological data with the Krishna legend from the textual sources due to the fragmentary nature of the excavated material. Due to the hot and humid climate and the acidic nature of the soil, very little organic material such as bones or wood remains from these early cities except for nonorganic objects such as those made from clay.

Krishna was born in 3228 BCE in Mathura from where he was immediately transferred by his father Vasudeva to Vraja. Krishna stayed at Vraja with his adopted parents, Yashoda and Nandagopa, during the first three years of his life. Here Krishna killed Kamsa's demons such as Putana, Sakatasura, and Trinavrita. Noticing these incessant demonic attacks and other premonitions, the Yadava elders decided to move the camp to another nearby town. Krishna then moved to Brindavan along with his parents and the Yadavas, where he stayed for about nine years (3225–3215 BCE) until he left with Akrura to participate in the wrestling match in Mathura. Krishna's life in Brindavan is the most loving phase of his divine incarnation on earth. Here, Krishna enchanted the *Gopis* and *Gopas* with his pranks, interspersed with divine revelations. Hence Brindavan is epitomized in several incidents connected with the plays (*lilas*) of Krishna, such as *Govardhanlila, Raasalila,* and *Danlila*. Krishna killed Kamsa and lived in Mathura for the next sixteen years (about 3200 BCE.), building the Yadava state and helping his kin. It was here that Jarasandha, Kamsa's father-in-law, defeated the Yadavas eighteen times, forcing Krishna to leave Mathura. Krishna subsequently founded his own empire centered in Dvaraka, a new capital city on the west coast of the Indian Ocean, built on land reclaimed from the sea, where he lived the next ninety-nine years of his life. During this period he also married his eight principal wives and, at their own request, the

16,100 princesses imprisoned by Narakasura. He vanquished Jarasandha with the help of Bhima, killed Kalayavana and Narakasura, and ruled from Dvaraka. Krishna's death occurred in a place called Prabhasa, not very far from Dvaraka, his capital, at about 3102 BCE. Most of the places associated with Krishna's life form part of the pilgrimage circuit of Mathura and are revered as sacred centers of Krishna.

See also: Bhima; Birth and Early Childhood of Krishna; Childhood of Krishna in Brindavan; Death of Krishna; Dvaraka; Jarasandha; Kamsa; Mathura; Narakasura; Nidra; Prabhasa; Yogamaya

Further Reading

Athavale, V. B. 1947. "A Summary of the Research Work Done with Regard to the Chronology and Geography of the Events in the Life History of Shri Krishna and the *Pandava Brothers*." *Poona Orientalist* 12: 1–4, 34–39.

Chandra, A. N. 1978. *The Date of the Kurukshetra War*. Calcutta, India: Ratna Prakasan.

Rao, N. 2014. *Sindu-Saraswati Civilization: New Perspectives*. New Delhi: D. K. Print World & Nalanda International.

Rosen, S. 1989. *Archaeology and the Vaishnava Tradition*. Calcutta, India: Firma KLM.

BIRTH AND EARLY CHILDHOOD OF KRISHNA

Krishna was born in Mathura to Vasudeva and Devaki in prison. He had to be moved to Vraja as soon as he was born to avoid being killed by Kamsa. It was foretold, soon after the marriage of Devaki to Vasudeva, that Krishna, the eighth son of Devaki, would be the killer of Kamsa. Kamsa reacted very violently to this message from the divine voice, trying to kill Devaki. Vasudeva convinced Kamsa to spare her life with the promise that he would stay in Mathura and hand over every child born to Devaki. Krishna was born in the prison and showed his divine form to his parents, Devaki and Vasudeva, telling Vasudeva to transfer him to Vraja. As soon as Vasudeva picked up the basket into which Krishna was placed, the locks on the doors of the prison broke open, while all the prison guards and the people of Mathura slipped into a deep slumber, overcome by Yogamaya, making it easier for Vasudeva to leave Mathura. As Vasudeva proceeded toward Vraja, it continued to

---

Butter Thief

The Braj *lila* (play of Braj/Vraja) of Krishna was dominated by his infant and childhood mischief of getting into everything and putting everything into his mouth. This stage of Krishna's life is emblematic of *vastalya bhava* (mood of affection), which was showered on baby Krishna by Yashoda, his doting mother, and her *Gopi* friends. The most remembered *lila* of Krishna from this stage of his life is stealing butter, not only from his own home, but also from any house he could get into in Vraja. *Lila* is where boundaries vanish; the most beloved lord becomes the most notorious thief in this episode. Hence, he is lovingly called *makhanchor* (butter thief) because of his mischief.

rain: the river Yamuna flowed full of water. Sesha, the divine serpent, made a path for Vasudeva while protecting Krishna from the rain by covering the basket with his hood. As Vasudeva left, Nanda's wife Yashoda gave birth to a girl in Vraja. As soon as Vasudeva reached Vraja, he met Nanda and handed him the child Krishna, who gave him the baby girl born to Yashoda in exchange. Vasudeva brought the child back and she was handed to Kamsa the next morning. Kamsa killed the child immediately by hitting her on rocks. But from that child the goddess Yogamaya rose to the sky, informing him that Kamsa's killer had been born somewhere else. Meanwhile Krishna was safe in Vraja and delighting everyone with his childish pranks.

Putana Killed

Kamsa deputed his demonic guards to find Krishna among the children born in his kingdom and kill him. Putana, the female demon, arrived in Vraja and, noticing the beautiful young child Krishna, transformed herself into a beautiful woman and approached Krishna. She took Krishna into her arms as if to cuddle him and then tried to breastfeed him, with the intention of killing him. She had previously smeared poison on her breasts. However, as Krishna suckled at her breast, she lost her life and fell down, assuming her original body as a female demon. Seeing the demonic body of Putana, Yashoda and the rest of the *Gopis* of Vraja were terrified and left, taking the baby Krishna away with them. Putana, however, obtained the grace of God even though she was only pretending love in order to breastfeed Krishna; her act of service was noted. Her body, which previously smelled putrid, now had a fragrant smell, and the people of Vraja arranged for the cremation of Putana's dead body. As her body burned, all the people of Vraja smelled the fragrance and wondered about it. Several other demons followed her and tracked Krishna, meeting a similar fate.

Trinavrita Killed

The demon Trinavrita created a whirlwind, assuming the form of a hurricane lifting everything in its way. However, Krishna, lifted into the air, got hold of Trinavrita's neck. Unable to move or escape from Krishna's grasp, Trinavrita died and fell to the ground.

Yamala-Arjuna Trees Fall

Krishna's childhood pranks included breaking a pot of milk, feeding butter to monkeys, and crawling in the house incessantly. One day Yashoda, when she wanted to prevent him from crawling away and getting into things, tied him to a mortar with a rope and went back to her chores. Krishna crawled off into the neighborhood dragging the mortar behind him. As he crawled between two Ashoka trees, the trees, making a stupendous sound, fell crosswise due to the pressure from the mortar. Nalakubara and Manigriva, two sons of Dhanada, treasurer of Kubera, emerged from the trees. Hearing the loud sound of the falling trees, the

Gopas and Nanda arrived, only to discover the fallen trees and Krishna, innocently crawling nearby and dragging a mortar. Nanda released Krishna and took him into his hand. However, the *Gopas* could not imagine how such large trees could have fallen to the ground. The *Harivamsa* also narrates another event following the fall of the Ashoka trees in Vraja, one that is not recollected in any other classical text of India. It is said that a number of wolves attacked the calves and terrorized the *Gopas* in Vraja. The wolves were dark in color and bore the *srivatsa* mark of Vishnu on their foreheads. It is clear that Krishna prepared the

Krishna kills the ogress Putana, folio from an illustrated *Bhagavata Purana* (*Ancient Stories of the Lord*) text, ca. 1675–1700, Rajasthan, India. (Los Angeles County Museum of Art)

Gopas to leave Vraja for their new encampment in Brindavan. However, the appearance of wolves is strange and cannot be clearly explained.

As an infant Krishna killed Putana and Trinavrita, and he also released two Yakshas, Nalakubara and Manigriva, from their curse. However, the elders of Vraja, who decided to move the camp to a nearby site known as Brindavan, saw these incidents as bad omens and signs indicative of impending danger. Krishna spent his childhood in Brindavan delighting the residents with his pranks, games, and miraculous deeds. Overall the early childhood of Krishna in Vraja could be categorized as a peaceful period.

See also: Balarama; Braj: Classical History; Childhood of Krishna in Brindavan; *Gopas* and *Gopis*; *Lila*; Mathura; *Maya*; Nidra; Vrishnis; Yashoda

Further Reading

Hawley, J. S. 1983. *Krishna, the Butter Thief.* Princeton: Princeton University Press.

BRAJ: CLASSICAL HISTORY

The classical history of Braj continues after the death of Krishna and the annihilation of a majority of the Yadavas at Prabhasa. Dvaraka, Krishna's city, was also submerged in the ocean. Braj was revived by Vajranabha, the great-grandson of Krishna, who was rescued and coronated king of the Yadavas in Mathura by Arjuna. At the death of Krishna, most of the Yadavas died in the battle, and Arjuna transported the remaining women and children at the request of Krishna. Therefore, for a long time after Krishna's death the sacred sites associated with Krishna's life were abandoned and became desolate.

The *Mausulaparva* of the *Mahabharata* and the *Bhagavatapurana* mention that Krishna sent Jara to fetch Arjuna to convey an important message to him before his death. When Arjuna had come, Krishna informed him that Dvaraka was about to be drowned by the ocean, and that Arjuna should transfer the women and other survivors of the Yadava clan from Dvaraka to a safe location. The death of Krishna marked the end of *Dvaparayuga* and the beginning of *Kaliyuga*, a degenerative age marked by low morals and difficult life. As Arjuna proceeded toward Indraprastha with the women, elders, and other survivors of the Yadava clan, they were attacked by Ahirs and other tribes who took away women and wealth that was being transported. Arjuna coronated Vajranabha, great-grandson of Krishna (son of Aniruddha and grandson of Pradyumna) as the king of the Yadava state, while he also crowned his grandson Parikshit, son of Abhimanyu and Uttara, as the king of the Pandava state, and left with his brothers on their final journey (*mahaprasthana*) to reach the other world. Vajranabha lamented to Parikshit that Mathura (known as Mathuramandala or Vrajabhumi in classical texts) and the places sacred to Krishna had been abandoned since a large section of the Yadava clan had been annihilated. Vajranabha wished to recover the sacred sites associated with Krishna. Parikshit and Vajranabha subsequently consulted the sage Sandilya, who was familiar with the life of Krishna and the region of Mathura. The sage Sandilya took Vajranabha on a tour of the sacred places associated with the life of Krishna, identifying the places where major events of Krishna's life had occurred. The sage Sandilya advised Vajranabha to establish villages near the sacred places so that Vajranabha could make arrangements for taking care of the river, hills, tanks, and groves of Mathura, and preserve the sacred places associated with Krishna for the future. Vajranabha began repopulating Mathura. While ruling from there, he constructed temples in important places associated with Krishna, and also took care of the natural areas of Mathura including the hills, tanks, and groves, to preserve the idyllic natural beauty of the region that once enjoyed Krishna's presence.

The repopulation and preservation of Mathura is narrated as another classical story in the *Skandapurana* and the *Gargasamhita*, which describes how Vajranabha enlisted the support of Kalindi (one of the eight principal wives of Krishna and a form of Yamuna) and Uddhava, a friend and follower of Krishna. Classical texts describe Vajranabha as the progenitor of devotional worship centered on Krishna. Vajranabha is said to have constructed the temples of Govindadeva and Harideva with the help of his great-grandmother Kalindi. Vajranabha then met Uddhava, who was said to have been living in the form of an evergreen creeper near Kusumsagar (Kusum Sarovar). Uddhava informed Vajranabha that he preferred to live in Vraja in any form, since Krishna sports eternally in the bowers of Brindavan. Uddhava also informed him that he would continue to reside near the Narad Kund and convey the message of the *Bhagavadgita* to the devotees. This is in accordance with the role of Uddhava narrated in the *Bhagavatapurana*. Uddhava conveyed the message of Krishna to the *Gopis*, and also Uddhava received another message from Krishna also known as the *Hamsagita* or the *Uddhavagita*. Why Uddhava chose to remain a creeper in Vraja may be puzzling, but it may indicate the evergreen and flowering nature of the creeper, as Uddhava is said to be ever present in Mathura, spreading

Krishna's message. Therefore, Uddhava, reminiscent in the ubiquitous plant, and Kalindi, present as the water body of Braj, symbolically indicate the conviction of Krishna devotees that Krishna's presence is felt though every plant and water body of Braj. Thus supported by Uddhava and Kalindi, Vajranabha recreated Vraja as it was known previously. Uddhava helped him with spreading Krishna's philosophical message, while Kalindi helped him recreate the physical representation of Krishna in the places where Krishna sported. Thus the physical and metaphysical imagery of Krishna is spread through devotion to Krishna as narrated in the texts. The *Skandapurana* and the *Gargasamhita* list a number of temples, *vans* (bowers), and tanks that Vajranabha supported. Vajranabha is said to have been the founder of images of Dirghavishnu and Keshavadeva at Mathura, Govindadeva at Vrindavan, Harideva at Govardhan, Gokulesha at Gokul, and Baladeva at Baldeo.

See also: Birth and Early Childhood of Krishna; Braj *Parikrama*; Brindavan; Caitanya; *Gargasamhita*; Govardhan; Mathura; Twelve Forests of Braj; Uddhava; Vallabha

Further Reading
Entwistle, A. 1987. *Braj: Center of Krishna Prilgrimage.* Groningen: Egbert Forsten.

BRAJ *PARIKRAMA*
Braj, also known as Vraja/Vraj in Hindu texts, is the most sacred and important region of pilgrimage for Vaishnavas. Numerous temples of various Vaishnava traditions have been constructed to mark its sacred nature. Visiting one or several places in the Braj region is part of the devotional practice. *Parikrama* (circumambulation) is a variation of the *pradakshina* (circumambulation) ritual conducted in the temples. In *pradakshina* a devotee may only walk around the inner sanctum of the temple or around the deity and the periphery of the temple inside the compound wall. This represents paying homage to the deity, while presenting oneself by walking around the sacred representation of the deity inside the temple. However, this ritual is extended to include a whole town and geographical landmarks (such as hills, rivers, or bowers) that are considered sacred due to the symbolic presence of the deity. The Braj region includes a number of landmarks that are considered sacred as the playground (*lila sthana*) of the child Krishna, the place where most of

---

Dandauti Parikrama

Dandauti parikrama is a laborious *parikrama* since the devotees do not walk during the circumambulation, but roll over the distance prostrate on the ground. Govardhan *parikrama* is generally undertaken for *Dandauti parikrama*, but it is not unusual for devotees to undertake other *parikramas* circumambulating an individual holy site connected to Krishna in a similar manner.

his childhood was spent. Devotees pay homage to Krishna by walking around these sacred places in Braj *Parikrama*.

Classical texts of India such as the *Mahabharata* and the *Harivamsa* (300 BCE–300 CE) praise the sanctity of Braj, while the later *puranas* include the standard list of pilgrimage sites of Hinduism. However, the Braj region underwent political instability and turmoil since the twelfth century with the establishment of Muslim rule in Delhi. Muslim invasions affected the Braj pilgrimage, and the sacred places around Braj became desolate. However, several Vaishnava gurus have visited the Braj region since the fifteenth century, trying to identify and revive the sacred places associated with Krishna's life. Narayana Bhatt's *Brajbhaktivilasa* describes all the sacred places in the Braj region, therefore it could be said that the Braj region has remained an important religious center, even though pilgrimages have been discouraged. Braj has been visited by the renowned Vaishnava saints and *acaryas,* including *acarya* Madhavendra Puri (1490), Vallabhacarya (1555, 1565), and Caitanya (1573). Caitanya was deeply moved by the desolation of the sacred places in Braj during his visit there. He later sent his disciples Rupa and Sanatana *Gosvami* to revive Braj.

Braj *parikrama* is a forty-day *yatra* (journey) covering all the sacred places associated with Krishna. However, there are also shorter pilgrimage trips to individual sacred sites in the Braj region, which may take only a day or two. Devotees may choose to undertake a short *parikrama* of specific pilgrimage sites or take several short trips to complete visiting all of the sacred sites in Braj. Alternatively, they can choose to undertake the complete Braj *parikrama* at one time, visiting all of the sacred sites in a single trip. The most commonly performed short *parikramas* of individual towns are to Mathura, Govardhan, and Brindavan. Other shorter *parikaramas* are Ramdal *parikrama* (15–16 days), Panctirth *parikrama* (5–6 days), and Antargrahi *parikrama* (Vishram *ghat* and its nearby regions, 1–2 days). Groups of devotees undertake the pilgrimage with the help of a guide, beginning their journey from Mathura.

See also: Braj: Classical History; Brindavan; Caitanya; *Gargasamhita*; Govardhan; Mathura; Twelve Forests of Braj; Uddhava; Vallabha

Further Reading

Anand, D. 2004. *Krishna: The Living God of Braj*. New Delhi: Abhinav Publications.
Mittal, P. D. 1968. *Braj Ke Dharam Sampradayon Ka Itihas*. Mathura: Sahitya Sansthan.

BRINDAVAN

Brindavan, also referred to as Vrindavana in classical texts, is located on the western bank of the Yamuna, which forms a beautiful semicircular border of the town. Brindavan is the place of *Krishnalilas* (*Raasalila, Govardhanlila*) and numerous temples of Krishna. The modern Birla temple on the Mathura road from Brindavan, built of red sandstone, contains a stone pillar inscribed with the entire *Bhagavadgita*. Brindavan also contains numerous temples dedicated to other minor Vaishnava deities related to Krishna as noted in the *Bhagavatapurana,* including the Akrura

Goddess Brinda as Tulasi

Brindavan is named after the goddess Brinda, the personified form of the *tulasi* plant (*Ocimum sanctum*), which is commonly found in Brindavan. Krishna always wore a garland of *tulasi* leaves and branches. The *Tulasi* Festival celebrates the marriage of Krishna and Tulasi symbolically with Tulasi represented by the *tulasi* plant and Krishna represented by the gooseberry plant in *Kartika suddha dvadasi* (October–November), called *Uttana dvadasi* or *Brinda dvadasi*.

temple, Bhatrod temple, and *Ashtasakhi* temple (Radha and her eight friends). The major temples of Krishna were constructed and are maintained by the various devotional traditions dedicated to Krishna, including the Krishna Balarama temple (ISKCON temple established by A. C. Bhakitvedanta Svami Prabhupada), Radha Damodar temple (by Jiva *Gosvami*), Rangaji temple (Ramanuja tradition after the Sri Rangam temple), Gopinath temple, Jugalkishore temple, Madan Mohan temple, Bankebihari temple (installed by Svami Haridas), Radhavallabha temple (temple constructed by Hit Harivams for Radha), Radharaman temple, and others. A number of groves and *ghats* (sacred lakes or ponds) are located on the three sides of Brindavan. The town of Brindavan itself is named after a forest and contains numerous forests. However, the most important groves in Brindavan are Sevakunj (Radhavallabha tradition) and Nidhivan (Haridasi tradition). There are a number of *ghats* in Brindavan, but the most important are Kaliya *ghat* (called Kalidah *ghat*), Praskandan *ghat*, Jugal *ghat*, Bihar *ghat*, Chir *ghat*, Keshi *ghat*, Akrur *ghat*, and Man *sarovar*.

Govindadev Temple

The most important temple of Brindavan is the Govindadev temple, an impressive temple built of red sandstone. The Govindadev temple is also considered the most sacred temple by the followers of Vaishnavism, since it is located on the *yogapitha* (seat of yoga) at the center of Brindavan, according to classical texts of Hinduism, which is also noted in an inscription found in the temple. The presiding deity of this temple, known by the name Govindadev, another name for Krishna, is represented in the gesture of playing the flute. The main idol installed in this temple appeared in a vision to Rupa *Gosvami*, and was later discovered by him in the vicinity of the current temple. Govindadev temple was built by Savai Man Singh in the sixteenth century (1577–1590) under the direction of Rupa *Gosvami*. However, the main idol of Govindadev had been moved to Jaipur in Rajasthan state during one of the raids by Aurangzeb, where it still remains in a magnificent temple. Aurangzeb destroyed part of the temple, which was later rebuilt, and a replica of the main idol is installed in the Govindadev temple. Aurangzeb is said to have destroyed the tall *shikhara* (tower) of the temple, and also the images around the temple. In addition to the main temple there are also two shrines in this temple complex dedicated to the goddesses Vrindadevi and Yogamaya, the sister of Krishna.

Madan Mohan Temple

The Madan Mohan temple is built for the deity Madan Mohan worshipped by Sanatana *Gosvami*. The deity was taken care of by the disciples of Sanatana *Gosvami* after his death before being installed in the temple. During the early seventeenth century under the fear of attack by Aurangzeb, the deity was moved to Rajasthan and worshipped in a *haveli* in Jaipur until 1728, when it was transferred to Karauli near Jaipur, where it still remains in a temple. Aurangzeb's army destroyed the original temple; a new Madan Mohan temple was built, where a replica of the deity Madan Mohan is worshipped, in the main temple in Brindavan. The original Madan Mohan temple is the tallest temple in Brindavan; it is sixty feet high and it is located on a fifty-foot-high hill. The original Madan Mohan temple was constructed in the Nagara style with a tall octagonal *shikhara* (tower) over the sanctum. The tower over the *mandapa* (hall) is shorter and square. Originally devotees entered a hall, topped with a pyramidal tower, through an ornate gateway with a nave, but currently a side entrance is being used to enter the temple. A new Madan Mohan temple was constructed in the nineteenth century, located at the bottom of the hill, and in the vicinity of this temple are the *samadhis* (memorials) of Sanatana *Gosvami* and numerous other disciples. There is also a *bhajan kuti* of Sanatana, which is used for devotional activities. East of the mound beneath the Modan Mohan temple are shrines of other deities, such as *Ashtasakhi*, Sitala, Shiva, and Surya. The Advaita *bat* (Advaita's banyan, after Advaita *acarya*), where Advaita *acarya* used to sit in meditation, is in the vicinity of the Madan Mohan temple. The original tree, lost in the floods, was replaced by another tree.

Bankebihari Temple

The icon of Bankebihari discovered by Swami Haridas in Nidhiban is housed in the Bankebihari temple. Haridas originally called the deity Kunjbihari (one who roams in the grove), later changed by his disciples to Vankevihari or Bankebihari (the letter V is often replaced by B in the local dialect), meaning one who roams the forest. This latter name has led some to interpret Bankebihari as "bent one who roams," since *banke* also means bent or crooked in the local dialect. The original temple of Bankebihari is in Nidhiban, while another Bankebihari temple is in Brindavan, maintained by the *gosvamis* of the Haridasi tradition. There is a dispute over the hereditary priesthood between the ascetics and priests of the Haridasi tradition. There are now numerous *gosvamis* eligible for temple service, drawing their line from the brother of the first priest appointed by Haridas, which is disputed by the ascetics of the Haridasi tradition, who claim that there were no hereditary appointments made by Haridas. The ascetics remain and control the shrine in Nidhiban, while the temple in Brindavan is managed by the hereditary *gosvami* priests.

However, the festivals involve the organized participation of the ascetics as well as the priests. The Bankebihari temple is one of the most popular and well-attended temples in Brindavan. Its festival celebrations draw large crowds of devotees. The Bankebihari temple follows its own *arati* schedule, which is offered only three times a day, and strangely the early-morning *arati,* called the *mangal arati,* is never offered. It is believed that the deities are up late in the night sporting in the groves and forests of Brindavan and need their rest in the morning, and therefore should not be disturbed early in the day. The temple takes pride in safeguarding the privacy of the central deity, Bankebihari. The use of conch and bells is restricted in this temple, because loud sounds may disturb the deities. Another custom is to close the curtain for a few seconds during the *darsan* period, while the temple is open and the *darsan* queue is proceeding. The temple is known for single-day festivals such as *Dolotsav* (the swing festival held in the month of *Chaitra,* March–April of each year) and *Akshay Tritiya* (the second day of *Diwali*). Special *pujas* are offered to the deities on the day of *Akshay Tritiya;* it is the only day of the year on which the deities' feet can be seen for *Darshan. Janmasthami,* marking the birth of Krishna, is also celebrated with special *pujas;* it is the only day of the year on which an early-morning *mangal arati* is offered in the Bankebihari temple. *Bihar pancami* (the day when Bankebihari was found by Swami Haridas) is another special festival day of the temple. On this day a festival procession is organized from Nidhivan to the temple, and the ascetics also organize *samaj gayan* as part of the celebrations.

Radhavallabha Temple

The image of Radhavallabha, found and worshipped by Hit Harivams, is housed in the Radhavallabha temple. The temple as well as the devotional tradition derive their name from the name of the image worshipped by Hit Harivams. There are two temples currently in use under this name. The first Radhavallabha temple was constructed during the lifetime of Harivams. However, the central deity, Radhavallabha, was taken to Kaman in the eighteenth century due to fear of Aurangzeb's destructive attacks. The main idol of Radhavallabha was brought back from Kaman to a new and magnificent temple in 1784, while the former temple is still used on special occasions and during festivals for *samaj gayan.* A special festival conducted in the temple is the *kichidi* festival on *Amavasya* (new moon) days during the months of *Pushya* and *Margashira.* During these days the deity is offered *kichidi* (rice and lentils) in the morning and prepared with appropriate clothing and ornaments (*sringar*), followed by special *darsan* during the day.

The old and new temples of Radhavallabha are located in a compound called Radhavallabha Ghera, where other small temples of the Radhavallabha tradition are also located such as Anandi Bai ka mandir and Kolkattawala mandir. In the vicinity of the Radhavallabha Ghera are other temples of the Radhavallabha tradition such as Radhamohan Ghera (founded by Krishnachandra, son of Hit Harivams), Bari Sarkar temple, and Choti Sarkar temple, behind which is a Balarama temple of the Vallabha tradition.

See also: Arati; Bhaktivedanta Swami Prabhupada; *Darsana*; *Gaudiya* Vaishnavism; ISKCON; Nimbarka Tradition; Radhavallabha Tradition; Rupa *Gosvami*; *Samaj Gayan*; Six *Gosvamis*

Further Reading

Vajpayi, K. D. 1958. *Braj Ka Itihas*. Parts 1 and 2. Mathura: Akhil Bharatiya Braj Sahitya Mandal.
Vaudeville, Ch. 1976. "Braj Lost and Found." *Indo-Iranian Journal* 18: 195–213.

BUDDHISM AND KRISHNA

The Krishna legend was well known in ancient India, established by the fact that variations of it are encountered in the early classical tales of other religions of India such as Buddhism and Jainism. Although the Buddhist story of Krishna is fragmentary and recollected as a story of the former life of the Buddha, it bears striking associations with the classical story of Krishna.

The *Ghatajataka* in the Pali canon includes a variant of Krishna's life. Although some incidents recounted in the *Ghatajataka* are similar to the Hindu classical texts, it differs significantly in most of its details. In the Buddhist story, Krishna is the eldest brother of ten siblings, while Baladeva (known as Balarama in Hindu texts) is the second and Arjuna is the seventh brother.

Mahakamsa had three children: Kamsa, Upakamsa, and Devagabba (Devaki in Hindu stories). On one of Devagabba's birthdays it was foretold that one of her children would destroy the lineage of Kamsa and bring an end to his kingdom. When Mahakamsa died, Kamsa became king and Upakamsa became viceroy. Thinking about the impending danger for them and their kingdom from Devagabba's child, her brothers decided to imprison Devagabba in an isolated tower, and decided never to marry her off to anyone lest she have children. They assigned to her a maid called Nandagopa.

In a nearby kingdom resided Upasagara, a friend of Upakamsa, who happened to visit Mathura and, observing the tower, saw Devagabba and fell in love with her. Devagabba also saw him and fell in love with him. Upasagara met the maid and requested her to arrange their secret meeting, and Nandagopa obliged happily. The brothers Kamsa and Upakamsa found out about it when they noted their sister was pregnant and questioned Nandagopa, the maid. The brothers did not want to kill their own sister, and they married her to Upasagara, but told them they would not spare their child if it were a boy. As a result of this first pregnancy, Devagabba gave birth to a daughter called Anjana. The brothers did not want to kill the child, so they let Devagabba keep her. Kamsa and Upakamsa then let Upasagara and Devagabba live in Govardhamana. Subsequently, Devagabba gave birth to nine boys, but knowing that her brothers might not spare the boys' lives, she sent them all to live with her maid Nandagopa and her husband Andhakavennu, where they grew up as Andhakavennu's children. In exchange Devagabba raised the daughters of her maid Nandagopa as her own. As the nine brothers grew up, they became strong and skillful wrestlers. They plundered Mathura and also took several other cities of India. They killed the wrestlers Mushtika and Canura in a wrestling match and took over the city (similar to the Hindu story). They also took Dvaraka from the Ass Demon, and finally they were attacked and their city was destroyed. Vasudeva and Baladeva went away into the forest leaving the city, in which everyone perished. Vasudeva died as Jara shot an arrow at him (similar to the Hindu story of the death of Krishna), and Baladeva was swallowed up by the demon Kalantika. Every single member of their family perished except for their sister Anjana.

Although the Buddhist story has some elements of similarity with the Hindu story of Krishna, such as Krishna's birth, death, and killing of Kamsa, it missed almost all the important aspects of his life depicted in the Hindu legends such as his divine play (*lilas*) of Vraja and Brindavan, and his involvement in the *Mahabharata* and the teaching of the *Bhagavadgita*. However, Krishna's wrestling match, growing up as a son with foster parents, his taking over the city of Dvaraka, and his death are strikingly similar to the Hindu story. It seems strange that the Buddhist *jataka* story does not mention the childhood events in Vraja and Brindavan, which form the central part of Hindu mythology as *Krishnalila*, inspiring devotional imagery in the worship of Krishna for numerious bhakti traditions of India, unless it could be understood as being intentionally eliminated to avoid conflict with the contemporary devotional traditions of Krishna.

See also: Brindavan; Devaki; Dvaraka; Jainism and Krishna; Mathura; *Maya*; Nandagopa; Nidra; Subhadra: Krishna's Sister; Vasudeva; Yashoda

Further Reading
Poussain, D. L., and E. J. Thomas. 2010. Reprint. *Pali Niddesa*. London: Pali Text Society.

C

CAITANYA

Caitanya (1486–1533), also commonly referred to as Caitanya Mahaprabhu, is the foremost Krishna devotee, recognized as a saint. He is also equated with Krishna as an incarnation of Krishna in a human form. Caitanya's teachings are organized in a collection known as *Sikshashtaka*, since it contains eight stanzas. These eight stanzas contain the essence of Caitanya's theological instruction on the nature of bhakti (devotion). Four stanzas (1–3 and 6) deal with *harinama japa* or *samkirtana*, while the remaining four stanzas describe the eternal relationship between individual souls and Krishna, along with *virahabhakti* and devotion. These are the two essential features of Caitanya's bhakti: the *namakirtana* (singing names) and *samkirtana* (devotional singing), while remaining conscious of the relationship of the individual with Krishna.

Caitanya's teaching of Krishna bhakti established five ways of devotional practice to reach Krishna: (1) be in the company of Krishna devotees, (2) chant and hear discourses on Krishna or names of Krishna, (3) participate in discourses on the names of Krishna, (4) visit Brindavan, and (5) worship the images of Krishna or perform *kirtan* (singing the names).

Caitanya is the progenitor of a devotional Vaishnava tradition known as *Gaudiya* Vaishnava *Sampradaya*. His disciples Rupa and Sanatana composed commentaries expounding Caitanya's teachings, thus popularizing them and making them accessible to succeeding generations.

Numerous biographies of Caitanya are available. The following are the most important texts: *Sri Krishnacaitanya Caritamrita* in Sanskrit by Murari Gupta, written during Caitanya's lifetime, served as the basic text for later biographies of Caitanya such as *Krishnacaitanya Caritamrita Mahakvya* by Kavikarnapura, Jayananda's *Caitanyamangala*, and Locanadasa's composition, also known as *Caitanya Mangala*.

Mayapur

Mayapur near Navadvip in the Nadia district of West Bengal, India, is identified as the birthplace of Caitanya. An annual festival marking Caitanya's birth, *Gaurapurnima* (full moon in March), is held in the temple of Caitanya here at *Yogapith*. *Navadvip parikrama*, a pilgrimage consisting of visiting the places associated with Caitanya's life, is also undertaken by the devotees of Krishna.

Kavikarnapura also wrote an allegorical drama on Caitanya's life known as *Caitanya Candrodaya Nataka*. Another biography, *Caitanya Caritamrita* by Krishnadasa Kaviraja, the most prominent work, enjoys immense popularity among the *Gaudiya* Vaishnavas.

Caitanya is identified as Krishna, and the followers of Caitanya are also identified with the *Gopis* and *Gopas* who were Krishna's close associates in Brindavan during the *Dvapara* age. Hence Caitanya's life is represented in a mandala akin to the *Krishnamandala*. Caitanya's life is exceptional and his contribution to Vaishnavism is unique. Caitanya's followers are credited with establishing and popularizing several schools of thought centered on Krishna, which brought Krishna bhakti to the masses not only in India, but also in numerous places around the world. Several events in Caitanya's life are narrated in great detail in his biographies. The following is a brief account of Caitanya's life and his later divinity. Caitanya was born during a lunar eclipse in the month of *Phalguna* (February–March) in 1486 in Navadvip to Brahman parents, Jagannatha Misra and Saci. He was named Vishvambhara, although he was called by his nickname, Nimai, before adopting his religious name, Caitanya. His birth is narrated as a cosmically and religiously purported event in his biographies. On the day of a lunar eclipse, it is particularly common for residents of Navadvip to recite the name "Hari" while standing in the waters of the river Ganga to ward off any evil. This public chanting is particularly noted as a divine portent indicating Caitanya's future work in the propagation of the recitation of divine names (*Harinama samkirtana*). Caitanya faced a number of sad events in the family while growing up, including his brother Vishvarupa's leaving the house never to return, the death of his father, and the death of his wife Laxmipriya. He married Vishnupriya at the behest of his mother, who also died young.

Young Caitanya was an accomplished scholar of Sanskrit and Hindu scriptures. Biographies of Caitanya depict him as winning debates against well-known *pandits* of the day, such as Kesava Bhatta, on Sanskrit prosody. However, the most important event happened on his pilgrimage to Puri to perform the *sraddha* rituals (last rites) for his father. Here Caitanya met Vaishnava ascetic Isvara Puri, who taught him the mantra for worshipping Krishna. Consequently, Caitanya became subsumed in Krishna worship, and he immersed himself in performing, listening, and acting in the service of Krishna, constantly singing the praises of Krishna rapturously. From then on *nama samkirtana* (singing the names) and *japa* (meditation on the names) became Caitanya's predominant spiritual practices.

Caitanya's participation in the Jagannatha *rathayatra* with his rapturous dance and song is recorded as a miraculous event. For the chariot procession of Jagannatha, Caitanya organized his followers into four groups, while Krishnadasa organized three groups. Krishnadasa noted the miraculous manifestation of Caitanya simultaneously in all seven groups, thus exhibiting one of the unique qualities associated with Krishna, that of simultaneous multiple manifestations noted in the *Bhagavatapurana* descriptions of *Raasalila*. Such public displays of devotion also led Caitanya into a conflict with the local *kaji* in Navadvip, where public *samkirtana* activities of Caitanya's followers were seen as objectionable activities according to Islam. The *kaji* and his men harassed Caitanya's followers, beating them, and he also threatened them with further action if they did not stop public chanting of the names (*nama samkirtana*). Caitanya called for a large public *samkirtana* attended by numerous followers and laypeople alike. In their ecstasy Caitanya's followers are said to have attacked the *kaji's* house, which broke his spirit. *Caitanyacaritamrita* provides additional details on this event. A dialogue took place between Caitanya and the *kaji*. Caitanya showed him the true meaning of religion and questioned him on practices such as killing cows. The *kaji* thoroughly regretted his own actions and also confessed to Caitanya that he had had a vision of Narasimha in his dream the previous night in which Narasimha had threatened the *kaji* with death if he did not stop harassing the devotees of Vishnu (Vishnu *bhaktas*). In the end, the *kaji* compromised and agreed not to cause any inconvenience to Caitanya's followers. This event is remembered as a turning point in the tradition of Caitanya. Another event of equal significance is Caitanya's attaining esteemed status among the learned circles of Puri. Soon after undertaking his *sanyasa* vows, Caitanya proceeded to Puri in Orissa following his mother's orders to stay in Puri. As soon as Caitanya reached Puri and entered the temple of Jagannatha, overcome by ecstasy, he fainted. He was carried to Vasudeva Sarvabhauma Bhattacharya's house. As he recovered from his unconscious state, a debate ensued between Caitanya and Sarvabhauma. Sarvabhauma recounted his stand from *advaita vedanta* for a week and invited Caitanya to expound his own meaning or refute that of Sarvabhauma's exegesis. The details of this debate are recorded in the *Caitanyabhagavata* and in greater detail in the *Caitanyacaritamrita*. Caitanya's expositions on philosophical and theological aspects of Vedanta in this debate later served as the basis for the philosophical arguments of his followers, such as Krishnadasa and Jiva *Gosvami*.

The most important event in Caitanya's life was his pilgrimage to Mathura in 1514, which led to the revival of Brindavan through his followers, Nityanand, Advaitanand, and then the six *gosvamis*. Caitanya visited sacred places in Mathura and went to the temple of Haridev near Govardhan. But by then the idol of Haridev had been moved to the village of Ghantoli for fear of Muslim destruction. Therefore Caitanya went to Ghantoli to offer his reverence to the deity. Caitanya circumambulated (*pradakshina*) the Govardhan hill and did not step on the hill, since it is considered an embodiment of Krishna. Caitanya's disciples Rupa and Sanatana also refrained from stepping on the Govardhan hill.

Although Caitanya was accepted as a form of Krishna himself during his lifetime, this aspect of his life acquired immense significance after his death. Caitanya is understood as representing the divine forms of Krishna and Radha together, which was later adopted by the Vaishnava *Sahajiyas*, giving rise to *sahajasadhana* (involving tantric sexual ritual practices). However, others only accept Caitanya as an incarnation of Vishnu or Krishna in the mood of Radha. Such accepted divinity of Caitanya resulted in the composition of varieties of eulogistic literature memorializing the significant features and notable events of Caitanya's life. A Bengali song series known as *Gauralila padas* (describing Gaura's/Caitanya's divine activities) is one such composition adopted easily for singing. Rupa *Gosvami*, a direct and principal follower of Caitanya, composed three *prarthanashtakas* (prayer verses in eight stanzas). Other texts such as *Caitanaycandramrita* and an *ashthaka* of Raghunandana Dasa are among the popular texts commonly recited that pay reverence to Caitanya. Several temples in Brindavan and states such as Orissa, Bengal, Assam, and Bangladesh also host images of Caitanya and offer regular worship by the devotees. Numerous manuals prescribing proper rituals for worship of Caitanya have been composed, among which *Bhakticandrika* by Lokananda *acarya* is significant. Several Caitanya mandala presentations are used in meditation practices, especially to seek devotional moods (*raganuragabhakti*). Several significant events in the life of Caitanya are marked by festival celebrations including his birth and advent (*Gaurapurnima*) during the *Holi* festival. Pilgrimage to Navadvipa, known as Navadvipa *parikrama* or Mayapuri *parikrama,* is also undertaken by the devotees of Krishna in memory of Caitanya.

See also: Advaita; Braj: Classical History; Brindavan; Jagannatha; Jiva *Gosvami*; *Kirtana*; Mathura; *Rathayatra*; Rupa *Gosvami*; Six *Gosvamis*

Further Reading

Chatterjee, A. N. 1983. *Srikrishna Caitanya: A Historical Study on Gaudiya Vaishnavism.* New Delhi: Associated Publishers.

Das, H. C. 1989. *Sri Caitanya in the Religious Life of India.* Calcutta: Association Press.

De, S. K. 1986. *Early Vaishnava Faith and Movement in Bengal from Bengal and Sanskrit Sources.* Calcutta: University of Calcutta.

Dimock, E. C., Jr. 1999. *Caitanya Caritamrita of Krishnadasa Kaviraja: A Translation and Commentary.* Harvard Oriental Series 56. Cambridge, MA: Harvard University Press.

Eidlitz, W. 1968. *Krishna Caitanya: Sien Leben und Seine Lehre.* Stockholm: Almqvist & Wiksell.

Kapoor, O. B. L. 1977. *The Philosophy and Religion of Sri Caitanya.* New Delhi: Motilal Banarsidas.

Kennedy, M. T. 1925. *The Caitanya Movement.* Calcutta: Association Press.

Majumandar, A. K. 1969. *Caitanya—His Life and Doctrines: A Study in Vaishnavism.* Bombay: Bharatiya Vidyabhavan.

McDaniel, J. 1993. "Dancing in the Hidden Vrindavana: The Service of Caitanya." *Journal of Vaishnava Studies* 1 (2): 72–82.

O'Connell, J. T. 1993. "Caitanya's Associates Were Not Sahajiyas." In *Shraddhalekhamala: Sukumar Sen Centennial Volume,* edited by P. Sarkar, 404–436. Calcutta.

Stewart, T. K. 2010. *The Final Word: The Caitanya Caritamrita and the Grammar of Religious Tradition.* Oxford: Oxford University Press.

CAITANYA VAISHNAVISM

see Gaudiya Vaishnavism

CALENDAR OF KRISHNA

The calendar of Krishna is dominated by festivals, *vrats* (religious vows), and rituals, which celebrate the major events of Krishna's life in Brindavan. The calendar is organized on a lunar-solar cycle. While the months are organized according to the moon cycle, the year is organized in the solar cycle. As a result of the discrepancy between the moon cycle and solar cycle, an excess of 10.87 days are left at the end of each year, which is corrected by adding an extra month every three years called *adhikamasa* (intercalary month). No celebrations or festivals can take place in this *adhikamasa*, so the festivals and auspicious days of the calendar stay the same each year. However, *adhikamasa* has a distinct role in the devotional practices associated with Krishna as it is dedicated to Krishna, and it is considered auspicious to hold special celebrations. *Bhandaras* are held at Govardhan frequently during the *adhikamasa*. The *navakalevara* ceremony of Jagannatha in the temple of Jagannatha in Puri is held when *adhikamasa* occurs in the month of *Ashadha*. Extra celebrations are also held in the temples of Krishna. For example, the Venkatesvara temple of Tirupathi holds additional *Brahmotsavam* in the month of *Adhika Ashadha*. Major festivals of Krishna are *Ekadasi, Janmasthami* (also known as *Gokulasthami*), *Holi, Diwali, Govardhanpuja*, and *Annakut* or *Chappanbhog*, which are celebrated with the utmost attention each year. *Caturmas* (four months of monsoon) and *Dhanurmas* (December–January) are vows lasting for a number of days involving fasts and ritual worship.

See also: Braj *Parikrama*; Brindavan; *Diwali; Ekadasi*; Govardhan *Puja; Holi; Janmasthami*; Uddhava; Vajranabha; Yamuna

Further Reading

Chaterjee, S. K. 1998. *Indian Calendric System.* Delhi: Publications Division, Government of India.

CANDIDASA

Candidasa (1400s) is also known widely as Baru Candidasa to set him apart from the other Candidasas known in later Bengali and Hindi literature. Candidasa's lyrics were discovered posthumously and published. Although several manuscripts have been discovered with the name Candidasa, only those bearing the colophon of Baru Candidasa are recognized as authentic compositions of Candidasa and included in his anthology, called *Srikrishnakirtana*. Not much information is known about Candidasa's life. He likely lived prior to Caitanya since his poems were familiar to Caitanya. Krishnadasa Kaviraja's biography of Caitanya written in Bengali mentions that Candidasa's poems greatly pleased Caitanya, and also that Caitanya was soothed by the recitation of Candidasa's verses during his ecstatic state of meditation. The title of Baru in Candidasa's name indicates that he might have belonged to the priestly community of Brahmans, although it is unknown if he is associated with any temple in Bengal. His name, Candidasa (servant of the goddess Candi), and the dedication lines in his verses in the name of Basali or Vasali (a popular form of goddess represented in varying forms), particularly worshipped in the Birbhum and Bankura districts, are interpreted as evidence of his association with a temple of the goddess in Bengal. However, due to lack of clear evidence, this could not be verified.

Candidasa's poems are composed in Bengali as long sequential poems describing Krishna and his play in Brindavan. His lyrics are noted for simplicity of language and intensity of passion. Candidasa's long poem, the *Srikrishnakirtana*, contains an extensive treatment of Krishna's early life in Vraja and Brindavan, especially the courtship of Radha and Krishna. The *Srikrishnakirtana* contains more than 400 songs. Candidasa provides the first extensive treatment of *danlila,* which only

---

Srikrishnakirtana

The *Srikrishnakirtana* is a trendsetter in the history and linguistics of the Bengali language. It is the second extant Bengali literary text composed in Middle Bengali next only to the Buddhist *Caryagitikosa* composed in Old Bengali. Although its dating is not clear, subsequent analysis has placed its composition prior to the fifteenth century. The *Srikrishnakirtana* contains 412 *kirtanas* (songs) divided into thirteen *khandas* (sections). Although the *kirtanas* may vary in length, more than half (about 226) of the *kirtanas* in the *Srikrishnakirtana* contain seventeen lines ending in a *bhanita* (signature) line. The signature lines simply identify the author by name, Candidasa, who in a few rare instances is also named Ananta or Ananta Baru Candidasa. Each of these *kirtans* begins with an assignment of musical notations, *raga* and *tala*, which indicates that they were intended to be sung at performances or private ceremonies. The subject of the *Srikrishnakirtana* roughly corresponds to the legend of Krishna narrated in the *Harivamsa*. The *Srikrishnakirtana* begins with the narration of the birth of Krishna and ends with Krishna leaving for Mathura to kill Kamsa.

---

appears briefly in classical texts. *Danlila* is described in more than a hundred songs in Candidasa's composition, the *Srikrishnakirtana*. Although Radha is described as a shy, ten- to twelve-year-old girl, she is also described as an independent girl in her own way. Radha was won over by Krishna with his tricks and clever schemes. Sanatana *Gosvami* noted the *danalila* and *naukalila* episodes of Candidasa's *Srikrishnakirtana* in his commentary on the *Bhagavatapurana*, the *Vaishnavatosani*. Sanatana's brother Rupa *Gosvami* composed the *Danakelikaumudi* in Sanskrit, describing the *danlila* episode between Radha and Krishna.

Baru Candidasa, however, does not depict Radha and Krishna as a married couple, which became conventional practice in later poetical and lyrical devotional traditions. The *Srikrishnakirtana* depicts Radha as much older than Krishna and as the wife of someone else (*parkiya*) named Abhimanyu, said to be a brother of Devaki. This gives rise to the *parakiya-vada*, which proposes that relationships of spirit are not bound by the etiquette of marital relationships. The common limitations of marriage, caste, or class do not apply to spiritual relations noted in the Krishna legend.

The lyrics of Candidasa's *Srikrishnakirtana* are set to music and are also used with a number of dance styles associated with Krishna such as *Manipuri* and *Odissi*. Candidasa's lyrics are also commonly sung in devotional circles and ceremonies.

The influence of the *kirtanas* of Candidasa on bhakti literature can be understood from the fact that devotional circles from the sixteenth century onward adapted a new lyrical language called Brajbuli, a mixture of the Braj language with the language structure of Bengali, to compose bhakti literature. However, the influence of Candidasa on eastern devotional traditions is direct and clear, while his influence on northern devotional schools is indirect. Overall, it could be said that Candidasa was one of the most influential bhakti poets of his time, whose legacy endures in the devotional traditions of India.

See also: Bhagavatapurana; Bhakti; Braj *Parikrama*; Brindavan; Childhood of Krishna in Brindavan; Radha

Further Reading

Bhattachara, D. 1967. *Love Songs of Candidasa*. London: George Allen and Unwin.

Sen, D. C. 1954. *History of Bengali Language and Literature*. Calcutta: University of Calcutta.

CATURVYUHAS

see Vyuhas

CHILDHOOD OF KRISHNA IN BRINDAVAN

Krishna arrived in Brindavan as an infant and lived there until he was twelve years old. Although Krishna was only a child in Brindavan, numerous incidents connected to his *lila*, popularly known as *Krishnalila* or *Raasalila* as well as *Govardhanlila*, were performed in Brindavan by Krishna. These incidents became part of the ritual and religious practice of several religious traditions in Hinduism.

It is said that as soon as they set up camp in Brindavan, the sight of the Brindavan groves, the sand banks on the Yamuna River, and the Govardhan hill gave Krishna great joy, as Krishna himself expressed it to Balarama. This feeling of joy pervades almost all the activities of Krishna in Brindavan. Krishna and Balarama began tending the cows in Brindavan along with other cowherd boys.

Vatsasura (Calf Demon)

One day Krishna saw a demon entering the herd of cows and assuming the form of a calf. Krishna grabbed hold of this demon and hurled him on to a *kapitha* (*Feronia elephantum*) tree. The demon died and fell down, bringing the tree down with him.

Raasalila

The most important episode of Krishna's childhood in Brindavan is the *Raasalila*, his dance with the *Gopis* during the autumn nights, when he was a mere child of ten or eleven years of age. *Raasalila* is the sacred love story of Krishna. Through this round dance Krishna showed his most devoted followers, the *Gopis*, the divine experience of nearness to the deity, which under normal circumstances could only be experienced after death. Although erotic, the *Raasalila* is seen as the union of longing souls with the divine. The *Raasalila* has been compared to the biblical "Song of Songs" (Song of Solomon). The *Raasalila* has been replicated in many art forms, among them dance, music, and painting. It is also depicted in lyrical poems, the most famous poem being Jayadeva's *Gitagovinda*.

Bakasura (Crane Demon)

On another day as Krishna, Balarama, and the other *Gopa* boys were drinking water on the banks of the Yamuna, they saw a large form that almost looked like a hill. However, Krishna realized it was the crane demon Baka. Krishna then grabbed hold of its beak and killed him, splitting his beak open.

Aghasura (Boa Constrictor)

Learning about the death of the crane demon, his brother Agha assumed the form of a large boa constrictor and came to Brindavan. He lay there pretending to be dead, luring the unsuspecting *Gopa* boys to climb into his mouth and slip into his stomach, while patiently waiting for Krishna. As Krishna came near the boa, he realized what was happening and climbed into the mouth of the boa to go inside his stomach to rescue the *Gopa* boys. As Krishna went inside the demon, the demon tried to crush Krishna by constricting his stomach muscles, but the breath inside him stopped, and his body then exploded, killing the demon Aghasura. Krishna then came out with the *Gopa* boys unharmed and safe.

God Brahma Submits: Krishna Becomes the *Gopa* Boys and Calves

One day Brahma took the *Gopa* boys, cows, and calves away from Vraja to test Krishna. Krishna searched for the *Gopa* boys and their calves. Not able to find them, Krishna realized it was Brahma's trick. Krishna then assumed the form of the *Gopa* boys and calves. Seeing this, Brahma felt repentant. He came to Krishna, admitted his mistake, and apologized to Krishna.

Kaliya Naga Subdued

Kaliya was a poisonous serpent demon that resided in Kalindi Lake in Brindavan. He spewed poison in the lake, making the water poisonous. Calves and the *Gopas* fainted after drinking the water from Kalindi Lake. Krishna jumped into the lake and got hold of the serpent, and after subduing him, he emerged out of the water, dancing on the hoods of the serpent. Kaliya's wives prayed to Krishna to spare his life, while Kaliya also pleaded with Krishna for forgiveness. Krishna then ordered him to leave the lake and move to the ocean.

Krishna Swallows the Forest Fire

One day the cows wandered off into the forest where fire broke out. The *Gopa* boys searched for the cows, and finding them in the middle of fires, they went to rescue the cows, but got stranded in the fire themselves. Krishna saw the plight of the cows and the *Gopa* boys; he immediately opened his mouth and swallowed the fire, consuming it.

Krishna Steals the *Gopis'* Clothes

In the month of *Hemanta* (October) young girls of Vraja undertook a vow, praying to the goddess Katyayani at dawn to obtain Krishna as their husband. They woke up early at dawn and calling one another's names, they went to Kalindi Lake. As usual they left their clothes on the banks and prayed to the goddess to make Krishna their husband. Krishna came there, took their clothes, and hid in the tree. He called the girls to come out of the lake. When they came out he told them that they should not take their clothes off, according to the rules of the vow. Since they made a mistake, Krishna told the *Gopi* girls to perform obeisance to him with up-lifted hands as purification. He then returned their clothes to them. The *Gopi* girls did not feel ashamed of what happened, and also they did not want to leave Krishna. Their minds were focused on Krishna. They only left after Krishna promised them that they would spend time in his company later. This episode of per-forming a vow by the *Gopis* (cowherd maidens), and their intense dedication and desire to be united with Krishna as one, is recollected by Andal *alvar* in her *Tirup-pavai* (*Thirty Poems*). The *Tiruppavai* is a narration of herself imagined as a cowherd girl, expressing her intense desire to marry and unite with Krishna not only for one life, but for eternity. She describes the undertaking of the vow (*pavai*) by her and her friends—other cowherd girls—for the purpose of uniting with Krishna in Vraja, and she performs a similar vow in the Sriranganatha temple in Srivilliputtur, Tamilnadu, in the ninth century. Following Andal *alvar,* currently women perform the *Dhanurmasa vrata*, and emulating Andal, they read the poems of *Tiruppavai* every day for the month of *Dhanurmasa* (mid-December to mid-January). There-fore the vow of the *Gopis* remains an enduring devotional practice by women, now focused on Krishna rather than the goddess Katyayani, as noted in this episode of Krishna's life in the *Bhagavatapurana* and the *Vishnupurana*.

Krishna Diverts Indra's Sacrifice and Lifts Govardhan Hill

One day the *Gopas* and *Gopis* were preparing food, as they were getting ready to offer the annual sacrifice to Indra. Krishna asked them what they were preparing. They said they were preparing for the annual sacrifice for Indra. Krishna told them they should not offer sacrifices to Indra, but to Govardhan Hill, which gave them the resources they needed for themselves and the cows. They prepared the food and other offerings to Govardhan, which infuriated Indra. Indra then rained heav-ily. The torrential rains did not stop, leaving the *Gopas*, their families, and their herds without shelter. They all came to Krishna seeking help. Krishna then lifted Govardhan Hill on the tip of the little finger of his left hand for a week. Indra was impressed by the mystic power of Krishna and withdrew his rain clouds.

Krishna Reveals His Abode to Nanda and the *Gopas*

One night after the *Ekadasi* fast, Krishna's father, Nanda, entered Kalindi Lake to bathe. He was caught by a demon servant of Varuna and taken to Varuna's world

(*Varunaloka*). It was forbidden to go into the lake at night; that was why Nanda was captured and taken away by Varuna's servants. The *Gopas* saw this and called for Krishna and Balarama. Krishna then went to Varuna. Varuna admitted the mistake of his servant and apologized to Krishna. Krishna then came back with Nanda. The *Gopas* were delighted to find Krishna and Nanda. Krishna transported them all to his own abode, *Vaikuntha*. Seeing the abode of Krishna, Nanda and the other *Gopas* were overcome with joy and ecstasy.

Raasalila

A detailed description of *Raasalila* is given in six chapters in the *Bhagavatapurana*, the largest space given to any one event in the Krishna legend in the *Bhagavatapurana*. On autumn nights when everything in Brindavan turned beautiful and fragrant with trees in full bloom, Krisha's mind turned to love and he invited his *yogamaya*. On the nights when the full moon showered his light rays on Brindavan, Krishna played the flute. When the *Gopi* women of Brindavan heard it, they left everything they were doing and rushed to meet Krishna. Krishna played the flute, filling everyone with joy.

The *Gopis* then became proud of their own fortune, and thought of themselves as the best women on earth. Krishna noticed this pride and disappeared from their midst in order to curtail their pride. The *Gopi* women became desolate and filled with remorse. Their minds were completely occupied by the thoughts of Krishna, as they behaved and imitated Krishna unknowingly. Each of the *Gopis* thought "I am Krishna." Singing loudly about Krishna, they searched for him in all the groves of Brindavan. In their desperation they talked to each animal, creeper, and lake or pond seeking information on Krishna's whereabouts. They enacted the childhood *lilas* of Krishna. Assuming herself to be the child Krishna, one of the *Gopis* kicked another *Gopi*, thinking it was Sakatasura (cart demon), while the other *Gopis* acted like the child Krishna and crawled around. They tried to find his footprints and to follow his path, but lost themselves again. Finally, the *Gopi* women returned to Lake Kalindi and sang about Krishna. The *Gopis* first sang of their longing for union with him, and then sang of their desperation to meet him. Finally, Krishna appeared, making the *Gopis* very happy. The *Gopis* complained to him about his disappearance and how desolate they became without him. Krishna consoled the *Gopis* by his sweet talk. Krishna explained to them that they had become exalted souls through their complete devotion. Following this exclusive and enlightening talk, the *Gopis* and Krishna danced the round dance. Krishna danced with each *Gopi* individually and simultaneously, while each *Gopi* thought that he was dancing exclusively with her.

After much dancing the *Gopis* were exhausted and took a bath in the lake. Exhorted by Krishna, they returned home to take care of their families.

Arista, the Bull Demon

One day a bull demon named Arista came to Brindavan and terrified the *Gopas* and their herds of cows. The *Gopas* and the cows ran away and took refuge with

Krishna. Krishna saw the bull demon and warned it. However, the bull demon was infuriated at this and instead of withdrawing, it started to charge at Krishna. Krishna then caught hold of its horns and slammed it to the ground, thus killing the demon.

Kesi, the Horse Demon

The horse demon Kesi came and terrified everyone in Gokula by running at the speed of thought and raising dust to the sky by knocking the ground with its hooves. Coming forward, Krishna challenged the horse demon, who was looking for him. The horse demon rushed forward with the speed of light and hit Krishna with its hooves. Krishna then caught hold of its front legs, whirled it around, and threw it with great force, which killed it instantaneously.

The Killing of Sankhacuda

One day the *Gopas* made a pilgrimage to the Ambika Forest on the banks of the Sarasvati River. They worshipped God Shiva and Goddess Ambika and fillfilled their vows. They camped in the Ambika Forest and rested for the night. While they were asleep a gigantic serpent began swallowing Nandagopa, Krishna's father. Nandagopa screamed for Krishna. The *Gopas* sleeping nearby came running and began hitting the serpent with firebrands from the campfire. The serpent, called Sankhacuda, continued to swallow even as the *Gopas* were hitting it with firebrands. Krishna arrived and touched it with his foot, which purified the serpent Sankhacuda of sins. The serpent changed its form and appeared as a celestial *Vidyadhara* called Sudarsana, who was cursed by the Angira sages due to his prideful and arrogant behavior toward them. He paid his reverence to Krishna and departed to the *Vidyadhara* world.

Vyoma, the Shape-Shifter Demon

Vyoma was a sky demon proficient in magic. Vyoma acquired the form of a *Gopa* and joined the *Gopa* boys, playing the game of role-play. As the boys were playing the lion and sheep game, he led the boys playing the part of sheep to a cave, under the pretext of hiding from the lion. He led almost all the boys into the cave and then closed it with a large stone. Krishna noticed that the demon was leading the boys away and seized him. Vyoma then acquired his original form, looking like a large mountain. However, he could not free himself from the grip of Krishna, and he fell down asphyxiated and died.

Krishna killed demons (calf demon, crane demon, bull demon, snake demon, horse demon, Vyoma, magician demon). He subdued four divine beings: the serpent Kaliya, (*nagas*), Indra (king of the gods), Brahma (the creator), Varuna (lord of the sky and dharma). He enchanted the *Gopas* with the vision of *Vaikuntha* and the *Gopis* with the experience of *moksha* in *Raasalila*. Numerous events of Krishna's life in Brindavan have become the basis of ritual celebrations for numerous Vaishnava devotational (bhakti) traditions. Lifting the Govardhan hill is epitomized in the Vallabha tradition by their central image of Srinathji, *Raasalila* by the *Sahajiyas* and Radhavallabhas, singing the names of Krishna by the Caitanya Vaishnava tradition, and so on. However, these events were only a prelude to the greater things Krishna accomplished in the later part of his life.

See also: Caitanya Vaishnavism; Haridasi *Sampradaya*; *Lila*; *Maya*; Radhavallabha Tradition; *Raasalila*; Vallabha Tradition

Further Reading

Matchett, F. 2001. *Krishna: Lord or Avatara*. Richmond: Curzon.
Schweig, G. 2005. *Dance of the Divine Love: The Rasalila of Krishna and the Cowherd Maidens of Vraj*. Princeton: Princeton University Press.

CHOKHAMELA

The *Mahar sant* (saint) of Maharashtra, Chokhamela, lived in Pandarpur in the fourteenth century, showing his unwavering devotion amid a discriminatory social structure that did not allow him even to enter the temple of his Lord, Vitthala, to whom Chokhamela had devoted his life and composed several *abhangs* declaring his passionate devotion. As is common with the legends of the *sants* of Maharashtra, numerous strands of his legend circulated as independent stories before Mahipati finally collected these stories, and a complete biographical account was composed and included in the *Bhaktamal*, an early hagiography consisting of the lives of *Varkari* saints.

The biography of Chokhamela links his birth to Vitthala. It is stated that once Chokhamela's parents-to-be were entrusted with carrying mangoes for Vitthala in the Pandarpur Temple. They met an elderly Brahman, who begged them for a mango as he was very hungry. Taking pity on him, Chokhamela's mother-to-be gave him a mango. The man returned it after taking a bite, saying it was sour. Chokhamela's mother wrapped the mango in the folds of her sari. As they reached Pandarpur, the couple were amazed to discover that the mango had turned into a child, whom they raised as their son, naming him Chokhamela, since Chokha means "to suck" and "to taste" in Marathi. Chokhamela lived his childhood and early life in Mangalvedha, but later moved to Pandarpur where he devoted the largest amount of his time to praising and praying to Vitthala through his *abhangs* while standing near the main gate of the temple, as he was not permitted to enter due to caste rules. However, his biography by Mahipati includes several miraculous incidents when Vitthala himself came out to meet Chokhamela and even to partake of dinner at Chokhamela's home. An overwhelming majority of Chokhamela's poems express his devotion to Vitthala, but also his desolation at the social status attributed to him by the caste system, which did not permit him to meet his beloved deity. Chokhamela, along with other members of the community, was hired by the local Muslim chief to construct fort walls in Mangalvedha. Part of a wall collapsed during construction, killing several workers including Chokhamela. However, he found the respect he deserved after his death. Namdev recovered his body from the ruins and brought it back to Pandarpur, saying that Lord Vitthala himself appeared in his dream and commanded him to bring back Chokhamela's body. Thus his remains were brought back to Pandarpur, and Chokhamela's *samadhi* was consecrated by Namdev at the same place where Chokhamela used to stand in front of the main entrance of the temple to offer his devotional prayers to Vitthala. Chokhamela's life is one of the simple tales of bhakti and devotional poetry in Maharashtra, although he experienced several hardships due to the social stratification in Indian society at that time. However, Chokhamela finally attained what he desired as the foremost devotee of Vitthala: a permanent place close to his deity.

See also: Bhakti; Eknath; Jnanadev; *Kirtana*; Namdev; Pandarpur Temple; Panduranga Vitthala; *Sants*; *Varkari* Tradition

Further Reading

Deleury, G. A. 1960. *The Cult of Vithoba.* Pune: Poona University.

Kadam, S. B. 1989, 2005. *Sant Chokkamela: Charitra ani Abhang.* Mumbai: Sabdalay Prakasan.

Mokashi-Punekar, R. 2010. *On the Threshold: Songs of Chokkamela.* New Haven: Yale University Press.

Novetzke, C. L. 2008. *Religion and Public Memory.* New York: Columbia University Press.

Ranade, R. D. 1961. *Pathway to God in Marathi Literature.* Bombay: Bharatiya Vidyabhavan.

Vaudeville, C. 1996. "Chokhamela: An Untouchable Saint of Maharashtra." In *Myths, Saints and Legends in Medieval India,* edited by V. Dalmia, 221–240. Delhi: Oxford University Press.

CHRISTIANITY AND KRISHNA

Legends of Krishna and Jesus have been compared by early scholars since the early eighteenth century, and current trends in comparative theology continue these comparisons. Events of their birth, divine conception, connectivity with devotees, and grace are noted as similar features. The celebration of the birth of Krishna at the festival of *Janmasthami* and the birth of Jesus at Christmas are also commonly compared. Mutual understanding arising from comparative studies of Krishna and Jesus is part of the early religious explorations of India. The events of the lives of Krishna and Jesus, such as their miraculous birth, their being divine (prophets), and their other childhood activities and sermons have been explored.

See also: Diwali; ISKCON; *Janmasthami*

Further Reading

Kennedy, J. 1907. "The Child Krishna, Christianity and the Gujars." *Journal of the Royal Asiatic Society,* 951–991.

Largen, K. 2011. *Baby Krishna and Infant Jesus.* New York: Orbis Books.

Jesus and Krishna

Besides their messages of peace and love, and the similarities between the names of Krishna and Christ, other parallels connect the two. Conceived supernaturally, both are considered sons of God; both were born in unusual and lowly places. Because of the cruelty of the kings Kamsa and Herod, there are massacres in each narrative, followed by a flight to Braj for Krishna and his parents, and to Egypt for Jesus and his parents. There are, of course, differences in their lives, but both appear at crucial times for their respective peoples and become the focus of devotion: one a shepherd, one a cowherd.

COSMOGONY

Although the material origin of the world is understood from the Vedic verse *Purusha Sukta* (*Rigveda* 10.90), followers of Krishna identify the primeval *purusha* with Vishnu. This version of the origin of the universe is also connected to the *Pancaratra* system, which proposes Vishnu as the material cause of the universe. It is explained in the *Pancaratra* system that Krishna is related to the universe as an incarnation of Vishnu. In the *Vishnupurana* version of creation, Vishnu forms an egg, which gradually expands like a bubble of water; the worlds are located in it, and Vishnu facilitates the origin of Brahma, who then proceeds with creation. As Vishnu, the god preserves the world by incarnating in the world (*avatara*) whenever the balance of good and evil is uneven. Creation is described as Vishnu's *lila*. However, the most detailed narrative of cosmogony is found in the *Bhagavatapurana*, the *purana* of Krishna, which contains the complete narration of Krishna's life. Vishnu born as Krishna lived on earth toward the end of the *Dvaparayuga*, the third *yuga*, of the *Kalpa* followed by the *Kaliyuga*, the fourth *yuga*. The events of Krishna's life are marked by festivals and observed as holy days with fasting and celebrations. The most important calendrical festivals of Krishna are *Janmasthami, Rathasamptami, Holi, Diwali,* and *Ekadasi.* These festivals are celebrated across India at homes and in temples. However, in Brindavan, they are celebrated in association with local traditions, since it is considered the place of Krishna's earthly life. Brindavan, as the place of Krishna's life, is considered the reflection of his divine

Gokula

Gokula is the earthly realm of the eternal paradise of Krishna, the *Goloka*. Elevated souls reach Krishna in *Goloka* and enjoy his company in the divine world similar to Gokula. Gokula is identified with the larger region of Brindavan, not any particular place, as the earthly realm of Krishna's divine play (*lila*). Gokula as an earthly image of *Goloka* inspired the living theology of Brindavan, the sphere of Krishna.

abode. Hence the Braj mandala is represented as a lotus, similar to the *Goloka*, which is arranged in the form of a lotus with the center occupied by Krishna and Radha.

See also: Bhagavatapurana; Braj *Parikrama*; Brindavan; *Dvaparayuga*; *Pancaratra*; Vishnu

Further Reading

Anonymous. 1952–1960. *Bhagavatapurana*. Gorakhpur: Gita Press.
Hume, R. E. 1931. *The Thirteen Principal Upanishads*. Oxford: Oxford University Press.
Kuiper, F. B. J. 1983. *Ancient Indian Cosmogony*. New Delhi: Vikas.
Rosen, S. 2006. *Essential Hinduism*. Santa Barbara: ABC-CLIO.
Wilson, H. H. 1961. *The Vishnupurana*. Calcutta: Punthi Pustak.

COSMOLOGY

The cosmology of Krishna broadly connects to the Hindu cosmology, which lists several worlds both below and above the earth, dedicated to sinners and the meritorious respectively. The abode of Krishna is known as *Goloka* (cow world); another is *Vishnuloka* or *Vaikuntha*, located above the *Brahmaloka* or *Satyaloka*. *Goloka* is where followers of Krishna proceed after attaining *moksha* (liberation). Descriptions of *Goloka* abound in Vaishnava classical texts. Some classical sources mention *Goloka* as part of the realm of *Vaikuntha*, while others mention it as a separate *loka* above the other divine realms of heaven. Since Krishna is considered Vishnu himself, *svayamvishnu*, so *Goloka* can be considered as the *Vishnuloka*. The *Bhagavatapurana* describes the return of Krishna to his own abode, where he is welcomed by Indra and other gods. The *Vaikuntha* is described as the topmost world above the *Satyaloka* (Brahma's world), where the *Goloka* of Krishna is located, which resembles a lotus. In the center of this world Krishna lives with Radha surrounded by his followers, friends, devotees, and former relatives in his life on earth as Krishna.

See also: Braj *Parikrama*; *Goloka*; Mathura; *Moksha/Mukti*

Further Reading

Deepak, A., and R. Sharma. 2008. *Dying, Death and Afterlife in Dharma Traditions*. Hampton, VA: Deepak Publications.
Rosen, S. J. 1997. *The Reincarnation Controversy: Uncovering the Truth in the World Religions*. Badger, CA: Torchlight Publishing.

D

DARSANA

Darsana, commonly known as *darsan*, has a special significance for the devotional practices connected with Krishna. *Darsana* is a Sanskrit word that means seeing, but in religious practice it acquires a deeper meaning than mere seeing. In the religious sense, it is a mutual act of seeing, a glance between the deity and the devotee that helps establish the divine connection. Although *darsan* has come to represent the divine connection between the deity and the devotee, the word has acquired multiple meanings; specifically, seeing the divine is considered an auspicious act in itself, implying a sense of achievement, which may mean an undertaking on the path of *moksha* (salvation). In a literal sense, as one opens one's eyes to the divinity, one's eyes may be opened to the deeper meaning of the word as theologically purported, leading to the ultimate reality.

Darsan acquired special temporal connotations in the living theology of devotional practices in Braj. Devotional (bhakti) practices of the Radhavallabha tradition, Haridasi tradition, Vallabha tradition, and Caitanya tradition employ *darsan* (seeing) as the primary mode of connecting with the deity. *Darsan* forms an important aspect of devotion to Krishna. It is said in the *Bhagavatapurana* that the *Gopis* and *Gopas* constantly pined to see Krishna and spend time in his company. Mere *darsan* of Krishna is said to have given the *Gopis* and *Gopas* immense satisfaction, as noted in the classical *purana* texts, the *Harivamsa,* the *Bhagavatapurana,* and the *Vishnupurana.* This serves as a theological basis for devotional traditions to insist on personal involvement with the deity through visiting temples and performing pilgrimage. Vaishnava temples, especially Krishna temples, remain busy with visitors throughout the year. Krishna has given the *darsan* of his divine persona to a select number of people associated with him, according to the Krishna legend in the *Harivamsa* and the *Mahabharata.* Krishna temples are said to contain the image of the deity that is considered the god himself as an incarnation in the worshipful form (*arcamurti*). Krishna temples in the Braj region, as well as regional forms of Krishna such as Venkatesvara in Tirupathi, Jagannatha in Puri, Panduranga Vitthala in Pandarpur, Ranganatha in Srirangam, and Guruvayurappa in Guruvayur, are the most visited temples in India. It is also said that envisioning (*darsan*) even the *shikhara* (temple tower) above the sanctum sanctorum (*garbhagriha*) itself is also capable of giving one salvation (*moksha*). Hence the temple towers are built at an elevated height so that devotees can constantly remember the deity and envision the *shikhara* in lieu of the regular *darsan.* This is especially the case when one is infirm or not healthy enough to move: one can get the satisfaction and the same merit of visiting the temple simply by looking (*darsan*) at the *shikhara* of the temple.

Deities are also taken out periodically in procession around town on special holy days, when devotees can have a *darsan* of the deity from their own locations, thus deriving merit. Large processions such as the Jagannatha *rathayatra* (chariot procession) are attended by large numbers of devotees. Annual festivals (*Brahmotsavams*) of temples in south India also involve processions of deities attended by numerous devotees. *Darsan* of the deity during the processions and festivals provides the same merit as *darsan* of the central deity of the temple.

See also: Asthana; Bhakti; Braj *Parikrama*; Brindavan; *Holi*; Mathura; *Seva*

Further Reading

Eck, D. 1998. *Darsan: Seeing the Divine*. New York: Columbia University Press.
Goswami, S., and Robyn Beeche. 2001. *Celebrating Krishna*. Brindavan, India: Srikrishna Prema Sansthana.
Haberman, D. 1988. *Acting as a Way of Salvation*. New York: Oxford University Press.

DEATH OF KRISHNA

The deaths of Krishna and Balarama and the annihilation of the Yadavas took place simultaneously due to a curse placed on Samba by the Brahmans angered by his prank. One day the Yadavas went for a picnic on the beach near Prabhasa. After partying late and drinking heavily, they started arguing among themselves. During a drunken brawl that followed, the Yadavas became infuriated and started hitting one another with reeds (*eraka* grass) on the beach. However, the reeds had been fortified by the fine grains of the iron pestle that was ground and thrown into the ocean by Samba and his friends when the sages cursed the Yadavas because they were infuriated by the prank of the pregnant lady played by the disguised Samba. The curse stated that Samba would in fact give birth to a pestle that would cause the end of the Yadava clan. When Samba removed his disguise, he found the pestle and the shocked *Gopa* boys brought it immediately to the notice of Yadava king Ugrasena, who had it ground and thrown into the Indian Ocean near Prabhasa to safeguard the Yadavas from the curse of the sages. However, the curse materialized, since the powder of the ground pestle became infused into the reeds (*eraka* grass), and the Yadavas died instantaneously as they hit one another with the reeds.

Ban ka Tirtham

Ban ka Tirtham near Prabhasa is identified as the place of Krishna's death as a result of the mortal wound from the hunter Jara's arrow. It is a pilgrimage site visited by the devotees of Krishna. Krishna is depicted in his yogic posture, while a kneeling Jara sits nearby. This sacred place is a memorial to the event of Krishna's death.

Seeing this, Krishna and Balarama realized that the end of *Dvaparayuga* was near, and it was time for them to leave the earth and return to their respective divine abodes. Krishna then left the beach, entered the forest, and sat in meditation under a banyan tree. An arrow hit the big toe of Krishna's left foot while he sat there a long time absorbed in meditation. The hunter Jara had shot his arrow, mistaking Krishna's big toe for the ear of a deer. However, he realized his mistake as soon as he approached Krishna, and deeply repented. By then the poison from the arrow had already begun spreading through Krishna's body. Krishna informed Jara that this was desired, and blessed Jara with heaven. Krishna's charioteer Daruka searched for him and arrived where Krishna was sitting. Seeing Krishna injured, Daruka wept uncontrollably. Krishna consoled Daruka and informed him that the sea would drown the city of Dvaraka. He also told Daruka to inform Arjuna of the impending deaths of Krishna, Balarama, and the Yadavas. Krishna then sent a message to Arjuna to take care of all the women, his parents, and other families. He instructed Daruka to move everyone from Dvaraka to Indraprastha, the city of Arjuna.

See also: Arjuna; Dvaraka; Eight Wives of Krishna; Prabhasa; Samba; Vajranabha

Further Reading

Frith, N. 1976. *Legend of Krishna*. London: Abacus.
Patro, J. B. 2014. *The Life and Times of Krishna*. New Delhi: Wisdom Tree.

DEVAKI

Devaki is the biological mother of Krishna and Balarama. Devaki's legend is the most complex story of the mother of a god in Hinduism. Six of her children were killed as soon as they were born; her seventh pregnancy appeared to have been aborted, while Goddess Nidra safely transferred the embryo to Rohini, another wife of Vasudeva, who gave birth to Balarama. Devaki's eighth child, Krishna, was transferred to Vraja soon after his birth. Devaki met her only surviving children, Krishna and Balarama, later in her life.

Devaki was the daughter of Ugrasena, king of Mathura, and was imprisoned by her brother Kamsa immediately after her marriage to Vasudeva, since the *akasavani* (divine voice from the sky) warned that Devaki's son would kill Kamsa.

Temple of Devaki and Krishna

A unique temple of Devaki is located in Goa. The central image of the temple depicts Devaki in a sitting position, while the child Krishna is standing in front. Local temple legends state that the image belonged to an ancient temple of Devaki in Marcel, which was moved to Mayem in Bicholim during the sixteenth century due to the Portuguese inquisition. However, a new temple was built and the central deities were brought back to the original location at Marcel, which is near Panaji.

Painting of Devaki and Vasudeva being freed from the prison in Mathura by Krishna and Balarama. (Dinodia Photos/Alamy Stock Photo)

Hearing this made Kamsa very anxious for his life, and he tried to kill Devaki immediately. Vasudeva stopped him and promised him that he would hand over every child born to Devaki soon after its birth. Devaki then stayed in the prison with her husband, while Kamsa killed all of her children as soon as they were born except for Krishna and Balarama, who were transferred to Vraja and grew up incognito among the *Gopas*. Devaki and her husband Vasudeva were freed from the prison by Krishna after he killed Kamsa in a wrestling match in Mathura, several years later, on the occasion of visiting his true parents Devaki and Vasudeva for the first time in the prison. During a conversation between Vasudeva and Balarama, Devaki noticed that Krishna had brought back the son of his guru, Sandipani, from the world of death. Devaki then requested that her six sons who were killed by Kamsa be brought back, as she wished to see them. Krishna consequently entered the Yogamaya and, along with Balarama, visited the underworld (*sutala*) ruled by Bali. Krishna told Bali that he wished to take his brothers back to Earth from where they could proceed back to their original abodes in heaven. Bali then agreed to return the six brothers (Svara, Udgita, Parishvanga, Patanga, Ksudrabrit, and Grina) to Devaki. Seeing her eight sons at once, Devaki was overjoyed and embraced them. The six sons then took leave of their parents and Krishna, and left for their original abodes in heaven. Jain stories of Krishna also preserve the myth of six children born to Devaki in the Jain *Harivamsapurana* of Punnata Jinasena. However, the six children of Devaki were transferred as embryos from Devaki to Sulasa and born as three sets of twins. They grew up as sons of Sulasa and Naga in a devout Jain royal family, became Jain monks, and obtained heaven at the end of their life on Earth. The Jain story of the six brothers differs slightly from the Hindu versions, in that they were not killed by Kamsa, but were transferred as embryos to Sulasa, living an enjoyable and happy life on Earth. However, Hindu and Jain stories both provide a happy ending with the six brothers finally reaching heaven.

Although Devaki is the birth mother of Krishna, her role is limited to the cosmological plan of bringing forward the incarnation of Vishnu to bring about the death of evil Kamsa. Devaki still has a special place as the mother of Krishna, but as a mother of the God, Krishna's adopted mother, Yashoda, is the receiver of most veneration from the followers of Vaishnavism. In fact, the central practice of the Vallabha tradition is based on the *vastalya bhava* (affectionate love of mother) of Yashoda, which is considered to represent one of the greatest modes of emotional connection with Krishna.

See also: Jainism and Krishna; Kamsa; Rohini; Sandipani; Yashoda

Further Reading

Suneson, C. 1993. "The *Shadgarbha* Tradition in the *Harivamsa*, the *Puranas*, and the *Krishna Caritranataka* of Ranjit Malla." *Proceedings of the VIII World Sanskrit Congress Wiener Zeitshcrift Kunde Sud- und Ost Asiens* 36: 197–211.

DIWALI

Diwali, originally called *Dipavali* in Sanskrit, means row of lights. It is one of the important festivals celebrated to mark good triumphing over evil, marking the occasion of Krishna slaying the demon Naraka (*Bhagavatapurana* 10.59). Hence, this festival is celebrated with utmost reverence in all the temples associated with Krishna. On the night of *Dipavali* Govardhan Hill, including the stairs (*ghats*) of Mansiganga Lake, is lit up with thousands of oil lamps. It is believed that Govardhan Hill is another form of Krishna, and the cowherd men and women lighted the hill to show their reverence for Krishna after he left Vraja. On the next day of *Dipavali* all the rock faces of Govardhan Hill are given *abhisheka* (anointed with milk or water) and prepared for worship. The hill face at Jatipura is decorated in the form of the Srinathji icon at the Nathdvara temple, one of the most important temples of Krishna. The five-day festival of *Diwali* is celebrated in all the Krishna temples of the Mathura region, Brindavan, Braj, Govardhan, Nandagaon, and so on. The first day of Diwali, called *Dhantrayodasi* (*Dhanteras*), is a day of shopping and gift giving. The second day is called *Naraka Caturdasi*, the day the demon Naraka was killed by Krishna, and hence it is seen as the end of evil and the arrival of peace and prosperity heralded by Krishna. Shooting off fireworks, lighting clay lamps,

Diwali Celebrations Across the World

Although the festival of *Diwali* is closely connected to Krishna and celebrated in Brindavan, it is also a pan-Indian festival celebrated by all the dharma traditions of India. Hence it is celebrated across the world wherever the Indian diaspora has settled in large numbers. One of the biggest and most popular celebrations of *Diwali* is in Trafalgar Square in London. Outside of India, *Diwali* is not merely a religious festival, but a cultural event.

and visiting Krishna temples to offer devotional worship are traditions that celebrate this day. The third day is the actual festival of *Diwali*, celebrated for two days in temples, towns, and homes. Laxmi *puja* (worship of Laxmi) is held at homes, temples, and shops on this day. The fourth day is the *Varsha-Pratipada*, celebrated as the beginning of the Hindu New Year in north India. The fifth day is *Bhaiduj*, a day for brothers and sisters who meet and express their love and affection for each other. It is considered auspicious for brothers and sisters to visit Yamuna River on this day.

See also: Govardhan; Govardhan *Puja*; Mathura; Narakasura; Srinathji *Haveli* Nathdvara; Yamuna

Further Reading

Devagupta, R. 2001. "Kindling the Deepa—The Tales behind the Hindu Festival of Lamps." *Parabola-Myth Tradition and the Search for Meaning* 26 (2): 74–79.
Gode, P. K. 1960. "Divali." *Studies in Indian Cultural History*. Vol. 5, pp. 187–260. Poona: Bhandarkar Oriental Research Institute.

DRAUPADI

Draupadi is the wife of Arjuna and is depicted as a relative of Krishna. She is esteemed as Krishna's beloved sister, and sometimes she is also called Krishnaa (ending in the long "a" representing a feminine epithet). Draupadi is also said to be dark in color like Krishna. Hence, the name Krishnaa is said to have been given to her to represent her color, similar to Krishna, who is described as dark blue, resembling a rain cloud. The Sanskrit word *krishna* means dark color, black, and so on. However, the similarity between the names Krishna and Krishnaa is unmistakable. Of all the women related to Krishna, Draupadi is different. She is strong willed, straightforward, and clever. Draupadi is the daughter of Drupada, king of the Pancala kingdom. She was born out of the sacrificial fire when King Drupada performed a sacrifice (*yajna*) to obtain children. Hence, she is also known as Yajnaseni.

Episodes in the *Mahabharata* portray her unique life and the tremendous support she obtained from Krishna during her troubles. Krishna is present in almost

---

Mastya Yantra

Drupada, the father of Draupadi, desired to marry his daughter to Arjuna. Knowing that Arjuna was the best archer, Drupada had the most difficult fish entrapment designed. A fish suspended on a rotating bar had to be shot while the archer looked at the image of the rotating fish in the water tank below. Drupada challenged the potential bridegrooms at his daughter's *svayamvara* (bridegroom-choice) to prove their prowess by breaking the *Mastya Yantra* and catching the fish. Arjuna successfully shot the fish and thereby won Draupadi as his bride.

Draupadi's meeting with Queen Sudeshna, folio from an illustrated *Mahabharata (Great War of the Bharatas)*, manuscript dated to 1670 from Seringapatnam, Karnataka, India. (Los Angeles County Museum of Art)

all the important episodes of her life. Even if Krishna was not present directly, he always answered her calls for help. For example, Krishna was present at her marriage, and he played a crucial role in convincing the five Pandava brothers to marry Draupadi together as their common wife. The *Mahabharata* described how the Pandavas attended the *svayamvara* (bridegroom choice) of Draupadi incognito, disguised as poor Brahmans. Arjuna won Draupadi in the *svayamvara* by winning the archery challenge, so technically he was her husband. However, as the five Pandava brothers reached home to announce this to their mother, Kunthi, she said, "Share it equally among the five of you." Only later did she find out that what they had brought home was actually a bride. Since Kunthi did not want to withdraw her command, the five Pandava brothers decided to do as she said. However, the Pandavas, as well as King Drupada, were concerned about her marrying the five brothers on the words of Kunthi, which urged them to "share equally." Krishna convinced the Pandavas as well as Draupadi's father to agree to this unusual marriage. As the brothers consummated their marriage with her, they entered into a marriage contract with Draupadi. Each husband would spend a month with Draupadi, when the other four were prohibited from entering her chambers, and if anyone happened to commit that mistake, he would have to take a pilgrimage for a year away from home.

Once Draupadi laughed at the inattentive Duryodhana as he fell into a pool of water that had been made to look like a paved floor by the skill of Maya, the divine architect, who designed and built the palace of the Pandavas in Indraprastha. Duryodhana could not forget this humiliation, and in retaliation, he invited Dharma (first of the Pandava brothers) to a dice game, defeated him, and stripped him and his family of all their possessions including their clothes. Duryodhana subsequently ordered Draupadi dragged into the court and disrobed publicly. Dussasana, brother of Duryodhana, dragged her to the court to disrobe her. This was another important episode of Draupadi's life during which Krishna saved her from public humiliation in the Kaurava court by providing her an infinite number of saris, which could not be taken off by Dussasana. During this episode Krishna was not present in the Kaurava court, but Draupadi's pleas for help received Krishna's attention. This episode clearly establishes the special bond and soul connection Draupadi had with Krishna.

Krishna also helped the Pandavas with their peace negotiations after their return from exile. Draupadi was adamant that war was inevitable, and even tried to dissuade peace talks between the Pandavas and the Kauravas. Although she did not fight in the war, a description in the *Mahabharata* includes her night prowl on the battlefield of Kurukshetra.

At the end of the Bharata war, when Asvatthama killed Draupadi's five sons during his night raid on the Pandava camp, Krishna was there to console her. Upon Draupadi's request, Krishna also blessed Uttara, the pregnant wife of Abhimanyu, to restore her embryo to life, so that the Pandavas would have an heir apparent.

It could be said that Draupadi complements the Pandavas and supports their efforts to regain their kingdom. In addition to Arjuna (*nara*) who shares a special bond of soul with Krishna as *Naranayana* (*Naranarayana* pair), Draupadi shares a sisterly bond of soul with Krishna. The *sakhyabhava* (mood of friendship) characterizes the relationship of Krishna with Arjuna and Draupadi, distinct only in gender. Draupadi is accorded special status as a goddess of fertility and feminine energy in Hinduism. Special festivals are held across India to celebrate her divinity, and oral tales narrate her life during the festival celebrations.

See also: Arjuna; Bhima; Krishna; Pandavas; Subhadra: Krishna's Sister

Further Reading

Hiltebeitel, A. 1988. *The Cult of Draupadi*. Chicago: University of Chicago Press.
Ray, P. 2011. *Yajnaseni*. New Delhi: Rupa.

DVAITA

Dvaita (dualism) places the god Vishnu and his *purna avatara* (full incarnation), Krishna, at the center of its theology and philosophy. Although *dvaita* is similar in conception to other theistic devotional schools such as *advaita* and *visishtadvaita*, with which the *dvaita* schools share Vedanta philosophy and the theistic devotional philosophy (bhakti) of medieval south India, it differs from the later Vedanta schools in advocating God as completely *svatantra* (independent) or separate from everything in the universe. *Dvaita* draws its philosophy from three source texts (*prasthanatraya*): the *Brahmasutras* of Badarayana, the Upanishads, and the *Bhagavadgita* in addition to the *Bhagavatapurana*.

Creation is not illusory but real, as is the Brahma, the universal soul, according to the *dvaita* philosophy. The creation and the creator are distinct and two different realities. The individual self is ignorant and experiences sorrow in this world, while the ultimate soul is omnipotent and omniscient.

Devotional traditions of Krishna are related to and partially derive from the *dvaita* philosophy, especially the theories of *bhedabheda* in understanding the nature of divinity. At the center of the *dvaita* philosophy is devotion to Vishnu, often translated as devotion to Krishna in practice, which is important for *moksha* (liberation). Liberation according to *dvaita* is achieved by intense bhakti (devotion to God), combined with the *jnana* (knowledge of God), which is only granted by God's *prasada* (grace). Therefore, there is a belief in predestination, according to which each individual *jiva* (life) is distinct and will have a distinct liberation, or final destination.

See also: Advaita; Bhagavadgita; Bhagavatapurana; Bhakti; *Dvaitadvaita (Bhedabheda); Gaudiya* Vaishnavism; Madhva; *Moksha/Mukti;* Vallabha Tradition

Further Reading

Sarma, D. 2005. *Epistemological Limitations of Philosophical Enquiry: Doctrine in the Madhva Vedanta.* London: Routledge.

Sharma, A. 2005. "*Jivanmukti* in Neo-Hinduism: The Case of Ramana *Maharsi.*" *Asian Philosophy* 15 (3): 207–220.

Sharma, D. 2003. *An Introduction to Madhva Vedanta.* Burlington, VT: Ashgate.

Srinivasachari, P. N. 1972. *The Philosophy of Bhedabheda.* Madras: Adyar Library and Research Centre.

DVAITADVAITA (BHEDABHEDA)

Dvaitadvaita (dualistic nondualism) also gives rise to the theory of *bhedabheda* commonly practiced by the devotional traditions of Krishna. *Dvitadvaita* proposes that the creator (god) and the created souls (beings) are distinct, but share an essential substance. *Bhedabheda* is an important doctrine in Caitanya's *Achintya Bhedabheda* (inexplicable identity-difference and indifference) and Nimbarka's *Svabhavaka Bhedabheda* (natural identity-difference and indifference). These doctrines are also referred to as *dvaitadvaita* (dual and nondual), because they explain Krishna as both absolute transcendent *sakti* (energy) and, together with Radha, as also dual and distinct. Although *bhedabheda* is utilized as a central philosophy of Krishna devotional schools, it had its origins in the Vedic notion that difference and unity (indifference) can coexist in intimate relation with each other, which finds explicit exposition in *Taittiriya Upanishad* 3.1. As stated in this verse unity is in nondifference, while also consisting of difference, implying *parinamavada* (theory of transformation). It explains that although individuals may appear separate and different from the source (the Brahma), they still maintain the essence of the source, situated within each individual as the individual's soul (*atma*). Although *bhedabheda* found its greatest utility in Krishna devotional traditions, as noted in the philosophical thoughts of Caitanya and Nimbarka, it was also significantly noted by other early Vaishnava thinkers such as Bhaskara and Yadavaprakasa.

See also: Caitanya; Caitanya Vaishnavism; Madhva *Sampradaya*; Nimbarka Tradition; Ramanuja

Further Reading

Nicholson, A. J. 2007. "Reconciling Dualism and Non-Dualism: Three Arguments in Vijnanabhiksu's *Bhedabheda Vedanta*." *Journal of Indian Philosophy* 35 (4): 371–403.

Ramaswamy, H. N., and K. Singh. 1985. *Taittiriya Upanishad*. Bombay: Bharatiya Vidya Bhavan.

DVAPARAYUGA

Dvaparayuga is the third *yuga* (age) in the *Mahayuga* (one time cycle), which consists of four *yugas*. Each *yuga* is considered more degenerate than the previous *yuga*. Hence *Dvaparayuga* is considered more degenerate than the first two *yugas* (*Krita* and *Treta*), which are called the Golden Age and Silver Age metaphorically. In another metaphorical comparison the dharma in each *yuga* is compared to a cow that walks with only two legs in *Dvapara*, while with only one leg in the *Kali* age. As the ages progress the succeeding age has only half the duration of the first age. For example, the duration of *Dvaparayuga* is 864,000 years, while *Kaliyuga*, its successor, lasts only 432,000 years. Krishna's incarnation is one of the major events of the *Dvaparayuga*, the end of which is marked by the death of Krishna. Krishna lived at the end of the *Dvaparayuga*, with his death considered to mark the beginning of *Kaliyuga*. With each passing age, the quality and nature of human life is halved, such as dharma (righteousness), life span, and physical strength.

See also: Cosmogony; Cosmology; Death of Krishna; Dvaraka; *Hiranyagarbha*; Prabhasa; Yamuna

Further Reading

Wilkins, W. J. 1900. *Hindu Mythology: Vedic and Puranic*. Calcutta, London: Spink.

DVARAKA

Dvaraka, also known as Dvaravathi, is the city of Krishna. The name Dvaraka is derived from the Sanskrit word *dvara*, which means door, signifying the city as a gated city or city of gates. It existed only for Krishna, who built it on land claimed from the ocean, and it was lost again to the ocean at Krishna's death. Krishna is referred to as Dvarakadhish (Lord of Dvaraka) in memory of his founding of the city, and for his rule from Dvaraka. The story of the founding of Dvaraka is narrated in Hindu, Jain, and Buddhist texts. According to the Hindu *puranas*, Jarasandha, the father-in-law of Kamsa, attacked Mathura and defeated the Yadavas sixteen times, wanting to kill Krishna to avenge the death of his son-in-law. In order to protect his kin from Jarasandha's repeated attacks, Krishna built a

---

Krishna Temples in Dvaraka

Dvaraka is the city of Krishna and hence considered an auspicious pilgrimage town for Krishna devotees. Dvaraka is one of the main centers of pilgrimage as part of the four sacred places (*Chardham*) of Hinduism. *Chardham yatra* (pilgrimage of four holy centers) is one of the most important pilgrimages undertaken by Hindus. The Jagat-mandir temple in Dvaraka and the Dvarakadhish temple in Bet Dvaraka are visited by Krishna devotees. Although Jagatmandir is considered a Krishna temple, it actually houses shrines for the four *vyuhas* (Krishna as Trivikrama, Balarama, Pradyumna, and Aniruddha). The Krishna temple in Bet Dvaraka houses the ancient image of Krishna that *acarya* Vallabha recovered from a well in Dvaraka.

---

new fortified city from reclaimed land on the shores of the Indian Ocean. A similar narrative is also preserved in the Buddhist story of *Ghatajataka*, with minor differences. According to the Buddhist story, an island fortified by hills on all sides was protected by an ass demon (*Gardabha*). Vaasudeva (Krishna) and his brothers defeated the demon and built a city in which to live peacefully.

Although Dvaraka is submerged under the ocean, efforts are currently underway to explore and recover evidence from the early historical city by archaeological agencies of India and other Western nations including the United States.

Braj, the Krishna pilgrimage center, preserves the memory of Dvaraka in its rituals and practices. Kosi, a place included in the Braj *Parikrama*, is referred to as Kushasthali, an alternative name for Dvaraka, to which it is said to correspond. A type of clay called *gopicandan*, which is used to make the Vaishnava forehead mark (*tilak*), is brought from Dvaraka.

See also: Braj *Parikrama*; Buddhism and Krishna; Jainism and Krishna; Mathura

Further Reading

Misra, D. P. 1971. *Proto-History of India.* New Delhi: Orient Longman.

Rao, S. R. 2001. *Marine Archaeology of India.* New Delhi: Publications Division, Government of India.

E

ECOLOGY

Krishna is closely connected to the environment, as depicted in numerous descriptions in the *Bhagavadgita*. In this text Krishna reveals his *visvarupa* (universal form) to Arjuna by providing his divine vision, in which Arjuna perceives the universe within the body of Krishna. This forms the basis of the Vaishnava belief that the world is part of God's body so that everything and every being in it need to be treated with respect (*Bhagavadgita* 11.7–20). Krishna further urges everyone to follow the *karmayoga* (path of action) for the welfare of all beings (*sarvabhutahita*) working for the preservation of the world. The geography of India with its sacred rivers, groves, and places interconnected by pilgrimage routes presents this sanctity, and everyone is expected to be responsible for taking care of the sacred regions. The area of Braj mandala, sanctified by the childhood play of Krishna (*lila*), is the focus of protection by numerous devotional groups of India. However, the modern government's developmental vision with incessant industrialization contributes to deforestation and polluting of rivers. Stories of Krishna and Balarama described in the *Harivamsa* and the *Vishnupurana* describe numerous events related to their protection of the lakes, groves, and forests of Braj. The *Bhagavatapurana*, especially, discusses how Krishna urged the *Gopas* to understand the importance of trees for humanity and coached them on the importance of protecting trees (*Bhagavatapurana* X.22.30–35). There is renewed pressure from several religious groups to protect the rivers and forests, while local opposition to mining and industrial development is mounting in modern India. However, with the largest number of vegetarians, India is still home to numerous species of animals, birds, and trees that have become extinct in other regions of the world. India needs to reinvest its vigor in continuing to protect its ecology.

See also: Braj *Parikrama*; Brindavan; Mathura; Twelve Forests of Braj; *Visvarupa*

Further Reading

Jain, P. 2011. *Dharma and Ecology of Hindu Communities*. Farnham: Ashgate.

Narayanan, Y. 2013. "Inspiring Sustainability beyond Sustainability: Sustainable Development and the Ultimate Hindu Purpose." *Nature and Culture* 8 (3): 301–323.

Nelson, L. E., ed. 1998. *Purifying the Earthly Body of God: Religion and Ecology in Hindu India*. Albany: State University of New York Press.

Patra, R. 2009. "*Vaastu Shastra*: Towards Sustainable Development." *Sustainable Development* 17 (4): 244–256.

Sullivan, B. 1998. "Theology and Ecology at the Birthplace of Krishna." In *Purifying the Earthly Body of God,* edited by L. Nelson, 247–267. Albany: State University of New York Press.

Tomlin, E. "The Limitations of Religious Environmentalism in India." *Worldviews: Environment, Culture, and Religion* 6 (1): 12–30.

EIGHT WIVES OF KRISHNA

Krishna married eight wives, and he also had to marry 1,600 princesses who expressed their wish to marry him when he was freed from prison when Narakasura was killed. Although the stories of Krishna's marriages to his eight wives are described in detail in the *Bhagavatapurana*, not much is known about each individual wife, except for Rukmini, Satyabhama, and Jambavati. The children of Rukmini and Jambavati play an important role in the *Bhagavatapurana*. Satyabhama's story is narrated in detail due to her naturally jealous temper as well as her behavior toward Krishna and his other wives. Only one wife of Krishna, Kalindi, is noted in the sacred narratives of Braj for her help in identifying the places associated with Krishna.

Rukmini

Rukmini is the daughter of Bhishmaka, king of Vidarbha. She was a typical young bride who went against her family to contact Krishna through a messenger to

Krishna with his wives, Rukmini and Satyabhama, and his mount, Garuda. Late 12th–13th century sculpture, copper alloy, Tamil Nadu, India. (Los Angeles County Museum of Art)

arrange her own marriage with him, which infuriated her brother Rukmi and made him a staunch opponent of Krishna. Rukmini is identified with Sri Laxmi, wife of Vishnu, who incarnates herself along with Vishnu during all his incarnations on earth. Therefore, Rukmini as an *avatara* of Laxmi is also the first and principal wife of Krishna. She is accorded a major role in the life of Krishna, which sometimes leads to other wives of Krishna becoming jealous of her. In particular, Satyabhama, another wife of Krishna, continued to have a competitive relationship with Rukmini out of jealousy. Rukmini is well remembered for bravely expressing her love for Krishna and inviting him to marry her. The episode of her marriage is the most appreciated chapter among those of the feminine counterparts of Krishna. Rukmini features most prominently in the legendary narratives and art of Krishna. Numerous literary and theatrical renderings of Rukmini's marriage to Krishna (*Rukmini Kalyanam*) are written in the many regional languages of India, in particular southern languages such as Tamil, Telugu, and Marathi. Krishna's marriage to Rukmini and images of her as one of the feminine counterparts of the central deity are a regular feature of the temples of Krishna in his allied forms, such as Venkatesvara, or Ranganatha in south India. Rukmini was the reason Krishna came to visit Pandarpur and became the presiding deity, Vitthala. Rukmini is the mother of Pradyumna and grandmother of Aniruddha. Thus she is directly related to three of the four *vyuhas* (*Caturvyuhas*), namely Krishna, Pradyumna, and Aniruddha, and indirectly related to the remaining *vyuha*, Balarama, as his sister-in-law. Rukmini is thus well represented in temples as well as in Hindu textual literature.

Satyabhama

Satyabhama was offered in marriage to Krishna when he brought back the *syamantaka* jewel to Satrajit, who at first thought Krishna had stolen it. To prove his innocence, Krishna undertook a search for it and returned it. Satrajit realized his mistake upon the return of the jewel and offered to marry Satyabhama to Krishna along with giving him the jewel. Krishna refused the jewel, but agreed to marry Satyabhama. Satyabhama tried to prove her superiority to the other wives of Krishna, especially the first wife, Rukmini. Her competitive nature is epitomized in the episode of *tulabharam* (weights on the weighing scale). According to the narration of this event in the *Bhagavatapurana*, Narada incites Satyabhama to undertake a *vrata* (vow), at the end of which she would have to donate her husband and then get him back by paying a quantity of gold equal to his weight. It so happened that at the end of the vow Satyabhama donated Krishna. In order to get him back she placed Krishna on one side of the weighing scale and placed all her fine gold jewelry on the other side of the scale, but the scale did not budge. Satyabhama did not know what to do, but Narada suggested she should invite Rukmini and request her help. Satyabhama swallowed her pride and requested Rukmini's help. Rukmini put a leaf of *tulasi* (basil) on the scale, and immediately it equaled the weight of Krishna. Everyone was amazed, and it is cited as one of the symbolic gestures of one's love for Krishna. Rukmini's leaf equaled Krishna and moved the scales, while all the jewelry of Satyabhama could do nothing.

Jambavati

Jambavati is significant among Krishna's wives, for she connects two *avataras* of Vishnu (Rama and Krishna) separated by two ages, *Treta* and *Dvapara*, and also her son Samba was instrumental in bringing about the death and destruction of the Yadavas, signifying the end of *Dvaparayuga*. Jambavati was married to Krishna while he went on a search for the *syamantaka* jewel, as it was thought that Krishna had taken it away, since in the past Krishna had asked that the jewel be given to Ugrasena, the king of the Yadavas. Therefore Krishna tried to recover it and return it to its owner, Satrajit, in order to clear his bad reputation because of the suspicious rumor generated out of Satrajit's misconceptions. While searching for the *syamantaka* jewel, Krishna went into a thick forest where he discovered a child playing with the jewel in a cave. This was a child of Jambavan, a principal associate of Rama, Vishnu's incarnation prior to Krishna, as narrated in the *Ramayana* (Legend of Rama), which occurred in an earlier era (*Kritayuga*). Jambavan was a minister and principal advisor to Sugriva, one of the close associates of Rama during his search and rescue of his wife Sita, who had been abducted by the demon Ravana. Krishna recognized him instantly as soon as he saw him, but Jambavan could not recognize him and engaged in a furious battle, since he thought Krishna had come to take the *syamantaka* jewel from his child. While wrestling with Krishna, Jambavan realized that he was none other than Rama, for whom he had worked in *Treta-yuga*. Jambavan immediately stopped the fight and prayed to Krishna, and after learning from Krishna the reason for his search, he ventured into the cave and offered the *syamantaka* jewel back, and he also requested that Krishna marry his daughter, Jambavati. Their marriage was conducted, and then Krishna returned to Dvaraka with Jambavati and returned the *syamantaka* jewel to Satrajit, who begged Krishna's forgiveness for blaming him, and offered to marry his sister Satyabhama to Krishna and give him the *syamantaka* jewel. Krishna agreed to marry Satyabhama, but refused the *syamantaka* jewel.

Kalindi

Kalindi was seen by Krishna and Arjuna during one of their hunting trips while Krishna was visiting the Pandavas after the marriage of the Pandavas to Draupadi. Kalindi is a minor river in north India, a tributary of the Ganga, along with the Yamuna. Kalindi is considered another form of the river goddess Yamuna. When Arjuna approached her at Krishna's prompting, she told him of her desire to marry Vishnu. Arjuna then brought her back and introduced her to Krishna, while mentioning to Krishna her wish to marry Vishnu. Krishna immediately accepted and married Kalindi. As a form of Yamuna, Kalindi has the longest continuous association with the Braj region. After the death of Krishna and the annihilation of the Yadavas, Kalindi is remembered for her important role in repopulating and reviving *Brajbhumi* (the land of Braj). She assisted Vajranabha, great-grandson of Krishna who visited Mathura to meet Uddhava, identify places associated with Krishna and establish temples for Krishna in Braj. Kalindi helped identify the places associated with the life of Krishna as well as with the carving of the images of Krishna installed in the temples marking the sacred spots of Krishna *lila* (play of Krishna).

Mitravinda

Mitravinda is the daughter of King Jayasena of Avanti. Although Mitravinda chose Krishna as her bridegroom in the *svayamvara* (bridegroom choice), her brothers Vinda and Anuvinda opposed this marriage as they were close friends of Duryodhana, and they did not view the relationship of Krishna to the Pandavas favorably. They wished her to marry Duryodhana. However, Mitravinda let Krishna know about it as soon as she chose him as her groom and requested him to take her away and marry her. Krishna followed her advice, took her away from the *svayamvara* by force, and defeated her brothers. Krishna married her according to Mitravinda's wishes.

Nagnajiti

Nagnajiti is the daughter of Nagnajit, king of Kosala. She is known by the patronymic Nagnajiti after her father's name, while she is also referred to as Satya, her given name. Nagnajit announced the bridegroom choice for his daughter Nagnajiti with the condition that whoever tamed the seven ferocious bulls in his kingdom could marry his daughter. The bulls were very ferocious, and those who tried to tame them were either injured or left unsuccessful. Krishna visited Kosala one day and expressed to her father Nagnajit his desire to marry the princess Nagnajiti. Nagnajit was delighted at the proposal, but indicated that he took a vow to marry his daughter to the one who could tame the seven bulls. Krishna then fulfilled that condition as he tamed the seven bulls easily and brought them all, tied to a rope, to Nagnajit, who then married his daughter to Krishna according to traditional customs.

Bhadra

Krishna married Bhadra, the daughter of his father's sister Srutakirti and Kaikeyi. Bhadra expressed her wish to marry Krishna to her brothers. Bhadra's brothers readily concurred and married her to Krishna, fulfilling her wishes.

Lakshmana

Krishna took Lakshmana away from the assembly hall where numerous princes were assembled for the *svayamvara*. She is the princess of the kingdom of Madra, the daughter of Brihatsena. Lakshmana is also an accomplished *vina* player.

See also: Aniruddha; Braj: Classical History; Braj *Parikrama*; Pradyumna; Samba; Vishnu; *Vyuhas*; Yamuna

Further Reading

Pauwels, H. 2007. "Stealing a Willing Bride: Women's Agency in the Myth of Rukmini's Elopement ('Krishna and Rukmini')." *Journal of the Royal Asiatic Society* 17: 407–441.

EKADASI

Ekadasi is one of the most sacred holy days of the Vaishnava calendar. It is thought that the doors of *Vaikuntha* open for anyone visiting the temple of Krishna or Vishnu on that day. *Ekadasi* literally means the eleventh day of the dark half or bright half of the month (*krishna paksha* or *sukla paksha*). Although *Ekadasi* occurs every fortnight of the month, one of the *Ekadasis*, known as *Mukkoti Ekadasi* or *Vaikuntha Ekadasi,* is held to be the most auspicious day for Hindus, and especially for Vaishnavas. *Vaikuntha Ekadasi* occurs on the *Suklapaksha Ekadasi* of *Dhanurmasa–Margasira* (December–January) of every year. It is also known as *Mokshada Ekadasi*, for it is believed that temples are like the entrance to heaven on that day, and anyone visiting the temple of Vishnu/Krishna is purified and granted *moksha* (release from samsara/heaven). Special *pujas* and rituals are offered in the temples. Devotees also perform special fasting, refraining from eating certain foods on that day.

Many Krishna temples, especially those in south India (Srirangam temple, Venkatesvara temple), have a special door called *Vaikuntha dvaram* on the north side of the main temple, which is opened only once a year on the day of *Vaikuntha Ekadasi*. Taking a view (*darsan*) of the deity on this day is considered efficacious for devotees, and is considered to purify one from all sins, and hence may lead to heaven.

See also: Guruvayurappa and Guruvayur Temple; *Moksha/Mukti*; Srirangam Temple; Venkatesvara

Further Reading

Jagannathan, M. 2005. *South Indian Hindu Festivals and Traditions*. New Delhi: Abhinav Publications.

EKNATH

Eknath was one of the most prolific *Varkari* saint poets of Maharashtra. Eknath was born in the caste of *Desastha* Brahmans and was raised by his great-grandfather Bhanudas, a renowned *Varkari* leader. A number of biographies recollect the life of Eknath.

Kesavasvami composed Eknath's biography in 1760, which served as a basic text for several other renderings of his later biographies. The *Pratisthanacharitra* and the *Bhaktalilamrit*, written by Mahipati, also contain the biography of Eknath. His significant contribution is the scholarly commentary and Marathi rendering of the *Bhagavatapurana*, known as the *Ekanathi Bhagavat*, along with several other contributions, such as the *Gitasar*, a new edition of Jnanadev's translation of the *Bhagavadgita* popularly known as the *Jnanesvari*, several philosophical treatises, and poetical works called *Gathas*, a Marathi rendering of the *Ramayana*, known as

Eknath in Popular Culture

A number of Marathi films portray the life of Eknath. The film *Sant Eknath* released in 1926 is the first Marathi film on Eknath while several films followed. Another Marathi film, *Sant Eknath Maharaj,* was released in 2012. Theatrical productions based on the life of Eknath and his writings are also common. Eknath is one of the most popular *sants* of the *Varkari* tradition.

the *Bhavarth Ramayana*, although left incomplete due to his sudden demise. Eknath composed numerous other popular texts such as the *Rukmini Svayamvar*, the *Prahlad Vijaya*, the *Ananda Lahari*, the *Svatma Sukha*, and the *Chiranjiva Pad*. Eknath is also credited with popularizing the devotional singing style of *Bharood*.

Eknath is described as a model *bhakta* (devotee) in his biographies, sometimes even identified as an avatar of Panduranga Vitthala himself, the main god of the *Varkari* tradition. Eknath was dedicated to the *advaita* philosophy of regarding the creator (Brahma) and creation (*jiva*) as one and indifferent. Hence, his practice transcended the restrictive social practices of caste prevalent in his lifetime during the sixteenth century. His behavior caused discomfort to his own family, as well as certain conservative Brahmans of the day. Biographies of Eknath recollect that conservative Brahmans did not associate with him. Even Eknath's son Haridas disagreed with his father's nontraditional view of associating with non-Brahmans, and Haridas left home to reside in Varanasi.

Eknath left Paithan at the age of twelve and became a disciple of Janardana in Daulatabad. At the completion of his discipleship, with the blessings of his guru Janardana, Eknath undertook a pilgrimage to the sacred cities of India, at the conclusion of which he married and settled down as a householder in Paithan. While living in Paithan, Eknath devoted his life to practicing his bhakti, editing and translating major Vaishnava texts for use by *Varkari* practitioners. His *Varkari* devotional practice is noted for its unique *kirtana* singing and religious discourse in public and at people's houses, standing right in front of their gates. Eknath was also noted for his willingness to eat food prepared by non-Brahmans, as well as serving food to non-Brahmans. Two temples were constructed for Eknath in Paithan. Eknath *shashti* is celebrated here, as well as at his shrine at Paithan, one of the main stopping points on the *Varkari* pilgrimage path; and his *padukas* (sandals) are taken in procession as part of the *Varkari* pilgrimage. Eknath's imprint on the *Varkari* tradition, philosophy, and culture of Maharashtra is distinct and enduring. Eknath *palki* is one of the largest and most well organized *palkis* that participate in the biennial *vari* to Pandarpur from across the state of Maharashtra.

See also: Jnanadev; *Kirtana*; Panduranga Vitthala; *Sants*; *Varkari* Tradition

Further Reading

Abbot, J. E. 1927. *The Life of Eknath*. Delhi: Motilal Banarsidass.

Keune, J. 2007. "Gathering the *Bhaktas* in Marathi." *Journal of Vaishnava Studies* 15 (2): 169–187.

Pangarkar, L. R. 1910. *Eknath Charitra*. Mumbai: Gita Press.

Phatak, N. R. 1950. *Sri Eknath: Vangmay ani Kavya*. Pune: Suvichar Prakashak Mandal.

Zelliot, E. 1980. "Chokhamela and Eknath: Two *Bhakti* Modes of Legitimacy for Modern Change." *Journal of Asia and Asian Studies* 15 (1–2): 136–156.

F

FORESTS OF KRISHNA

Numerous forests (groves and arbors) are mentioned in the *Harivamsa*, the *Bhaga-vatapurana*, and the *Gargasamhita* as favorite places of Krishna to play with his friends the *Gopas* and also to sport with Radha and the *Gopis*. Several forests around Brindavan are identified and maintained by devotional groups, and form part of the regular itinerary of the devotees participating in the pilgrimage of Braj *parikrama* (circumambulation of Braj). Twelve major forests and twelve minor forests form part of the Braj *parikrama* and are listed in the pilgrimage manuals. The twelve major forests are Mahavana, Kamyavana (also known as Kaman, short for Kam-van), Kokilavana (Kokilaban), Talavana (Talban), Kumudavana (Kumudban), Bhandiravana (Bhandirban), Chatravana (Chhata), Khadiravana (Khaira), Loha-vana (Lohban), Bhadravana, Bahulavana (Bahulaban), and Bilvavana (Belban). This is the standard list of the sacred forests associated with the life of Krishna, although modern pilgrimage lists may add forests or replace some of these forests with other forests that are convenient to visit or close to popular temples or *tirthas*. In local usage *van,* a variant of *vana* in local language, is transformed into *ban* (current usage indicated within parentheses), or the *vana* or *ban* may be dropped from usage altogether in some cases; hence the names may sound different, but in reality the currently used names are shortened names of the original Sanskrit names mentioned above. These alternative names may sometimes cause confusion and create issues with identification of the forests. The twelve minor forests also routinely listed in the pilgrimage circuits of Mathura are Brahmavana, Apsaravana, Vihvalavana, Suvarnavana (Sonehara), Kadambavana, Surabhivana, Premavana, Mayuravana, Manengitavana, Seshasayanavana (Shekhsai), Naradavana, and Para-manandavana. In addition to these major and minor forests, numerous arbors and groves are also listed as places of meditation (*tapovana*), *moksha* (salvation), service (*sevyakavana*), desire (*kamavana*), material gain (*arthavana*), duty (*dharmavana*), and spiritual realization (*siddhavana*). Numerous banyan trees are also listed in the pilgrimage lists; the most important trees are Bhandiravata (at Bhandirban), Srin-garavata (at Brindavan), and Vamsivata (at Brindavan). Bhandiravata is the large banyan tree in the legendary Bhandiravan in which Balarama killed the demon Pralambha. A temple of Balarama near the Bhandiravat marks the sacred spot of this pastime (*lila*) of *Pralambavadha* (killing of Pralamba). Vamsivata is identified with Krishna's *Raasalila* during which Krishna enchanted the *Gopis* with music played on his flute (*vamsi*). Sringaravata is a banyan tree located on the banks of the Yamuna on the way to Kesighat. It is also associated with the *Raasalila* of Krishna. It is mentioned in the *Bhagavatapurana* that during the *Raasalila* Krishna

disappeared with his favorite *Gopi*. Sringaravata is associated with the secret ran-
dezvous of Krishna and his favorite *Gopi*, identified as Radha. Sringaravata is also
called Nityanandavata, since Nityananda, the close associate of Caitanya, spent
time under the tree.

See also: Balarama; Braj *Parikrama*; Brindavan; Caitanya; Krishna; Mathura; Radha;
Twelve Forests of Braj

Further Reading

Goswami, S. 2001. *Celebrating Krishna*. Vrindavan: Sri Caitanya Prem Samsthana.
Haberman, L. 1994. *Journey through the Twelve Forests: An Encounter with Krishna*. New
    York: Oxford University Press.
Malhotra, K., Gokhale, Y., Chatterjee, S., and Srivastava, S. 2007. *Sacred Groves of India*.
    New Delhi: Aryan Books International.

G

GARGASAMHITA

The *Gargasamhita* is attributed to the sage Garga, the family priest of Nanda, the adopted father of Krishna. The *Gargasamhita* is especially important in the Vallabha tradition for its central treatment of Govardhan as a sacred place. The *Gargasamhita* presents the story of Krishna as told to Garga, based on the account of Narada as narrated to Bahulashva, a king of Mithila. The centrality of narration of the events and places associated with Krishna makes the *Gargasamhita* the most popular *purana* among the devotees of Krishna. The *Gargasamhita* describes the events of Krishna's life in ten books, associating these events with sacred places in Braj, including descriptions of pilgrimages and festivals. The first book, known as *Golokakhanda*, describes Krishna's birth and childhood. Book two, known as *Brindavanakhanda*, is an important section of the book, for it not only narrates the events of the life of Krishna with his favorite *Gopi*, Radha, and the other *Gopis* (cowherd maidens) and *Gopas* (cowherds), but also identifies the numerous forests and sites where the events took place in the *Mathuramandala* (Mathura region). The third book, known as *Girirajakhanda*, narrates the divinity of Govardhan Hill and its festivals. The third book describes the Govardhan *puja*, the *Annakut* festival, and *Chappanbhog* in detail. The fourth book, known as *Madhuryakhanda*, describes the love plays of Krishna in Brindavan. The fifth book, known as *Mathurakhanda*, describes Krishna's return to Mathura and the wrestling match in which Kamsa was killed by Krishna. The sixth book, known as *Dvarakakhanda*, describes the foundation of the city by Krishna, including a detailed description of the city. The seventh book, *Vishvajitkhanda*, describes Krishna's worldly exploits and his divinity. The eighth book, known as *Balabhadrakhanda*, describes the exploits of Balarama in Vraja and his divinity. The ninth book, *Vijnanakhanda*, appears as a concluding chapter, which states that the nine books are like the nine gems, as if there were only nine books in the *Gargasamhita*, while the tenth book concludes the earlier chapters and describes the return of the Yadavas to *Goloka*. However, it contains an additional chapter, which forms the tenth book of the *Gargasamhita*, called *Asvamedhakhanda*. The tenth book does not continue with the narratives of the nine chapters preceding it, but describes Ugrasena's *asvamedha* sacrifice. Chapter ten also contains some late references about the *catuh sampradayas* (the four devotional traditions), and the emergence of Shrinathji at Govardhan, which led scholars to consider these parts as later additions to the *Gargasamhita*. The narration of the text itself also lends support to this view that the tenth chapter might have been a later addition to the text. The pilgrimage descriptions of the *Gargasamhita* list sacred *vans* (forests or arbors), lakes, and several important places associated with Krishna's life, and their recovery and foundation by Vajranabha, grandson of Krishna. The *Gargasamhita* describes Brindavan, Govardhan, and Dvaraka as the most important sacred places associated with Krishna. The *Gargasamhita* describes Brindavan as the center of the *Mathuramandala* (Mathura region), which constitutes the area of the *caurasikos parikrama* (the eighty-four *kos,* or 2.26 miles, circumambulation). It is described as containing numerous forests where Krishna and the other *Gopas* took the cows for grazing, including Govardhan Hill, Barsana, and Nandgaon. Twelve forests are mentioned as settings for Radha and Krishna's love play and also the *rasa* dance, as well as other events in the life of Krishna. The *Gargasamhita* also contains descriptions of several practices associated with devotional worship, such as worship of the *tulasi* (basil) plant, Govardhan, and reverence to Yamuna, and it also includes the list of Yamuna's thousand names. The *Gargasamhita* also lists the thousand names of Krishna and his worship, along with the thousand names of Balarama and his worship, as well as the rituals and rules for observance of *Ekadasi*.

See also: Braj *Parikrama*; Brindavan; *Ekadasi*; *Gopas* and *Gopis*; Govardhan; Govardhan *Puja*; Mathura; *Raasalila*; Radha; Vajranabha

Further Reading

Holtzman, D. (Goswami, D). 2006. *Gargasamhita*. Kansas City, MO: Rupanuga Vedic College.

GAUDIYA VAISHNAVISM

Gaudiya Vaishnavism, also referred to as Bengal Vaishnavism as well as Caitanya Vaishnavism, is a distinct religious group devoted to Krishna. Caitanya is the principal founder of this tradition, as indicated by one of the names by which this tradition came to be known. *Gaudiya* Vaishnavism notes that its origins were derived from Madhavendra Puri (thus connecting to the Madhva tradition), while the next stage of its development is due to Caitanya, with support from nine other peers of Caitanya. Caitanya's association with *advaita* traditions including Ramanuja's *visishtadvaita* (qualified monism) tradition of Srirangam is noted in traditional sources. The role of Madhavendra Puri (his disciple Isvara Puri initiated Caitanya) and a number of the other peers of Caitanya during the early stages of his spiritual progress is nominal, although notable. Three of Caitanya's associates, Advaita (Kamalaksha Bhattacarya), Nityananda (Kuvera Pandita), and Gadadhara, and his disciples Jiva, Rupa, and Sanatana, along with numerous other devotees have contributed significantly to the development of the *Gaudiya* tradition, which emerged as one of the most popular Vaishnava traditions of India. *Gaudiya* Vaishnavism faced opposition from the Muslim rulers of Bengal during its early phases. The *Caitanyacaritamrita* mentioned objections raised by a local Muslim *kaji* to the *samkirtana* (public chanting) practices of *Gaudiya* Vaishnava devotees, which was solved amicably by Caitanya in a meeting with the *kaji*. Caitanya received honor and support from the local ruler, Prataparudra, as he came to Puri in Orissa.

Caitanya had visited Braj on a pilgrimage and expressed concern at the desolation of the sacred sites related to Krishna's life. His disciples Rupa and Sanatana *Gosvami*, along with Jiva *Gosvami*, Raghunathabhatta *Gosvami*, Gopalabhatta *Gosvami*, and Raghunathadasa *Gosvami* (also known as the six *Gosvamis*), settled in Braj, working for the revival and restoration of the sacred sites associated with Krishna's life. The *Gosvamis* were able to secure the financial support of Raja Bhagavandas, king of Amber, and his son Mansing (1589–1614) in building the Govindadeva temple at Vrindavan (Brindavan in current usage), and several other temples in Mathura, Govardhan, and surrounding regions, entrusting the temples to the care of *mahants* (temple priests). However, the neutral attitude of the Mughal Empire did not last long, finally resulting in persecution from Aurangzeb (1658–1670). Aurangzeb's raids forced numerous temples to close, and the central images of Krishna from numerous temples in Mathura and Brindavan (including the Caitanya tradition's Govindadev temple and Madanmohan temple, the Vallabha tradition's temple of Srinathji, and the *Janmasthan* temple) were moved to safe places. The central images of the Govindadev temple were moved to Jaipur state under the patronage of Savai Jaisingh II. In addition to moving toward western India for safety, the *Gosvamis* of the Caitanya tradition also began establishing their devotional centers in Bihar and Bengal in eastern India. *Gaudiya* Vaishnavism was established by Srinivasa *Gosvami* in Bankura, southwest of Bengal, with support from Vir Hambir (1575–1576), the Malla chieftain. Several temples were built here in a new and innovative style known as *ratna* (jewel—a particular style of architecture popular in Bengal) with walls richly adorned with terracotta panels depicting *Krishnalila*, leaving a large place for the devotees to gather for *kirtans* and so on. One of the best-known temples for its terracotta panels is the Madan Mohan temple in Vishnupur (Bishnupuar). Srinivasa also established distinct *sevas* (services) in the temple, along with *prasadam* distribution. He made *kirtan* singing a regular activity in these temples in Bankura. This style of devotional singing is recognized as a distinct style of musical performance known as *Vishnupur Gharana,* for its association with the Gaudiya temples in Vishnupur. Narottamadas, another *Gosvami*, moved back to his own home town, Kheturigram in the Rajshahi district of present-day Bangladesh, and with support from his cousin, Santoshadatta, the local raja, Narottamadas was able to institute the celebration of Caitanya's birthday as an annual event of celebration as well as doctrinal disputation to bring close understanding among the several Vaishnava groups of that period. This established Caitanya Vaishnavism on a firm footing in both west Bengal (India) and east Bengal (Bangladesh), spreading to northeastern states including Assam, Manipur, and Tripura. Caitanya Vaishnavism is also a major force in Uttar Pradesh in the Mathura and Braj regions, extending into Rajastan and northwestern India. Therefore, it can be said that before 1750 the Caitanya Vaishnava tradition had spread and established itself in all of north India. During colonial rule (1857–1947), Bengal went through severe economic upheavals and political changes. However, under the able and effective leadership of Kedarnath Datta Bhaktivinoda and his son, Bhaktisiddhanta Saraswati, Vaishnavism continued to increase its support base and attract English-educated modern Indians as

The famous Madanmohan temple located in Bishnupur (Vishnupur), West Bengal, India. (Nilanjan Bhattacharya/Dreamstime.com)

its followers. Bhaktisiddhanta increased the institutional efforts by establishing monastic centers (*mathas*) and encouraging his followers to establish *mathas*, thereby beginning the missionizing activities. Caitanya Vaishnavism was introduced to America by A. C. Bhaktivedanta Swami, who established ISKCON (International Society of Krishna Consciousness), which continues to thrive in the United States, while it has also spread to numerous countries across the world.

A court order in 1948 divided *Gaudiya* Math into two: Shri Chaitanya Math (Sridham Mayapur, west Bengal) and *Gaudiya* Mission (Baghbazar, Calcutta), each with their branch *mathas*.

The *Gaudiya* Vaishnava tradition has been a major influence on the religious practice of Brindavan through the dedicated service of Caitanya and his followers. Sri Caitanya Mahaprabhu, his disciples Rupa and Sanatana *Gosvami*, and their nephew Jiva *Gosvami* lived in Brindavan and contributed to the revival of the sacred sites associated with Krishna's life. Rupa *Gosvami* was instrumental in the construction of the Govind Dev temple in Brindavan, as well as the revival of numerous other temples in the Braj region. The international unit of the Caitanya Vaishnava tradition, founded by A. C. Bhaktivedanta Svami Prabhupada (ISKCON), constructed the Krishna Balaram temple and was one of the major religious groups in Brindavan.

A large compendium of texts written by the *Gosvamis* and several gurus and followers enriches *Gaudiya* Vaishnavism. The *Gaudiya* literary tradition contains several biographies of Caitanya, as well as other disciples. Eight Sanskrit verses known as *Sikshashtaka* are attributed to Caitanya. Rupa *Gosvami's Bhaktirasamritasindhu* prescribes the types of bhakti and practices. Jiva *Gosvami's Bhagavatasandarbha* is another important text explicating the philosophical and theological doctrines of the *Gaudiya* Vaishnava tradition. *Jiva Gosvami's Vaidhibhaktisadhana* lays down the rules for bhakti practices outlined in the *Bhaktirasamritasindhu* of Rupa *Gosvami*. Another important text of this tradition is the *Haribhaktivilasa*, which is a detailed manual on ritual practice for daily worship and special occasions. Sanatana *Gosvami's Brihatbhagavatamrita* is a two-part narrative. Numerous collections of devotional songs also form part of the *Gaudiya* Vaishnava literary treasury, which includes important texts such as the Narottamadasa's *prarthana*, written in Bengali, unlike the above texts, which are written in Sanskrit.

See also: Bhakti; Bhaktivedanta Swami Prabhupada; Caitanya; Jiva *Gosvami*; *Raganuraga*; Rupa *Gosvami*

Further Reading

Chakravarti, R. 1977. "*Gaudiya* Vaisnavism in Bengal." *Journal of Indian Philosophy* 5 (1–2): 107–149.
Rosen, S. 1992. *Vaishnavism: Contemporary Scholars Discuss the Gaudiya Tradition*. New York: Folk Books.

GITAGOVINDA

The *Gitagovinda*, composed by Jayadeva, is a book of songs describing the sensuous and boldly erotic Brindavan wanderings of Krishna and the *Gopis* (cowherd maidens), termed *Raasalila*, on full-moon nights of autumn. The tale of *sringara* (romance), describing the night exploits of the god Krishna with women of the town, has raised some eyebrows since its composition, and opinion is still divided on how religious the text is in its form and treatment of the subject. However, this has not stopped the *Gitagovinda* from being widely used by devotees in their song and dance or musical performances revering Krishna on any occasion. In fact, the *Gitagovinda* is the most often sung and performed text of this type from the twelfth

---

Sringara Rasa

The credit for bringing *sringara rasa* to the center of devotional activity and literature in India goes to the *Gitagovinda*. Although initial responses to the *Gitagovinda* lamented the erotic expressions of the text, it remains a trendsetter inspiring later literary compositions of numerous devotional traditions in India as *rasa* became an important aspect of devotional experience.

century onward. The *Gitagovinda* is absolutely unique in its treatment of the subject matter, simplicity of language, and poetical style.

Jayadeva, composer of the *Gitagovinda,* was a Bengali poet associated with the Sena dynasty (Lakshmanasena, 1178–1205). Jayadeva's poetry was popular among literary circles in Bengal and the rest of north India during the twelfth and thirteenth centuries, which is indicated by the inclusion of his poetry in an anthology, the *Sringarapaddhati,* a thirteenth-century text from Rajasthan. However, it is unknown whether the poems of *Gitagovinda* were performed or known to the common public during this time. Nonetheless its preference in devotional circles of the temples is significant. It is notable that *Gitagovinda's* performance in musical and dance recitations is noted in the Jagannatha temple in Puri dating from the fifteenth century. An inscription written in Oriya, dated to the fifteenth century, in the Jagannatha temple issued on the occasion of the consecration of the images of the doorkeepers of the temple, Jaya and Vijaya, notes that the *Gitagovinda* is offered in song and dance performances for Jagannatha in the temple. It is a notable fact that among *Gaudiya* Vaishnavas the poetry of the *Gitagovinda* has been immensely well received since the fifteenth century, as attested by the emphasis of Rupa *Gosvami's* thesis on devotional intimacy with God with aesthetics understood in a theological framework. The followers of *Gaudiya* Vaishnavism quote the *Gitagovinda* verses extensively, and it may have formed part of the processional singing of this group too. From the sixteenth century onward the *Gitagovinda* experienced a meteoric rise in popularity, which attracted admiring followers from different religious groups, including Sikhism, in addition to various Vaishnava groups, as well as lay artists, performers, and composers.

The *Gitagovinda* contains twelve chapters (*sargas*), each of which contain one to four songs, for a total of twenty-four songs. *Gitagovinda* is written in Sanskrit, which is lyrical and metrical in style, and uses simple words in composition, making it easier for anyone to sing or recite even without much training in language or music. The *Gitagovinda* is noted for its use of images of sound (*sabdalankaras*) and *upamanas* (comparative analogies), which can be appreciated without fully grasping the meaning, and that helps even the illiterate to grasp the general meaning of the verses. Each song in the *Gitagovinda* ends with a signature line (*banita*), which is ubiquitous in bhakti poetry, but the *Gitagovinda* also includes a unique arrangement of words (*padavali*) that were later adopted in regional languages of the Ganga-Yamuna basins of north India, such as Maithili, Bengali, and Brajbuli. Jayadeva's *Gitagovinda* could be classed as the harbinger of the *padavali* style of bhakti poetry. This style of poetry inspired bhakti poets across India and even spread to south India with *padakirtans* composed by major poets of Andhra Pradesh including Tyagaraja and Annamayya.

The subject of the *Gitagovinda* poetry is the love dalliances of Radha and Krishna. Separation (*viraha*) and union, two modes of love, found expression in this fantasy-laden world. The world of Vraja is transformed in the poems of the *Gitagovinda* into a heavenly, blissful place, where only happiness is found and thoughts of Krishna pervade. While the *Raasalila* section of the *Bhagavatapurana* spans five chapters of the tenth book, it does not mention Radha explicitly, but mentions the *Gopis* only as a generic term, while including descriptions of a special *Gopi* as the favorite of Krishna. By including Radha as the full-fledged partner of Krishna, the *Gitagovinda* diverges from the original, although it deals in a similar way with the concept of *Raasalila* as described in the *Bhagavatapurana*, which also includes the "separation-union" anxiety of lovers represented by Krishna and the *Gopis*.

Overall the *Gitagovinda* has several unique qualities in addition to its literary merits, which places it at the top of literary texts of India devoted to Krishna. First, it brought forward a new style of poetical composition, *padavali*, which became a ubiquitous feature of bhakti poetry in several regional languages. Second, the *Gitagovinda* made the concept of aesthetic theology accessible to the common public through its compositions. Third, it brought Krishna to the devotees as someone to be adored and intimately loved, not merely revered and worshipped.

See also: Bhagavatapurana; Bhakti; Braj: Classical History; Braj *Parikrama*; Brindavan; *Gopas* and *Gopis*; *Kirtana*; *Lila*

Further Reading

Siegel, L. 1978. *Sacred and Profane Dimensions of Love in Indian Traditions as Exemplified in the Gitagovinda of Jayadeva.* Delhi: Oxford University Press.

Vatsyayan, K. 2006. "The *Gitagovinda*: A Twelfth-Century Sanskrit Poem Travels West." *Studying Transcultural Literary History* 10: 221–231.

GOLOKA

Goloka is the heavenly realm of Krishna *Gopala* (Krishna the cowherd). It is the cosmic world of Krishna filled with happiness, similar to Brindavan, where everyone enjoyed the presence of Krishna, while forgetting about the worldly limitations of living life on earth. *Goloka* is synonymous with *Vaikuntha*, also known as *Vishnuloka*, since Krishna is himself the full incarnation of Vishnu, which is sometimes conceptualized to mean that Krishna is Vishnu. Some devotional traditions even consider Vishnu as an emanation of Krishna. *Goloka* is a world with several layers arranged in concentric circles, resembling the arrangement of petals in a lotus flower. Krishna and Radha are located at the center of this *Goloka*; others connected with Krishna surround him in the petals of the lotus, arranged in circular layers, overlapping but individual at the same time. Everyone on these lotus petals directly connects with Radha and Krishna in the center. A similar concept of *lotiform* is also seen in the depiction of the *Vrajamandala* drawings and drawings of other mandalas incorporating Vaishnava saints such as Caitanya. Mandala diagrams of Krishna, Caitanya, and *Goloka*, also called *yantra,* are used as helpful meditative and contemplative tools by Krishna devotees. The *Gargasamhita* describes the *Gopas* as reaching *Goloka* when Krishna left the earth and returned to his own abode in *Goloka*. While *Goloka* is the divine world, modeled on the earthly abode of Krishna in Brindavan, the region of Brindavan is considered auspicious because it holds a reflection of the divine world of Krishna where he once lived. For the pilgrimage chronicles narrating the sacred centers of Krishna in Braj, *Goloka* is the divine world that is reached after attaining *moksha* (salvation), which could also be experienced in Braj, because it holds the idyllic natural settings that once hosted Krishna.

See also: Braj: Classical History; Braj *Parikrama*; Brindavan; *Gargasamhita*; Krishna; Mandala; Mathura; *Moksha/Mukti*

Further Reading

Dasa, K., and Dasa, P. *Glory of Sri Goloka: Sri Goloka Mahatmya of Sanatana Gosvami.* Calcutta: Rasbihari Lal & Sons.

GOPALACAMPU

Written by Jiva *Gosvami*, the *Gopalacampu* is an important contribution to the Caitanya Vaishnava corpus in particular and Sanskrit literature in general. The *Gopalacampu* is a book of verses written in the *campu* style of poetry. *Campu* is a simple style of writing in which prose passages (*gadya*) alternate with poetical stanzas (*padya*). Hence the *Gopalacampu* is an accessible devotional text composed in simple language interspersed with poems that can be easily set to musical notes.

The *Gopalacampu* provides descriptions of the pastimes of Krishna in Brindavan. The *Gopalacampu* is divided into two sections: the *purva* (former) and the *uttara* (later). Although both the *purva* and *uttara* sections describe Krishna's pastimes in Vraja and Brindavan, the *uttara* section is particularly important for its lyrical *kirtanas* used for meditation, worship, and *bhajan* ceremonies.

See also: Bhakti; Brindavan; Caitanya Vaishnavism; Childhood of Krishna in Brindavan; Jiva *Gosvami*; *Lila*

Further Reading

Dasa, K. 2009. *Gopala Campu of Srila Jiva Gosvami.* Vrindavan: Ras Bihari Lal & Sons.

GOPAS AND *GOPIS*

The *Gopas* and *Gopis* form the community of Krishna. They are almost like his extended family. Even though Krishna was born a Satvata prince as the son of Vasudeva, he spent part of his life with the *Gopas* and *Gopis,* intimately playing and enjoying life with them and then founding a new empire in Dvaraka, protecting the larger Yadava community. However, it is these *Gopa* boys and the *Gopi* girls that feature prominently in the bhakti literature centered on personal devotion (*seva*) and self-surrender (*prapatti*) to Krishna. While the Yadavas Sridama and Uddhava were great friends of Krishna, other *Gopas* also received the pleasure of his company and cherished his presence. Although there were several *Gopi* maidens that desired the company of Krishna, only one *Gopi*, Radha, acquired the special position of being Krishna's favorite cowherd maiden. The *Gopis*, as described in the *Raasalila*, connect with Krishna and surrender to him completely. Self-surrender of the *Gopis* is indicated by two incidents narrated in the *Bhagavatapurana*: Krishna stealing the *Gopis'* clothes, and engaging in the *Raasalila* dance with the *Gopis* on autumn nights in Brindavan. Krishna's constant

Ashtasakhis

The *Ashtasakhis* (eight friends), along with Radha, form the *Gopi* group most favored by Krishna. The *Ashtasakhis* are Radha and her friends. Although they are not named in the *Bhagavatapurana*, later *purana* texts provide their names: Lalitha, Visakha, Campakalatha, Citra, Tungavidya, Indulekha, Rangadevi, and Sudevi. These eight friends always provide Radha with companionship and any help she may need in meeting her beloved Krishna. In the bhakti milieu of Brindavan between the thirteenth and sixteenth centuries, it was common for the devotees to imagine themselves as one of the *sakhis* of Radha in order to find closeness and intimacy with Krishna and participate in *Krishnalila*. Haridas, one of the three Haris (*Haritray*), imagined himself as Lalitha, serving Radha and Krishna in their pastimes in Brindavan. *Ashtasakhi* temples are found in the Mathura region, in Brindavan, and in Barsana, accompanying Radha.

engagement with the *Gopas* and *Gopis* is an illustration of *sakhyabhava* (mood of friendship), which is one of the important modes of connecting with the god in the bhakti tradition of worship.

The *Gopis* and *Gopas* missed Krishna once he left Vraja. Although Krishna never visited the *Gopis* again, he sent them a message through his friend Uddhava. He only met them as adults in Samantapancaka during the great eclipse. Krishna talked to them and instructed them in spiritual matters. They in turn, seeing Krishna, filled their hearts with him and became absorbed in his thoughts, which destroyed all their sins.

See also: Birth and Early Childhood of Krishna; Braj: Classical History; Braj *Parikrama*; Dvaraka; *Lila*; *Raasalila*; Uddhava

Further Reading

Goswami, S. 2001. *Celebrating Krishna.* Vrindavan: Sri Caitanya Prema Samsthana.

Gopis (cow maidens) and cows in the divine embrace of Krishna. Master at the court of Mandi (active, ca. 1710–1750), Himachal Pradesh, India, ca. 1700–1725, watercolor on paper. (Los Angeles County Museum of Art)

GOVARDHAN

Govardhan is a small town near Mathura surrounded by hills, lakes, and bowers. The Govardhan hill is a ridge of rocky outcrops stretching from the township of Govardhan to Puchhari, and its highest elevation can be found between Anyor and Jatipura, where the Srinathji temple is located. The hill diminishes in height toward Lake Kusum Sarovar, and only a few rocks protruding above ground are noticed near the lake. The Govardhan hill is also known as *giriraj* (king of mountains or mountain king) or *girisa* (lord of mountains) for the central position it holds in the Krishna myths. *Govardhanadharanlila* (lifting of Mount Govardhan), also called *Govardhanlila,* was mentioned in the *Harivamsa* when Krishna exhorted the Yadavas to divert the offerings to Govardhan from Indra, who was regularly worshipped with annual offerings. This *lila* of Krishna is mentioned in numerous classical texts of Hinduism, and also in numerous texts in regional languages, such as Brajbhasha. The Vrindavan Research Institute preserves copies of early manuscripts in regional languages epitomizing the *Govardhanlila*. These are also preserved in the local temples, and *prarthana* poems, which are familiar to local devotees, are sung in temples.

Classical texts also imagine Govardhan in a physically imaginable form through an expression of protruding rocks. The *Gargasamhita* refers to the *tirthas* (holy lakes or ponds) as parts of the body of Govardhan. The face is where the annual *Annakut* festival is celebrated, with Manasiganga identified as its eyes, Chandrasarovar as its nose, Govindkund as its lips, and so on. Three separate rocks are marked as the face of Govardhan in particular, called *Mukharavind* (lotus face); in addition the tongue and tail of Govardhan are also distinctly identified and marked. The tongue is located near Krishnakund, and legend says that blood issued from it when workers were digging there to construct a well. It is said that Krishna appeared in their vision in the night and explained to them that they should stop digging immediately and worship the hill with milk offerings. The hill was then dug out and a shrine was constructed, and milk offerings continue to be offered regularly, especially during the festival of *Diwali*. There is a shrine at Puchhari marking the tail of the Govardhan; the deity is known as *puchari kau lautha*.

It is said that Nandagopa (adopted father of Krishna) along with his clan moved to Brindavan on the advice of the *Gopa* elders, worried that the child Krishna was in danger in the town of Braj. The move was considered both particularly ominous and joyful. The *Bhagavatapurana* mentions that Krishna expressed his joy to

---

Mukharavind Temple

There are two naturally formed central images in the Mukharavind (lotus mouth) temple. One is considered the face and mouth (*mukharavind*) of the Govardhan hill, and the other is considered to be Krishna. Devotees can enter the temple, worship, and offer their food and other offerings all through the mornings. Both the Mukharavind and Krishna are adorned and prepared with similar dress each afternoon, reflecting the belief that Govardhan is a form of Krishna.

Balarama when they moved there, saying that the hills, bowers, and lakes were very pleasant.

Govardhan *lila* is one of the most important episodes in the life of Krishna, remembered as one of the important revelations of Krishna and as a symbol of protection. The Govardhan *lila* episode narrates that Krishna diverted the offerings the *Gopas* traditionally offered to Indra every year. Krishna convinced the *Gopas* that the offering should be made to the Govardhan hill, as it was the Govardhan hill that provided them with resources such as grazing grounds for the cattle. Hearing this, the *Gopas*, led by Nandagopa, diverted their offerings to the Govardhan hill and performed ritual worship for the hill. This infuriated Indra, who rained down for a week, which flooded the town, making the *Gopas* destitute. In order to protect the *Gopas,* Krishna immediately lifted the Govardhan hill on the tip of his little finger, under which the *Gopas*, their families, and their cattle took shelter. Indra then realized the divinity of Krishna and submitted to him. This event is epitomized in the image of Srinathji, the central deity of the Vallabha tradition. Srinathji is depicted as the child Krishna of about ten years old with an uplifted hand indicating the lifting of the Govardhan hill, considered a symbol of protection offered by Krishna to his followers.

Vallabhacarya founded the temple of Srinathji at Govardhan in 1559. However, during the Muslim raids the original icon was removed and taken to Nathdvara near Udaipur in Rajasthan, where the Srinathji *haveli* now houses the icon, which became a major pilgrimage center for Krishna devotees. However, the original temple founded by Vallabhacarya is still in use in Govardhan and is considered one of the main temples for the followers of the Vallabha tradition.

Govardhan *parikrama* involves walking around the town of Govardhan, especially the large hill and numerous small hills around it. It is a twenty-one to twenty-four kilometer (about twelve to fifteen miles) walking pilgrimage known as a seven *kos parikrama* encircling the circumference of the Govardhan hill. While conducting the walking pilgrimage of Govardhan, devotees stop to worship at a number of temples located on the way, such as the Haridev *mandir*, Danghati *mandir*, and Mukharavind temple, in addition to the sacred spots on Mansiganga Lake. Pilgrims may also perform *dudhdhara ki parikrama* (circumambulation with dripping milk), which involves walking around the Govardhan hill while dripping a continuous stream of milk through a hole in the bottom of a clay pot.

Two festivals that are central to Govardhan are the second day of *Diwali* (*Dipavali*) and *Gurupurnima*, when elaborate festivals are celebrated for Govardhan. On *Diwali* all the rock surfaces of Govardhan are adorned with clay oil lamps, and on the second day of *Diwali* the surfaces are washed and offered worship and ritual food.

See also: Braj *Parikrama*; Childhood of Krishna in Brindavan; *Diwali*; *Gargasamhita*; Govardhan *Puja*; *Harivamsa*; Srinathji *Haveli* Nathdvara

Further Reading
Vaudeville, Ch. 1980. "The Govardhana Myth in Northern India." *Indo-Iranian Journal* 22: 1–45.

GOVARDHAN *PUJA*

Govardhan *Puja* (*Annakut/Chappanbhog*) is celebrated in the temples of the Mathura region with an offering of fifty-four varieties of dishes to the god Krishna.

Mount Govardhan's arrival in Brindavan and its sacredness is narrated in the
Gargasamhita. The *Gargasamhita* narrates that Govardhan was a son of the Drona
hill, born on the western island of Shalmali. The sage Pulastya liked the Govardhan
hill so much that he decided to move it to the sacred city of Varanasi, so that he
could sit on the hill to perform his austerities and meditation. However, Govardhan did not show any interest in moving to Varanasi, but finally had to consent to
the move in response to pressure from his father Dronacala (the Drona hill), who
was worried that the sage might curse Govardhan if he were angered with Govardhan's refusal to move. The sage began the move toward Varanasi along with the
Govardhan hill, but when they reached Brindavan, it dawned on Govardhan that
it was his duty to be present there to participate in the sports of Krishna (Krishna
lilas), and he refused to move any further. This angered the sage Pulastya, who
cursed him, saying he would decrease in size by the amount of a mustard seed each
day as long as he stayed in Brindavan. Govardhan, however, was the playground of
Krishna in Brindavan as described in the *Harivamsa* and the *Bhagavatapurana* in
detail. The Govardhan hill has a special relationship with Krishna. In the *Bhagavatapurana* and the *Harivamsa* Krishna diverted offerings from Indra to the Govardhan hill, saying that it was Govardhan that was helpful to the *Gopis* and *Gopas* and
their cows. This angered Indra, who poured rain for a week, causing floods.
Krishna then lifted the Govardhan hill under which the cows and cowherd folk
took shelter. As a reminder of this incident of lifting the Govardhan hill, Krishna is
given the name Govardhandhari, holder of Govardhan. This is the image worshipped by the Vallabha tradition. Thus Krishna began the worship of the Govardhan hill by offering food. On the night of *Diwali* all the rock surfaces of Govardhan
are washed and lit with clay oil lamps symbolizing *Diwali*. On the next day of *Diwali* all the rock surfaces are cleaned and offered sweets and milk. Temples prepare
annakut (a mountain of food) with a variety of foods known as *Chappanbhog* (fifty-
four varieties) as an offering for Govardhan. People decorate their front yards with
little cow-dung representations of the Govardhan hill, or *sanjhi/rangoli* drawings of
the Govardhan hill. In addition to *annakut*, devotees also celebrate a feast known
as *kunvarau*. This feast is offered to Govardhan when *bariyatra* arrives at Jatipura.

Chappanbhog

Chappanbhog and *Kunvarau* are offered frequently at the Govardhan hill during the
bari yatra season. When *bari yatra* arrives at Jatipura, massive amounts of food offerings are displayed at the Mukharavind temple. Food offerings are arranged in concentric circles in a pattern resembling a lotus. *Chappanbhog* and *Kunvarau* feasts are
symbolic reminders of offerings the *Gopas* made to the Govardhan hill at the urging
of Krishna, foregoing the traditional offerings for the god Indra.

People gather at a temple in Kolkata to celebrate Govardhan *Puja*, also called *Annakut* (meaning a heap of grain) and to commemorate the victory of Lord Krishna over Indra. It is held on the fourth day of *Dipavali* (*Diwali*), the Hindu festival of lights. According to legends, Lord Krishna taught people to worship the supreme controller of nature, Govardhan, a manifestation of Krishna, and to stop worshiping Indra, the god of rains. (Subhendu Sarkar/NurPhoto/Corbis/AP Images)

A part of the rock face of Govardhan known as *mukharavind* (lotus face) is anointed by the *Gosains* in milk, followed by water from Manasiganga Lake, and then offered the *kunvarau* feast.

The Govardhan hill itself is considered sacred, since it was touched by the feet of Krishna. Several traditions about its sacredness are known in the area, which reveres the stones as Krishna himself. Caitanya Vaishnava tradition maintains that Caitanya and his disciples Rupa *Gosvami* and Sanatana *Gosvami* refrained from entering there, lest they defile the sacred hill by walking on it. However, it is said that Caitanya took a small rock with him to Puri, which he revered as the body (*kalevara*) of Krishna. Govardhan stones are placed in temples in Krishna shrines and worshipped. One can also see Govardhan stones in small shrines on the street corners, as well as placed in pots along with basil (*tulasi*) and revered in daily worship. As the popular legend of Srinathji narrates, the icon of Srinathji gradually rose from the ground on Govardhan, and the image was given milk by a cow belonging to Saddupande. Krishna later informed Vallabha in a dream vision of his appearance as Srinathji in Govardhan. Subsequently Vallabha came to Govardhan searching for Srinathji. He met Saddupande, recovered the image of Srinathji, constructed a shrine for Srinathji, and made arrangements for regular worship.

See also: Braj *Parikrama*; Brindavan; Childhood of Krishna in Brindavan; *Diwali*

Further Reading

Goldman, R. P. 1986. "A City of the Heart—Epic Mathura and the Indian Imagination." *Journal of the American Oriental Society* 106 (3): 471–483.

GURUVAYURAPPA AND GURUVAYUR TEMPLE

Guruvayurappa is the popular name of Krishna, the major deity in the temple established by Sankara (788–820) in Guruvayur, Kerala. Guruvayur is considered to be the "Dvaraka of the South," after Dvaraka, the submerged capital city of Krishna. It is said that the image of Krishna is called *svayamvyakta* (self-revealed) since the image appeared to Sankara while he was traveling in the Guruvayur area. Sankara subsequently constructed the temple in Guruvayur in which he installed the image of Krishna he found. As a temple of *svayamvyakta* Krishna, for the presence of the god himself, this temple is also known as *Bhuloka Vaikuntam* (Vishnu's Heaven on Earth). Narayana Battatiri (1560–1646) composed *Narayaniyam*, a long text based on the *Bhagavatapurana* and the *Bhagavadgita*, which also includes praise of Guruvayurappa. The *Narayaniyam*, popularly known as the "Gospel of Guruvayur," contains the most detailed descriptions of Guruvayurappa and the sacred city of Guruvayur.

Guruvayurappa appears as the child Krishna with four arms, which was his *nija svarupa* (original form) revealed to his parents, Devaki and Vasudeva, soon after his birth in the prison in Mathura. The central icon of Krishna is four feet tall, holding his characteristic adornments: the Sudarsana *cakra* (wheel) and *pancajanya sankha* (conch) in his upper right and left hands respectively, the lotus (*padma*) in one of the lower hands, the other resting on his waist. Daily *pujas* (worship) and festival *pujas* are offered to Krishna (Guruvayurappa) according to the sacred calendar of Krishna throughout the year. There are five daily *pujas* performed in the Guruvayurappa temple called the *Pancamahapujas* (the Five Great *Pujas*). Early-morning *puja* (*Ushah puja*) is conducted at 6 a.m., mid-morning *puja* (*Pantirati puja*) is conducted from 9 a.m. to 10 a.m., midday *puja* (*Uccha puja*) is conducted from 11:45 a.m. to 12:45 p.m., and the temple is closed between 1 and 4 p.m. Evening *puja* (*Attara puja*) is conducted at 5 p.m., and the last *puja* is conducted from 9 to 10 p.m., after which the temple is closed for the night. *Diparadhana* is conducted at 6 p.m. in the Guruvayur temple, during which numerous small oil lamps are lit in the sanctum showing the deity in brilliant light. Numerous lights are also lighted in the compound of the temple on *dipa/vilakku sthambhas* (pillars of lights) and *vilakku mandapam* (hall of lights), making the temple shine brightly in the flickering light of the lamps amidst the darkness of the night.

Special Festivals of Guruvayur

Two festivals form the most important celebrations in the Guruvayur temple. *Ekadasi*, held in the month of November–December, is a special day permitting everyone entry into the temple for *darsan*. Celebrations begin eighteen days prior to *Ekadasi* and end on the next day after *Ekadasi*. These nineteen days mark the busiest days in the temple, which is visited by thousand of devotees, since it is considered very auspicious to visit the temple and have a *darsan* (view) of the deity during this time of the year. *Vilakkumatam* is a special feature of the Guruvay-urappa temple in which the walls and pillars of the temple are lighted with oil lamps every evening. *Ekadasi* is a special holy day for Vaishnavas and hence it is celebrated at all the Vaishnava temples. However, followers of Guruvayurappa con-sider that a visit to the Guruvayurappa temple and a *darsan* (seeing) of the central lord Guruvayurappa and the *Ekadasi villakku* in the temple cleanses one of all one's sins and ensures direct passage to heaven.

The annual festival of Guruvayur is called *Utsavam*, conducted each year during February–March for ten days. As an annual festival of the temple, it includes a number of festival processions, a ritual of temple *kalasam* (pitcher) and flag hoist-ing. The streets and gateways are decorated with banana leaf arches, and clay lamps are lighted on *vilakku sthambams* and *vilakku mandapam* during the evenings. Light fireworks are used in the evening, but no loud explosive fireworks are used in Gu-ruvayur, unlike at other temples in Kerala. The presiding deity, Guruvayurappa, is taken in procession on an elephant in the morning and evening every day. The procession of decorated elephants (about fifty) is one of the major attractions of the Guruvayur temple. Numerous elephants historically have been donated to the temple by the devotees. The elephants are well taken care of by the temple and are brought out for the festival processions. Other rituals such as the elephant race (*aanayottam*), and *palliveta* (hunting expedition) are mock events and indicate the play aspect of divinity associated with Krishna. Celebrations are also marked by music and dance (*kudiattam* and *krishnattam*) performances in the temple.

See also: Arati; *Bhagavadgita*; *Bhagavatapurana*; *Darsana*; *Ekadasi*; *Krishnattam*; *Lila*; *Moksha/Mukti*; Vishnu

Further Reading

Khan, D. S. 2012. *Sacred Kerala: A Spiritual Pilgrimage*. New Delhi: Penguin Books.
Vaidyanathan, K. R. 1974. *Sri Krishna: The Lord of Guruvayur*. Bombay: Bharatiya Vidya Bhavan.

H

HARIAUDH

Hariaudh (1865–1947), born Ayodhya Singh Upadhyay, was one of the most famous poets of the modern Hindi language. Although he worked as a tax professional by occupation, his passion was in literature. He was an active participant in
the literary and cultural movement of Banaras, Uttar Pradesh. He also chaired the
Hindi Sammelan, which earned him the *Vidyavacaspati* award. Hariaudh was naturally talented in languages, learning numerous languages including Persian, Urdu,
and English, along with Hindi and Sanskrit. The last two were his favorite languages, and Sanskrit literary texts most influenced his poetical talents.

Priyapravas (Sojourn of the Beloved) has several firsts to its credit, and also won
critical acclaim and awards. Although the subject of the text is not new, it dealt
with emerging literary Hindi (Khadiboli), instead of the Brajboli in which other
devotional poetry of Krishna is commonly written. Hence, it was a new poetical
and literary genre. Hariaudh also deals with Radha in a way unlike the Braj poetry
of earlier periods. It won the Mangal Prasad award for best literary poetical work.
After retiring from his job Hariaudh taught Hindi at several places, including the
Banaras Hindu University. Hariaudh also composed nationalistic poems influenced
by the independence movement current in India at that time. Three of his books
deal with the subjects of Krishna's three famous feminine counterparts, Radha
(*Priyapravas*), Satyabhama (*Parijata*), and Rukmini (*Rukmini Kalyan*). Hariaudh
presents his heroines, Radha, Satyabhama, and Rukmini, in a new style of interpretation as strong and independent women.

See also: Brindavan; Eight Wives of Krishna; *Haritray*; Krishna; Kumbhandas
Gorva; Mathura; Surdas

Further Reading

Ritter, V. 2004. "The Language of Hariaudh's *Priya Pravas*: Notes Towards an Archaeology
of Hindi Language." *Journal of the American Oriental Society* 124 (3): 417–438.

HARIDASA THAKURA (1450–1520)

Haridasa Thakura was a follower and close contemporary of Caitanya Mahaprabhu.
Haridasa Thakura and Nityananda were the principal followers of Caitanya and
were responsible for establishing Caitanya Vaishnavism in Bengal by popularizing
the *samkirtana* (chanting the sacred names). Haridasa is noted for his incessant
chanting of the names of Krishna (*Nama samkirtana*) loudly throughout the day
wherever he was or whatever he might be doing. In fact the *Caitanya Caritamrita*

Siddha Bakul at the Puri Jagannatha Temple

A banyan tree in the Jagannatha temple complex known as the Siddha Bakul is said to mark the place of Haridasa Thakura's *japa* (recitation of the names of Krishna). A memorial shrine of Haridasa Thakura is also located in Puri. Pilgrims visit the Siddha Bakul and the shrine of Haridasa Thakura to pay homage to the memory of Haridasa.

---

notes that he completed chanting almost 300,000 names each day prior to his only meal of the day around noon, and completed almost one million chantings of the name of Krishna every day.

Although not much is known about his childhood, it is said that Haridasa was born in a Muslim family, but converted to Hinduism, inspired by Caitanya's teachings. Haridasa Thakura's biography is recorded in the *Caitanya Caritamrita* and the *Caitanya Bhagavata*. However, these texts record his life and achievements as a Vaishnava, and do not recollect much about his earlier life prior to his conversion. Three strands are commonly noticed in Haridasa's biographies: first, Haridasa's commitment to *Nama samkirtana*; second, his conflict with Muslim *kaji*; third, his debates with devotees of other Hindu gods and goddesses, especially the *Smarta Brahmans*. Haridasa's *Nama samkirtana* is said to have infuriated the local *kaji*, who is said to have ordered Haridasa to be publicly whipped to death. However, Haridasa is said to have survived this punishment miraculously without any harm. This amazed the *kaji,* who is said to have converted to Vaishnavism. Similarly, Haridasa's debates stirred Brahmans, who objected to Haridasa Thakura's loud chanting, saying that it disturbed the peace of the divinity and might disturb the balance of the world. However, Haridasa was an erudite scholar of Sanskrit and debated the Brahmans by quoting Sanskrit texts. Thus convinced by him, many of the Brahmans also became devotees of Krishna. Both of these events describe the commitment of Haridasa Thakura to Caitanya and also his enthusiasm for converting others to Caitanya Vaishnavism. During the last days of his life Haridasa lived in Puri under the care of Caitanya before passing away there.

See also: Caitanya; *Gaudiya* Vaishnavism; Puri Temple; Six *Gosvamis*

Further Reading

Hein, N. 1976. "Caitanya's Ecstacies and the Theology of the Name." In *Hinduism: New Essays in the History of Religions*, edited by L. S. Bardwell. Leiden: Brill.

HARIDASI *SAMPRADAYA*

The Haridasi *sampradaya* (tradition) is one of the important Krishna devotional traditions of Mathura, founded by *Svami* Haridas (1480–1575). Haridas discovered the image of Bankebihari in Braj and constructed a monastery with a shrine in Nidhivan. He appointed Jagannath as the priest to perform daily services to

Dhrupad and *Samaj Gayan*

The three Haris (*Haritray*) are noted for popularizing a special style of devotional singing in Brindavan during the early sixteenth century. Even though all three are considered experts in music, Svami Haridas is considered to be an expert musician with particularly notable skill in *Dhrupad sangit*. Haridas is credited with imparting musical techniques to Tansen, a musician at the Mughal court. Svami Haridas played an important role in the evolving musical tradition of the devotional traditions of Braj, which later gave rise to the *samaj gayan* of north India. In memory of his service to musical traditions, festivals of music (*Svami Haridas Sangit Sammelan*) are held in different cities of north India. Festivals held in Mumbai and Vrindavan last for days and attract highly qualified performers.

Bankebihari in the temple, although it is not known if he nominated a successor to his priestly order, the *Gosvamis,* or appointed Jagannatha, his first priest, as progentitor of the permanent priestly line of the Bankebihari temple. The descendants of Jagannath claim their appointment is hereditary. However, the sadhus of the Haridasi tradition are not married and do not have a hereditary succession. The sadhus also oppose the practice of hereditary succession for the priestly line descending from Jagannatha. The sadhus, who derive their monastic order from Haridas himself and elect their own leaders, claim that Haridas did not appoint any hereditary priests for the Bankebihari temple as well. The sadhus claim that they reserve the right to nominate priests from time to time. The monastic order of Haridasi sadhus was reformed and organized in its modern form in the 1700s under the leadership of Biharinidas, and also his disciples Govinddas and Lalitkisoridas. The ashram of the ascetics in Brindavan is known as Tatti Asthan, or Tatiya Sthan. Associated with the Nimbarka *sampradaya*, the Haridasi ascetic order is one of the most conservative devotional groups in Brindavan.

Although such procedural differences continue to occur between the temple and the monastic order as noted in the paragraph above, the Bankebihari temple is one of the most famous temples in Brindavan. The sadhus organize *samaj gayan* in the temple, and they also conduct annual festivals of *samaj gayan* competitions in Brindavan, which are very popular among the lay devotees of Krishna; they are the most well-attended public performances. Festival celebrations with *samaj gayan* are organized on the birthday anniversary of *acaryas* and *Radhashtami*. Incidentally, the birthdays of Radha and of the founder of the Haridasi tradition, Haridas, are the same day, and they are honored with festivities and *samaj gayan*.

The scriptural base of Haridasi *sampradaya* is represented by the poems, which are written exclusively in *Brajbhasha*. Hence, theological and religious views of Haridasi *sampradaya* can only be gleaned from Haridas's compositions. *Svami Haridas* composed the *Astadas Siddhanta* and the *Kelimal* in *Brajbhasha*. The *Astadas* (Hindi word meaning eighteen) has only 18 *padas*, as the name indicates, but *Kelimal*, his main work, contains 110 *padas*. For Haridas, the central *bhava* to reach

Krishna is *Madhuryabhava* (love) of Krishna and Radha, so Radha and Krishna are worshipped in a joint form (*yugalsvarupa*) in recognition of their pastimes in Braj (*nityavihara*). As is common among the *Haritray*, Haridas's poems also indicate his participation in Krishna's *Raasalila* as one of the *Gopis*. Haridas himself is recognized as Lalita, one of the eight cowherd maidens. The understanding of the religion and theology of Haridasi tradition therefore involves the *Raasalila* of the couple Radha and Krishna and the cowherd maidens (*Gopis*) that serve them. Through accomplishing an imagery of them by saying the *padas* and singing, Haridas imagines nearness to Krishna in order to experience Krishna's presence, which is the goal of the meditative practice. Through his *padas*, Haridas also contemplates *maya* and the physical world. He considers Bankebihari (Krishna) as the creator, and considers that without the grace of God it is impossible to reach the divine world of Krishna. Bankebihari's image, given to him by Radhakrishna himself, was housed by him in a small temple in Nidhivan, which was later shifted to the Bankebihari temple by the *Gosvami* priests, because of a dispute with the sadhus of the tradition about the hereditary succession of the priests. The *seva* in the temple consists of only three *aratis* and brief *darsan* periods between 7:45 to 12 noon and 5:30 to 9:30 p.m., which allows lay devotees to view the deity Bankebihari briefly. Sounds and music are not permitted in the temple so as not to disturb the love play of Radha and Krishna. A brief *darsan* is followed by *Prasadam* distribution. On festival days the Bankebihari temple is decorated with an exquisite arrangement of flowers and lights called the *phul bangla* (flower house), which is a favorite sight for devotees to visit. There are three levels of initiation available for the devotees of the Haridasi tradition. All initiates receive mantras for recitation consisting of twelve syllables. Devotees of the second stage receive the *gopimantra*, while the advanced devotees of the third stage receive the *yugalmantra*. In addition, the guru administers some individual mantras and meditation techniques that involve very esoteric meditation practices and rituals. The afternoon activity of the *sadhus* is devoted to singing the *padas* of Haridas and practicing meditation.

It is said that Haridasis did not adopt *samaj gayan,* one of its signature features, until the eighteenth century. Currently only initiated monks perform *samaj gayan*. Haridasis perform *samaj gayan* on the birth anniversaries of their *acaryas*, organizing a four-day or five-day singing in the traditional style of *samaj gayan*, with a *mukhia* (main singer), *pakhavaj* (musical accompaniment), and *jhelas* (assistant singers). The Haridasis also sponsor musical festivals (*sammelan*) in Brindavan where several invited musical groups participate and compete for prizes.

Haridasi *sampradaya* is simple in its practice, placing centrality on the love play (*keli lila*) of Radha and Krishna, with the service centered on offering musical compositions as a way of achieving closeness with Krishna. It attracts followers from the Braj area as lay followers, while it has a strong priestly community (*Gosvamis*) and ascetic community (sadhus) who keep the tradition in order and keep the tradition close to the original precepts of its founder Haridas.

See also: Braj *Parikrama*; *Diwali*; Mathura; Nimbarka Tradition; *Radhashtami*; *Samaj Gayan*

Further Reading

Datt, G. 1977. *Svami Haridasa Ka Sampradaya Aur Uska Vanisahitya.* New Delhi: National Publishing House.

Haynes, R. D. "Svami Haridas and the Haridasi Sampradaya." PhD Dissertation. University of Pennsylvania: Electronic Thesis and Dissertation Center.

HARITRAY

Haritray literally means the Three Haris, devotees of Krishna: Hariram Vyas (1492–1552), *Svami* Haridas (1480–1575), and Hit Harivams (1502–1555). The Three Haris lived in Braj, composing, singing, and worshipping Krishna. Haridas and Harivams have been succeeded by devotional traditions following their style of worship, which are still active in Brindavan.

Hariram Vyas (1492–1552)

The three Haris, *Svami* Haridas, Hariram Vyas, and Hit Harivams, were bhakti poets of Braj, composing poems on the *Raasalila* of Krishna in Braj. In addition to composing poems on Radha and Krishna's love play, Hariram Vyas also composed poems about other saints, including a number of saints of the day: Mira, Haridas, Hit Harivams, and many others. Hariram Vyas and Haridas also imagined themselves as taking part in the round dance (*Raasalila*) among the retinue of *Gopis* and playing *Raasalila* with Krishna, composing poems of their experiences and observations as such. Hariram Vyas's *Ras Pancadhyayi* is a poetical composition of the five chapters of *Raasalila* from the *Bhagavatapurana*. Hariram Vyas is not associated with founding any traditions, unlike his friends *Svami* Haridas (founder of Haridasi *sampradaya*) and Hit Harivams (Radhavallabha *sampradaya*), but he continued to compose beautiful lyrical poems for Radha and Krishna.

Svami Haridas (1480–1575)

Haridas founded a devotional tradition dedicated to Radha and Krishna in Braj known as the Haridasi tradition. A master musician, he composed several devotional songs for Krishna. He is also known as the teacher of Tansen, a musician of the Mughal court. Although Vallabha *sampradaya* (*Pushtimarga*) claims that Haridas is associated with their tradition, Haridas functioned as an independent ascetic. No evidence of his initiation into any formal devotional group of Braj is known.

Haridas founded his own devotional tradition, known as the Haridasi tradition after his name, which is an offshoot of Nimbarka *sampradaya.* Very scant information is available on the birth and early life of Haridas. However, it is said in his biographies that he arrived in Braj as a young man in his mid-twenties and settled there, spending his days singing devotional songs for Bankebihari and Syama. Nabhadas's *Bhaktamal* includes poems commemorating Haridas among the two hundred other significant religious teachers of Braj he chose to describe in the text.

There are also two other versions of Haridas's life preserved by his followers. The *Gosvamis* (priests of the Bankebihari temple) collected ten volumes on the life of Haridas from oral accounts of the devotees. The sadhus (monastic disciples of Haridas) have a text on Haridas known as *Nizamat Siddhanta*, composed by Kisoridas.

Svami Haridas's songs are written for singing in the *dhrupad* style. Even though Haridas did not sing publicly, his close friends who heard him sing recollect fond memories of his singing talents, and all his *pada* compositions are marked with the *raga* (musical note) in which the songs must be sung, attributed to Haridas himself.

Hit Harivams (1502–1555)

Hit Harivams is one of the major Vaishnava poet saints of Vrindavan. His contribution is notable in the revival of Vrindavan, the sacred land, and also in Krishna poetry. Hit Harivams is respected as one of the triumvirate of the *Haritray* (Three Haris), along with Svami Haridas and Hariram Vyas, for their contribution to the Radhavallabha concept and philosophy, and for inaugurating a temple music genre. Numerous biographies and texts are written about Hit Harivams. Some of the important biographies are the *Sri Hitaharivamsa Candrashtaka* and the *Vrinda-vanamahimamrita* by Krishnadas, son of Hit Harivams; the *Bhaktanamavali* by Dhruvadas; the *Sevakvani* by Damodardas; and the *Hitacaritra* by Uttamdas. Among these texts, the *Hitacaritra* of Damodardas is the most notable and commonly served as the basis for later biographies about Harivams. Harivams was born to Vyasa Misra and his wife Tara Rani in 1502. His childhood, early devotional (bhakti) teachings, and *kirtans* (song compositions) were recorded in detail. It is described in his biographies that hearing the name Radha delighted Hit Harivams and also that Radha had revealed to him the *yugalmantra* in a dream vision. He developed his own unique concept of bhakti with Radha and Krishna at the center of its theology.

Numerous important poetical compositions on Krishna were written by Hit Harivams. However, one of the most important compositions of his central texts is the *Caurasipad*, a text of 84 verses describing the *nikunjavihara*, love pastimes of Krishna and Radha during the nights in Brindavan. Hit Harivams's texts also include the *Sriradhasudhanidhi* and the *Sphutavani*. The *Sriradhasudhanidhi* contains 270 verses describing Radha's supremacy within Hinduism, lauding her as "the secret of the *Upanishads*."

Hit Harivams's poems have been adopted for *samaj gayan* (public and temple singing), which is one of his major contributions, still sung and performed every day in the Radhavallabha temple he established in Mathura. Theologically, Hit Harivams is the founder of the Radhavallabha tradition, which is a *yugal* (dual) tradition of worshipping Radha and Krishna as dual aspects of one deity rather than worshipping Radha or Krishna as two separate deities. The concept of *do deh ek pran* (two bodies one soul) is illustrative of the Radhavallabha tradition. Radha is the primary center of worship and a way to reach Krishna through bhakti.

See also: Bhakti; Braj *Parikrama*; Brindavan; *Lila*; Mathura; Nimbarka Tradition; *Samaj Gayan*; *Seva*; Vallabha

Further Reading

Beck, G. L. 1996. "Vaishnava Music in the Braj Region of North India." *Journal of Vaishnava Studies* 4 (2): 115–147.

Beck, G. L. 2011. *Sonic Theology: Ritual and Music in Hindu Tradition.* Columbia: University of South Carolina Press.

Entwistle, A. W. 1987. *Braj: Center of Krishna Pilgrimage.* Groningen: Egbert Forsten.

Gosvami, S. B. 1966. *Krishnabhakti Kavya me Sakhibhav.* Benaras: Chowkhamba Vidyabhavan.

Pauwels, H. 2009. "Imagining Religious Communities in the Sixteenth Century: Hariram Vyas and the Haritraya." *International Journal of Hindu Studies* 13 (2): 143–161.

Pauwels, H. 2009. *Krishna's Round Dance Reconsidered: Hariram Vyas's Hindi Ras Pancadhyayi.* London: Routledge.

Pauwels, H. 2009. "The Saint, the Warlord, and the Emperor: Discourses of Braj Bhakti and Bundela Loyalty." *Journal of the Economic and Social History of the Orient* 52: 187–228.

Rosenstein, L. L. 1997. *The Devotional Poetry of Svami Haridas: A Study of Early Braj Bhasha Verse.* Groningen: Egbert Forsten.

Sastri, G. S. 1996. "*Samaj Gayan* in the Haridasi *Sampradaya.*" *Journal of Vaishnava Studies* 4 (2): 137–144.

Snell, R. 1991. *The Eighty-four Hymns of Hita Harivamsa: An Edition of the Caurasi Pada.* Delhi: Motilal Banarsidass.

Thielemann, S. 2001. *Musical Traditions of Vaishnava Temples in Vraja: A Comparative Study of Samaja and the Dhrupada Tradition of North Indian Classical Music.* New Delhi: Sagar.

White, C. S. J. 1977. *The Caurasi Pad of Sri Hit Harivams.* Honolulu: University of Hawaii.

HARIVAMSA

The *Harivamsa* takes its name from Hari, another name for Vishnu, while the title itself means "dynasty of Hari" or "lineage of Hari." The *Harivamsa,* which was also compiled by Vyasa, is similar to the *puranas,* epics, and other major texts of Hinduism. Although the text is not classified as part of any traditional genre of religious texts of India, it is variously known as a *purana, mahakavya, carita,* and *akhyana,* while the *Mahabharata* regards it as a *khila,* an appendix. Hence the critical edition of the *Mahabharata* also includes the critical edition of the *Harivamsa.* Therefore, the *Harivamsa* now exists in two versions: the critical edition and the vulgate. Although both editions are similar in containing three sections (*Harivamsaparva, Vishnuparva,* and *Bhavishyaparva*), the critical edition of the Harivamsa contains reduced sections: the critical edition contains 45 chapters in the first section (the vulgate has 55 chapters); the critical edition contains 68 chapters in the second section (the vulgate has 128 chapters); and the critical edition contains only 5 chapters in the third section (the vulgate has 135 chapters).

As far as the Krishna legend is concerned, the *Harivamsa* could be considered a *khila* (appendix) to the *Mahabharata* as the text claims, since it provides the earlier part of the life story of Krishna missing from the *Mahabharata.* The first section,

Harivamsaparva, narrates the cosmology and *avatara* stories, and the lineage of Hari, while the second section, the *Vishnuparva*, contains stories of the birth of Krishna and Balarama (also known as Samkarsana) and the founding of a new city, Dvaraka. The other parts of the story of the adult life of Krishna are of course found in the *Mahabharata,* including the story of Krishna's death. As a text, the legend of Krishna in the *Harivamsa* could be considered the earliest for its lack of structural refinement and the presence of stories that are not commonly found in any other *purana* texts including the *Bhagavatapurana*. An example is the story *Vrikadarsana* (The Wolves Are Seen). In this story Krishna expresses his disgust at the forests of Vraja and wishes to move to Brindavan. During the night wolves seem to appear and terrorize the pastoral settlement of Vraja. The wolves bear the mark of *srivatsa* and are dark in complexion, bearing a direct link to Krishna, although the text does not directly connect the wolves to Krishna. Thoroughly terrified, Krishna's parents and other elders of Vraja plan to move their encampment to Brindavan. This strange story is not found in any other *puranas* and may indicate the earliest composition of the text among the *puranas* containing the Krishna legend. Therefore the *Harivamsa* is considered one of the earliest texts containing the legend of Krishna.

See also: Balarama; *Bhagavatapurana*; Brindavan; Childhood of Krishna in Brindavan; *Mahabharata*

Further Reading

Brinkhaus, H. 2001. "*Ascaryakarman* and *Pradurbhava* in the 'Harivamsa' (Sanskrit poetry)." *Journal of Indian Philosophy* 29 (1–2): 25–41.

Coleman, T. 2010. "*Viraha-Bhakti* and *Stridharma*: Re-Reading the Story of Krishna and the Gopis in the *Harivamsa* and the *Bhagavata Purana*." *Journal of the American Oriental Society* 130 (3): 385–412.

Couture, A. 1986. "Akrura and the *Bhagavata* Tradition According to the *Harivamsa*." *Studies in Religion–Sciences Religieuses* 15 (2): 221–232.

Filliozat, M. Pierre-Sylvain. 2007. "The Vision of Markandeya and the Manifestation of the Lotus, Ancient Histories Taken from *Harivamsa*." *Comptes Rendus des Seances de l'Academie des Inscriptions & Belles-Lettres* 2: 687–688.

Ludvik, C. 2004. "A *Harivamsa* Hymn in Yijing's Chinese Translation of the '*Sutra of Golden Light*'." *Journal of the American Oriental Society* 124 (4): 707–734.

Osto, D. 2009. "The Supreme Array Scripture: A New Interpretation of the Title '*Gandavyuha-sutra*.'" *Journal of Indian Philosophy* 37 (3): 273–290.

Vemsani, L. 2006. *Hindu and Jain Mythology of Balarama*. Lewiston, NY, and Kingston, Canada: Edwin Mellen.

HAVELI SANGIT

Haveli Sangit is associated with Krishna temples of the Vallabha tradition (*Pushtimarga*). Its early lyrics are in the *dhrupad* style and composed by Surdas, and are collected in *Sursagar*. It is famously said that Krishna himself came to listen to Surdas sing his couplets. Surdas is one of the *Ashtachap* (eight seals), the eight composer-singers of the Vallabha tradition. The others are Nandadas, Paramanandadas,

Krishnadas, Govindasvami, Citsvami, Kumbhandas, and Caturbhujdas. The *Haveli sangit* involves elaborated daily singing in the *Haveli* temples. Each day is divided into eight services, and each service includes renditions of music in a certain style. Festival days and other special days may have elaborate musical performances.

See also: Kumbhandas Gorva; Surdas

Further Reading

Goswami, S., & S. Thieleman. 2005. *Music and Fine Arts in the Devotional Traditions of India.* New Delhi: A. P. H. Publishing.

HIRANYAGARBHA

Hiranyagarbha, a Sanskrit word translated as "golden egg," is one of the most important concepts associated with Vishnu. Although *Hiranyagarbha* is identified with Vishnu, its form came into existence prior to the beginning of creation. According to Hinduism, at the beginning of a *Kalpa* (age with four *yugas*), there is only darkness, and creation begins in the form of *Hiranyagarbha*. At the beginning the four *vyuhas* (Samkarsana, Vaasudeva, Pradyumna, and Aniruddha) emerge, making way for the creation; from them arise *Trimurtis* (Vishnu, Shiva, and Brahma), and creation begins. To maintain the creation Vishnu then descends to the world in his various incarnations (*avataras*). *Hiranyagarbha* is then everything that emerges at the beginning of creation in a *Kalpa* and is identified with Vishnu. As Vishnu is *Hiranyagarbha*, so also is Krishna, who is identified as *purna avatara* (full incarnation) according to the devotional traditions such as Srivaishnavism and Caitanya Vaishnavism.

Lotus

The lotus is a special symbol associated specifically with Lakshmi and Vishnu. Vishnu, as Padmanabha (Lotus Navel), appears at the beginning of creation. The lotus is also associated with Krishna. The divine *Goloka* is imagined in its earthly form represented by Brindavan as portrayed in the form of a lotus. Vishnu usually holds a lotus in his lower left hand, while Lakshmi holds a lotus in her right hand; she is also usually depicted as sitting or standing on a lotus. *Padmasana* (Lotus seat) is the first posture in yoga, indicating the beginning of a serious practice session.

See also: Avatara; Bhagavan; Lila; Vishnu; *Vyuhas*

Further Reading

Chenet, F. 2008. "Seeing and Appearance." *Journal of the American Oriental Society* 128 (1): 147–151.

Terrin, A. N. 2011. "*Ap m Nap t*: Il Mito Delle 'Acque Primordiali' Nella Cosmogonia *Vedica*. (Italian)." *Hermeneutica*, 101–138.

HISTORICAL KRISHNA

The legend of Krishna places his life in the world of 3000 BCE, for which little historical evidence is available. Marine explorations near the coast of Dvaraka and Prabhasa found scarce information, which shows that not much could be understood about life five thousand years ago, since sea water and waves might have destroyed a significant amount of historical material over such a long span of time. However, from the middle of the second millennium BCE (about 1500 BCE) occupational levels that could be identified with epic culture are noted in marine archaeology. Clear literary and archaeological evidence pointing to Krishna devotional traditions are noted from at least 600 BCE, if not earlier. Vedic evidence, although scanty, places the worship of Krishna at about 1300–1000 BCE.

Vedic References

The *Chandogya Upanishad* (III.17.6), dated to have been composed prior to 800 BCE, refers to *Gopa*, son of Devaki, but does not provide any details associated with Krishna. Hence, this evidence is considered questionable by a number of scholars; but devotees consider the mere indication of Krishna in a Vedic text as evidence of an early reverence for Krishna. Several other occurrences of Krishna are recorded in the *Vedas*, but these are all used in reference to "dark," rather than the god Krishna. Occurrence of the word *Yadava,* referring to a tribe, is also recorded in the *Vedas*, including the *Rigveda*, although its connection to Krishna is not clear. Therefore Vedic evidence could be noted as inconclusive for establishing early worship of Krishna. The *Vedas* contain only cryptic information about popular deities of Hinduism, and, based on the above evidence, it could be said that information about Krishna in the *Vedas* exceeds reference to any other popular deities of Hinduism, which in itself could be understood as evidence of the importance of Krishna.

Early textual references to Krishna are available in Vedic texts but only provide scant evidence; however, they provide typical information on Krishna and devotional traditions of Krishna. The earliest reference to Krishna in the *Rigveda* (1.22.164) mentions the cowherd who never stumbles, and another verse in the *Rigveda* (8.96.13) mentions Krishna who is like a black drop. Although there are numerous other early references to Krishna in the Vedic texts such as the *Rigveda,* the reference in the *Chadogya Upanishad* (III.17.6), dated between 900 and 800 BCE, mentions the clearest evidence stating the reference for Krishna Devakiputra. It not only mentions Krishna, but also mentions that he is the son of Devaki. Even though the other early evidence from Vedic sources is ruled out as ambiguous by some scholars, the evidence of the *Chandogya Upanishad* establishes unequivocally that traditions of Krishna were well established by the turn of the first millennium

BCE. The *Satapathabrahmana* (900 BCE) and *Aitareya Aranyaka* (600 BCE) mention Krishna of the Vrishni clan.

Numerous nonreligious texts such as grammar texts and history texts also provide early evidence of Krishna. Yaska's *Nirukta*, an etymological dictionary dated to 600 BCE, mentions the *syamantaka* jewel in the possession of Akrura. Panini's *Ashtadhyayi* (500 BCE), a grammar text, mentions Vaasudeva Krishna and his contemporaries Kaurava and Arjuna.

Patanjali's text, the *Mahabhashya* (400 BCE), mentions musical group performances (*samsadi*) in the temple of Krishna, which brings forward not only the evidence for the existence of temples for Krishna, but also establishes the fact that music and performance traditions are associated with devotional traditions of Krishna at this early date.

Megasthenes's account of India, *Indica*, includes descriptions of the supreme god of Mathura, Heraklese, which was derived from *Harikuleya* (*Harikula* or *Harivamsa*—lineage of Hari), meaning Krishna, born in the lineage of Hari.

Although the historical data are slight, the early evidence nonetheless establishes worship of Krishna at least from the middle of the second millennium BCE, and evidence of Krishna is found in numerous later creations in art, literature, and architecture since the turn of the first millennium CE.

The *Mahabharata,* including the text of the *Bhagavadgita* and its appendix the *Harivamsa,* provides complete evidence of Krishna and his devotional worship. Numerous inscriptions also provide early evidence on devotional traditions of Krishna before the beginning of the first millennium. Hindu sources note that its central text, the *Bhagavadgita,* is revealed by Krishna to Arjuna while the armies are arrayed on the battlefield of Kurukshetra.

Indus Valley Culture

Numerous seals, figures, and structures identified as religious in nature were found in excavations in Indus valley cities such as Harappa, Mohenjodaro, Chanhudaro, Lothal, and Dholavira. Important among these finds are the symbols of the swastika, the wheel, and a well shaped in the form of a banyan (*Vata* in Sanskrit) leaf, which can be connected to Krishna. The wheel is the quintessential symbol of Krishna, while the swastika is a symbol that connects him to Vishnu as maintainer of the balance of the world. The banyan leaf is connected to the creation myths associated with Vishnu, who appears as *Hiranyagarbha* at the beginning of creation. The *Markandeyapurana* provides the description of a vision the sage Markandeya encountered. In this vision, Markandeya found a child peacefully lying on a banyan leaf, which was floating on water. This vision is epitomized as the child Krishna floating on a banyan leaf at the beginning of creation. This is one of the most commonly depicted images of Krishna. Thus banyan leaf designs or banyan leaf motifs on pottery as well as the well in the shape of a banyan leaf might have some symbolic connection to Krishna. Other Harappan cities and archaeological excavations yielded clearer data. The site of Kurukshetra and other epic sites identified with Pandavas such as Hastinapura, Ahicchatra, and Kausambi show

Seal from the Indus Valley. Thousands of terracotta seals unearthed in archaeological excavations portray gods and goddesses, in addition to several symbols associated with Hinduism. (Angelo Hornak/Corbis)

occupational levels as early as 3000 BCE to 1100 BCE. Another interesting fact from these sites is that late Harappan pottery is found together with typical epic pottery (called painted gray ware). This supports the correspondence and coexistence of prehistoric cultures of the Ganga-Yamuna *doab* (area of Krishna's influence) and Indus-Saraswati civilization in northwestern India. Marine archaeology also confirmed the existence and submergence of the city of Dvaraka after the death of Krishna, and the abandonment of Hastinapur by Parikshit, grandson of the Pandavas, due to floods. Such close correspondence of events of the *Mahabharata* with archaeological data is cited as evidence for the historical Krishna, who ruled from Dvaraka at about the same period. Although broad and general, evidence of the close correspondences between cultural levels of these cities and the *Mahabharata* cannot be ignored, and it is hoped that clear evidence in the form of coins or inscribed pottery will be discovered one day from these lost prehistorical habitations.

Gandhara Sources: Coins, Petroglyphs, and Inscriptions

Sporadic finds of coins, sketches, and inscriptions are preserved in museums and private collections and provide early evidence of Krishna and Balarama from the Afghanistan and Pakistan regions. That any historical evidence has survived at all from the ancient Gandhara region (present-day Kandahar in Afghanistan and Peshawar in northeast Pakistan) is impressive in itself, let alone any evidence on Krishna, owing to the fact that the region of Afghanistan and northwestern Pakistan has been engaged in wars continuously since the late seventeenth century with one or another of the major powers with only intermittent and short-lived peace. Bearing in mind the predicament in Afghanistan, the presence of any or fractional evidence should predict a substantial presence of Krishna devotees in this area during its early history. Vaasudeva appears on Indo-Greek coins of King Agathocles (180–165 BCE), as well as Kushana coins. Vaasudeva and Balarama are found inscribed on the weight stones used by wrestlers. Although fragmentary, evidence, including the depictions on coinage and epithets on weight stones, helps us understand the popularity of Krishna worship in this region before the Common

Era. Figures of Balarama and Krishna dated to about 200 BCE are also found with their names inscribed on the hillsides of Chilas in the northwestern borders between Afghanistan and Pakistan.

Early Inscriptions from India

The Gosundi inscription, the Mora well inscription, and other inscriptions from Rajasthan (near Chittore), Madhya Pradesh, and Maharashtra (Nanaghat) refer to the worship of Krishna as *Bhagavan*. The frequency of inscriptions increases with the Gupta Empire (325 CE onward), and Gupta emperors referred to themselves as *parama bhagavata*, indicating their devotion to *Bhagavan*, clearly established Krishna as the supreme deity by the third century CE.

Early Textual Sources

The *Ashtadhyayi* (600 B.C.E.) of Panini describes Krishna using his patronymic as Vaasudeva, meaning son of Vasudeva, which is also the name of the Vyuha Vaasudeva, which emerges at the beginning of creation. The *Arthasastra* refers to the temple of Vaasudeva, along with other temples of Kubera. Hala's anthology of stories, the *Gatha Sattasai*, and Bhasa's play, the *Balacarita*, dated to the turn of 100 CE also describe the childhood exploits of Krishna. Megasthenes, Greek ambassador at the court of Chandragupta Maurya, includes descriptions of the Indian Hercules in his book *Indica*, considered to be a Hellenistic adaptation of the name of Harikulesa, another name for Krishna. In Tamil literature, the *Silappadikaram* also mentions Krishna, while poems of the *alvars* epitomize the divine play of Krishna in its various human emotions. Although early Vedic references are notable, consistent references to Krishna since 1500 BCE onward establish the historical worship of Krishna in India.

See also: Avatara; Bhagavan; Bhagavatas; Bhakti; Narayana; *Pancaratra;* Vishnu; *Vyuhas*

Further Reading

Bryant, E. 2003. *Krishna: The Beautiful Legend of God*. London: Penguin Books.
Chanda, R. P. 1920. *Archaeology and the Vaishanva Tradition*. New Delhi: Archaeological Survey of India.
Majumdar, B. 1969. *Krishna in History and Legend*. Calcutta: University of Calcutta.

HOLI

Holi is the Indian spring festival of colors, celebrated about ten days after the arrival of spring. *Holi* is a celebration of fun and religion mixed with spontaneity. Several temples in the Braj region hold *Holi* festivals in their own individual style. In Barsana, the sacred place where Radha was born, people recall the pranks of Krishna, the play (*lila*) and love between Radha and Krishna, and perform dances and shows featuring Krishna *lila*. The men of Nandgaon carry the flag from the

---

Holi in the United States

Holi is celebrated across the world, and it is also celebrated in almost all the major cities across the United States. *Holi* celebrations in New York, Salt Lake City, and San Francisco are popular and attract a large number of participants.

---

temple of Shriji and arrive in Barsana, where they are received with devotional singing. The men of Nandgaon, pretending to be the *Gopas* of Nandgaon, arrive in the afternoon in Barsana to play *Holi* and are beaten with bamboo staves by the women of Barsana, pretending to be the *Gopi* women of Barsana, while the men try to protect themselves with shields. Folk music and dance interrupt the attacks, and everyone is filled with a sportive, joyful mindset. This celebration in Barsana is followed on the next day by the returning *Gopas*, who also bring the *Gopas* of Barsana with them to Nandgaon. Men and women play with color, dance to music, and women try to hit men with bamboo sticks (this is the reason it is called *lath mar Holi*, hitting with sticks, in Mathura).

The sprinkling of color, the folk music and dances follow the celebration. At the *Dauji*, it is celebrated in the Balarama temple. Baskets of powdered color are released from the rooftop of the temple, covering everyone and everything with a haze of color. However, in *Dauji*, hitting with sticks is not part of the *Holi* celebration, as it is in Mathura. *Holi* is celebrated with the marriage of Radha and Krishna in the Radhavallabha temple followed by *samaj gayan* celebrations. *Rathothsava*

Holi festival celebrations at the Gopi Krishna Temple, March 2012, Kolkata, West Bengal, India. (Samrat35/Dreamstime.com)

conducted as part of the *Brahmotsav* at the Rangji temple marks the end of the month-long celebration of *Holi* in Brindavan. *Holi* is celebrated with fun across India, and it is also celebrated as a festival of colors in many cities across the world.

See also: Balarama; Barsana; Braj *Parikrama*; Brindavan; *Lila*; Mathura; Radha

Further Reading

Kandodwala, D. 2006. *Holi: The Hindu Festival of Colors.* London: Evans Brothers.

Sanford, W. 2005. "Holi Through Dauji's Eyes: Alternate Views of Krishna and Balarama in Dauji." In *Alternative Krishnas,* edited by Guy L. Beck, 91–113. Albany: SUNY Press.

ISKCON (INTERNATIONAL SOCIETY FOR KRISHNA CONSCIOUSNESS)

The International Society for Krishna Consciousness (ISKCON) was founded by A. C. Bhaktivedanta Swami Prabhupada in New York in 1967, and the organization soon spread to several other cities in the United States and then to other countries. The practice of Krishna consciousness includes living in a semimonastic mode, wearing Indian dress and the *tilaka* (*urdvapundra*—a Vaishnava marking on the forehead), and abstaining from alcohol or other intoxicants, meat dishes, gambling, and illicit sex. ISKCON is a Western offshoot of the Caitanya Vaishnava tradition, which is well known for its traditional *kirtan* singing and *raganuraga bhakti* practice. The twenty-first–century practitioners of ISKCON come from diverse backgrounds in India and across the world. The number of ethnic Indians participating in ISKCON temple activities in the West, as well as in India, has increased in the twenty-first century. ISKCON temples number almost ten across India, while

Yard of Shri Krishna-Balaram Mandir, Vrindavan, the most famous temple of ISKCON in India. (Viacheslav Belyaev/Dreamstime.com)

New Brindavan

One of the most important temples of ISKCON (International Society for Krishna Consciousness) is located in New Brindavan, an unincorporated town in the state of West Virginia. New Brindavan contains elaborate gardens, a lotus pond, the Palace of Gold (Prabhupada's prayer hall), a Krishna temple (Sri Radha Vrindavancandra Temple), and a cow shelter (*gosala*). New Brindavan is one of the tourist attractions included on a number of travel lists.

---

its African, East Asian, and Southeast Asian centers also have a nontraditional ethnic attendance.

See also: Bhaktivedanta Swami Prabhupada; Caitanya; *Puja; Raganuraga; Seva*

Further Reading

Bryant, E., and M. L. Ekstrand, eds. 2004. *The Hare Krishna Movement: The Post-Charismatic Fate of a Religious Transplant*. New York: Columbia University Press.

ISLAM AND KRISHNA

Although it is possible that followers of Krishna may have existed in the Middle East during 600–700 CE, early Islamic sources do not mention Krishna or his followers. Early interactions of Islam with Hinduism prior to the fifteenth century in the Braj region were not pleasant. However, the change of policy toward non-Muslim religions by Akbar, the Mughal emperor, and also his creation of Din-i-Ilahi, a new religion combining the traditional beliefs of India with Islam, changed India's religious landscape. Numerous later religious sects in Islam, such as the Ahmadiyas, include Krishna in the list of prophets recognized by Islam and venerate him as such. Krishna devotional traditions, such as Pranamis, also accept the Qur'an as a sacred text and include it in their scripture. The Nizamiya branch of the Chishti Sufi sect amalgamated numerous belief systems traditionally associated with Hinduism. Its Hindu aspects of belief are evident in the hundred Hindi verses included in its central text, the *Rusdnama* (Treatise on Righteousness). Abul Fazl was familiar with Surdas and was noted as a pupil of Svami Haridas, founder of the Haridasi tradition of Mathura. Abul Fazl notes the *Bishnupad*, while Akbar, the Mughal emperor, is said to have composed verses in the Hindi language that mention Krishna.

The Ahmadiya sect of Islam, which was founded by Mirza Ghulam Ahmad in Lahore during the early 1900s, regards *avatara* and prophet as synonymous. Hence, Krishna, Buddha, and Christ are accepted as prophets and revered within the Ahmadiya sect. This has put the Ahmadiyas in an uneasy relationship with orthodox Muslim groups of India and Pakistan. In Pakistan the Ahmadiyas are not recognized as a legitimate Islamic sect, just as several Muslim groups of India such as the Deobandis do not recognize the followers of Ahmadiyas as Muslims. However, the Ahmadiya sect survives in India and other Western countries such as the

United Kingdom, Australia, and numerous countries in Africa, and Krishna continues to be revered by the Ahmadiyas as one of the past prophets.

A special local tradition in Andhra Pradesh links several Muslim groups to the Venkatesvara of Tirupati, the supreme God of Andhra Pradesh. Although the Wakf Board of Andhra Pradesh does not recognize the Ahamdiyas and several Sufi groups as Muslims, they continue to practice a syncretistic religion, attending Hindu temples and celebrating Hindu festivals such as *Diwali*. Local temple traditions of Venkatesvara in Tirupathi and Andhra Pradesh narrate that Venkatesvara married Bibi Nanchari, a Muslim woman. Hence many Muslims, who also travel on pilgrimages to the Venkatesvara temple in Tirupathi, regard Venkatesvara as the beloved Lord of Muslims. Venkatesvara is unmistakably connected to Krishna, and their reverence also includes devotion to Krishna and other deities of Hinduism. Muslim women read and recount the stories of Ramayana on *Diwali*.

Hindu traditions also regard the Prophet Muhammad as one of the appearances of the divine on the earth. In particular, Krishna devotional traditions such as the *Pranamis* consider the divinity of Muhammad and accept the Qur'an as one of the revealed texts. Srila Prabhupada, the founder of ISKCON, is credited as having said that Islam was a simplified form of Vaishnavism and explained that Muhammad taught the religion according to time, place, circumstances, and intellectual level. The *Pranami* tradition is a liberal blend of teachings of the Qur'an and the *Bhagavadgita*. The major text of the *Pranamis* is the *Tartham Sagar*, containing a compilation of basic teachings on heaven, life, and God, from the Qur'an, the Torah, the *Vedas*, and the *Bhagavadgita*. Although the supreme God is referred to as "Raj ji," Krishna is worshipped as the central deity. Even though Krishna is commonly worshipped, *Pranami* tradition prefers non-idolatry-based practices such as singing *bhajans* (devotional songs) or reciting from the holy text. Strict vegetarianism and abstention from spirits such as alcohol and from smoking are among the basic personal rules of practice for the followers of the *Pranami* tradition.

See also: Bhagavadgita; Bhaktivedanta Swami Prabhupada; ISKCON

Further Reading

Qasim, A. 2012. "Lord Krishna Prophet of Allah." *Huffington Post—Religion*, August 9, http://www.huffingtonpost.com/qasim-rashid/lord-krishna-prophet-of-allah _b_1759049.html

J

JAGANNATHA

Jagannatha is the established form of Krishna in the temples in Orissa, especially the major temple built by the Eastern Ganga Dynasty in Puri, also known as *Purushottama Ksetra* in the *puranas*. Puri is one of the *char dhams* (four sacred places) that a Vaishnava should visit on pilgrimage. Jagannatha is seen here with Balabhadra (Balarama) and Subhadra, his elder brother and his younger sister respectively. Central icons in this temple are made of wood, which is a unique practice. The images of Jagannatha, Balabhadra, and Subhadra are also unusual and incomplete. There is an important religious story concerning the origin of the images and the reasons for their strange appearance. The legend has it that Jagannatha appeared as a log after King Indradyumna requested him to stay in Puri and receive his prayers. Vishvakarma, the divine sculptor, volunteered to carve the images, but on the condition that no one should disturb him for twenty-one days. As Vishvakarma worked behind closed doors, sounds of woodworking could be heard for two weeks, after which time everything fell absolutely silent. Unable to understand what was going on, King Indradyumna's wife, Gundica, made him open the doors and check. As they opened the doors before the agreed-upon time of twenty-one days, Vishvakarma left the unfinished images and disappeared. The king then installed the unfinished images in the temple as he had found them. New images are installed every twelve or nineteen years carved from the wood of a neem tree specially identified by the priests of the temple. This may represent the material aspect

---

Rathayatra

The largest *Rathayatra* procession, called Jagannatha *Rathayatra,* is celebrated each year in June or July and draws close to a million pilgrims to Puri, the holy city in Orissa, one of the four holy cities of pilgrimage (*chardham*) in India. Jagannatha *Rathayatra* is celebrated in the month of *Ashadha* (June–July) of the Hindu calendar. However, prior to the *Rathayatra* another ceremony takes place in the Jagannatha temple during which time (*Jyestha*, May–June) the images of Jagannatha, Balabhadra, and Subhadra are kept in the "sick chamber" and the temple is locked, so no usual worship or *darsan* takes place. When the idols are returned to health, they are taken out in the *Rathayatra* procession from the main temple to their summer residence, the Gundica temple, from where they return to the main temple four days later.

Navakalevara

Navakalevara is a special ritual associated with the Jagannatha temple in Puri. New images of Jagannatha, Balabhadra, and Subhadra replace the old images once in seven or nine years, whenever the *adhikamasa* (intercalary month) occurs in the month of *Ashadha* (July–August). The *Navakalevara* ritual begins in the month of *Caitra* at the beginning of the new year of the Hindu calendar with identification of the neem (*Azadirachta Indica*) trees, which are then harvested ritually to procure the wood for the images.

The current images of Krishna, Balabhadra, and Subhadra were installed on June 16, 2015. The *Navakalevara* ceremony is a two-and-a-half-month process, which began on March 29, 2015, when the temple priests set out on a quest to find the neem trees adorned with specific auspicious marks showing that they were suitable for making the idols. The sacred neem trees were identified in the forests of the Jagatsinghpur and Khurda districts of Orissa. Once the idols were ready, the *Brahmapadartha* (soul) was transferred from the old images to the new images. Transferring the *Brahmapadartha* is an esoteric ceremony. During the ceremony the hands and eyes of the *Badagrahis* are tied with cloth; they cannot touch or see the *Brahmapadartha*. After the transfer ceremony the old images are buried in Koilbailkuntha, and the *Badagrahis* observe mourning rituals for ten days. The *rathayatra* with the new images was held on June 18, 2015.

---

of *purusha*, as represented in the *Purushasukta*, where the body of *purusha* is not permanent but sacrificed in order to become everything else in the world.

See also: Balarama; Caitanya; *Purusha*; Subhadra: Krishna's Sister; Vishnu

Further Reading

Couture, A., and C. Schmid. 2001. "The Harivamsa, the Goddess Ekanamsa, and the Iconography of the *Vrsni* Triads." *Journal of the American Oriental Society* 121 (2): 173–192.

Misra, K. C. 1971. *The Cult of Jagannath*. Calcutta: Calcutta University Press.

Mohaptra, G. 1979. *The Land of Vishnu: A Study of Jagannatha Cult*. Delhi: B. R. Publishing.

JAINISM AND KRISHNA

Krishna and Balarama are depicted as the cousins of Neminatha, the twenty-second Jain *tirthankara*. Therefore, Krishna and Balarama are considered minor deities in Jainism. Krishna and Balarama are depicted as the ninth incarnations of Vaasudeva and Baladeva, minor gods accompanying the Jain *Salakapurushas* (illustrious persons), and hence Jain texts describe the complete life story including past life stories of Krishna in detail, although with major theological differences. While Krishna's brother Balarama is depicted in a positive light as an incarnation of Baladeva (a category of special beings in Jainism, the *salaka purushas*) and as a follower of dharma (right/duty), Krishna is depicted in the Jain texts as Vaasudeva

Neminatha and Krishna

Krishna is the cousin of Nemi, the twenty-second Jain *tirthankara*; both are considered *salakapurushas* in Jainism. However, in Jainism Krishna is still not close to his enlightenment and hence he is depicted only as a minor god. The largest number of texts and sculptural depictions of Krishna, next only to those in Hinduism, are found in Jainism.

(a category of special beings in Jainism, the *salaka purushas*), a conniving and not fully mature person in following the dharma, and, in particular, he is described as a sinner in almost all the Jain texts that contain the Krishna story. The earliest legend of Krishna, although brief, is noted in the Svetambara canonical text, the *Antagada dasao,* and the *Vasudevahindi* (parts containing the story of Krishna are dated to 300 CE). Although all the Jain texts containing the myths of *Tirthankara* Neminatha contain information on Krishna, the most detailed narration of Krishna is found in the *Harivamsapurana* (783 CE) of Digambara Jain *acarya* Punnata Jinasena, the *Cauppannamahapurusacariyam* (868 CE) of Svetambara *acarya* Silanka, and the *Trishashtisalakapurushacarita* (1160–1172 CE) of Svetambara *acarya* Hemacandra. The *Harivamsapurana* provides the most complete and detailed account of the story of Krishna's life, although it is infused with typical Jain adaptations.

Vaasudevas are a category of special beings in Jainism known for their amazing actions, known as *karmavir* (action hero) and *ascaryavir* (wonder hero). In general, the Jain narration of the life of Krishna depicts that in each birth as Vaasudeva Krishna's life follows a pattern of regression in which he loses his greatness, as opposed to the patterns of incarnations noticed in Vaishnavism, in which the greatness of Vishnu is revealed in a progressive manner, while in Krishna is revealed the full manifestation of the supreme God, *Bhagavan* Vishnu. Krishna is the eighth incarnation of Vishnu and Vishnu himself (*purna avatara*), not a partial incarnation as in the earlier incarnations of Vishnu. On the contrary, Jain stories, especially those of the past lives of Krishna included with Neminatha's legends, depict Krishna as a compulsive sinner, always destined for hell.

Krishna Vaasudeva, the Wonder Hero

Krishna is the ninth Vaasudeva, a cousin of the twenty-second Jain *Tirthankara* Neminatha. Krishna is subordinate to his cousin Neminatha; a clear Jain bias can be noticed in the narration of the events of Krishna's life. Krishna's birth is narrated as similar to the Hindu legend of Krishna, and Krishna was born in prison, as his uncle Kamsa imprisoned his parents. Miraculous events surrounding Krishna's birth and childhood are either omitted or attributed to other beings such as angels to minimize the effect of Krishna's potential achievements. As Krishna was born in prison, his guardian deities helped Vaasudeva by putting the prison guards to sleep and unlocking the prison gates. Krishna was exchanged with Nanda, the cowherd, whose child was brought back in his place. As a child Krishna was passive in the cowherd village, while two demonesses (*khecharis*: Sakuni and Putana) attempted to kill him. Krishna's guardian angels overturned the cart and killed both the demonesses. Some cowherds who witnessed the event assumed that Krishna had killed the demonesses and informed other cowherds, including Nanda. Therefore, the stories of Krishna's miraculous strength as noted in the Hindu stories were presented in the Jain stories as arising out of the misunderstanding of a few innocent cowherds. Krishna's mischievous pranks are portrayed as an obstacle to good discipline, rather a disquieting quality and definitely not an indication of greatness. His love and play with the cowherd maidens (*Gopis*) is described as a "disease," which makes them neglect their work. Balarama, who is absent in the stories of Krishna up to this point, was sent by their father Vasudeva after he learned about the love play of Krishna with the *Gopis* of Brindavan and worried that Kamsa might learn about Krishna's location from rumors of his exploits in Brindavan. Krishna's relations with the Pandavas, narrated in the *Mahabharata,* are also part of these narratives, but they lack most of the distinct imagery associated with Krishna in the *Mahabharata.* The miraculous deeds of Krishna such as the demonstration of his *visvarupa* (universal form) are absent from the story, as also in the *Bhagavadgita.* However, Krishna assists his cousins the Pandavas and rescues Draupadi from being kidnapped, very different from the Hindu story in which Krishna saves Draupadi from public humiliation in the Kaurava court. The arch nemesis of Krishna in the Jain stories is not Kamsa as in the Hindu stories, but Kamsa's father-in-law Jarasandha, included in a separate category in Jainism known as *prativaasudevas* (opponents of Vaasudevas). The war between Krishna and Jarasandha is described as a major battle involving *Tirthankara* Neminatha, the Pandavas, Balarama, and Vasudeva on Krishna's side, while Jarasandha is joined by the Kauravas. A terrible war ensues, with Neminatha taking an active part in the war. However, Neminatha does not kill Jarasandha, knowing that it is the duty of Vaasudeva to kill *prativaasudeva.* In the Hindu mythology, Krishna does not kill Jarasandha. Bhima, the third Pandava, kills Jarasandh in a long, grueling wrestling match that lasted for several days. Jain stories of Krishna also alternate the weapons of Krishna with others. In a strange turn the wheel, a typical weapon of Krishna in Hindu myths, is a weapon of Jarasandha. Not only did Jarasandha use the wheel as his weapon, but he also assaulted Krishna with it, an action that was interrupted by Krishna. Krishna offered to spare Jarasandha's life if he were to change his ways and agree to live a peaceful life. Jarasandha refused to do so and was killed by Krishna with the wheel, which was, incidentally, Jarasandha's weapon.

Krishna's death is narrated in the Jain texts following the basic outline found in Hinduism, with minor changes. Krishna wandered off in the forests and was accidentally hit by a hunter's arrow. He then performed a *nidana* (a sinful resolution) of revenge before his death. As he performed this *nidana* and died with sinful thoughts, the Jain *puranas* state that Krishna was destined for hell. Although Jain sources do not accept the superior status of Krishna as a god in his current life, Jain sources make amends for it by noting that he would be reborn eventually as a *Tirthankara,* the highest divinity of Jainism in a future era (*utsarpini*).

Past Lives of Krishna: Regression, Rather Than Progression

Krishna is the ninth Vaasudeva (each Vaasudeva has a different life, similar to the Hindu incarnations of Vishnu), born as the cousin of Neminatha. His past lives are narrated with minor differences in the *Harivamsapurana* and the *Trishashtisalaka-purushacarita*. The *Harivamsapurana* narrated three past lives of Krishna, while the *Trishashtisalakapurushacarita* narrates only two past lives, leaving out the first past life of Krishna described in the *Harivamsapurana*.

Krishna in his first past life was born as a cook of meat dishes who was called Amritarasayana. He was a royal cook and enjoyed the patronage of the king, who appointed him the head cook with a position of lord of ten villages. However, the king had a change of mind and became a Jain ascetic after he listened to the sermon of a Jain sage known as Sudharma. As the king abstained from eating meat dishes, the cook of meat dishes, Amritarasayana, lost his position and became the lord of only five villages, instead of ten villages. This made Amritarasayana very angry with the sage. Amritarasayana then prepared a curry made from a poisonous cucumber and gave it to the sage, which killed the sage instantly. As a result of this sin, Amritarasayana went to the hell called *Valukaprabha* and, falling from there, was born as an animal in the forest. In Krishna's second past life, he was born as a villager with an underdeveloped brain called Yakshilaka, and he intentionally killed a two-headed mother snake. In his third life, he was born as the hated son of the female snake who was born human in the next life, who gave him away as soon as he was born, which made his life poor and difficult although he was born a prince. The *Trishashtisalakapurushacarita* contains only the last two stories with minor differences.

Krishna's story is narrated, with major differences, in each text of the Jain tradition, and it lacks the uniformity of subject line observed in the Hindu tradition. This makes the veracity of the Jain tradition on Krishna questionable, and gives rise to the view that the stories may have been received from Hinduism.

See also: Arjuna; Balarama; Birth and Early Childhood of Krishna; Childhood of Krishna in Brindavan; Jarasandha; Pandavas

Further Reading

Johnson, H. 1931–1962. *Trishashtisalakapurushacaritra*. Vols. 1–5. Baroda: Gaekward Oriental Institute.

Muni, D. 1971. *Bhagavan Arishtanemi aur Karmayogi Sri Krishna: Ek Anusilan*. Udaipur (Rajasthan): Sri Tarak Guru Jain Granthalaya.

JANMASTHAMI

Janmasthami (August–September), also known as *Krishnajanmasthami*, marks the birthday of Krishna, celebrated in all Krishna temples across India and the world by a large attendance of devotees. It is celebrated to commemorate the birth of Krishna on the eighth day of the dark half of the Hindu month of *Bhadrapada* (*Bhadon*). *Krishnajanmasthami* is also referred to as *Gokulashtami*. This is the largest public celebration associated with Krishna. Numerous temples in the Braj region

---

Dahi-handi

Celebrations of Krishna's birth in the month of *Bhadrapada* (August–September) begin at sunset as soon as the moon is visible in the dark sky. The celebrations continue late into the night with cultural shows, tableaux depicting Krishna's birth, and a variety of competitions. An important attraction of the festival is the pot-hitting (*Dahi-handi*) competition attempted by young boys in a specifically constructed entrapment, which pulls the pot away just when someone is about to hit it. *Dahi-handi* commemorates the fun and frolic of Krishna as an infant in Govraja stealing and distributing butter, curds, and milk to one and all, including the monkeys.

---

perform *Mahabhishek* in the morning followed by cultural shows, which are organized for the rest of the day, until midnight. At midnight a special celebration takes place honoring the birth of Krishna. Almost all the temples in India celebrate Krishna *Janmasthami* with processions and cultural shows. However, in Pakistan and Bangladesh it is a subdued celebration. Pakistan banned public processions of Hindu festivals in 1948, but Bangladesh lifted the ban on *Janmasthami* processions in 1989.

See also: Braj *Parikrama*; Caitanya Vaishnavism; Mathura

Further Reading

Bahadur, O. *The Book of Hindu Festivals and Ceremonies.* Delhi: UBS Publishers.

JANMASTHAN TEMPLE

The *Janmasthan* temple in Mathura, also known as the *Janmabhumi* temple, marks the exact place of Krishna's birth. Hence this temple is one of the most visited temples in India. Festivals connected with the life of Krishna such as *Janmasthami, Diwali*, and so on are celebrated with a large attendance in this temple. This temple sustained numerous destructive attacks from invading Muslim armies since the twelfth century. However, the temple was destroyed completely and a mosque was built on the grounds in the seventeenth century. The present *Janmasthan* temple was rebuilt from the ruins of the previous temple, although part of the complex was occupied and used by a local Muslim general to build a mosque. The mosque currently stands on the temple grounds next to the *Janmasthan* temple in the place of its former *mahamandap* (hall). The Krishna *Janmasthan* temple is a sacred complex, which contains the tank Potrakund/Pavitrakund, the *Janmasthan* temple, the Kesavadev temple, and the Bhagavatabhavan. Potrakund is a small stepped tank, the water of which was said to have been used for the first bath and cleaning of the child Krishna soon after his birth. Vajranabha, the great-grandson of Krishna, constructed the original Kesavadev temple, installing the image of Krishna prepared according to the instructions of Kalindi (Yamuna), one of Krishna's wives. The Bhagavatabhavan contains a number of temples including the Radhakrishna temple, the Jagannath temple, the Sitaram temple, and the Kesavesvar temple (Shiva temple with mercurial *linga*). Nearby is located the temple to the goddess Mahamaya, also known as the Mahavidya temple, a temple for Krishna's sister Yo-gamaya, who was killed by Kamsa on the day of Krishna's birth.

See also: Braj *Parikrama*; Brindavan; Childhood of Krishna in Brindavan; *Diwali*; *Janmasthami*; Mathura; *Radhashtami*

Further Reading

Growse, F. S. 1979 reprint. *Mathura: A District Memoir*. New Delhi: Asian Education Services.

JARASANDHA

Jarasandha means "joined by Jara," a name by which the father-in-law of Kamsa was known in the Krishna legend in the Hindu *puranas*. Jarasandha replaces Kamsa as the central antihero in the Jain mythology, and hence he is commonly called *prativaasudeva* (enemy of *vaasudeva*).

According to the Hindu legends, Jarasandha is the father-in-law of Kamsa and the sworn enemy of Krishna. Kamsa's wives, Asti and Prapti, went back to their paternal home with great sorrow at the death of their husband. Jarasandha, their father, vowed to annihilate the Yadavas and take revenge on Krishna for killing Kamsa. Jarasandha declared war on the Yadavas and invaded Mathura. The Yadavas prepared well for the war under the leadership of Krishna and Balarama, defeating Jarasandha in the eighteen wars he declared on them. However, to avoid destruction and loss of life of the Yadavas, Krishna built a great city, Dvaraka, by claiming land from the Indian Ocean, which formed a beautiful island impregnable to attacks from Jarasandha. Krishna is also known as Dvarakadhish, Lord of Dvaraka, because he ruled the Yadavas safely in Dvaraka. Balarama, his brother, ruled Vraja and was known as Brajaraja. During one of the final battles, Jarasandha was defeated badly and was caught and tied up by Bal-arama. However, Krishna set him free, giving Jarasandha an opportunity to change his ways before his fate (karma) came to fruition. Krishna then had him defeated and killed by Bhima.

Bhima is the second Pandava and a close cousin of Krishna. Bhima helped Krishna vanquish Jarasandha, one of his sworn enemies. As the Pandavas began preparations for *Rajasuya yaga*, Krishna, along with Arjuna and Bhima, reached Girivraja, the city of Jarasandha, under the guise of Brahmans. Jarasandha received them, thinking that they might be Kshatriyas dressed as Brahmans. He wondered if he had seen them somewhere earlier, as they seemed vaguely familiar. However, Jarasandha served the Brahmans and said he would offer anything they might de-sire. Krishna declared that they were not Brahmans, but Kshatriyas, introduced them, and then said that they desired to have one-to-one combat. Krishna chal-lenged Jarasandha to fight with any one of them he chose. Ruling out Krishna as cowardly for previously withdrawing from the battlefield, and Arjuna as younger and weak, Jarasandha said he would fight with his equal in strength, Bhima. A fight ensued between Bhima and Jarasandha that lasted for seven days. Bhima became tired and approached Krishna to ask how Jarasandha could be defeated. Krishna symbolically indicated a plan by splitting a twig and throwing the pieces crosswise, not side-by-side. Bhima subsequently took hold of Jarasandha by his legs, split him open, and threw him away crosswise, so the body parts did not come together to fuse. Thus he died.

Jarasandha's strange death is related to his birth, which was also a miraculous event. Brihadratha, Jarasandha's father, was king of Magadha, but did not beget any children from his wives, twin sisters. Brihadratha then left his kingdom and served a sage, Chandakausika. Knowing the king's desire for children, Chandakausika gave him a mango and informed him to give it to his wife, so that she could bear a son. However, the king had two wives, and therefore he cut the mango in half and gave it to both of them equally, informing them that it was given by the sage to beget a son. Both of his wives got pregnant, but when they delivered only half a child each, the king ordered the guards to leave the lifeless parts of the baby in the forest. A demoness, Jara, saw the parts of the baby and approached it to eat it. However, as soon as she picked up the parts, brought them together, and joined them, they fused and the baby started crying. The demoness then gave the child back to King Brihadratha and informed him of what had happened. Since the baby was born joined by Jara, he was named Jarasandha (joined by Jara). Hence it was impossible to kill him by any other manner other than separating his body lengthwise into two parts.

Krishna then met the 20,800 kings imprisoned by Jarasandha. He gave them the vision of his four-armed form (*caturbhuja bhagavan*), with his typical adornment, and received their homage. Krishna informed them that they were free to return to their kingdoms. He then returned with gifts to the Pandavas' capital, Indraprastha, with Arjuna and Bhima, where Dharma, the eldest of the Pandavas, was preparing to hold the sacrifice of *Rajasuya*, performed by the greatest kings on Earth.

Jain texts present Jarasandha as the main rival of Krishna, calling him *prativaasudeva* (anti-Vaasudeva), as Krishna is depicted as the ninth Vaasudeva. Vaasudeva stands for a category of special men (*salaka purushas*) in Jainism condemned to living in hell. According to Jain traditions Krishna killed Jarasandha with his own weapon, the wheel, by obstructing it and hurling it back at Jarasandha in the war.

Hindu and Jain *puranas* narrate the story of Jarasandha with minor differences. However, in both stories Krishna was responsible for the death of Jarasandha. According to Hindu *puranas* Jarasandha's life ended when Bhima separated the two halves of his body at the direction of Krishna and prevented them from joining together. In contrast, the Jain *puranas* mention that he was killed by Krishna with Jarasandha's own weapon, the Sudarsana *cakra* (wheel).

See also: Bhima; Kamsa; Pandavas

Further Reading

Katre, S. 1933, 1934. "Krishna and Jarasandha." *Indian Historical Quarterly* 8: 500–508, and *Indian Historical Quarterly* 9: 854–865.

JATRA

Jatra of Bengal is an open-air musical theater performance that originated in the bhakti tradition. Caitanya, founder of the *Gaudiya* Vaishnava tradition, is said to have composed and participated in the *jatras* of Krishna. Several theater groups still perform the *purana* stories of Krishna and other major Hindu themes, but the Bengali *jatra* theater has adapted itself to modernity. Secular theater shows of everyday life are common in present-day Bengal and Bangladesh, and the *jatra* theater tradition has lost its originality. However, the *jatra* has retained its original religious nature in neighboring eastern states of India including Bihar and Orissa (*Danu jatra*), where the *jatra* is still associated with temples and performances are conducted on the occasion of festivals. The *Danu jatra* of Orissa is a performance of the Krishna story from the *Bhagavatapurana* in the Oriya translation. Krishna's childhood episodes from the medieval Oriya epic *Mathuramangala* commonly form the subject of the *jatras* in Orissa.

See also: Bhagavatapurana; Caitanya; *Gaudiya* Vaishnavism

Further Reading

Guha-Thakurta, P. 2001. *The Bengali Drama: Its Origin and Development*. London: Routledge.

JAYADEVA

Jayadeva lived in the twelfth century in Orissa, where he composed his famous poetical text, the *Gitagovinda*, describing the pastimes of Krishna. This text has attained a tremendous following among Krishna devotees, literary circles, and the common public as one of the most famous texts on Krishna. It was also performed during the daily ritual in the Jagannath temple at Puri. Biographers of Caitanya also note that Caitanya and Jayadeva met during Caitanya's stay at Puri. As a court poet of the Sena Empire of eastern India, Jayadeva's influence not only extended to the poetical and literary circles of the day, but also to the Sena rulers who were taught and coached by him in the Sanskrit language and linguistics. Jayadeva's poems, especially the *Gitagovinda,* found a transcontinental following in the later Rajput rulers of western India. Numerous commentaries were written about the *Gitagovinda*, including the prominent commentaries composed by Rajput rulers Raja Mananka and Rana Kumbha. Jayadeva's *Gitagovinda* received acclaim from his contemporaries, and still receives acclaim after several centuries from generations of people in the East and West for its scholarly merits, lyrical qualities, and enthusiastic representation of divine love, which evokes awe and a sense of exuberance within anyone's heart. Jayadeva's poetical style, *padavali* (row of words), is unique, and its use is now ubiquitous in the bhakti lyrics in vernacular Hindi, such as Maithili, Bengali, Brajboli, and so on, and also in southern languages such as Telugu, in which the prototypical *padas* of Tyagaraja and Annamayya form popular bhakti verses. The sources of *padavali* can be located in prototypical *bhanita* verses as well as Bengali *caryagiti* or *caryapada*. However, their influence on Jayadeva is unknown, and the use of *padavali* is unique and widespread in Jayadeva's poetry.

Any poetry of similar style was unknown in Indian poetical literature until Jayadeva popularized it with his *Gitagovinda*; even though the origin of *padavali* is not known, its popularization could be certainly attributed to Jayadeva. Krishna and Radha's mutual adoration and separation anxiety (*viraha*) formed only a minor sidetrack in the larger Krishna legend prior to Jayadeva's *Gitagovinda*. This scarce attention to Radha and Krishna's relationship may have been caused by the stigma attached to the sexual imagery of such poetry. Jayadeva's poetry successfully overcomes the prevalent stigma in popularizing the concept of the separation of Krishna and Radha, adapting it to the bhakti milieu and presenting it as an allegory of the longing of evolved souls for union with Krishna, the divine, as depicted in the *Raasalila* section of the *Bhagavatapurana*.

See also: Bhakti; Bilvamangala Svami, Lilasuka; Caitanya; Candidasa; Jagannatha; Puri Temple

Further Reading

Gerow, E. 1989. "Jayadeva's Poetics and the Classical Style." *Journal of African and Oriental Studies* 109 (4): 533–544.

Knutson, J. 2010. "The Political Poetic of the Sena Court." *Journal of Asian Studies* 69 (2): 371–401.

Knutson, J. 2011. "The Vernacular Cosmopolitan: Jayadeva's Gitagovinda." In *South Asian Texts in History: Critical Engagements with Sheldon Pollock*, edited by Y. Bronner, W. Cox, and L. McCrea, 125–149. Ann Arbor: University of Michigan Press.

Pollock, S. 1998. "The Cosmopolitan Vernacular." *Journal of Asian Studies* 57 (1): 6–37.

Sandahl-Forgue, S. 1997. *Le Gitagovinda de Jayadeva: Tradition et Innovation dans le Kavya*. Stockholm: Olms.

Telang, M. R., and V. D. Laxman, eds. 1899. *Gitagovindakavyam: With the Rasikapriya of Kumbhakarna and the Rasamanjari of Sankaramisra*. Bombay: Bharatiya Vidyabhavan.

JHULA SEVA/DHOOL SEVA (SWING FESTIVAL) OR *DOLOTSAV/OONJALE SEVA*

The swing festival of Krishna is celebrated during October–November. The swing festival may be celebrated for a single day or as many as eight days. The Sriranganathasvami temple in Srirangam celebrates the festival for eight days before *Mukkoti Ekadasi*. *Jhula seva* or *oonjale seva* involves placing Krishna in a swing, which is also the last service before the deity retires to his bed. Devotees participate in offering *jhula seva* in the late evening following the late evening *arati* and *naivedyam* offering before the deities are retired to rest. In the Venkatesvara temple in Tirupathi and other south Indian temples, it is performed in the *mandapam* for the *utsava vigrahas* placed in the swing; therefore, participants can take part in it and a large number of other devotees can watch. This festival is called *Phul Dol* in the Srinathji temple at Nathdvara. This festival is celebrated during the dark half of the month of *Caitra* (mid March–April) around the time of the *Holi* festival. The main icon of the temple Navnitpriyaji is placed in a flower-decorated swing attended by devotees. Temples in Brindavan have their own traditional *dolotsav* (swing festival). The Bankebihari temple celebrates *dolotsav* only on one day of the year, in the month of *Sravan* (July–

August), while most other temples of Brindavan celebrate it for fourteen days during the bright half of the month of *Sravan* in the Hindu calandar.

The *Jhula* festival is also celebrated for newly married women and young women during July–August. The *Jhula Yatra* of Krishna is performed during this time in Brindavan. Radha and Krishna, seated on their swing, are taken out in procession. This festival is held for five days in a number of temples in Brindavan. Each temple has its own *jhula kunja* (swing garden) appropriately prepared for this occasion. Performances of *Gaurangalila* (based on the life of Caitanya) and *Krishnalila* (based on the life of Krishna) are performed during this time.

See also: Arati; Bhakti; Braj *Parikrama*; *Holi*; *Lila*; *Raasalila*; *Seva*

Further Reading

Packert, C. 2010. *Sringar: The Art of Loving Krishna*. Bloomington: Indiana University Press.

Vaswani, J. P. 2003. *What Would You Like to Know about Hinduism*. Berkshire, UK: Sterling.

JIVA *GOSVAMI* (1517–1608)

Jiva *Gosvami* was the most prominent of the six *Gosvamis* ensuring the successful transmission of Caitanya's teachings for posterity. He is appreciated by his successors in the Caitanya Vaishnava tradition in particular, as well as scholars of Vaishnavism in general, for his prolific writings and versatility. Jiva was a nephew of Rupa and Sanatana *Gosvami*, under whose guidance Jiva learned, although he owed his early learning to his guru, Nityananda, who sent him to join his uncles in Brindavan. Although numerous biographical accounts of Jiva's life are known, the most extensive account of his life is available in the *Bhaktiratnakara* of Narahari Cakravarti in Navadvip. One of the remarkable achievements of Jiva in Brindavan was obtaining official recognition from Akbar, the Mughal emperor, for the Madanamohan temple and from the Rajput king, Todarmal, for the Govindadeva temple. Jiva also contributed to the ritualistic and theological framework of the *Gaudiya* Vaishnava movement through his work, the *Bhagavatasandarbha*, as well as training the next generation of Vaishnavas of the Caitanya tradition. Jiva was also unique in leaving a will concerning how the *Gosvami* temples, libraries, and other assets should be managed in his absence. It is estimated that Jiva may have written about 400,000 verses epitomizing Krishna. Among the texts, the *Bhagavatasandarbha* and the *Gopalacampu* are most notable and received immense attention from his disciples and followers of Caitanya Vaishnavism. The theological and philosophical contributions of Jiva *Gosvami* are important in ensuring a balance between Vedanta and bhakti in the Caitanya Vaishnava practice. In this respect, the *Bhagavatapurana* is explained in the light of the *Brahmasutrabhashya* of Sankara. Jiva utilized the first five verses of the *Brahmasutras* in his text, the *Bhagavatasandarbha*, which is an early instance of a *purana* explained in the light of Vedanta philosophy. There is only one goal in Caitanya Vaishnavism, that of unmotivated and spontaneous love (*prema*) for Krishna. Jiva's philosophy successfully supersedes the previously

---

Bhagavatasandarbha

The *Bhagavatasandarbha* was composed by Jiva *Gosvami*. *Sandarbha* literally means "arranging" or "weaving." In the *Bhagavatasandarbha*, Jiva *Gosvami* thematically arranged the *Bhagavatapurana*, expounding Caitanya Vaishnava theology, philosophy, and practice. Hence the *Bhagavatasandarbha* serves as a general handbook of Krishna devotion for the Caitanya Vaishnava tradition. The *Bhagavatasandarbha* explains the rational theology of Vaishnavism in six books called *sandarbhas*. The first four *sandarbhas* (*Tattvasandarbha*, *Bhagavatsandarbha*, *Param tmasandarbha*, and *Krishnasandarbha*) discuss the relation between God and his energies, while the fifth (*Bhaktisandarbha*) describes devotional practice (bhakti), and the sixth (*Pritisandarbha*) deals with the love of individuals (*atma*) for God.

---

established four goals of life according to Hinduism (dharma, *artha*, karma, and *moksha*) to establish *prema* toward Krishna as the only and ultimate goal of life. Jiva *Gosvami* is the first religious preceptor to expound on *acintyabhedabheda*, the central doctrine of Caitanya Vaishnavism. This explains the fundamental doctrine of Krishna in relation to his devotees. According to *bhedabheda*, the divine is the same and different, at the same time, with individuals of the creation, which is unthinkable to the human mind and hence *acintya* (inconceivable). One of the remarkable achievements of Jiva *Gosvami* is his contribution to Caitanya Vaishnava theology by distilling through a number of traditions current during his time, including the Vedanta, the ecstatic bhakti movements, a variety of Sanskrit poetics, and the *puranas,* which are the backbone of popular Hindu praxis.

See also: Bhakti; Caitanya; *Gaudiya* Vaishnavism; *Raganuraga*

Further Reading

Broo, M. 2006. "Jiva Gosvami and the Extent of the *Vedic* Paradigm." *Journal of Vaishnava Studies* 15 (1): 5–29.

Brzezinki, J. 1992. "*Goloka Vrindavana*: A Translation of Jiva Gosvami's *Gopala-Campu* (Chapter One)." *Journal of Vaishnava Studies* 1 (1): 61–98.

Brzezinki, J. 1996. "Verse and Prose Poetry in Gopalacampu." *Journal of Vaishnava Studies* 4 (4): 105–138.

Brzezinki, J. 2007. "Jiva Gosvami: Biography and Bibliography." *Journal of Vaishnava Studies* 15 (2): 51–80.

Elkman, S. M. 1986. *Jiva Gosvami Tatvarthasandarbha: A Study on the Philosophical and Sectarian Development of the Gaudiya Vaishnava Movement.* Delhi: Motilal Banarisdas.

Gupta, R. M. 2008. "On Conceiving the Inconceivable: Jiva *Gosvami's* Presentation of *Acintya-Bheda-abheda*." *Journal of Vaishnava Studies* 16 (2): 103–117.

JNANADEV (1275–1296)

Jnanadev is one of the most well-known *sants* (saints) of the *Varkari* tradition. He is most famous for his translation of the *Bhagavadgita* into Marathi, which came to

Jnanadev in Popular Media

Numerous films based on the life of *sant* Jnanadev have been produced in several Indian languages including Marathi, Telugu, Kannada, and Hindi. While the first film was produced in Marathi in 1940, a recent Hindi film was produced in 2012. TV shows and regional theater shows are numerous and continue to be staged across southern India, mainly in Maharashtra, Karnataka, and Andhra Pradesh.

be known, after his name, as the *Jnanesvari*. Jnanadev's biography is narrated in Marathi oral lyrical texts as well as sacred biographies of Maharashtra. Oral texts are organized in three sections, *Adi*, *Tirthavali*, and *Samadhi*, describing different parts of the life of Jnanadev, while the most well-known biography of Jnanadev is included in the Marathi text, the *Bhaktavijay,* written by Mahipati. Jnanadev's life was riddled with a number of hardships, which were not under his control, but arose due to the rigid social customs prevalent during thirteenth-century India. Jnanadev was born to Vitthal and Rukmini, incidentally named after the central deities of Pandarpur. Vitthal was excommunicated by their caste as he adopted *Nathyogi* tradition and became a mendicant renouncer, and hence Jnanadev was treated as casteless and had a hard time entering educational institutions. The four children of Vitthal and Rukmini, including Jnanadev, were admitted back into the caste by the caste council in Paithan after much ridicule and testing, while their parents were ordered to commit ritual suicide, which resulted in Jnanadev and his siblings growing up as orphans. Jnanadev's childhood and his admission into the caste are narrated, interspersed with the miraculous events of his supernatural qualities. However, it cannot be ignored that his childhood might have been extraordinarily difficult, owing to all the peculiar events he faced. Yet his extraordinary achievements starting in his teen years dominate his life stories and obscure his early life. Jnanadev was only a teenager when he translated the *Bhagavadgita* into Marathi, a translation popularly known as the *Jnaneswari*. This is one of the few instances in Indian literary history that a person's name becomes the name of an important religious text such as the *Bhagavadgita,* which indicates the merit of Jnanadev's translation and also its primacy of place in the religious literature of Maharashtra. Jnanadev is described as having had good relations with other *Varkari* saints. Jnanadev visited Namdev in Pandarpur, while Eknath is said to have visited Jnanadev's tomb and described his real-life experience of meeting Jnanadev, even though Jnanadev was not alive at that time. The *samadhi* of Jnanadev is described as *sajiva samadhi*, which means that he was entombed while still alive. It is said that Jnanadev informed his family and friends about his departure from the world, said goodbye to everyone, and then entered a small structure and sat in meditation while his friends and family closed the structure from outside and built a tomb. Jnanadev is said to be living there as a thin "breath" of life within the tomb in Alandi. Jnanadev wrote four texts: the *Jnaneswari* (translation of the *Bhagavadgita*), the *Gatha* (anthology of short devotional verses), the *Anubhavamrit* (Nectar of

Experiences), and the *Cangadevprasasti* (Praise of Cangadev). Of these texts, the most accessible text for ordinary people is the anthology, the *Gatha*. Most of the *Gatha* songs are devotional in nature with a spiritual message. The *Gathas* address the childhood stories of Krishna in the temple of Pandarpur. The most popular *Gatha* from this anthology is adapted for the *Varkari Kirtan Haripath* (twenty-seven-verse *abhanga*), which is recited during *Varkari* pilgrimages and other events.

Jnanadev left his characteristic imprint on the religious life of Maharashtra. His legacy endures in the festivals celebrated at his *samadhi* and the biennial *vari* pilgrimages in which Jnanadev *palki* is one of the regular attractions.

See also: Bhakti; Panduranga Vitthala; *Sants*; *Varkari* Tradition

Further Reading

Abbott, J. E., and N. R. Godbole. 1982. *Stories of Indian Saints: A Translation of Mahipati's Marathi Bhaktavijaya*. Delhi: Motilal Banarsidas.

Bahirat, B. P. 1984. *The Philosophy of Jnanadeva: As Gleaned from the Amritanubhava*. Delhi: Motilal Banarsidas.

Kripananda. 1989. *Jnanesvar's Gita: A Rendering of the Jnaneswari*. Albany: SUNY Press.

Ranade, R. D. 1994. *Jnaneswari: The Guru's Guru*. Albany: SUNY Press.

Vadeville, C. 1969. *L'Invocation: Le Haripath de Dnyanadev*. Paris: Ecole de Paris.

K

KALAYAVANA

Kalayavana is an enemy of the Yadavas, who harassed them with battles from time to time, supported by Jarasandha. However, Krishna devised a clever plan to eliminate him without causing any loss of life or resources to the Yadavas. Krishna, knowing that the Yadavas were engaged in continuous wars with Jarasandha, did not want them to encounter another enemy and face large losses of lives and resources. As Kalayavana laid siege to the city of Mathura with a large army, Krishna came out of the city as though he were leaving. Kalayavana thought that Krishna was fleeing and chased him. Krishna continued to walk, pursued by Kalayavana and his army, eventually disappearing into a dark cave. Kalayavana, finding no alternative to catching Krishna, also entered the cave. As soon as he entered the cave, he found someone sleeping. He thought it was Krishna sleeping in the cave and kicked the person. The person slowly woke up from his deep slumber and opened his eyes. As soon as his gaze reached Kalayavana, Kalayavana was burned to ashes. Krishna then came out of the cave and, along with Balarama who was waiting outside the cave, jumped down the tall mountains and left for Mathura without anyone noticing them. Jarasandha, meanwhile, approached and surrounded the mountains with his army, but was not able to find anyone coming out of the cave, so he went inside to check. He found only ashes in the cave. Assuming that those ashes belonged to Balarama and Krishna, Jarasandha withdrew his army and went back to Magadha. Thus Krishna averted the danger of two wars from the enemies of the Yadavas, Kalayavana and Jarasandha, and annihilated Kalayavana effortlessly.

See also: Bhima; Jarasandha; Krishna; Pandavas; Vasudeva

Further Reading

Banker, A. 2010. *Slayer of Kamsa.* New Delhi: HarperCollins.

KAMSA

Kamsa was anxious that his future killer might be growing up somewhere, as foretold by the child goddess Nidra, whom he killed. Kamsa heard about the unusual deaths of his fellow demons in Brindavan, and he became suspicious about Vraja in general. The sage Narada visited Kamsa one day and informed him that Balarama and Krishna were, in fact, the sons of Devaki and Vasudeva growing up in Vraja. Hearing this from the sage Narada confirmed Kamsa's suspicions, so he dispatched Akrura, his old friend, to bring Krishna to Mathura on the pretext of participating in a wresting match during the bow festival in Vraja.

Akrura visited Krishna's family and explained that he had come to fetch the boys Balarama and Krishna, now twelve years of age, to participate in the wrestling match in Mathura. Balarama and Krishna accompanied Akrura to Mathura, as the *Gopis* cried inconsolably on seeing Krishna leaving Vraja. As Krishna reached Mathura he and Balarama went around Mathura amusing themselves in the market, taking clothes, perfumes, and flowers from Kamsa's washerman and other royal servants. The perfume carrier for the royal household, Trivakra (one with three bends on her body), gave the perfumes to Krishna, and she became straight from Krishna's touch. Nanda, along with the other *Gopas*, also arrived at Mathura under the pretext of paying his annual taxes. The next morning it was announced in the arena that Krishna and Balarama would fight the wrestlers Canura and Mustika. Krishna and Balarama defeated the wrestlers easily. Krishna then jumped on the platform where Kamsa was sitting, grabbed him by the hair, and killed him instantly. The people of Mathura shouted for joy at the death of Kamsa, the evil king. Krishna and Balarama then went to meet their parents, Vasudeva and Devaki, in the prison. Krishna declared Ugrasena, Devaki's father, the king of Mathura. The *upanayana* ceremony (rite of passage) was performed for Balarama and Krishna, after which they left for their education to the *gurukula* of Sandipani in Avanti. While leaving on his educational travels, Krishna dispatched his friend Uddhava with a message to console the *Gopis* in Vraja, and sent Akrura to Hastinapura to meet the family of Kurus, especially his aunt Kunthi, to inform her about the happenings in Mathura and Vraja.

The Jain *puranas* preserve a story of Kamsa that differs from the Hindu story in minor details. According to the Jain texts, the name of Kamsa is derived from *kamsya*, meaning bronze, since Kamsa was found in a bronze box that was floating down the river. Kamsa was described as an evil king of Mathura, similar to the Hindu *puranas*. Kamsa learned the prophecy about his death during the wedding of Devaki, but in a slightly different manner than in the Hindu narrative. In the Jain story, Kamsa's wife became drunk at the wedding of Devaki and Vasudeva, and made fun of the sage Atimuktaka. The sage prophesied that the eighth child of Devaki would kill her husband. Kamsa took a promise from Vasudeva to hand over the children born to them. However, Krishna was transferred to Nanda and Yashoda in Braj by gods who also brought their daughter back and handed her to Kamsa. Krishna grew up in Braj and later marched on Mathura and killed Kamsa.

Kamsa's cruelty is depicted in detail in Hindu and Jain stories, although Krishna's life is depicted differently in the Jain texts.

See also: Braj: Classical History; Brindavan; Childhood of Krishna in Brindavan; *Janmasthami*; *Janmasthan* Temple; Mathura

Further Reading
Banker, A. 2010. *Slayer of Kamsa*. New Delhi: HarperCollins.

KARMA

Karma is a central concept closely connected to Krishna. Krishna lays down in the *Bhagavadgita* that it is impossible for anyone to live in this world without performing karma (action): according to Krishna even the *sanyasi* (ascetic) is not excluded from action. Karma as action that could result positively (merit) or negatively (sin) is an ancient religious ideal found in the *Vedas*, which was dealt with in detail in the later Hindu classical texts. Krishna also discusses karma, especially encouraging unattached karma as a solution to samsara, which leads one to *moksha*. Toward this end, Krishna proposes a new yoga called *karmayoga* (the yoga of action), by which one performs required action according to the *varnasrama dharma*, but one's mind is focused on Krishna, not desiring the fruits of the action, submitting oneself to the supreme deity. Engaged in this type of action, one attains the supreme status purified by the mind.

Historically, karma is understood as three varieties, which follow the individual soul (*atma*) from one life to the next in the eternal cycle of samsara (cycle of life). *Prarabdhakarma* is inherited karma to which one keeps adding karma from one's current life. Since history does not permit changing the past, one can only hope to change one's karma of the future. This is one of the ways one's fortunes or misfortunes are explained. *Kriyakarma* is the karma one acquires in one's current life through actions. Unlike the *prarabdhakarma,* this can be changed, and can even serve to expiate the *prarabdhakarma* from past life. And, as Krishna advised in the *Bhagavadgita*, one can even attain the *sayujya* of Krishna by devoting all actions (karma), as well as oneself, to Krishna with a steadfast mind. *Sancitakarma* is another kind of karma inherited by someone, but it is not activated in the current life, staying in the background.

Karma is a religious concept with strong repercussions for each individual. One's past, current, and future lives are all connected by karma (one's actions). It has a strong pedagogical and social message through which one can face the results of one's actions, if not in this life, then in another life (*Bhagavadgita* 6.45).

Karma is a central doctrine of Hinduism, and Krishna, through his *karmayoga*, brings forth the centrality of action, especially conscious action, putting one in charge of one's life.

See also: Arjuna; *Bhagavadgita*; Bhakti; *Moksha/Mukti*; Pandavas

Further Reading

Austin, C. R. 2009. "Janamejaya's Last Question." *Journal of Indian Philosophy* 37 (6): 597–625.

Carlisle, S. G. 2008. "Synchronizing *Karma*: The Internalization and Externalization of a Shared, Personal Belief." *Ethos* 36 (2): 194–219.

Granoff, P. 1998. "Cures and *Karma*: Healing and Being Healed in Jain Religious Literature." *Self, Soul, and Body in Religious Experience* 78: 218–255.

Kent, E. F. 2009. "'What's Written on the Forehead Will Never Fail': *Karma*, Fate, and Headwriting in Indian Folktales." *Asian Ethnology* 68 (1): 1–26.

Kochappilly, P. 2000. "Varnadharma, Nishkama *Karma* and Practical Morality." *Journal of Dharma* 25 (3–4): 427–432.

Lehtonen, T. 2000. "The Notion of Merit in Indian Religions." *Asian Philosophy* 10 (3): 189–204.

Luis, K. N. 2012. "*Karma* Eaters: The Politics of Food and Fat in Women's Land Communities in the United States." *Journal of Lesbian Studies* 16 (1): 108–134.

Ohami, I. 1993. "On a Comparison between the Theory of Movement and the Theory of *Karma* in Vaisesika System in Ancient India." *Kagakushi kenkyu. [Journal of the History of Science, Japan]* 32 (186): 75–83.

Okundaye, J. N., C. Gray, and L. B. Gray. 1999. "Reimaging Field Instruction from a Spiritually Sensitive Perspective: An Alternative Approach." *Social Work* 44 (4): 371–383.

Sen, T. 2001. "In Search of Longevity and Good *Karma*: Chinese Diplomatic Missions to Middle India in the Seventh Century." *Journal of World History* 12 (1): 1–28.

KEDARNATH DATTA BHAKTIVINODA (1838–1914)

Kedarnath Datta Bhaktivinoda is a major figure in modern *Gaudiya* Vaishnava history. His early life was not much different from the Bengali *Bhadraloka* society of the early nineteenth century. He was an English-educated member of the colonial administration of Bengal at a time when Bengal was undergoing its cultural renaissance. He was initially infatuated by Western literature, similar to the other English-educated young men of colonial India at that time: he was drawn only later in his life to Vaishnava literature, and especially the *Caitanyacaritamrita*, which had a profound influence on him. His self-discovery continued as he persevered in his study of classical Indian literature. A prolific writer, Bhaktivinoda contributed numerous works to Bengali journals and wrote pamphlets and books. Discouraging others from joining *Brahmasamaj*, he directed them toward the *Gaudiya* Vaishnava tradition founded by Caitanya. Bhaktivinoda also became an itinerant preacher visiting villages, establishing grassroots assemblies wherever he visited. Bhaktivinoda revived the celebration of Caitanya's birthday in Mayapur, and he also changed the organizational structure of *Gaudiya* Vaishnavism by instituting voluntary contributions and service by practitioners rather than depending on the aristocracy (*Zamindars*) for donations and support. He also formed a voluntary organization under the name *Navadvipa Pracarini Sabha* to fund the festivals, celebrations, and other regular on-site activities of the organization. Bhaktivinoda's contributions to Caitanya Vaishnavism (*Gaudiya* Vaishnavism) are significant and brought enduring traditions into practice through publications and the creation of local and regional organizations (*namhatta* and *pracarini sabha*). Bhaktivinoda's son, Bhaktisiddhanta Saraswati, continued the traditions, undertaking other necessary reforms for a successful organization, such as denouncing internal caste distinctions within *Gaudiya* Vaishnavism, establishing *mathas* (monasteries), and structuralizing devotional activity by requiring *murti puja* (Radha-Krishna and Caitanya) in the *mathas*. One of his disciples, Bhaktivedanta Swami Prabhupada, is credited with establishing ISKCON, the most successful Caitanya Vaishnava tradition in the West.

See also: Bhaktivedanta Swami Prabhupada; Caitanya; *Gaudiya* Vaishnavism; Jiva *Gosvami*; *Puja*; Rupa *Gosvami*; Six *Gosvamis*

Further Reading

Das, S. 1996–1997. "The Krishna-Samhita and the Adhunika-vada: Thakur Bhaktivinode and the Problem of Modernity." *Journal of Vaishnava Studies* 5 (1): 127–150.

Fuller, J. D. 2009. "Modern Hinduism and the Middle Class: Beyond Reform, and Revival in the Hindu Historiography of Colonial India." *Journal of Hindu Studies* 2 (1): 158–176.

Valpey, K. R. 2006. *Attending Krishna's Image: Caitanya Vaishnava Murti-seva as Devotional Truth*. London: Routledge.

KIRTANA

Kirtana is a popular form of singing the names or stories of the god in a particular ritualistic style considered as song offering (*kirtan seva*). Patanjali's *Mahabhashya* notes *samsadi* (musical performance) at temples of Krishna, which establishes that musical performances were associated with worshipping Krishna as early as 400 BCE. *Kirtana* is most commonly used by the devotees (*bhaktas*) of Krishna. Singing the names of Krishna is universal among Krishna devotees, although the style of singing and presentation may differ. The *Varkari* saints of Maharashtra are known to have composed and sung *kirtans*. The *Bhagavata katha* or *Harikatha* involves only one narrator, while the *Burrakatha* performances usually contain three performers: two supporting performers accompany the central narrator with musical instruments such as drums. The central narrator of *Burrakatha* also uses a stringed musical instrument similar to *kirtana* performance. Closely allied forms of this art form in southern India are *bhagavatakatha* (Karnataka, Andhra Pradesh, and Tamilnadu), *harikatha, burra katha* (Andhra Pradesh), and *kirtana* (Maharashtra, Andhra Pradesh, Karnataka, and north India). All of these art forms are not stationary but nomadic. Unlike the *Bhagavatamela*, they do not require a particular place for performance. The performance is constant but evolving. The singers move from house to house and village to village singing their *puranas* and *kirtans*. *Bhagavatars* use few musical instruments, but rely on their own oratorical skills to bring the events of the *Bhagavan* Krishna's story to life. Although poems are sung in literary Telugu, Kannada, Marathi, Sanskrit, or Tamil, the meaning is conveyed in simple words spoken by the common people. Although the singers are known by a variety of names such as *haridasus, kirtankars, bhagavatars*, and so on, their main avocation is singing the names of God in general or Krishna stories in particular for the public. *Haridasus* are Vaishnava followers of the Madhva tradition, mostly patronized by the Vijayanagara Empire, and are found in south India, including Karnataka,

---

Padavalis **and** Padas

Padavalis, commonly composed and sung in Bengali, are said to have originated with the poets Candidasa and Jayadeva. This tradition of singing the praises of Krishna is also prevalent in Andhra Pradesh. Numerous *padakartas* (composers of *padas*) including Annamayya, Kshetrayya, and Tyagaraja have distinguished themselves through their compositions. The *Muvvagopala Padalu* of Kshetrayya illustrates the childhood plays (*lilas*) of Krishna.

Andhra Pradesh, and Tamilnadu. *Haridasus* are mostly male, itinerant spiritual singers performing at individual households, mostly in informal settings similar in nature to the *Baols* of north India and the *kirtankars* of Maharashtra, while the *bhagavatars* can be either male or female and perform to audiences at a temple or in an auditorium in a formal setting. Singing *kirtanas* is also one of the special features associated with the Caitanya Vaishnava tradition. Caitanya himself composed and sang *kirtans*. *Samaj gayan* is a highly ritualized singing tradition that is a specialized form of *kirtan* singing commonly associated with the Haridasi and Radhavallabha traditions. *Pada Kirtan* is one of the most common modes of worshipping or meditating on Krishna.

See also: Bhakti; Music and Krishna; Performing Arts and Krishna; *Samaj Gayan*; *Varkari* Tradition

Further Reading

Hate, N., and G. N. Koparkar. 1982. *Kirtanachi Prayog Prakriya*. Pune, India: Kirtan Mahavidyalaya Prakashan.

Kelkar, M., and K. Mahabal. 2007. *Kirtanrang*. Mumbai, India: Akhil Bharatiya Kirtan Sanstha.

Koparkar, G. N. (2000). *Katha Haridasanchi*. Pune, India: Kirtan Mahavidyalaya Prakashan.

KRISHNA

see Biography of Krishna; Birth and Early Childhood of Krishna; Childhood of Krishna in Brindavan; Christianity and Krishna; Death of Krishna; Eight Wives of Krishna; Historical Krishna; Islam and Krishna; Jainism and Krishna

KRISHNATTAM

Krishnattam (dance of Krishna) is a ritual dance drama performed as an offering to Guruvayurappa in Guruvayur, Kerala. The *Krishnattam* is performed by only one troupe based at the Guruvayur Krishna temple in Kerala. The *Krishnattam* has its origins in the story of the *Krishnagiti* and the *Narayaniyam*, written in the early 1600s in Kerala, which was adopted for eight plays based on the *Bhagavata-purana* narration of Krishna. Manavedan (1595–1658) composed the *Krishnattam* plays, which are commonly performed in the Guruvayur temple. The plays are the *Avatara, Kaliyamardana, Rasakrida, Kamsavadha, Svayamvara, Banayuddha, Vivida Vadha,* and the *Svargarohana.* The first eight plays of the *Krishnattam* tradition, not including the *Svargarohana,* are known as the *Krishnagiti.* The *Krishnattam* is performed as an offering and temple ritual. The theme of the *Krishnattam* is closely tied to the wishes of the devotees. For example, episodes of Krishna's childhood are enacted in relation to a devotee's wish for offspring. Hence, similar to *puja* offered by the devotee, the dances could be offered as a ritual of *upacara* (*seva*).

See also: Ankiya Nat; Bhagavatapurana; Guruvayurappa and Guruvayur Temple; *Kirtana; Kuchipudi; Lila; Manipuri* Dance

Further Reading
Ashton-Sikora, M. B. 1997. *Krishnattam*. Oxford: Oxford and IBH Publishing.

KUCHIPUDI

The *Kuchipudi* style of dance was created by Siddhendra Yogi in the village of Kuchipudi in Andhra Pradesh, from which it derives its name. Initially, *Kuchipudi natyam* was only practiced and performed by men; however, currently both men and women can learn and perform it. The *Kuchipudi* dance was created as a devotion to Krishna, and the most popular and commonly performed *Kuchipudi* dances are *Bhamakalapam* and *Krishnalila tarangini*. *Bhamakalapam* is a dance based on Krishna and Satyabhama's love, their separation, and the anxiety and jealousy of Satyabhama, while *Krishnalila tarangini* is based on the *Raasalila* episode of the *Bhagavatapurana*.

Siddhendra Yogi

Siddhendra Yogi (1500s) was the founder of the *Kuchipudi* dance style in Andhra Pradesh. The town of Kuchipudi, in the Krishna district, is located about twenty-one miles away from Vijayawada, the district capital. Siddhendra Yogi is the composer of the most distinguished dance *Kuchipudi*, the *Bhamakalapam*.

See also: Bhagavatapurana; Raasalila

Further Reading
Hanna, J. L. 2003. "Aesthetics—Whose Notions of Appropriateness and Competency, What Are They, and How Do We Know? (Dance)." *World of Music* 45 (3): 29–55.
Kothari, S. 1983. "The Kuchipudi Dance-Drama Tradition." *Dance Research Annual* (14): 120–125.
Kothari, S. 1997. "Kuchipudi: The Dance-Drama Tradition Came into Being as a Result of the *Bhakti* Movement." *Ballet International* 7: 44–45.
Kothari, S. 2001. *Kuchipudi: Indian Classical Dance Art*. New Delhi: Abhinav Publications.

KULASEKHARA ALVAR

Kulasekhara *alvar* (the royal *alvar*) is regarded as an *amsa* of the *kaustubha*, a gem on the chest of Vishnu. Kulasekhara was a prince of the Chera dynasty, proficient in Sanskrit and Tamil. Kulasekhara *alvar* lived during 800 CE in Tondaimandalam and was an ardent devotee of Vishnu. Very scant information is available from historical sources about the cause of his transformation and initiation into Vaishnavism. For most of his life he lived near Kanchi, dedicating his life to Vishnu.

Mukundamala

Kulasekhara *alvar*'s devotional prayer, the *Mukundamala,* is a *stotra* (praise poem) text composed in Sanskrit. Kulasekhara *alvar* praises Krishna in concise, beautifully composed verses that are lyrical when recited. As a *stotra* text it focuses on concise presentation rather than detailed treatment of plot. Hence the exploits (*lilas*) of Krishna are presented in short verses, emulating true devotion and passionate worship of Krishna. Kulasekhara completed *Mukundamala* at the Srirangam temple.

Kulasekhara wrote *Mukundamala* in Sanskrit. He composed the *Perumal Tirumoli* in Tamil, which was included in the *Nalayira Divya Prabandham.* The *Perumal Tirumoli* contains 105 verses, roughly divided into 10 decads. In the first five verses, Kulasekhara praises Ranganatha, his favorite god of the Srirangam temple; in the next five decads he praises the lords of Tirumala-Tirupathi (Andhra Pradesh), Chidambaram, and Tiruvangadu (Kerala). The main subjects of his texts are Rama's mother Kausalya and Krishna's mother Devaki, who endured separation from their divine children. Kulasekhara's verses express the pain of separation Rama's mother faced during his exile, as well as the pain of separation Devaki faced while living in prison awaiting her son's return.

See also: Alvars; Ranganatha; Srirangam Temple; Srivaishnavism; Venkatesvara

Further Reading

Chari, S. M. S. 1997. *Philosophy and Theistic Mysticism of the Alvars.* Delhi: Motilal Banarsidas.

KUMBHANDAS GORVA (1468–1582)

Kumbhandas's life is recounted in the *Caurasivaishnavon ki Varta* as one of the eminent *bhaktas* of Braj and a follower of Vallabha. When Vallabha found the image of Srinathji in Govardhan, he constructed a small temple and appointed Haridas Chauhan to conduct daily *sevas.* Kumbhandas was also part of the temple *sevas,* performing singing and music for Lord Srinathji as part of the daily rituals. Although Kumbhandas was ten years older than Vallabha, he was one of Vallabha's first disciples. Kumbhandas, along with his son Caturbhujdas, is also recognized as a member of the *Ashtachap* poets of Braj. Kumbhandas was a farmer from Jamnauta. Well known as the *bhakta* and poet of Krishna, he is the contemporary of other poet *bhaktas,* including *Haritray* (The Three Haris). Hit Harivams is mentioned as requesting Kumbhandas to compose a poem for *Svaminiji* (Radha) and Krishna's *lila* (play) in Braj. Several incidents of his life are mentioned in his biographies to demonstrate his strong devotional attachment to Krishna, such as his son's death, and his refusal to join Vitthalnath on a tour to raise funds. Although he was forced to visit the court of the Mughal emperor on his invitation to sing, he only did it at the compulsion of the Mughal courtiers. He also refused to visit Raja

Man Singh, for he refused to part with his beloved god even for a day. His biographies also narrate his devotion to Krishna and his refusal to part with Krishna for any reason including wealth.

See also: Braj *Parikrama*; Brindavan; Vallabha Tradition; Vitthalnath

Further Reading

Barz, R. 2007. "Kumbhan Das: The Devotee as Salt of the Earth." In *Krishna: A Source Book*, edited by E. Bryant. Oxford: Oxford University Press.

Mathur, S. 1968. "Bhakt Kumbhandasji." *Sri Vallabh Vigyan* 8 (3): 12–15.

LILA

Lila, a Sanskrit word, simply means play, dalliance, sport, or merely a pastime, but this word is infused with important religious connotations in Hinduism when it is used in the theological and philosophical context. *Lila* is also closely related to other words in Sanskrit such as *keli*, words that are also used in theological contexts, but not used as commonly as *lila* in connection with the divine. Any act of the divine on Earth is considered to be *lila,* since the activity is devoid of a motive on the part of the divine. The god participates in the play as an actor participates in acting a role in the theater. According to *lila,* God's role in the world is similar to that of an actor in a play. The actor is not the actual character being portrayed on stage, but a different individual. For example, in the *Brajlilas* Krishna is a child, but in reality he is the incarnation of the supreme God, Vishnu. Hence, his actions (*lilas*) acquire divine meaning. *Lila* has had a dense theological meaning since its first occurrence in Badarayana's *Brahamasutras* (also known as the *Vedantasutras*), while noting the creation as mere sport for Brahma (*Brahmasutra* II 1.32–33). Although *lila* is an aspect of the divine, its most elaborate development is found in the sacred texts of Krishna, expressed most imaginatively in dance, music, theater, and literary creations associated with Krishna. Krishna explicitly states in the *Bhagavadgita* that he does not need to take any action; even so, he engages in action (*Bhagavadgita* 3.22). Krishna descends to Earth as an *avatara* to destroy evil and restore dharma (*Bhagavadgita* 4.7–8). Krishna acts without purpose with regard to his earthly self, but with a divine purpose accorded by his divine self (*paramatma*). Everything he does on Earth is the purpose of his divine self, not the earthly self that is visible to everyone. He is not the innocent little child everyone sees in his *Brajlilas,* but the Lord accomplishing cosmic, protective, and ethical purposes of the divine. Hence Krishna's actions (*lilas*) should be seen as signifying a cosmic meaning rather than what is visible to the common eye at the moment. Several *lilas* of Krishna are, therefore, illusions (*maya*) that in fact establish a deeper and theologically significant meaning. Several *lilas* of Krishna are interpreted as such to explain inner theological definitions. The *Raasalila* (amorous play) of Krishna on autumn nights in Brindavan is one such example. At a cursory glance, it might seem like an adulterous extravagance on the part of Krishna; however, a deeper analysis makes it clear that it is a play of the divine self (*paramatma*) with the individual souls (*atmas*) that find release and ecstatic joy through such union. The *Gopis,* with their souls immersed in the thoughts of Krishna, are thus the elevated souls obtaining *sat-cit-ananda* (true eternal joy). Thus for the divine self it is an

expression of the joy within him, which is shared intimately with the individual souls.

Lila is a major aspect of the legend of Krishna. *Krishnalila* is a commemorative theater or dance-drama based on several such *lilas* of Krishna. *Krishnalila* plays are enacted to bring back the memory of *Brajlilas* by recreating it, and by helping devotees with the *manana* (remembering) and *smarana* (reciting) practices of bhakti, creating a meditative focus.

Due to these deeper theological and cosmological implications in the *lilas* of Krishna, many devotional schools consider it as a path to attain *moksha*. *Krishnalila*, followed through any of the bhakti methods such as remembering, listening, reciting, or singing, can help devotees attain inner peace and final *moksha*. The Caitanya Vaishnava tradition incorporates *lilasmarana* (remembering the *lilas*) as an im-

Watercolor representing *Raasalila* (dance) of delight from Bundi, Rajasthan, India, ca. 1675–1700. (Los Angeles County Museum of Art)

portant meditative technique. In fact, sixty-four *vaidhi* rituals outlined by Rupa *Gosvami* are designed to celebrate the various moments in the play of Krishna, known as *Brajlilas*. *Lila* is hence closely associated with Krishna, so it is used most commonly at festivals and in the theater, music, meditation, and ritual traditions associated with Krishna.

See also: Bhakti; Caitanya Vaishnavism; Krishna; *Maya*; Radha; Radhavallabha Tradition

Further Reading

Coomaraswamy, A. K. 1941. "Lila." *American Journal of Oriental Society* 61: 98–101.
Haberman, D. L. 1988. *Acting as a Way of Salvation.* Oxford: Oxford University Press.
Hawley, J. S. 1981. *At Play with Krishna.* Princeton: Princeton University Press.
Kinsley, D. R. 1979. *The Divine Player (A Study of Krishna Lila).* Delhi: Motilal Banarsidas.
Sax, W. S. 1997. "Fathers, Sons, and Rhinoceroses, and Garhwal Drama, '*Mahabharata*': Masculinity and Violence in the '*Pandav Lila*'." *Journal of the American Oriental Society* 117 (2): 278–293.

Schweig, G. M. 2005. *Dance of the Divine Love: The* Rasa Lila *from the Bhagavatapurana.* Princeton: Princeton University Press.

Schweig, G. 2007. *Bhagavad Gita*: San Francisco: Harper.

Srirama, M. 2004. "Dancing the Self: Personhood and Performance in the *Pandav Lila* of Garhwal." *Journal of Asian Studies* 63 (2): 540–541.

MADHURAKAVIALVAR
see Nammalvar and Madhurakavialvar

MADHVA
Madhva (1197–1280) was the founder of the *dvaita* (dualist) philosophy. The non-dualist *Brahma-Atma* unity (*advaita*) is the most commonly accepted philosophical tradition based on the teachings of the major *acaryas* of Hinduism, such as those of Shankara, the most important Hindu philosopher. However, as a dualist thinker, Madhva's influence can be seen in the numerous Vaishnava devotional traditions (*sampradayas*) of Braj, including the Radhavallabha and Caitanya traditions. Madhva's dualist philosophy establishes Vishnu as the superior and independent God. Although numerous biographies were written about Madhva soon after his death, the *Manimanjari* of Narayan Panditacarya contains the most exhaustive and authentic biography. Madhva is considered to be an incarnation of the god Vayu (God of Wind), son of Vishnu. This puts Madhva in indirect relationship with Vishnu as the direct incarnation of the god; he is known as a son of Vishnu.

Madhva was born near Udupi, Tulunadu, to Sivalli Brahmans in Karnataka. He was initially educated in the *advaita* classics. He was then appointed as the head of the *matha* known as Anandatirtha. Madhva was also commonly known by the name Anandatirtha in addition to his other name, Purnaprajna. Madhva traveled extensively through southern India meeting and debating some of the *advaitavadis,* followers of Ramanuja. According to Madhva's *dvaita* philosophy, God and the created

---

Udupi

Udupi became a sacred center for Krishna worship because of the temple of Krishna established there by Madhva *acarya*. The image of Krishna is one of the unique representations of Krishna's childhood play. He is portrayed holding the butter churn that he took from his mother Yashoda's hand. Madhva *acarya* discovered the image in the Indian Ocean, covered in a thick layer of clay (referred to as *Gopicandana*), which cleared off easily, revealing the image. The image is connected directly to Krishna in Dvaraka. It is said that Krishna had the image made for Rukmini because she requested an image of him in his childhood play. However, the image was lost when Dvaraka was submerged under the Indian Ocean at the end of the *Dvaparayuga*.

objects are two distinct entities. Madhva states, "There are two orders of Reality," the dependent and the independent. Madhva claims that God is the independent reality, while the rest of the universe, containing all that is not God, is dependent reality.

Madhva traveled across India widely preaching and expounding the principles of Vedanta and bhakti. He debated with philosophers and preachers of many religions across India, and he also learned Persian so he could understand and debate with the mullahs of his time.

Madhva was a prolific writer of thirty-seven primary works on Hindu philosophy and theology. His major theoretical treatise is the *Sarvamulagrantha*. He also wrote commentaries on important classical texts such as the *Bhagavadgita*, the *Anuvyakarana*, and the *Brahmasutrabhasya*. Madhva accomplished the monumental task of analyzing the Hindu texts from the perspective of the dualist philosophy he proposed through his analytical commentaries and his theoretical compendium.

For the followers of Krishna, Madhva's *Vishnutattvanirnaya* and his commentary on the *Bhagavatapurana* are important. The *Krishnamritamaharnava* is a 242-verse text of praises of Krishna. Madhvacarya founded eight *mutts* (*mathas*) to continue the *dvaita* legacy after Madhva, and he also established the Srikrishna temple in Udupi, Karnataka. Madhva expounded Indian classical texts in a new way of understanding that was not common in India during the first millennium CE. His unique contribution to Hindu philosophy and theology is different from the commonly established traditions.

See also: Advaita; Bhakti; Caitanya Vaishnavism; Madhva *Sampradaya*; Radha; Radhavallabha Tradition; Vallabha

Further Reading

Puthiadam, L. 1985. *Vishnu the Ever Free: A Study of the Madhva Concept of God*. Madurai: Arul Anandar College.

Rau, S., and H. S. Olcott. 1900. *The Dvaita Philosophy of Madhvacarya*. Madras: Theosophical Society.

Sarma, D. 2003. "Madhvacarya and Vyasatirtha." *Journal of Vaishnava Studies* 15 (2): 145–168.

Sharma, B. N. K. 1986. *Philosophy of Sri Madhvacarya*. Delhi: Motilal Banarsidas.

MADHVA *SAMPRADAYA*

The Madhva *sampradaya* (tradition), also known as the *dvaita sampradaya* (dualist tradition), was founded by Madhvacarya (1238–1317). Madhva *sampradaya* is also popularly knowns as Brahma *sampradaya*. Madhva is considered the incarnation of Vayu (the Wind God). Madhva contends that Vedanta is not interpreted correctly through the *advaita* (nondualism) philosophy, and he proposed *dvaita* (dualism) as the rightful philosophical basis for understanding Vedanta. He supports the theological conception of Vishnu as the highest god, and characterizes him as the beginning and end of creation similar to the other Vaishnava traditions. However, *jivas* and the universe are distinct and real, unlike the *advaita* philosophy, which considers the Brahma (universal soul) as real and creation (*jagam*) as imaginary and illusory. The creator and the created universe are two distinct and separate entities. The creator is superior to the creation, and hence *moksha* according to the Madhva tradition comes only from the grace of Vishnu, but not from effort. The Madhva system considers the relation between God and the created universe to be *bhedabheda* (similar and different). His devotion to Krishna is governed by his understanding of *dvaita*, and the Madhva tradition places *bhedabheda* and grace at the center of its practice. The Madhva tradition also proposes eternal release and damnation. Those who attain eternal release (*moksha*) and those subjected to eternal damnation are exempted from birth and rebirth.

Madhva found an icon of Krishna encased in mud in the ocean one day while he was performing his morning bath and *sandhya* rituals. He cleaned off the mud and installed the icon in the Balakrishna temple in Udupi, where it is still worshipped today. He also established a *mutt/matha* (monastery) there, and seven other *mutts* elsewhere in India, all of which are referred to as a group: the *ashtamathas* (the eight *mutts*). Madhva also ordained eight monks, nominating them as *svami* (chief preceptor) of each *mutt*. The eight *mutts* are known by the names of the places where they are located: Palimar, Admar (Adamar), Krishnapur, Puttige, Shirur (Sirur), Kaniyur (Kanur), Pejawar, and Sode *mutts*. Madhva also ordained his younger brother, Vishnusvami, and nominated him as the *svami* of Sode *mutt*. Initially, while Madhva was alive, he acted as the leader of the eight *mutts*, overseeing all eight *svamis*. However, he established a *paryaya* (rotation) system to carry on the leadership after him. According to this system, each of the eight *mutts* acts as leader for a term of two years. Therefore each *mutt* gets the leadership for two years once every sixteen years. Although several *mutts* of the Madhva tradition are established with Krishna-centered devotion, Udupi remains the most important center of the Madhva tradition. Bhakti is a very important path of self-realization in Madhva's Vedanta philosophy. *Karmayoga* (path of action) in itself is not sufficient in attaining self-realization, but needs devotion (*Bhakti yoga*) to be fruitful. Followers of Madhva *Sampradaya* are commonly encountered in the western Indian states of Karnataka and Maharashtra. Although primary texts of the Madhva tradition are written in Sanskrit, numerous commentaries and additional texts on philosophy are written in Kannada, the regional language of Karnataka.

See also: Advaita; *Dvaita*; Madhva

Further Reading

Rao, K. R. 2012. "Complementarity of Advaita Non-dualism and Yoga Dualism in Indian Psychology." *Journal of Consciousness Studies* 19 (9–10): 121–142.

Sarma, D. 2003. *An Introduction to Madhva Vedanta*. Burlington, MA: Ashgate.

Sharma, B. N. K. 2008. *History of the Dvaita School of Vedanta and Its Literature*. Delhi: Motilal Banarsidas.

MAHABHARATA

Krishna appears in the *Mahabharata* as the supreme deity showing his universal form (*visvarupa*) twice, repeatedly praised by the most renowned *Mahabharata*

Mahabharata in Persian

The Mughal emperor Akbar commissioned the translation of the *Mahabharata* into Persian. The abridged free translation has the title *Razmnama*. One of the special features of the *Razmnama* is the colorful paintings of Krishna accompanying the narrative of the *Mahabharata*. The manuscript, now preserved in the Jaipur palace museum, depicts important events of Krishna's life in the paintings. The *Harivamsa*, considered an appendix to the *Mahabharata*, was also translated in a separate abridged volume with fourteen illustrations as part of the Persian translation project of the Mughals.

---

characters, including Bhishma, in the most exalting words. In the *Mahabharata*, Krishna performs a number of miracles, including saving Draupadi from the humiliation of disrobing in the Kaurava court, and most importantly delivers the preeminent text of Hinduism, the *Bhagavadgita*, to Arjuna at the beginning of the *Mahabharata* war. The Krishna of the *Mahabharata* is the fully evolved Krishna, determined to establish dharma, unlike the playful child Krishna one encounters in Brindavan and Vraja, eloquently described in the *Harivamsa*, a *purana* text considered to be an appendix of the *Mahabharata*. The adult Krishna captures the imagination and inspires literary and artistic expressions as much as the child Krishna. Krishna's driving of Arjuna's chariot during the war described in the *Mahabharata* is one of the most frequently depicted images of Krishna from the *Mahabharata*, followed by the depiction of his *visvarupa* form and his delivering the *Bhagavadgita* to Arjuna on the battlefield of Kurukshetra.

The *Mahabharata* is the longest epic in the world, containing about 230,000 verses. Several versions of the *Mahabharata* are available, although the critical edition of the *Mahabharata* published by the Bhandarkar Oriental Research Society is considered to be the most authoritative text for research purposes. The final composition of the *Mahabharata* in written form is dated between 300 BCE and 200 CE, although it might have existed in oral tradition since 1500–1000 BCE in India. Krishna appears in almost every episode of the *Mahabharata*, especially during the Pandavas' trials and tribulations. Krishna is related to the Pandavas through his father Vasudeva, a cousin of Kunthi, mother of the Pandavas. Krishna and Vasudeva visited the grief-stricken Pandava family after the death of Pandu during their exile in the Himalaya Mountains. Subsequent to the death of Pandu, Vasudeva had invited Kunthi and the Pandavas to Vraja to live with her maternal family. However, Kunthi chose to take the children to Hastina and raise them in the Kuru household. Krishna was present, but incognito, at the *svayamvara* of Draupadi, where Arjuna won Draupadi. Although the Pandavas were disguised, Krishna believed that it must have been Arjuna and his siblings attending the *svayamvara*. Krishna followed them to their home to confirm that his conjecture was right. It so happened that the Pandavas escaped from a burning wax house in Varanavata, where they were vacationing on the advice of Dhritarashtra, their uncle, the blind

The chariot of stone, at Vitthala Temple at Hampi, is a representation of the divine chariot of Vishnu. Its wheels decorated with lotus motifs can be revolved, representing movement in place. The chariot is situated in front of the *maha mandapa* of the Vitthala Temple. Vitthala Temple is the most ornate temple of Vijayanagara Empire located in Hampi, in the Karnataka state of India. (Dr. Pramod Bansode/Dreamstime.com)

king of the Kuru Empire. The house had been set on fire by his son Duryodhana. Krishna noticed that the rivalry between the cousins, the Pandavas and the Kauravas, was taking a turn for the worse, and therefore advised the Pandavas to stake their claim to a share of the kingdom to protect themselves from Duryodhana. Krishna then supported the Pandavas as they lay claim to their share of the Kuru Empire, while Duryodhana, out of his arrogance, only agreed to give them the Khandava forest. Krishna, along with Arjuna, burned down the Khandava forest, where the Pandavas had built a great city and fortress and invited all of their relatives, friends, and family for the inauguration. Two untoward incidents happened in the Pandava assembly: Krishna beheaded Sisupala in the full assembly for unruly behavior and for hurling abuse at Krishna; Draupadi laughed and humiliated Duryodhana, who became lost while visiting the palace. Duryodhana vowed to take revenge on Draupadi for that humiliation and cleverly executed a dice game, subjecting the Pandavas to fourteen years of exile, after attempting to disrobe Draupadi in the assembly; however, she was rescued by Krishna miraculously. Although Krishna was not present in the Kaurava court at the time of this event, he released an infinite number of saris for Draupadi in response to her pleas for help, as Dusshasana proceeded to disrobe her. As a result, an infinite number of saris issued forth from the single robe Draupadi was wearing until a tired Dusshasana stopped his attempts to disrobe her. Krishna visited the Pandavas in exile and supported them in their peace negotiations upon their return. Failing that, Krishna supported the Pandavas in their war, in every way contributing to their success. Krishna gave the vision of his *visvarupa* (universal form) for the first time during the peace negotiations, infuriated by Duryodhana's inappropriate attempt to capture and entrap Krishna, an envoy. Sanjaya, narrating the progress of the war to Dhritarashtra, also saw this second vision of the *visvarupa* indirectly, as it was given to Arjuna. The *Bhagavadgita*, a discourse given to Arjuna at this time on the battlefield of Kurukshetra, thus became part of the narration as retold by Sanjaya to Dhritarashtra. These two events established Krishna as the supreme God, Vishnu himself, although his status as supreme deity is evident in each book of the *Mahabharata*. The *Mahabharata* establishes several concepts of divinity connected to Krishna, such as *Narayana, Naranarayana (Krishna Arjuna), vyuha, avatara,* and *atma-paramatma*.

See also: Arjuna; *Avatara; Bhagavadgita;* Bhima; Draupadi; Jarasandha; Narayana; Pandavas; Vishnu; *Visvarupa*

Further Reading

Austin, C. 2011. "Draupadi's Fall: Snowballs, Cathedrals, and Synchronous Readings of the *Mahabharata*." *International Journal of Hindu Studies* 15 (1): 111–137.

Austin, C. 2013. "Narrative Art in the *Mahabharata*: The Adi Parva." *International Journal of Hindu Studies* 17 (1): 87–92.

Baltutis, M. 2011. "Reinventing Orthopraxy and Practicing Worldly *Dharma*: Book 14 of the *Mahabharata*." *International Journal of Hindu Studies* 15 (1): 55–100.

Brook, P., and J. Kalb. 2010. "The *Mahabharata* Twenty-Five Years Later." *Paj-a Journal of Performance and Art* (96): 63–71.

Buehnemann, G. 2013. "Bhimasena as Bhairava in Nepal." *Zeitschrift Der Deutschen Morgenlandischen Gesellschaft* 163 (2): 455–476.

Lutgendorf, Philip. 2012. "Epic Nation: Reimagining the *Mahabharata* in the Age of the Empire." *Journal of Contemporary Asia* 42 (2): 338–340.

Reich, T. 2011. "Ends and Closures in the *Mahabharata*." *International Journal of Hindu Studies* 15 (1): 9–53.

Vassilkov, Y. 2011. "Indian 'Hero-Stones' and the Earliest Anthropomorphic Stelae of the Bronze Age." *Journal of Indo-European Studies* 39 (1–2): 194–229.

Wang, H. 2012. "Research on the Theme of Curse and Prayer in *Mahabharata*." *Foreign Literature Studies* 34 (2): 63–71.

West, E. 2010. "A Quartet of Graeco-Aryan Demi-Goddesses: Leukothea, Eidothea, Ulupi and Varga." *Journal of Indo-European Studies* 38 (1–2): 147–171.

MANDALA

A mandala is linked to ritual space, with theological significance centered on Krishna, and is generally referred to as *Vrajamandala*. The *Vrajamandala* is the idyllic natural setting of Vraja, where Krishna reveled and played with *Gopas* and *Gopis*, pleasing one and all alike. A mandala diagram is a miniscule representation of the world of Krishna in a drawing. A mandala is normally drawn with Krishna in the center, surrounded in the first circle by close associates, followed by the next intimate associates represented in the next circle. The arrangement of the inner circle and concentric circles thereafter does not necessarily represent kin association but closeness in divine union, represented by souls related to Krishna.

Sacred geography and holy saints are mapped on the mandala in a circular diagrammatic fashion. The *Vrajamandala* is in the shape of a lotus with Brindavan at its center, while other sacred places, groves, and tanks around Mathura are represented as petals on the lotus around Brindavan in this conception of the *Vrajamandala*.

The mandala also maps the devotees' lineages connected to Krishna. Each community of Krishna is seen to represent a petal of *Goloka*, a heaven on earth with its own mandala. Krishna devotional tradition is also familiar with the mandala of Caitanya, called *pancatatvamandala*, commonly used by the followers of the Caitanya tradition. Caitanya is represented in the center in the *pancatatvamandala*, along with Nityananda, Srivasa Pandita, Gadadharadasa, and Advaitacharya flanking his four sides as four petals.

The *Vrajamandala* is represented in the form of a lotus, considered to be the yogic meditative device for the eternal activities of the holy Brindavan; in other words, it represents the eternal *Krishnalila*. In this mandala, Radha and Krishna are made up of two interlocking triangles (with the masculine pointing up and the feminine pointing down) in the shape of a star. The interlocking stars indicate a union marked by simultaneous distinction and nondistinction (*acintyabhedabheda*). This triangle is encircled by three concentric circles representing Krishna in the first circle, Krishna and the *Gopis* in the second circle, and Krishna with Radha as well as the *Gopis* in the third. The third circle therefore replicates everything that was in the circles before it. The mandala diagram represents the esoteric connection of a devotee to Krishna through the concept of the Krishna mandala, which is then spread to several of the petals in concentric circles of eight each, in two or more concentric circles. Similar mandalas are also commonly prepared in the case of Vaishnava saints, such as Caitanya *Mahaprabhu*, who is thought of as Krishna himself (*svayam Krishna*). The Caitanya mandala is very similar to the Krishna mandala in concept and representation. The basic outline of the mandala noted above also serves as the basis for the *Yantra* and the *Yogapitha* representations. Such *Yantras* are also used as efficacious and powerful representations of the divine. The Krishna mandala represents divine Krishna with his accompanying followers in the *dhama* (divine world) of Krishna. This concept of representing the divine world through the geometric design of the mandala takes another form in the *Vastupurusha* mandala, which is drawn on paper and laid on the ground to geographic scale before temple construction begins, thus implanting the divine mandala in the temple grounds. The mandala surpasses its geometrical meaning and acquires deep theological and divine meaning in Hinduism, and especially in Krishna devotion.

See also: Braj *Parikrama*; Brindavan; Caitanya Vaishnavism; *Gopas* and *Gopis*; *Lila*; Mathura; Radha; Vallabha Tradition

Further Reading

Brauen, M. 2009. *Mandala: Sacred Circle in Tibetal Buddhism*. Stuttgart: Arnoldsche Art Publishers; New York: Rubin Museum of Art.

Tucci, G. 1969. *The Theory and Practice of the Mandala.* Translated by A. H. Broderick, 1973. London: Rider; New York: Dover.

MANIPURI DANCE

The *Manipuri* dance originated in the state of Manipur in India in the late sixteenth century as part of the bhakti religion centered on devotion to Krishna. The term "*Manipuri* dance" encompasses several individual dance and drama styles of Manipur such as the *Nupipala* (performed by women), *Ojhapala, Lai Haroba, Thambal Chongbi, Meitei Jagoi,* and *Pena.* The *Lai Haroba* is a forty-day ritual performance involving a congregational gathering. The *Pena* is a unique storytelling tradition of Manipur involving a drum and solo performer called the *Wari Leeba.* The *Meitaie Jagoi* consists of five distinct *Rasa* dances related to the five seasons of the year, which are based on different events of Radha and Krishna's *Rasa* dance narrated in the *Bhagavatapurana.* Devotional practices centered on Radha and Krishna, especially the *Raasalila,* form the basic subject of the *Manipuri* dances. Krishna's play forms the central theme of the performances of the *Manipuri* dance-theater. The most important dance-theater of *Manipuri* dance is *Raasalila,* a purely religious subject based on Krishna's play. *Raasalila* dance is choreographed with Vaishnava *padavalis,* set to music with traditional *Manipuri* musical instruments such as the *pungi, kartal, sembong,* harmonium, and so on. Although the *Manipuri* dances originated in the devotional religion of the sixteenth century, the dances are also commonly performed by children in secular settings such as schools or public theaters. Maharaja Bhagyacandra (1759–1798) composed three *Raasalilas* popularly known as the *Maha Ras, Basanta Ras,* and *Kunja Ras,* which are performed regularly in the Govindaji temple in Imphal. King Bhagyacandra is also credited with designing the costumes of the *Manipuri* dance and organizing the musical tone and dance moves. The *Manipuri* dance uses graceful movements of the body, with hand and facial gestures. Foot movements are subtle, unlike those in other traditional dances of India such as the *Bharatanatyam.*

The *Sansenba* and *Gosthalila* have their origins in the courtly arts of Manipur in the mid-eighteenth century (1779) and owe their origin to the Krishna devotional tradition. However, these dances also flourished beyond the courtly culture of eastern India. The *Gosthalila* performances, which are among the popular classical dances of India, are also popular outside of Manipur. Nobel Laureate Ravindranath Tagore is said to have watched one of the performances of the *Gosthalila* and invited the eminent performer of *Manipuri* dance, Guru Naba Kumar, to introduce the subject of *Manipuri* dance in the university and teach the *Gosthalila* at Shantiniketan, a university founded by Tagore, in Bengal. Guru Nabakumar, joined by Guru Amubi Singh, another eminent *Manipuri* dance teacher, helped develop the *Santiniketan* style of dance, attracting popular attention to the *Manipuri* and *Kathakali* style of dances. Guru Amubi Singh was a Vaishnava devotee of Krishna in the Caitanya tradition, who had spent part of his life at the Radhakund temple in Vrindavan. With his background in the Meitei culture and his exceptional talent in *Samkirtana* and *Rasa* dance, Guru Amubi transformed and imparted the pure art of the *Manipuri* dance to many of his student disciples.

The *Sanseba* and *Gosthalila* also evolved as children's theater in modern India, with children enacting the playful life of cowherd Krishna, based on the *Bhagavatapurana* narratives. *Manipuri* language and typical style of dress dominate these performances, which developed from the regional style of dance centered on Krishna devotion. In addition to *Manipuri* verses and compositions, *Manipuri* dance also uses Sanskrit, Brajbhasha, and Bengali compositions in its performances. The *Gitagovinda* of Jayadeva and Candidasa's poems are also commonly used in *Manipuri* dance.

Professional *Manipuri* dancers in traditional attire, enacting the love story of Lord Krishna and Radha, during a national dance festival in India. (Mangalika/Dreamstime.com)

See also: *Bhagavatapurana*; Candidasa; *Gitagovinda*; Jayadeva; *Krishnattam*; *Lila*; *Raasalila*; Radha

Further Reading

Doshi, S. 1989. *Dances of Manipur: The Classical Tradition.* New Delhi: Marg Publications.

MANTRA

A mantra is also referred to as *mahamantra* when it is required as a verse for regular recitation. It is an esoteric formula imparted by a preceptor (*acarya* or guru) to a disciple in a number of bhakti traditions associated with Krishna. The sanctity of the divine word and the proper way of saying it are typical characteristics of Hinduism, as noted in the *Vedas*, and also of Hindu-affiliated religious practices such as Buddhism, Jainism, and Sikhism. Although defined in various ways by the commentators of the *Vedas*, the Vedanta *acaryas*, the central purpose of the mantra can be understood as a formula to be used in sacrifices, rituals, *pujas, sevas*, and meditation, to serve the purpose of the devotee/religious performer by allowing her or him to achieve a closeness to God and to his or her desired goals in life. However, the mantra has to be uttered in the right way, for saying it in the wrong way can produce exactly the opposite—negative results rather than positive. Mantras possess immense power and provide efficacious results, but only when used in the proper context. Devoid of the proper method, the words themselves do not have any meaning and do not result in anything positive for the devotee.

The bhakti traditions associated with Krishna adopt popular forms of worship along with esoteric mantras, which are taught by the guru to the disciple. While some traditions, such as the Caitanya Vaishnava tradition, impart a single mantra to all devotees, leaving it up to the devotees to attain perfection, others, such as the Haridasi tradition, distinguish three levels of devotees by imparting different mantras in recognition of each level of devotional achievement. To protect the sanctity of the sacred words of the mantra, according to the Vallabha tradition, the *mahamantra* can be imparted only by the male successors of Vallabha, genealogically related to him through his sons. Hence, only the male successors of Vallabha can initiate disciples into the Vallabha tradition.

See also: Bhakti; Caitanya Vaishnavism; Haridasi *Sampradaya*; ISKCON; *Seva*; Vallabha Tradition

Further Reading

Amodio, B. A. 1992. "The World Made of Sound, Whitehead and Pythagorean Harmonics in the Context of Veda and the Science of *Mantra*." *Journal of Dharma* 17 (3): 233–266.

Burchett, P. E. 2008. "The 'Magical' Language of *Mantra*." *Journal of the American Academy of Religion* 76 (4): 807–843.

Chen, P. Y. 2005. "Buddhist Chant, Devotional Song, and Commercial Popular Music: From Ritual to Rock *Mantra*." *Ethnomusicology* 49 (2): 266–286.

Chethimattam, J. B. 1984. "Religious Monograms and *Mantras*." *Journal of Dharma* 9 (2): 142–149.

Cousens, D. 2009. "Bringing the Gods to Mind: *Mantra* and Ritual in Early Indian Sacrifice." *South Asia: Journal of South Asian Studies* 32 (3): 558–559.

McDermott, A. C. S. 1975. "Towards a Pragmatics of *Mantra* Recitation." *Journal of Indian Philosophy* 3 (3–4): 283–298.

Paradoux, A. 1990. *Vac: The Concept of Word in Selected Hindu Tantras.* Albany: SUNY Press.

Thimalsina, S. 2005. "Meditating *Mantras*: Meaning and Visualization in *Tantric* Literature." In *Theory and Practice of Yoga*, edited by K. A. Jacobson, 213–235. Leiden: Brill.

Wheelock, W. 1980. "A Taxonomy of the *Mantras* in the New-Moon and Full-Moon Sacrifice." *History of Religions* 19 (4): 349–369.

MATHURA

Mathura is one of the foremost sacred places associated with Krishna, since it is his birthplace. The greater Mathura region, known as the *Mathuramandala,* functions as the early realm for Krishna's life as well as the representation of his divine realm on Earth. Mathura is on the right bank of the Yamuna River, about ninety miles south of Delhi, the capital city of India, and thirty miles north of Agra, the legendary capital of the Mughal Empire. Prehistoric habitations are noted at the site of Mathura and its surroundings, which are dated from at least 5000 BCE. However, its rise to popularity begins with the legendary Shurasena Empire of the Yadavas, into which dynasty Krishna was born. Mathura was sacked by Aurangzeb in the late seventeenth century. Aurangzeb destroyed numerous temples, which could be one of the reasons for the lack of historical continuity in Mathura. Numerous

---

Ugrasena

Visitors to Mathura are greeted by a statue of seated Ugrasena in the center of the town. Ugrasena is the grandfather of Krishna and the father of Kamsa and Devaki, the mother of Krishna. After the death of Kamsa, Krishna freed his parents and crowned Ugrasena as the king of Mathura.

---

ancient monuments were excavated from Mathura, dated to as early as 300 BCE. However, a despoliation of sacred places between 1300 and 1500 CE is noted in several pilgrimage manuals, since pilgrimages and several festivals were banned by the successive Muslim states established in Delhi from the early thirteenth century, which controlled most of the Mathura region. It was only after Akbar lifted the ban on pilgrimages in the late sixteenth century that sacred places in Mathura were revived and new temples were constructed in the well-known places associated with the life of Krishna. However, this religious freedom was short lived as persecution of Hindus and destruction of temples resumed with Aurangzeb in the seventeenth century.

Mathura is the nucleus of *Brajbhumi* (the land of Braj) and is a sacred spot on the Braj *parikrama*. The sacred region of Mathura is designated as *Mathuramandala*, including the sacred places in and around Mathura that are connected with the life of Krishna.

The most important temple in Mathura is the Krishna *Janmabhumi* (place of birth) temple in the *Janmabhumi* temple complex, marked by a marble pavilion. An underground cellar of this pavilion is marked as the exact place of Krishna's birth, said to be the prison where Devaki and Vasudeva were imprisoned. On the western side of the *Janmabhumi* temple is a quadrangular tank of solid masonry known as Potrakund. The ancient temple at the Krishna *Janmabhumi* was destroyed and a mosque was built over the ruins of the temple during the raids by a general of the Mughal emperor Aurangzeb. Now, a mosque adjoins the restored temple at the *Janmabhumi* temple complex.

The Dvarakadhish temple is another important religious site in Mathura. Gokulpati Singh, a treasurer of the Scindhia dynasty of Gwalior, built this temple in 1815. The Dvarakadhish temple is maintained and administered by followers of the Vallabha tradition (*Pushtimarga*); hence the temple contains a number of paintings and art associated with this tradition. The interior walls of the Dvarakadhish temple courtyard are painted with magnificent murals depicting episodes from the life of Krishna and Radhakrishna as well as Krishna listening to Surdas singing his poetry. The *Garbhagriha* (sanctum) is covered by a domed ceiling, unlike the other temple ceilings usually seen in Mathura, giving it the appearance of a palace, which also demonstrates the influence of the Vallabha tradition, in which a temple is designated as *haveli* (palace).

Walking down to the Yamuna River, one reaches Vishramghat (the stairs of rest), so-called because the legend says that Krishna and Balarama rested here after killing Kamsa in a wrestling match. Further to the southwest of Mathura is Madhuvan, a beautiful and serene forest area known to have been a place of meditation in the past. The Govardhan hill is located about two and a half miles west of Madhuvan. This mountain is noted in Krishna legends as having been lifted by Krishna to guard the people of Vraja against torrential rains. The circumference of Govardhan is about fifteen and a half miles. These hilly ranges are venerated, and devotees undertake the pilgrimage of Govardhan *parikrama* by going around the Govardhan hill. Eminent Vaishnava *acaryas*, such as Caitanya, Vallabha, Sur Das, and a number of others, are said to have meditated on the Govardhan hill. Near Govardhan is a large natural lake known as Manasiganga, with the Giriraj temple near it; a bit farther away is the stepped tank of Kusum Sarovar, and a little bit further are the two stepped tanks known as Radhakund and Shyamakund (Krishnakund) respectively. The twin ponds of Radhakund and Krishnakund are surrounded by meditation *asrams*, *samadhis* of saints, and temples.

Mathura, designated as *Mathuramandala* theologically, represents the realm of Krishna. Every hill, plant, pond, and lake in *Mathuramandala* is connected with Krishna through mythology and represents the living theology of Krishna.

See also: Braj *Parikrama*; Brindavan; *Lila*; Radha; Vallabha Tradition

Further Reading

Hartel, H., and V. Moeller, eds. 1993. *Excavations at Sonkh: 2500 Years of a Town in Mathura District*. Berlin: Dietrich Reimer Verlag.
Srinivasan, D. 1989. *Mathura: The Cultural Heritage*. New Delhi: American Institute of Indian Studies.

MAYA

The term *maya* has been used in three contexts within the classical imagery associated with Krishna. First, on the cosmic level, *maya* or *yogamaya* is the inert energy of Vishnu associated with his slumber at the *Yuganta*, which is also commonly associated with Krishna. Second, the cosmic energy of Vishnu that takes form as Goddess Maya, who protects God Vishnu while he is asleep, is also commonly known as Nidra. Third, *maya* (illusion) envelops creation, including everyone and everything within, so that one is not able to visualize the purpose of Krishna's life or the divine within the creation. In this context *maya* is denoted as a veil that clouds the wisdom of beings. *Maya* is seen in these three contexts in the narratives of Krishna. *Maya* is also referred to as Nidra in another form, as awakened energy of Vishnu, as she is the personification of the energy arising out of the restful Vishnu, and considerable differences are noticed between the activities and personalities of the goddesses Maya and Nidra. While Nidra is active when Krishna is sleeping or inactive, Maya is active while Krishna is active and awake. Maya, or Yogamaya, also has an important cosmic role in her impersonal manifestation as illusion as well as personified manifestations as Maya or Nidra.

In the first context as the inert energy of Vishnu, Maya envelops Vishnu and also the whole universe. Everything is in darkness, while Nidra stays alert to protect

Vishnu who is in deep slumber. While Vishnu is in his play (*lila*) as Krishna in Brindavan, Maya envelops the town so it goes into deep slumber. Maya appears several times in this role as sleep enveloping Mathura and Vraja during several *lilas* of Krishna. As *maya* she also envelops Mathura during the birth of Krishna; overcome by her, the town of Mathura sleeps deeply as Vasudeva is transferring Krishna to Vraja. *Maya* also envelops Vraja during Krishna's *Raasalila*, while the *Gopis* join him in the night during the autumn months for the round dance; the town is in deep slumber under the influence of *maya*.

In the second context, as Nidra she appears in her role as protector of Krishna when he is born as Krishna. Nidra was born as the daughter of Yashoda in Vraja and exchanged with Krishna, and she was then handed over to Kamsa in place of Krishna as the newborn daughter of Devaki. Kamsa, assuming her to be the daughter of Devaki, immediately killed the child, who then rose to the sky and proclaimed the death of Kamsa at the hands of Krishna.

In the third context *maya* appears as a cosmic illusion that envelops the creation in which the dream seems real, while the real purpose of life is lost. The individual forgets that he or she is, in fact, an *atma*, which should return to the divine. The individual's wisdom is clouded by the curtain of *maya* and sees the earthly life as real, forgetting/not understanding the divine path that leads him or her to *moksha* (release from samsara). Samsara itself is an illusion, while the divine, and a soul's return to the divine realm, is real. In this role as a cloud that mystifies life on Earth, *maya* known as *avidya* (ignorance), she is delusional. This aspect of *maya* has been well known since the early Vedic period, when she is referred to as illusion and magical in the *Vedas*. However, in the *Bhagavadgita*, Krishna describes *maya* as delusional, veiling the divine Krishna, due to which, not being able to realize Krishna, individuals fall back into ignorance (*Bhagavadgita* 7.14).

Maya is an ancient and distinguished concept well established in Hinduism. The concept of *maya* has been shown in its complete theological purport in the Krishna legend as a symbolic concept, a personified goddess, and a cosmic dream vision that clouds the vision of the real nature of the divine and creation.

See also: Bhagavadgita; *Gopas* and *Gopis*; *Lila*; Nidra; Radha; Vishnu

Further Reading

Goudrian, T. 1978. *Maya Divine and Human*. Delhi: Motilal Banarsidas.

Reyna, R. 1962. *The Concept of Maya from the* Vedas *to the 20th Century*. New York: Asia Publishing House.

MIRABAI

Mirabai (1500s) is the most renowned bhakti saint of India. Although born in a royal household, she gave up riches to adopt a mendicant lifestyle, one of devotion and simplicity. Her simplicity and exceptional poems for Krishna have acquired for her an immense following, although she faced the wrath of society due to her disregard for the gender norms and social etiquette prevalent in high-class Rajput society during the period 1400–1500 CE. Several biographies of Mira memorialize

Mirabai sculpture, Loutolim, Goa, India. (Dinodia/
Corbis)

her life. An early biography of
Mira, written by Nabhadas in his
Bhaktamal, set the trend for later
biographies. The basic details of
Mirabai's life do not vary among
the versions of the numerous
extant biographies, except for
the narration of each event of her
life. There is a general consensus
both on the basic details of
her early life, and her later
renouncer-mendicant life as a
wandering devotee of Krishna
singing Krishna *prem* (love of
Krishna) and *viraha* (separation).
Mira was unique among the female ascetics for her fearless nature and singular lifestyle. She
faced unique challenges due to
gender expectations, such as the
wrath of her husband and in-
laws, lustful overtures from fellow *bhaktas*, and the refusal of
recognition from fellow devotees
(*bhaktas*) of Krishna. However,
for Mira all of these societal
problems were nonissues, as her
only concern in life was her quest for the supreme, Krishna, whom she believed to
be her partner. She lived her life as the *Bhagavadgita* and the *Bhagavatapurana* depict the life of a devotee completely absorbed in *Krishnalila,* oblivious to the world
around her. Mira was born in the royal household of Merta, a principality in Marwar, and was married to the Rana of Mewar, another independent principality in
Rajasthan. Her ways of devotion to Krishna raised concerns soon after her arrival
at the palace of her in-laws, where she refused to worship the *kuladevata* (family
deity), causing anxiety among her husband's family. Later events of her life were
complicated by various attempts by members of her family to dissuade her from
her bhakti in order to bring her back into the mainstream feminine life of the palace. Mira's father-in-law sent her away to live in an isolated palace, her sister-in-law
tried to poison her, and her husband tried unsuccessfully to prove her infidelity. As
numerous attempts proved unsuccessful in bringing Mira back into family life,
they became indifferent to her, and she eventually left her family to become a wandering mendicant.

Three major events are noted during this phase of her life as a mendicant: meeting, in order, a scheming sadhu (mendicant), the emperor Akbar, and Jiva *Gosvami*.
The sadhu approached her and said that Krishna had ordered her to surrender her

---

Mirabai in Popular Culture

Mira's life and poems have had a lasting impact on India. Several retellings of her life in almost all media, including music, dance, drama, animation, cartoon, and film in addition to paintings and ritual traditions, indicate her enduring popularity in Indian culture. Her story inspired nationalists. Tagore's story "Letter from a Wife" and Gandhi's autobiography, *My Experiments with Truth*, make references to Mira. Films have been produced based on her life. The first film about her was produced in 1945, starring M. S. Subbulakshmi as Mira. The second film was produced in 1979, and it is still known for its musical compositions and wide availability. Mira's story was also televised in a 1993 television series for popular audiences, reaching even rural communities.

---

body to his lust, to which Mira agreed and asked him to come later that night. She then arranged a bed in the midst of the devotees and told the sadhu that if Krishna had ordered such an action, then there should be no shame in its public performance, to which the sadhu had no answer but left in shame. It is said that while living in Braj, she sent a message to Jiva *Gosvami* to meet her, to which Jiva refused, saying that as an ascetic he did not meet women. However, he later decided to meet her, understanding her superior devotion to Krishna. The Moghul emperor Akbar and Tansen are said to have visited her in disguise and, impressed with her devotion, offered a necklace to Krishna. Various scholars interpret Akbar's visit differently. It is suggested that Akbar's visit might suggest his attempt to slight the royal family of Mewar, which was the last of the major independent states in Rajasthan that did not surrender to the emperor.

Later retellings of Mira's story include her depiction as a disciple of Ravidas, an untouchable *Chamar* saint of Punjab. Mira's life ended mysteriously in all of the legends that narrate her story. Eventually, Mira's husband realized her devotion and sent messengers instructing her to return home. However, as the messengers were preparing to leave with her, Mira went to her image of Krishna and, as everyone was watching, she became absorbed into the picture, never to be seen again. Mira is thus said to have departed from this world mysteriously. Her legacy endures among the ordinary population, even though the orthodoxy never accorded her any special respect. Numerous temples host her images, as well as her poetry recitals, popularly known as Mira *Bhajans*, which form part of major celebrations there, as well as at festivals and fairs.

See also: Bhakti; Brindavan; Jiva *Gosvami*; Mathura; Ravidas

Further Reading
Alston, A. J. 1980. *The Devotional Poems of Mira Bai*. Delhi: Motilal Banarsidas.

MOKSHA/MUKTI

Moksha and *mukti* are two words that each denote the final goal of life in Hinduism. *Mukti* is derived from the Sanskrit root *mud* (happiness or joy), and *moksha* is derived from the Sanskrit root *muc*, meaning release or liberation. Although its early use is noted in Hinduism, this concept of happiness through release is ubiquitous in other Indian religions such as Buddhism and Jainism. *Mukti* in Hinduism is finding unity with the divine soul (Brahma), which leads to *sat-cit-ananda* (true-eternal-joy), when the individual soul (*atma*) rests contentedly and desires nothing. Several Vaishnava traditions utilize the same concept, but ask that the devotees desire unity with Vishnu/Krishna, or to reach the *Vishnuloka/Goloka* to live in perpetual and limitless happiness. Thus, they are liberated souls, which do not return to life on Earth. It will be helpful to analyze *moksha/mukti* in Krishna traditions here.

Although *moksha* has its origins in the *Vedas*, its clear depiction, enunciated in an important Vedanta text by Badarayana in his *Brahmasutras*, is important for Krishna traditions. According to Badarayana, although the liberated souls are defined as pure consciousness, they may exhibit some qualities of the supreme reality (*Brahmasutras* 4.4.5–7), and they may have some embodiment (*Brahmasutras* 4.4.8–9). Badarayana also proposed several levels of liberation (*Brahmasutras* 4.3.7–16), a concept that later finds expression in the views of *kramamukti* (gradual liberation) known in the Krishna bhakti (devotional) traditions based on the *Advaita Vedanta* and *Dvaita Vedanta*.

Krishna lays down a clear examination of liberation in the *Bhagavadgita*, in which he explains that a sage is qualified to become Brahma, the supreme soul (*Bhagavadgita* 18.15). Krishna himself is identified as Supreme Brahma (*param brahma* or *paramatma*). Krishna also clearly states that a liberated soul will attain him (*Bhagavadgita* 4.9; 7.23; 8.7; 10.10; 12.8; 18.55, etc.). In fact, according to Krishna, the liberated soul goes "beyond *maya*," never again to be reborn (*Bhagavadgita* 7.14; 4.9; 5.17; 8.15–16). Vaishnava traditions, accepting the thought of Ramanuja, Madhva, Vallabha, Rupa *Gosvami*, and Jiva *Gosvami*, follow the general theoretical purport of the *Brahmasutras* and the *Bhagavadgita*. Hence, for the Vaishnava devotees of these schools, the spiritual selves (*atma, jiva*) may obtain eternal, blissful communion with the supreme deity in heaven (*Vaikuntha* or *Goloka*). A number of Vaishnava traditions centered on Krishna, however, concur on the differing degrees of liberation with the supreme deity in *moksha*: *salokya* (residence in the same realm), *samipya* (proximity to the Lord), *sarshti* (same power as the Lord), *sarupya* (enjoying a divine form), *ekatva* or *samaikya* (oneness with God).

Madhva is known to have purported that not all souls are destined for *moksha*; while some may confine themselves to samsara, others may be destined for hell, according to the premise of predestination of souls. The Nimbarka and Vallabha traditions do not emphasize the eternal fate of souls; however, they confirm the role of predestination that may lead souls to their final *moksha*.

Alternatively, as emphasized in the *Bhagavatapurana*, bhakti (devotion) in itself is the end, but not the means, to liberation (*Bhagavatapurana* 7.8.42; 11.14.4). Several devotional traditions of Krishna, including Caitanya Vaishnavism, deemphasize the *moksha* in preference to bhakti, which in itself is designated as the goal of life (*pancamapurushartha*). Hence, *moksha* has a special meaning for the devotional traditions (bhakti *sampradayas*) in addition to the commonly accepted features of *moksha* noted in classical Hinduism.

A related concept is *jivanmukti*. While the concept of *moksha* in general deals with what happens after death, *jivanmukti* denotes a state of liberation that can be enjoyed while still living in this world. Although this state is not very common, references to *jivanmukti* can be found in the Vedanta and other later bhakti traditions. The *Samkhya* and *Yoga* schools of thought and practice support the view of *jivanmukti*, while the *Advaita Vedanta* of Sankara also supports it, although several Vedanta schools (Vallabha *sampradaya*, Nimbarka *sampradaya,* and so on) do not support it.

See also: Advaita; *Bhagavadgita*; *Bhagavatapurana*; Caitanya; *Dvaita*; Madhva; Ramanuja; Vallabha

Further Reading

Fort, A. O., and P. Mumme, eds. 1996. *Living Liberation in Hindu Thought*. Albany: SUNY Press.

Rensoli, L. 1998. "Levels of *Moksha* in the *Bhagavad-Gita*." *Pensamiento* 54 (209): 245–264.

Sribhashyam, T. 2011. *Way to Liberation, Moksa Marga: An Itinerary in Indian Philosophy*. New Delhi: Motilal Banarsidas.

MUSIC AND KRISHNA

Performing arts, sculpture, painting, and literature are tremendously influenced by the *Krishnalilas* (Plays of Krishna), which take inspiration from numerous events in the life of Krishna narrated in the *Bhagavatapurana* and the *Mahabharata*. Dances based on events narrated in the Krishna legend such as the *Kaliyadamana* (the submission of the serpent Kaliya), and the *Raasalila* of Brindavan provide recurring themes serving as constant inspiration for the evolution of a number of dance styles and theater performances across India. Some traditions, such as the *Satriya*, *Manipuri* dances, *Jatra*, *Kirthana*, and *Haridasu*, originated within Krishna devotion and continue to thrive on religious performances held during festival days.

Performance arts have always held a special place in Hindu religious life. Dance is a sacrifice in Vedic practices, while in relation to Krishna, dance and music became an essential part of the "divine *lila*" in the *puranas* and the *Mahabharata*. Performing arts (dance, drama, and music) fulfill a dual role of celebration and offering. The *Pancaratra agamas* note dance, music, and enacting (theater) for Vishnu as one of the important forms of ritual offerings of service (*seva/upacaras*). The arts have a special place in devotional (bhakti) traditions of Krishna to celebrate the deity and make offerings similar to the *sevas* (services) offered to the deity during *puja*. Krishna bhakti contributed to the development of numerous performance traditions and regional styles in India. *Satriya* dance and *Ankiya Nat* in Assam owe their origin to the Krishna devotional tradition founded by Sankaradeva in Assam, while *Jatra* in Orissa and Bengal owes much of its popularity to Caitanya. The Maharashtrian saints' (*Varkari* tradition) contribution to the *kirtan*

Flute of Krishna

The flute is a simple musical instrument fashioned out of a stalk of bamboo with eight holes, one of the most ancient musical instruments of India. The *Bhagavatapurana* describes Krishna playing the flute for his *Gopa* (cowherd) friends and cows in the afternoons in the Brindavan and Govardhan region. Another incident described in the *Bhagavatapurana* depicts Krishna playing the flute during the *Raasalila* in Brindavan. It is this incident that is interpreted theologically to represent the divine call, only heard by enlightened souls, that certain *Gopis* (cowherd maidens of Brindavan) played during the quiet nights of autumn. Hence, the flute has come to represent Krishna.

---

tradition, and the *samaj gayan* tradition developed by Haridasi *sampradaya* of Hit Harivams, owe their origin to the *Krishnalila* tradition and Krishna bhakti. The *yaskshagana* popular in Karnataka and Andhra Pradesh, and the tradition of *Haridasus*, *Bhagavatakaras*, popular across southern India, took their inspiration from the devotional traditions of Krishna following the *acaryas* Madhva and Ramanuja. The unique dance style of Andhra Pradesh, *Kuchipudi*, as well as *Manipuri* dance (Manipur), *Ankiya Nat* (Assam), and *Krishnattam* (Kerala), owe their origin to Krishna devotion too.

See also: Ankiya Nat; Bhakti; Haridasa Thakura; Haridasi *Sampradaya*; *Haritray*; *Kuchipudi*; *Lila*; Madhva; *Manipuri* Dance; *Maya*; *Pancaratra*; Ramanuja; *Samaj Gayan*; *Seva*

Further Reading

Gupta, R. K. 1984. *The Yoga of Indian Classical Dance: The Yogini's Mirror*. Innner Traditions/Bear.

Jhaveri, D. 1997. "Manipuri Indian Dance Form Portrays the Divine Love of Krishna and Radha." *Ballet International* (7): 32–33.

Kinsley, D. 1972. "Without Krishna There Is No Song." *History of Religions* 12 (2): 149–180.

Nanddas. 1973. *Round Dance of Krishna and Uddhav's Message*. London: Luzac.

MUTATALVARS

The first three *alvars*—Poigaialvar, Peyalvar, and Bhutatalvar—together are known as the *Mutatalvars*, a Tamil word meaning three *alvars*. Poigaialvar was found near a pond known as Poigai in Kanchi. Hence, he was named Poigai. Although Poigai lived during 700 CE, legends date his life to 4000 BCE. The text of a hundred poems known as the *Mutal Tiruvantati*, composed by Poigaialvar, are included in the *Nalayira Divya Prabhandham*. All his poems contain his signature line: "I am singing these garlands of verses, whose vision I had in the flame of the lamp of Earth with the sun as the light and the oceans as the oil," imagery presenting the sun and earth as the clay lamp commonly used in temples to light lamps during festivals and vows. Poigai's verses are written in the *antati* style, in which the last word/syllable of the preceding poem is used as the first word/syllable of the succeeding poem, thus creating beautiful chain-poems, which Poigai refers to as garlands of poems. Peyalvar was a contemporary of Poigaialvar. Peyalvar composed a hundred poems known as the *Munram Tiruvantati* in a style similar to the *antati* style, which are also included in the *Nalayira Divya Prabandham*. He described the form of Narayana with his attributes: *shankha* (conch), *chakra* (wheel), *gada* (mace), *padma* (lotus), and his wife Srilaxmi. Bhutatalvar was found in a flower in Mahabalipuram. He composed the *Irantam Tiruvantati*, a hundred poems for Vishnu in the *antati* style, which are included in the *Nalayira Divya Prabandham*. Not much is known about the life of Bhutatalvar, other than the legend that he was looking for shelter one rainy night in Tirukkoilur and found himself staying with the other two *alvars*, Pey and Poigai, who were already taking shelter in a small room that barely had enough room for one. The poems of these first three *alvars* are comparable in style and composition.

See also: Alvars; *Nalayira Divya Prabandham*; Ramanuja; Ranganatha; Srirangam Temple; Srivaishnavism

Further Reading

Narayanan, V. 2008. "'With the Earth as a Lamp and the Sun as a Flame.'" Lighting Devotion in South India." *International Journal of Hindu Studies*11 (3): 227–253.

NALAYIRA DIVYA PRABANDHAM

The poems of the *Nalayira Divya Prabandham* (The Divine Collection of Four Thousand) were composed by Vaishnava saints known as the *alvars*. The poems were composed before 900 CE but were lost, only to be collected in early 1000 CE by Nathamuni, the first *acarya* (preceptor) of the Srivaishnava tradition, and organized as the *Nalayira Divya Prabandham*. Nathamuni arranged the poems into groups of a thousand, each closely following the conventions of structure and function of the group. For example, all the *antati* poems are grouped together, which could be memorized through their internal links innate to the *antati* style of poetry.

The *Nalayira Divya Prabandham* was almost lost until it was accidentally discovered and compiled by Nathamuni. It is said that Nathamuni was struck by the unique qualities of the *pasurams* (verses) sung at a temple in Kumbhakonam by some devotees. Driven by intellectual curiosity, Nathamuni enquired about the poems. The devotees gave him the ten verses they had, which launched him on a quest to recover more poems. Nathamuni collected the rest of the poems by traveling widely, following clues the devotees gave him, and successfully tracking down the rest of the four thousand verses. The *Nalayira Divya Prabandham* is divided into four parts, containing a thousand verses in each section.

First Thousand
1. Periyalvar: *Tiruppallantu* and *Periyalvar Tirumoli*
2. Andal: *Tiruppavai* and *Nacciyar Tirumoli*
3. Kulasekharalvar: *Perumal Tirumoli*
4. Tirumalisai: *Tiruccantaviruttam*
5. Thondaradipodialvar: *Tirumalai* and *Tiruppalliyelucci*

Tiruppavai

Andal *alvar* composed the *Tiruppavai*. Poems (*pasuralu*) from the *Tiruppavai* are read by female devotees during the holy month of *Dhanurmasam* (December–January) across India and in other Hindu temples in the West that contain her shrine. Although Andal faced initial resistance for acceptance as one of the *alvars*, she is one of the most worshipped saints of present-day Hinduism, as at least one full month each year during December and January (*Dhanurmasam*) is devoted to her across India, a rare honor in the busy twenty-first century.

6. Tiruppanalvar: *Amalanatippiran*
7. Madhurakavialvar: *Kanninu Ciruttampu*

Second Thousand
1. Tirumangaialvar: *Periyatirumoli*
2. Tirumangaialvar: *Tirukkuruntantakam* and *Tirunetuntantakam*

Third Thousand
1. Poigaialvar: *Mutal Tiruvantati*
2. Bhutatalvar: *Irantam Tiruvantati*
3. Peyalvar: *Munram Tiruvantati*
4. Tirumalisai: *Nanmukan Tiruvantati*
5. Nammalvar: *Tiruviruttam, Tiruvaciriyam,* and *Periyatiruvantati*
6. Tirumangaialvar: *Periyatirumatal*

Fourth Thousand
1. Nammalvar: *Tiruvaymoli*

NAMDEV (1270–1350)

Namdev, referred to by many names such as Nama, Namdeo, or Namabhagat, was a saint with a considerable following among various bhakti traditions, including Sikhs as well as *Varkaris, Dadupanthis,* and *Kabirpanthis*. Indeed, his influence extends far beyond Maharashtra, his birthplace, and poems attributed to him are known in several languages including Hindi, Punjabi, and Rajasthani, in addition to Marathi. Namdev was born into a family of tailors. His parents, Damaset and Gonai, taught him their traditional family profession. Namdev's family also included another distinguished *Varkari* saint, Janabai, who was found, raised, and adopted by Namdev's parents. Although Janabai is known as Namdev's "maidservant," she played a major role as his biographer and as a poet. Namdev is also associated amicably with his contemporary bhakti saints including Jnanadev, his wife Rajai, Narahari, and Chokhamela. Namdev's legacy can also be seen in later saints including Tukaram, who claimed to have a dream vision of Namdev as he embarked on Namdev's life goal of composing a thousand poems, which remained unfulfilled for

---

Janabai

Janabai was an adopted child in the house of Namdev, and she may have been a little older than him. Surrounded by the religious atmosphere of the household where she served, she herself was totally immersed in devotion to Vitthala; she composed a number of *abhangas* expressing her devotion to him. She is remembered as a *sant* (saint) in the *Varkari* tradition for her devotional practices and contributions to devotional literature. She appears prominently in the film *Sant Namdev* released in 1995, true to the biographic songs attributed to her in Marathi. The film, in fact, was scripted as a memory of Janabai, who narrated the life of Namdev through her *kirtans*.

Namdev. Namdev lived in Pandarpur during his early life, composing beautiful *abhanga* poems expressing his deep devotion to Vitthala, a form of Krishna in revered Pandarpur, Maharashtra. Namdev subsequently set these poems to music and danced in the temple of Vitthala singing them, thus starting the tradition now known as *kirtana*, a major aspect of Marathi devotional culture. In fact, the popularity of his *kirtans* reached Jnanadev, which prompted him to come to Pandarpur to meet Namdev. Several religious pilgrimages were undertaken by these two saints, on which they had religious debates and exchanged poems. Namdev's legacy persists in northern India among several religious traditions due to his travels there. However, not much is known about his death. Several traditions claim separate places for Namdev's death. *Varkaris* claim that he returned to Pandarpur in the last days of his life and died there, while Sikhs claim that he died in Ghuman in the state of Punjab in northern India. Namdev's following is not only found among Sikhs outside of the *Varkari* tradition of Maharashtra; numerous other devotional groups claim affiliation with Namdev. He is said to be the guru of the priest of the deity Madanmohan, housed in the temple Kaladhari Mandir in Brindavan, who migrated from Multan after Pakistan became a Muslim theocratic state. They are said to have inherited the *gaddi* of Namdev in Multan, commemorated with a *samadhi* in the temple. Namdev is one of the most renowned saints of Maharashtrian origin, with a widespread following across India. An annual *Varkari* pilgrimage is undertaken in his memory. Namdev's legacy also endures in films, theater, and music.

See also: Bhakti; Chokhamela; Eknath; Jnanadev; *Sants*; Tukaram; *Varkari* Tradition

Further Reading

Nath, J. 1983. *Namdev, the Saint Poet*. New Delhi: Namdev Mission Trust.

Novetzke, C. 2008. *Religion and Public Memory: A Cultural History of Saint Namadev in India*. New York: State University of New York Press.

Prill, Susan. 2009. "Representing Sainthood in India: Sikh and Hindu Images of Namdev." *Material Religion* 5 (2): 156–179.

Vaudeville, C. 1996. *Myths, Saints and Legends in Medieval India*. Delhi: Motilal Banarisdas.

NAMGHAR

The *namghar* of Krishna in Assamese villages is an integral aspect of devotion in Assamese culture centered on Krishna. Introduced by Sankaradeva, the *namghar*, roughly translated as the "House of Names," is a simple congregation hall where followers of Krishna assemble to venerate him, recite his names, or perform dance and music. A *namghar* is usually built facing east and consists of sections known as the *monikut* (the sanctuary) and the *mandap* (assembly space). The *monikut* (jewel house) houses the *singhasan* (throne) or the altar. Devotees sit facing the *singhasan* in the *mandap* while performing *Nama sankirtan* (singing names). A unique architectural element of the *namghars* is the *ghai khuta* or *lai khuta*, often an oversized column in the *mandap*, usually identified by a *gamosa* (rope) tied around it. No one is allowed to sit near this pillar as it is considered the seat of the *burha dangoriya* (the holy spirit). When the *mohaprasad* (offerings) are distributed after a service, they are first offered to the pillar. There are *namghars* in most Hindu villages in Assam. Unlike temples, *namghars* are not for everyday use, but are locations of assembly for special religious events and memorial services. Private family *namghars*, although rare, are known to exist, patronized by the local landed aristocracy.

See also: Ankiya Nat; Performing Arts and Krishna; Sankaradeva; *Satra*

Further Reading

Choudhury, R. D. 1985. *Archaeology of the Brahmaputra Valley of Assam*. Delhi: Abhinav Prakasan.

Goswami, K. D. 1982. *Life and Teachings of Mahapurusha Sankaradeva*. Patiala: Punjabi University.

Sarma, P. C. 1982. *Architecture of Assam*. Gauhati: Gauhati University.

NAMMALVAR AND MADHURAKAVIALVAR

Nammalvar (our *alvar*), also known as Catakopan, has been regarded as the foremost *alvar* since 1100 CE. His composition *Tiruvaymoli* is regarded as the equivalent of the *Samaveda*. Nammalvar's life is shrouded in mystery, with scant details available from later hagiographies. According to the legends, Nammalvar did not speak. His parents tried various methods but could not stimulate him to talk. As his parents gave up hopes of his speaking and being a normal boy, he climbed a tamarind tree and continued to live in it. While he was there Madhurakavialvar, who had been led by a shining star from the north to the south, where Nammalvar was living in the tamarind tree, found him. Madhurakavialvar spoke to Nammalvar and recorded his compositions, collected as the *Tiruviruttam*, the *Tiruvaciriyam*, the *Periyatiruvantati*, and the legendary *Tiruvaymoli*. Madhurakavialvar is credited with recording Nammalvar's poems included in the *Nalayira Divya Prabandham* and is considered an incarnation of Garuda, the mount of Vishnu. Madhurakavi was born in Tirukkolur near Alvar Tirunagari. Madhurakavi's poem, the *Kanninu Ciruttampu* of eleven poems, is also included in the *Nalayira Divya Prabandham*.

Tiruvaymoli

Tiruvaymoli, containing 1,100 verses that are included in the *Nalayira Divya Prabandham*, was composed in Tamil by Nammalvar and is equated with the *Vedas*. Nammalvar said in a verse in the *Tiruvaymoli* (sacred word or sacred utterance) that God speaks through him. Therefore, the *Tiruvaymoli* is considered revelation of the divine truth. Hence *Tiruvaymoli* has a special place in the religious practice of south India, especially for the Srivaishnava tradition. Working on the text in any form, recitation, singing, and commenting are all considered devotional service. The annual *Tiruvaymoli* festival is held in Srivaishnava temples across India during which the *Tiruvaymoli* is recited and the ascension of Nammalvar is enacted (*Adhyayana utsava*). The *Adhyayana utsava* is held for ten days beginning on the *Ekadasi* (eleventh day after the new moon) in the month of *Margasira* (December–January).

See also: Alvars; *Nalayira Divya Prabandham*; Ramanuja; Srirangam Temple; Srivash-navism; Tirupathi

Further Reading

Clooney, F. 1991. "Nammalvar's Glorious Tiruvallavar: An Exploration in the Methods and Goals of Srivaishnava Commentary." *Journal of African and Oriental Studies* 111: 260–276.

Ramanujan, A. K. 1981. *Hymns for the Drowning: Poems for Vishnu by Nammalvar*. Princeton: Princeton University Press.

NANDAGOPA

Nandagopa was the chief of the *Gopas* of Vraja, living in the village of Nandgaon. Nandagopa was the adopted father of Krishna and the best friend of Vasudeva, Krishna's biological father. Nandagopa is also sometimes noted as the cousin of Vasudeva, although supporting evidence is lacking to establish this relationship. Nandagopa's wife, Yashoda, was the doting innocent mother of Krishna, who was not aware of the child exchange and raised Krishna as her own biological son. Nandagopa took an active role in the child exchange, exchanging his newborn daughter for Krishna as soon as Vasudeva reached Vraja. He kept this as a permanent secret in his own mind without revealing it to anyone. Nandagopa kept a close watch on Krishna in Vraja, noticing Krishna's childhood with pleasure. Nandagopa met Vasudeva in the prison every year when he came to Mathura to pay his annual tax. Nandagopa would share the details of Krishna's childhood and life in Govraja (Vraja). Nandagopa took note of the deaths of demons in Vraja close to the presence of Krishna, such as Putana, Sakatasura (cart demon), and the falling of ashoka trees. Considering these as bad omens, in consultations with other village elders, Nandagopa moved the camp to Brindavan. Although Krishna was a child, Nandagopa always heeded his advice. When Krishna advised them that the *Gopas* should offer a ritual annual offering of food to the Govardhan hill, rather than to Indra, Nandagopa obliged, allowing his fellow *Gopas* (cowherds) to make the annual offerings to the Govardhan hill. Although this ritual led to the wrath of Indra, who lashed Brindavan with cataclysmic rain for a week, flooding the Yamuna River, Nandagopa's faith in Krishna was unwavering. Krishna saved the *Gopas* (cowherds), and *Gopis* (cowherd maidens) by lifting the Govardhan hill and sheltering them. Nandagopa was always aware of Krishna's divine birth, although he never spoke of it with anyone. Nandagopa, who never revealed the divine secret of Krishna, noted with respectful silence the divine play of Krishna in Brindavan and his interaction with numerous evil forces that troubled the *Gopas*. Nandagopa was an important player in the divine play of Krishna; although central to Krishna's life, he was always silent and never boastful. Nandagopa gave a tearful farewell to Krishna, along with the rest of the cowherds and cowherd maidens of Brindavan, when Akrura brought Kamsa's invitation to participate in the wrestling match in Mathura. He did not stay back, but came to Mathura on the pretext of paying annual taxes along with the other cowherds. He watched Krishna's wrestling match anxiously, along with everyone assembled in the arena. Nandagopa was elated when Krishna defeated Kamsa. Krishna and Balarama came to Nandagopa at the end of the wrestling match, hugged him, and told him that they would come back to visit him after staying for a while in Mathura. Although the intimate relationship of Nandagopa and Yashoda with Krishna lasted only twelve years, it was the most remembered and revered stage of the life of Krishna. Several bhakti traditions derive their central philosophy from the intimate relations Krishna displayed toward the *Gopas* and *Gopis* during this stage. *Vastalyabhava* (affection of mother), *sakhibhava* (affection of friends), *raganuragabhava* (affection of intimacy), and *sringarabhava* (romantic love) serve as the philosophical bases for bhakti traditions (*sampradayas*) such as Haridasi *sampradaya*, Vallabha *sampradaya*, Radhavallabha *sampradaya*, and Caitanya Vaishnava *sampradaya*.

The Buddhist story of the *Ghatajataka* attributes an even more responsible role to Nandagopa, although giving his character a different name, Andhakavenhu. While the nine sons of Devagabba (Devaki in the Hindu story) were raised by Andhakavenhu and his wife Nandagopa (Yashoda in the Hindu texts), their daughters were raised by Devagabba in turn, since Upakamsa (Kamsa in the Hindu texts) did not kill female children. Therefore, unlike the Hindu story, all the children of both parents survived. The Buddhist story avoids the violence in Krishna's childhood and narrates the story according to the Buddhist vision.

The Jain stories of Krishna's parentage are also slightly different from the Hindu ones. Krishna was transferred right after his birth to Nanda and Yashoda. However, his childhood pranks are not narrated with the same unapologetic delightful style as in the Hindu *puranas*. Nanda, the adopted father of Krishna, also plays a minor role, as Balarama, the elder brother of Krishna, takes care of him as a father figure.

Nandagopa plays an important role in the childhood of Krishna in Hindu, Jain, and Buddhist stories. His role as the adoptive father of Krishna is an established fact in the traditional mythology of India. Nandagopa remains the beloved father figure of the Krishna stories, along with Yashoda, who was the beloved mother of the Lord.

See also: Birth and Early Childhood of Krishna; Brindavan; Buddhism and Krishna; Childhood of Krishna in Brindavan; Devaki; Jainism and Krishna; *Lila*; Vasudeva; Yashoda

Further Reading

White, C. 1970. "Krishna as a Divine Child." *History of Religions* 10 (2): 69–86.

NANDGAON

Krishna's childhood town was Nandgaon, which is located about a mile from Barsana, Radha's hometown. Nandgaon and Barsana have acquired a special renown due to the relationship of Radha and Krishna. Surrounded by tanks and ponds, groves and arbors, Nandgaon was frequented by Krishna and Balarama in their childhood while grazing calves and cows. Nandgaon is included in the pilgrimage itineraries of the Braj *parikrama,* which takes at least three days to complete, visiting the sacred places of Nandgaon associated with Krishna's childhood, including a temple dedicated to Nandbaba, father of Krishna, on top of a hill. As one reaches the Nandababa temple at the top of the hill, one can catch a beautiful view of the sprawling Mathura valley below. The Nandababa temple contains the images of Krishna and Balarama as well as the parents, Nanda and Yashoda. Within the outer courtyard are a number of images of Krishna depicting various episodes of his life, Krishna *lila* (plays), *Raasalila* (play of *Raasa*), and as Radhavallabha. Although most structures near this temple are dated to the early eighteenth century, an older temple may have existed here previously, since an early inscription found on the site is dated to 1578. Caitanya visited this temple during his visit to Mathura, and Sanatana *Gosvami* discovered the icons of the main temple in a cave on the hill, which also supports the view that an earlier temple might have been destroyed there, while the icons might have been hidden in the cave.

On the northern side of the village is the lake Pavan Sarovar (popularly known as Pan Sarovar), which is paved by stairs (*ghats*), and near it are located the temple of Bihariji and *baithak* (meditation sites of *acaryas*) shrines to Vallabha and Sanatana *Gosvami*. Numerous tanks are located near Pan Sarovar, called Dohanikund, Taragtirth, and Motikund (Pearl Lake). Motikund is mentioned in the *Gargasamhita* with an interesting story connected to Krishna. A narrative event connected with Motikund mentioned in the *Gargasamhita* notes that Radha's father, Vrishabhanu, sent a gift of a tray of pearls, which made Nanda sad as he was not able to reciprocate with an equally valuable gift. To placate his father, Krishna planted a hundred pearls, which grew into trees and produced fruits laden with pearls. Motikund is supposed to be located where the pearls were planted. This legend is interpreted to indicate that a gift of one pearl here equals that of many hundreds more. Three tanks are located near Motikund, known as Isarapokhar, Sanskund, and Phulvarikund. Near Phulvarikund is a large banyan tree called Bilas Bat, under which is located a *baithak* of Krishna.

On the east side of Nandgaon is a pond called Kund, near which is located a grove called Terkadamb (bent Kadamb), where Krishna and the *Gopa* boys used to rest. Near this place are also the huts of Rupa *Gosvami* and Sanatana *Gosvami*. Rupa *Gosvami* is said to have meditated in this grove. On the east side are also located seven other tanks, known as Jalbiharkund, Bahak, Morkund, Chachikund, Harikund, Krishnakund, and Jogikund. North of Jogiyakund is a garden referred to as Yogiyasthana, which is said to be the place where Uddhava met the *Gopis* upon his return from Mathura.

On the south side of Nandagaon are also located numerous ponds, many of which are named after the friends (*sakhis*) of Radha, such as Lalitakund (with a *Gaudiya* temple dedicated to Lalithbihari), Akrurkund, Jhagarakund, Vishakhakund, Purnamasikund, Runaki, and Jhunakund. Southwest of Lalitakund is Uddhavkyari, a flower garden (flower bed) where Uddhava, as a messenger sent by Krishna, spoke to the *Gopis* to pacify them for missing Krishna.

On the southwest side of Nandgaon is Vimalkund, where a number of small enclosures for images of four lion-like monsters are located, referred to as the representations of *hava* or *hau* (Kamsa's demon associates) that once tried to frighten the infant Krishna. The Dauji temple and Bhandiravan mark the places of Krishna and Balarama's childhood play near Nandgaon. On the southwest side are also located Yashodakund, Yashoda's churning place, the *baithak* of Nandagopa, a large pond known as Madhusudhankund, and a small shrine to Narasimha. On the northern side of Madhusudhankund is a small extension of the Nandgaon hill known as Caranpahari, bearing the footprints of Krishna.

Next to Nandgaon is Mahaban (Mahavan in classical texts), which contains large trees and important sacred places connected with the life of Krishna. Mahaban is also known as Gokul in classical texts such as the *Padmapurana*. Numerous events of Krishna's infancy are located in and around the village of Mahaban. Most important among the buildings in Mahaban is the *Chaurasikhamba* (*assikambha*) temple, which means temple of eighty-four pillars. Devotees consider this to be the remainder of the original residence of Nanda (Nand Bhavan) before it was moved to Brindavan. It is said to be the place where Krishna was brought right after his birth. The Chaurasikhambha temple contains images of Krishna and Balarama, Krishna's cradle (representing the *Chathipuja* conducted on the sixth day after his birth), and a large stone mortar (*ulukhala*), representing the mortar Yashoda tied to Krishna in order to stop him from getting into mischief. Wish-granting trees are an ancient practice in Vraj, also mentioned in the *Harivamsa*. When Yashoda, tired of the pranks of Krishna, tied him to a mortar, he knocked down two ashoka trees with the mortar by crawling about with it. These two ashoka trees were noted as wish-granting trees in the *Harivamsa*. Along the path behind the Chaurasikhamba temple can be found small shrines commemorating incidents connected to the infancy of Krishna, such as the place of overturning the cart (killing of the cart demon Sakatasura); the place where the whirlwind demon was defeated (Trinavrita subdued); the place called Putanakhar, where Putana (the wet-nurse demon) was killed; the Yamala-Arjuna *kunda* where Krishna uprooted the two ashoka trees, which is also commemorated by a small shrine; and two trees on the edge of Mahaban next to the path leading to Brahmand Ghat. Brahmand Ghat commemorates the incident, marked by a small temple called Mrittikabihari, where Yashoda is said to have seen the universe in Krishna's mouth when she scolded him for eating dirt. Other notable places in the Mahaban are the temple of the Shyam or Shyamlala (where Nidra was born), Gopan ki haveli, Nandakup (Nanda's well), Karnavedhikup (where Krishna's ears were pierced), Saptasamudrikakup, and Gopiswar. Raman Reti is an area on the sandy riverbank between Mahaban and Gokul, said to be the place where Krishna played in the sand as a child.

See also: Balarama; Barsana; Childhood of Krishna in Brindavan; *Gopas* and *Gopis*; Nandagopa; Nidra; Radha; Twelve Forests of Braj; Uddhava; Yashoda

Further Reading
Entwhistle, A. 1987. *Braj: Center of Krishna Pilgrimage*. Groningen: Egbert Forsten.

NARAKASURA

The killing of Narakasura is considered to be one of Krishna's greatest deeds. Narakasura, also known as Bhauma (son of Earth), was a victorious king. He had defeated numerous kings and also Indra, lord of the gods. Hence, Narakasura is considered the most evil demon. The gods celebrate the death of Narakasura as the end of evil on earth and in heaven. *Dipavali (Diwali)*, the festival of lights, is celebrated to denote this event as the end of evil and the arrival of goodness on earth.

Narakasura also took away Indra's umbrella, his mother Aditi's earrings, and Indra's residence on the mountain Amara. Hearing of atrocities concerning Naraka, Krishna, along with his wife Satyabhama, mounted Garuda and laid siege to the city of Narakasura. Naraka's fort was made impenetrable by hill fortifications and guarded by elemental forces of air, fire, and water. Krishna cut through the mountains with his divine weapon, the Sudarsana *cakra* (wheel), and defeated the elemental forces with his sword. Naraka's generals retaliated with their large armies, which rained down weapons on Krishna. Krishna, who was invisible, cut their arms into small pieces and defeated them all. In the end, Bhauma hurled his club at Krishna, which he easily deflected and broke into pieces. Krishna then beheaded Naraka with his *cakra*. Some regional versions of the episode provide an alternative ending to the story. According to Telugu and Assamese regional traditions, Krishna was slightly injured by Narakasura toward the end of the battle, and he fainted. Satybhama then took Krishna's place and injured Naraka with an arrow, thus killing him. The goddess Bhumi (Earth) then appeared, presented Krishna with the *Vaijayanti* garland (the never-fading garland), and returned the earrings of the divine mother Adithi, the umbrella, and other jewels taken from Indra earlier by Bhauma Narakasura. The goddess Earth paid homage to Krishna and requested him to purify the sins of Narakasura and offer protection, which Krishna granted. Krishna entered the palace of Naraka and found sixteen thousand women who had been imprisoned by Naraka after he defeated and killed their husbands, rulers of numerous kingdoms on earth. As soon as the imprisoned queens saw Krishna, their hearts and souls filled with joy. They prayed for him to be their husband. Krishna agreed and sent them to Dvaraka, where he constructed a house for each one of the queens provided with servants and equipped with all the facilities necessary for a comfortable life. Krishna is said to have married each one of them individually in their houses. These were the sixteen thousand wives of Krishna, in addition to his eight principal wives.

Krishna then proceeded to visit Indra in heaven, along with his wife, Satyabhama. Indra along with thirty-two other gods worshipped Krishna and Satyabhama.

Death of Narakasura

The death of Narakasura is narrated variously in the regional literatures of India. In the *Bhagavatapurana* Narakasura is killed by the Sudarsana *cakra* (wheel) hurled at him by Krishna. However, in some regional versions of the episode popular in Bengal and Andhra Pradesh, his wife Satyabhama kills Narakasura. It is said that Krishna was overcome with exhaustion during the battle and passed out. Satyabhama carefully laid him on his chariot, while quickly grabbing a bow and shooting Narakasura with an arrow, which killed him immediately.

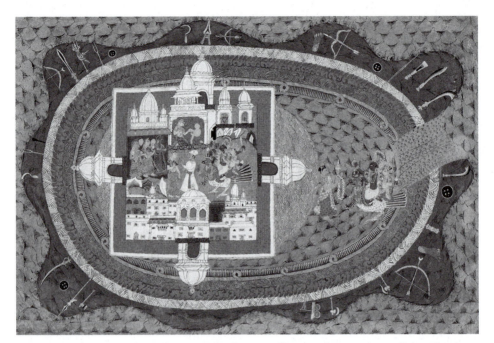

Scene from the story of Narakasura, folio from an illustrated manuscript of the *Bhagavata Purana* (*Ancient Stories of the Lord*), watercolor dated to 1775–1800, from Nepal. (Los Angeles County Museum of Art)

Satyabhama then prodded Krishna to pluck the *Parijata* tree from Indra's garden. They brought the heavenly tree and planted it in Satyabhama's garden, where its blooms produced the heavenly scent that filled Dvaraka. Bringing the *Parijata* tree immensely satisfied Satyabhama, for she had always been interested in having the *Parijata* tree in her back yard, since Rukmini had been presented with a *Parijata* flower, which Satyabhama greatly liked. Her desire was finally fulfilled after the death of Naraka. The story of *Parijathapaharam* (stealing the *Parijata* tree) forms the major story line of numerous regional narratives and theatrical performances across India in regional languages such as Assamese, Telugu, Kannada, Marathi, Tamil, and Malayalam. The divine tree, *Parijata*, that was brought to earth by Sathyabhama because of her true wish to have it in her earthly garden, can be seen throughout South Asia and Southeast Asia. It is commonly grown in the gardens of numerous temples and its flowers are used in worship. Although *Parijata* is a fragrant flowering tree, it is also identified with *Kalpataruvu* (wish-granting tree), which is not an earthly tree, but it is not unusual for a number of older trees or special trees across India to be identified with that name and revered as *Kalpavriksha*.

See also: Diwali; Eight Wives of Krishna

Further Reading

Bryant, E. 2003. *Bhagavatapurana*. X. 59, 253–259. London: Penguin Classics.
Devagupta, R. 2001. "The 'Slaying of Narakasura' (Hindu tale)." *Parabola-Myth Tradition and the Search for Meaning* 26 (2): 80–81.

NARASIMHA MEHTA

Narasimha Mehta (1414–1481) was a legendary bhakti poet of western India whose poems are sung in religious as well as nonreligious performances. Narasimha Mehta's biographies are found in several languages from the states of Gujarath, Rajasthan, and Uttar Pradesh. His biography is contained in Nabhadas's text *Bhaktamal* and also Priyadas's book *Bhaktirasabodhini*. A long poem in Rajasthani known as the *Narsi ji ro Mahero,* composed by a certain female poet, Mirabai (not to be confused with the saint Mirabai), also narrates Narasimha Mehta's biography. Narasimha Mehta was born in Talaja, a small town in Junagadh, Gujarat, in the community of *Nagara* Brahmans. Narasimha Mehta spent most of his time in the company of religious men, learning about religion. His parents got him married, hoping that it would change his mind and help him focus on family life. However, he did not develop any attachment to his wife, and for that reason he was taunted by his sister-in-law. He then left his home and wandered off, where he met Shiva, the deity of *Nagara* Brahmans, and also envisioned Krishna performing *Raasalila* in his eternal abode. He was blessed by both Shiva and Krishna to sing *bhajans*; thereafter he returned to Junagadh and continued to compose poems for Krishna and sing the *bhajans* in the temples. His popularity grew, although opposition also developed to his ways. Narasimha Mehta's biographies describe a number of events related to both his association with untouchable *bhaktas* and his poverty. Numerous manuscripts of his poems were found dated between the sixteenth and nineteenth centuries. The major subjects of his poems include *Krishnalila* and the nature of the divine. Narasimha Mehta's poems describe *Krishnalila*, the childhood and adolescence of Krishna in Braj, although most of his poems are devoted to the love of Radha and Krishna in beautiful, lyrical Gujarati. Narasimha Mehta's legacy endures in Gujarati poetry.

See also: Bhakti; Childhood of Krishna in Brindavan; *Lila; Raasalila;* Radha

---

Legacy of Narasimha Mehta

Narasimha Mehta's legacy in Gujarat extends beyond Hinduism and religion. Narasimha Mehta's poems are also found in the devotional compositions of Ismaili Muslims. The Gujarati language and social movements in Gujarat draw on his poetry for inspiration. Narasimha Mehta is recognized as the *Adikavi* of Gujarati poetry. His poems form part of Gujarat language teaching resources for schools. Films, TV series, and music about him are very popular in India. Nationalist leader K. M. Munshi wrote a biographical sketch of Narasimha Mehta. Gandhi was especially drawn to Narasimha Mehta's songs of spiritual and moral reflection. One of Gandhi's favorite *bhajans* was Narasimha Mehta's "*Vaishnava jan ke,*" which Gandhi frequently sang, and this *bhajan* continues to be sung at peace gatherings in India. Gandhi also pointed to Narasimha Mehta's association with untouchables in his fight against caste discrimination.

Further Reading

Asani, A. 1992. *The Harvard Collection of Ismaili Literature in Indic Languages: A Descriptive Catalog and Finding Aid*. Boston: Harvard University Press.

Bhagat, N. 1999. "Twenty-five Lyrics of Narasimha Mehta." In K. A. Panikkar. *Medieval Indian Literature and Anthology*. Vol. II, edited by K. A. Panikkar, 89–101. New Delhi: Motilal Banarsidas.

Shukla-Bhatt, N. 2007. "Govind's Glory: *Krishnalila* in Songs of Narasimha Mehta." In *Krishna: A Source Book,* edited by E. Bryant. New York: Oxford University Press.

The Hindu god Vishnu in his form as Narayana, Bangladesh, ca. 1000, schist sculpture. (Los Angeles County Museum of Art)

NARAYANA

Narayana is another ancient name for Vishnu, similar to the name Purushottama, which indicates his cosmological significance. As a name Narayana appears for the first time in the Vedic text *Satapata Brahmana*, as Purusha Narayana. While Purusha is a cosmic primeval man identified with Vishnu, Narayana is more philosophical in nature, variously identified with water and life as such, and noted as a companion or helper of humans in the compound term Nara-Narayana used in the *Mahabharata*, representing Krishna and Arjuna. While Nara (human) is Arjuna, Narayana is Krishna in this pair. Based on this *Mahabharata* representation, Narayana and Krishna are identified as one and the same, while Krishna is also known as Purusha (Purushottama) and Vishnu. Narayana, Purusha, and Vishnu are three terms that may represent the distinct supreme and cosmological aspects associated with Krishna rather than three divine persons. Vishnu is the *guna-vatara* representing the *satva* nature of Krishna; Purushottama represents his supreme personality; Narayana represents the absolute divinity connected to the *nara* (humans). For this reason, devotional texts call Krishna Purushottama, Vishnu, or Narayana simultaneously.

See also: Arjuna; *Avatara*; Krishna; *Lila*; *Purusha*; Vasudeva; Vishnu

Further Reading
Grunendahl, R. 1997. *Narayaniya Studien.* Tubingen: Otto Harrasowitz.
Krishna, N. 1980. *Art and Iconography of Vishnu-Narayana.* Bombay: D. B. Taraporewala.

NIDRA

Nidra, also referred to as Yoganidra, is the sister of Krishna and a personification of his sleep, hence she is called Nidra, a Sanskrit word for sleep. Although Nidra is identified with Maya, there are subtle differences that keep them clearly distinct. Nidra is a Vedic goddess whose narratives are described in detail in the *puranas.* Nidra is also connected to Balarama, with whom she acts as an ally to protect Krishna. Nidra is identified with Subhadra, sister of Krishna and Balarama. Overall, Nidra's relationship to Krishna and her representation in the *Ekanamsa* triads, flanked by Balarama and Krishna, has attracted much scholarly attention, leading to more ambiguity than clarity about her stature as a goddess. Analyzing Tamil textual sources led to the confusion that Nidra, also known as Ekanamsa, could be either wife or sister or both. Sanskrit textual sources concerning Nidra are not that ambiguous about her status, and she is clearly identified as the sister of Balarama and Krishna. In fact, her depiction may show her as a unifying force between the brothers. Nidra is said to have been reborn as Subhadra to Rohini and Vasudeva, after Krishna and Balarama freed Vasudeva from prison in Mathura, making her much younger in age than they were. Nidra's role in the legend of Krishna, before and after his birth, is described in detail in the *puranas* (*Harivamsa* 49.29–46; *Harivamsa* 51.1–16). Before the birth of Krishna, Nidra transferred six embryos (previously sons of Hiranyakasipu) from the underworld to Yashoda; Kamsa killed them soon after their birth, due to their curse in their previous life. Nidra also transferred Balarama as an embryo, during the seventh month of pregnancy, from Devaki to Rohini, another wife of Vasudeva. Hence, in relationship to Balarama, Nidra is like both mother and sister. Nidra was born as the daughter of Yashoda in Vraja soon after Krishna was born in Mathura, from which place he was brought to Vraja and exchanged for Nidra, the newly born baby girl of Yashoda. The child Nidra was taken to Mathura where Kamsa smashed her on the rocks and killed her. She rose to the sky and proclaimed the death of Krishna. Nidra's role as the protector of embryos and newly born children is obvious in this myth; hence, pregnant women worship Nidra for protection even now. The *Harivamsa* (*Harivamsa* 47.45) also reveals that Nidra undertook *kaumarika vrata* (the vow of nonmarriage) and was said to travel between the three worlds: earth, heaven, and the underworld. Nidra was adopted by Indra as his sister, thus giving her his *gotra* name of Kausika *gotra* (lineage), connecting her to the Brahmans of Kaushika *gotra*, who are traditionally associated with conducting the goddess worship. She is also described as a terrible goddess who could be propitiated with animal sacrifices. Nidra is also mentioned as a slayer of the demons Madhu and Kaitabha in *Pancaratra* literature, which connects her to Maya (Yogamaya), who works in collaboration with Vishnu in his divine play. However, Maya and Nidra are distinct in their features and personalities, except for their common activity of killing Madhu and Kaitabha. Nidra is depicted as the protector of embryos, handling embryos for transfer, and in the end she herself was transported, only to be killed by Kamsa. Apart from the *Ekanamsa* triads, a number of solitary figures also depict her, which indicates that Nidra may have been revered as an important goddess in ancient India.

Jain texts describe the worship of Nidra as an individual goddess, unconnected to any formal religion, in the forests. The Jain *Harivamsapurana* of Jinaprabha Suri states that the guards of Kamsa who were assigned to kill Nidra instead left her in a forest and showed the eyes of a deer to Kamsa as an evidence of her death. Nidra grew up in the forests by herself, spending her time in meditation. Nidra also does not perform any embryo transfers in the Jain myths, which are typical of her Hindu myths. As Nidra was deep in her meditation one day, some animals left parts of a hunted animal near the tree where she was meditating. She was then found by some forest bandits, who revered her as a forest goddess, offering her animal sacrifices, since they saw the leftovers of dead animals near her. The Jain story presents Nidra simultaneously as a meditating *sadhvi* and a terrible goddess accepting animal sacrifices, thus including elements of Hindu stories. What is common to both Hindu and Jain texts is the acknowledgment of her status as an independent goddess worshipped for her blessings, rather than as a goddess in combination with other deities.

See also: Arjuna; Balarama; *Maya*; Rohini; Subhadra: Krishna's Sister; Yashoda

Further Reading

Couture, A. 1999. "The Problem and Meaning of Yoganidra's Name." *Journal of Indian Philosophy* 27: 35–47.

Ghosh, J. C. 1936. "Ekanamsa and Subhadra." *Journal of Royal Asiatic Society Letters* 2: 41–46.

Hudson, D. 1982. "Pinnai, Krishna's Cowherd Wife." In *The Divine Consort: Radha and the Goddesses of India,* edited by J. S. Hawley and D. M. Wulff. Berkeley: University of California Press.

NIMBARKA TRADITION

Historical evidence is lacking for the Nimbarka tradition prior to the thirteenth century, although the tradition claims to be one of the four authorized Vaishnava traditions (*Catuh Vaishnava sampradayas*), originating in *Sanakadi sampradaya* and establishing itself as one of the oldest Vaishnava traditions in India. It is also called *Sanakadi* or *Hamsa sampradaya,* deriving these names from its ancient founders. Nimbarka *acarya*, the historical founder, lived in Nimgaon near Govardhan. Traditional accounts identify Nimbarka *acarya* with Bhaskara (1130–1200), the eminent astronomer of India. Although born in south India in a Telugu Brahman family, Bhaskara (Nimbarka) lived most of his life in Mathura. Traditional accounts narrate an interesting story about how Bhaskara acquired the name Nimbarka. It is said that one day Bhaskara was lost in theological discussions with an ascetic and it grew late. As a rule of his tradition no food can be taken after the sun sets. However, Bhaskara caught hold of a few last rays (*arka*) of the setting sun and hung them on a nearby *nimba* tree. Hence the meal could be prepared and eaten, because the sun's rays were still shining. He was then called Nimbarka in memory of this incident. Following his name the tradition also came to be known as the Nimbarka tradition.

The Nimbarka tradition is one of the dualist schools of Vaishnavism, in which Radha and Krishna are worshipped together as representing one divinity. It is said that Jayadeva, the author of the text *Gitagovinda,* was a friend of Nimbarka and shared the theological views of Radha and Krishna as dual expressions of the supreme God. The Nimbarka *sampradaya* has ascetic (*vairagi* or *bairagi*) and householder devotees among its initiated followers.

Although the Nimbarka tradition is said to possess extensive literature on Vaishnavism, a large part of its collection was destroyed during the conquests of Aurangzeb (1659–1709). Of the surviving texts, the two most important texts, the *Dasasloki* and the *Vedantaparijatasandarbha*, are attributed to Nimbarka. The *Dasasloki* mentions Krishna and Radha as supreme objects of devotion. The *Vedantasandarbha* is a commentary on the *Brahmasutra* (also known as the *Vedantasutra*). Nimbarka discusses the important issues of the nature of brahma (universal soul) and *atma* (individual soul), and the doctrine of *Bhedabheda*. Although scholars consider that Nimbarka's views show some resemblance to Ramanuja's views, Nimbarka's views do not support *jivanmukti*; according to Nimbarka *moksha* is attaining *samya* (similarity) for the *atma* with the brahma.

The Nimbarka tradition is recognized as one of the four Vaishnava traditions (*Catuh Vaishnava sampradayas*): Ramanuja, Madhva, Vishnusvami, and Nimbarka. The Krishna devotional tradition of Mathura, Haridasi *sampradaya*, is affiliated with the Nimbarka tradition. The Nimbarka tradition also has an affiliated ascetic order consisting of eight *akharas* or sadhus. The *Vaishnava naga* sadhus (*akharas*) are devotees of Krishna and Rama. The *Catuh Vaishnava sampradayas* only meet with their affiliated *akharas* every three years during the *Kumbhmela* when all the

---

Nimgaon

Nimgaon is a small town near Govardhan on the road to Barsana. Nimgaon is considered sacred and important in the Nimbarka tradition. According to the Nimbarka tradition, the founder, Nimbarka, performed his ascetic practices while living in a cave there, which disappeared as the Govardhan hill gradually shrank in size. The temple of Sudarsanji has an icon of Nimbarka, and the pond there is referred to as Sudarsankund or Nimbark Sarovar.

naga sadhus also hold their camp to discuss important matters of doctrine, elect representatives, and meet the chief *mahant*.

Each of the four Vaishnava traditions (*Catuh Vaishnava sampradayas*) has its own *mahants* overseeing the matters of the *akharas* affiliated with them. Although the Nimbarka tradition has householder devotees, it is considered to be primarily an ascetic order. Hence the Nimbarka tradition assigns two types of initiations and two types of *sadhanas* (practices). The first type of initiation and *sadhana* is reserved only for men of high birth, while the second one is for women and people of low birth. Initiates of the second order surrender directly to Krishna (*prapatti* or *saranagati*), a practice that can be adopted by all irrespective of birth or social status. However, initiates of the first order have elaborate initiation rites and wear twelve Vaishnava *tilak* marks on the body. They undertake three forms of *sadhana* (practice): *vidya* (learning), *upasana* (homage or prayers and worship), and *jnana-yoga* (meditation). There is also a third practice reserved for ascetics. An initiated ascetic disciple of the third order obtains direct contact with Krishna by surrendering himself completely to his guru (teacher). *Rasopasana* (contemplation on the love play of Radha and Krishna) is also one of the spiritual paths of the Nimbarkas. The sadhus (ascetics) take a secret name of one of the female companions (*sakhis*) of Radha to help them participate in the *Raasalila* (divine play) of Radha and Krishna in the forests of Brindavan.

Ascetics of the Nimbarka tradition are said to have been active in Braj since the thirteenth century. But from the nineteenth century numerous temples were built by the Nimbarka tradition, and its popularity grew due to *Svami* Haridas (1512–1607) in the early sixteenth century. During the late eighteenth century, the temples of Chatur Shiromani and Anandmanohar Mandir (also known as Shriji Kunj, which served as the main center of the Nimbarka *sampradaya* in Braj) were affiliated with the Salemabad *Gaddi*. The temples of Radhagopal (Brahmachari ji ka mandir) and Madhav Vilas in Brindavan (Jaipurwala mandir) were also built during the late eighteenth century by the ascetics of the Nimbarka tradition with monetary help from the Jaipur royal house. Thatti Astan continues to be the main residential site for the ascetics of the Haridasi tradition, which houses the most popular bhakti tradition within the Nimbarka *sampradaya*. Most of the followers of Nimbarka are local *Chaubes* (*Chaturvedi* Brahmans), one of the most popular devotional groups in Braj, noted for their *samaj gayan* held on the birthday of Haridas, also the birthday of Radha (*Radhashtami*), and their special temple decoration known as *phul bangla* (the flower house). Ascetic followers of Nimbarka have a temple of their legendary founders, the Sanaka brothers, near Govardhan, and they are also responsible for building the temple of Narada in Nimgaon and installing an image of Narada at Narada Kund.

Although the Nimbarka tradition may not seem a very centralized institution, it is one of the most influential schools of Vaishnavism in India. Nimbarkas provide guidance on several practices of Hinduism.

See also: Bhakti; Brindavan; Govardhan; Haridasi *Sampradaya*; Mathura; *Radhashtami*

Further Reading

Beck, Guy L. (2005). "Krishna as a Loving Husband of God." *Alternative Krishnas: Regional and Vernacular Variations on a Hindu Deity.* Albany: SUNY Press.

Brajvallabhasarana, ed. 1972. *Sri Nimbarka Aur Unka Sampradaya.* Vrindavan: Nimbarkapitha.

Clementin-Ojha, C. "Ascetics' Rights in Early 19th Century Jaipur (Rajastan)." In *Asceticism and Power in the South and South-Asian Context*, edited by P. Flugel and G. Houtman. Richmond: Routledge.

Mital, P. 1968. *Braj ke Dharmsapradayom ka Itihasa.* Delhi: National Publishing House.

Pinch, W. R. 2000. *Warrior Ascetics and Indian Empires.* Cambridge, UK: Cambridge University Press.

NIRGUNA/SAGUNA

Nirguna and *saguna* are derivatives of the Sanskrit word *guna*, which could be translated as "attributes" or "qualities." *Nir* is a negative prefix, hence the word *nirguna* stands for "without attributes/qualities" while *sa* is an affirmative prefix, so the word *saguna* stands for "with attributes/qualities." However, both of these words are equally significant for Krishna devotional traditions. As some gurus or *acaryas* propagated devotion to the *saguna* form of the deity, who appears with anthropomorphic qualities, others supported devotion to the *nirguna* form of the deity, the divine absolute, without anthropomorphic qualities. Devotional groups of *saguna* are convinced that worshipping the deity in easily understandable and relatable human form is conducive to self-realization and, thereby, *moksha*. However, the devotional groups of *nirguna* consider that one must pass beyond anthropomorphic understanding of divinity to reach self-realization. Both *saguna* and *nirguna* concepts are complementary and found expression in Krishna theology. While the *saguna* bhakti utilizes visual modes of mindful meditation, the *nirguna* bhakti utilizes aural modes of mindful meditation as a way to find unity with Krishna. Both forms are found among the Krishna bhakti (devotional) traditions. Sometimes *saguna* and *nirguna* supporters might even exist within the same tradition, as noted in the *Varkari* tradition. Namdev, a *sant* (saint) of the *Varkari* tradition, is noted for his support for *nirguna* bhakti; however, others in the same tradition, such as Eknath and Chokhamela, are known supporters of *saguna* bhakti. Although the *Bhagavatapurana* and the *Bhagavadgita* both note the nature of devotion to a personal deity in the form of Krishna, they also note the need for the devotees to progress beyond this personal deity to realize the true reality (*Bhagavadgita* 2.45), the ultimate supreme deity who is formless (*nirguna*).

Humans as living beings are endowed with *gunas* (qualities), generally classified as *satva* (clarity, light, happiness), *rajas* (dust, agitation, vigor), and *tamas* (darkness, confusion). The predominance of one or the other of these three qualities determines the quality of a person's life on Earth. *Satva, tamas,* and *rajas* are also attributed to gods, and the appearance of Vishnu, Brahma, and Shiva, at the beginning of creation is called *gunavatara*, since they manifest to carry on the creation, maintenance, and destruction of the world. However, in their pure form gods are *nirguna* and do not possess the qualities that are commonly associated with the earthly realm.

See also: Advaita; *Avatara*; *Bhagavadgita*; Chokhamela; Eknath; Namdev; *Varkari* Tradition

Further Reading

Carr, B. 1999. "Sankara and the Principle of Material Causation (Hindu Religious Philosophy)." *Religious Studies* 35 (4): 425–439.
Singh, R. R. 2006. *Bhakti and Philosophy*. New York: Lexington Books.
Werner, K. 2013. *Love Divine: Studies in "Bhakti" and Mysticism*. London: Routledge.

P

PAINTING AND KRISHNA

Using illustrations as part of storytelling is an ancient technique practiced in India. Scrolls, murals, and sculpted panels on the walls of temples may have been used as supplemental illustrations to the oral narrative traditions, which commonly recount the *purana* narratives for the information of the common people and visitors to the temple. This might have been a popular mode of learning in ancient and medieval India since few people were literate, and books were not freely and easily available. Temple sculptures may have been replicated from paintings of the events of the life of Krishna, for example, which may have existed previously in paintings on paper or cloth. The lighter styling of the sculptures, almost like a line drawing, along with surrounding scenery including trees, birds, and so on indicates such influence. The Vallabha tradition uses paintings, art, and craftwork as a major part of devotion in temples as well as homes. Although other devotional traditions may also use paintings, they may employ them only as devotional objects. The Vallabha tradition uses the paintings as devotional objects, but also as narrative panels on the walls of its temples. Several regional and folk traditions also depict the events of Krishna's life as a major part of the tradition. Krishna is depicted in a number of ways on calendar art. Miniature paintings of the Rajasthani (Mewar, Udaipur), Bundi, Kotah, Marwar (Jodhpur), Bikaner, Jaipur, and Kishangarh art styles depict *Krishnalila* (the play of Krishna) from the *Bhagavatapurana*. Avadhi paintings are noted for depictions of Krishna from the poetry of Surdas. Several tribal styles of paintings from Santal regions are also well known for depicting the life of Krishna. *Patacitra* originated in the rituals of the Jagannatha temple, depicting events in Krishna's life. It still continues to be a popular art form portraying religious

---

Themes of Painting

Although murals are not uncommon, miniature paintings abundantly depict the life of Krishna. Numerous paintings of Krishna vanquishing the demons, as well as his pastimes in Brindavan with Radha and the other *Gopis* (cowherd maidens) form the major subjects of the paintings of Krishna. The *Bhagavatapurana* and the *Gitagovinda* form the background of the *Krishnalila* paintings, especially those involving Radha and the *Gopis*. The *ragamala* (musical notes) theme, *baramasa* (twelve months) theme, or *ruturaga* (seasons with musical overtones) form the variety of paintings of Krishna with Radha and the *Gopis*.

The reversal of roles (*lila hava*), scene from the *Krishna Lila* (*The Play of Krishna*), folio from an illustrated *Sur Sagar* (*Ocean of Melody*) watercolor series from Udaipur, Rajasthan, ca. 1725–1735. (Los Angeles County Museum of Art)

subjects, although certain secular subjects could also be depicted sometimes.

Paintings of Krishna in the Vallabha tradition are called *pichvai* (back side), because they are traditionally hung on the back wall behind the central icon of the image of Krishna in the temples. Traditional *pichvais* are only drawn by professional painters associated with Vallabha temples. Although some artists not associated with the Vallabha tradition are attempting currently to draw and sell similar paintings on the open market, these are sold in the temple itself. Most of the *pichvais* depict Srinathji in events from the *Bhagavatapurana*, thus epitomizing the central icon of the lord for devotees to take home. Another painting style that emerged along with the Krishna devotional tradition is the Tanjavur style (Tanjore, Tamilnadu) of painting, which mostly depicts Krishna in his childhood exploits and *Krishnalila* events. One specialty of Tanjore paintings is the use of precious stones and gold within the painting, giving it a very pleasing and rich look.

See also: Krishna; *Raasalila*; Surdas

Further Reading

Caitanya, K. 1994. *A History of Indian Painting*. Delhi: Abhinav Publications.
Chakraverty, A. 1996. *Indian Miniature Painting*. Delhi: Roli Books.
Kramerisch, S. 1994. *Exploring India's Sacred Art*. Delhi: Indira Gandhi Center for the Arts.
Vatsyayan, K. 2004. *Dance in Indian Paintings*. Delhi: Abhinav Publications.
Vyas, C., and T. Daljeet. 1988. *Paintings of Tanjore and Mysore*. Jhansi: Gita.
Welch, S. T. 1985. *India: Art and Culture*. New York: Metropolitan Museum of Art.

PANCARATRA

The *Pancaratra* tradition is one of the oldest schools of Vaishnavism in India. Its earliest beginnings are traced to at least 200 BCE, and its traditions are followed by later Vaishnava *sampradayas*, such as the Srivaishnava tradition. The earliest evidence for the *Pancaratra* tradition comes from a 500 BCE text, Panini's *Ashtadhayi*

(4.3.98), which analyzes the word *Vaasudevakas* (follower of Vaasudeva), which demonstrates that the worship of Vaasudeva was well established by that time. Vaasudeva Krishna and his brother Samkarsana are also depicted on a silver coin of the Indo-Greek King Agathocles from Ai-Khanoum (Afghanistan), and on rock cliffs at Chilas (Pakistan), dated to 200 BCE. Both show the images identified as Vaasudeva Krishna and his brother Balarama (Samkarsana). The Satavahana queen Naganika's inscription in the Nanaghat cave in Maharashtra, dated to 100 CE, begins with an invocation to Samkarsana and Vaasudeva. *Pancaratra* may have its origins in the *Pancavira* tradition of northwestern India. The Mora well inscription in Mathura mentions construction of a temple for the *pancaviras* of the Vrishni clan. Although the names of these heroes are not mentioned in the inscriptions, the *purana* texts mention them as Samkarsana, Vasudava, Pradyumna, Samba, and Aniruddha. The list includes Krishna's elder brother Samkarsana (also known as Balarama), two of his sons (Pradyumna and Samba), and a grandson (Aniruddha). The centrality of Krishna in this group is unmistakable. The Besnagar Garuda pillar inscription mentions that a Greek ambassador, *Bhagavata* Heliodorus, erected a Garuda pillar for Vaasudeva.

Scholars as well as its practitioners have interpreted the name *Pancaratra* variously. Several scholars interpret *Pancaratra* as denoting Vishnu teaching all knowledge and ritual in five nights (including days). Others interpret it as imparting the knowledge to five disciples over five nights. The *Pancaratra* tradition states that five nights perish after the five senses reach the light (enlightenment), which may only indicate a symbolic meaning for the word *pancaratra* (five nights). However, it is notable that all the definitions interpret *panca* as five and *ratri* as night, the usual meaning of the Sanskrit words. Therefore, it can be understood as a type of ritual lasting five nights, maybe with one participant or many to lead to the light (*moksha* or enlightenment). From these explanations it can be deduced that *Pancaratra* practice involved meditation rituals over five nights.

A large compendium of classical Sanskrit literature is attributed to the *Pancaratra* tradition, including the *Narayaniya* section of the *Mahabharata*, as well as the *samhita* texts such as the *Jayakhyasimhita*, *Ahirbudhnyasamhita*, *Lakshmitantra*, and *Padmasamhita*.

The philosophical and cosmological concepts of *Pancaratra* are very complex. *Pancaratra* theology states that the Supreme Being is manifested in five different ways: *para* (supreme form, beyond cognition and recognition), *vyuha* (emanation), *vibhava* (incarnatory form), *avatara* (incarnation), and *antaryami* (form that dwells in the hearts of all). According to the textual sources, the cosmology of *Pancaratra* begins with the emanation of four *vyuhas* (*Caturvyuhas*) referred to as Samkarsana, Vaasudeva, Pradyumna, and Aniruddha, although some texts also mention twelve *vyuhantaras* that arise from the four *vyuhas*. These twelve *vyuhantaras* are also known as the tutelary deities of the months in the ritual calendar. According to the concept of *vibhavas*, numerous incarnations could arise at a single event such as the thirty-eight *vibhavas* that arise from a luminous pillar (*visakhayupa*); sometimes secondary emanations known as *vibhavantaras* are also described in the *Pancaratra* texts. Almost all the names that are mentioned in these lists are identified with forms of Vishnu and appear in the list of the 108 names of Vishnu. *Pancaratra* consists of the most elaborate theology depicting the icon as the earthly manifestation of the god for worship (*arca avatara*), hence considered an incarnation of the deity himself.

The concept of God is understood as transcendent and immanent in the *Pancaratra* tradition, which notes that the *jiva* (soul) of an individual is a form of God. As a ritual-based tradition, *Pancaratra* consists of several mantras for various rituals. It also includes specific initiation rites called *diksha*. Three types of rituals are usually described in the *Pancaratra* texts: *Nitya* (daily rituals), *Naimittika* (the ritual for special occasions), and *Kamya* (rituals to fulfill desires).

Pancaratra, being one of the oldest Vaishnava traditions, remains a trove of knowledge on the practice, ritual, and theology of the later Vaishnava traditions that have evolved since 900 CE.

See also: Avatara; Narayana; Vishnu; *Vyuhas*

Further Reading

Rastelli, M. 2009. "Perceiving God and Becoming Like Him: Yogic Perception and Its Implications in the Visnuitic Tradition of *Pancaratra*." *Yogic Perception, Meditation and Altered States of Consciousness* 794: 299–317.
Schrader, F. O. 1916. *Introduction to the Pancaratra, and Ahirbudhnya Samhita.* Madras: Adyar Library and Research Center.
Schreiner, P., ed. 1997. *Narayaniya Studien.* Wiesbaden: ZDMG.
Vemsani, L. 2006. *Hindu and Jain Mythology of Balarama.* New York: Edwin Mellen.

PANCAVIRAS
see Vyuhas

PANDARPUR TEMPLE

The Pandarpur temple of Krishna, locally known as the Panduranga or Vitthala temple, is the most important Krishna temple in Maharashtra. Pilgrimage to Pandarpur (*vari*) occurs twice a year (on *Ashada Ekadasi* and *Kartika Ekadasi*) from all across Maharashtra, with thousands of pilgrims traveling hundreds of miles, walking in groups known as *dindis*. The Pandarpur temple is a large complex with a separate shrine for Krishna's wife Rukmini. There are six entrances to the temple complex. The main one is on the east, which is also called the Namdev Gate because it is marked by the devotion of Namdev and Chokhamela. In front of that main entrance is a small memorial shrine (*samadhi*) dedicated to Chokhamela. It is a rare posthumous honor that immortalizes the devotion of Chokhamela in the form of a *samadhi* dedicated to a devotee, established right in front of the sacred temple. Namdev recovered the body of Chokhamela from a collapsed building where Chokhamela was working and had the *samadhi* constructed in front of the temple at the main gate, where Chokhamela used to stand and offer his prayers to the central deity of the temple, Vitthala. Thus Chokhamela's devotion and dedication to Vitthala is epitomized in the shrine memorial at the Pandarpur temple. Namdev's devotion is memorialized as the first step of the main entrance at the temple. The first step is called *Namdev chi payari*, meaning "the step of Namdev." The temple legend recounts that once Namdev's mother had asked him to offer *Naivedya* (a ritual food offering to God), as she was away on some urgent work. Namdev offered the *Naivedya*, but God did not touch it. In his childhood innocence, Namdev cried and bashed his head on the stairs in front of the temple. The god Vitthala then appeared and tasted the *Naivedya* offered to him. This pleased Namdev, and the first step at the main entrance memorializes this devotional moment of Namdev with Vitthala, the central deity of the temple. Devotees entering the temple offer their obeisance to the first step in the memory of Namdev before entering the temple.

The temple itself contains numerous shrines within the compound. The main temple has a square-shaped floor plan with a pyramidal *shikhara* (tower) above the *garbhagriha* (sanctum sanctorum). The *garbhagriha* houses Krishna in his simple two-armed form, with his arms resting on his waist, locally known as Vitthala (Vithoba) or Panduranga. Shrines for Shiva, Pundalik, and Rukmini are also found in the temple complex. The temple of Vitthala is located on the banks of the Chandrabhaga River on a high platform. An image of Namdev is also housed in the temple complex. Numerous saints of Maharashtra (Namdev, Jnanadev, Eknath, Tukaram, and Chokhamela) are devotees of Vitthala (Krishna) in the Pandarpur temple, composing numerous *abhangs* about the god Vitthala, which form part of Marathi culture and are commonly sung in *kirtan* performances.

Krishna appears as a simple householder in this temple, unlike any other temple legends associated with Krishna. Devotion to Vitthala (Krishna) in Pandarpur has shaped the culture of Maharashtra in a unique manner. The *Varkari* pilgrimage is undertaken twice a year, and *kirtan* performances across the state form the unique cultural matrix of Maharashtra.

See also: Chokhamela; Eknath; Jnanadev; Namdev; Panduranga Vitthala; *Sants*; *Varkari* Tradition

Further Reading

Deleury, G. A. 1960. *The Cult of Vithoba*. Pune: Deccan College.
Novetzke, C. L. 2005. "A Family Affair: Krishna Comes to Pandharpur and Makes Himself at Home." In *Alternative Krishnas*, edited by G. L. Beck. Albany: SUNY Press.

PANDAVAS

The Pandavas, also known as *Pancapandavas* (the five Pandavas), are the five sons of Pandu, called Dharma, Bhima, Arjuna, and the twins Nakula and Sahadeva. While Dharma, Bhima, and Arjuna are the sons of Pandu's first wife, Kunthi, the twins Nakula and Sahadeva are the sons of Madri, Pandu's second wife. Although the Pandavas are the sons of Pandu, they were born of divine conception. The *Mahabharata* narrates that Pandu was cursed to face death any time he desired sexual union with a woman. Hence, Pandu and his wives were living an ascetic life in the mountainous region of the Himalayas. However, Pandu was always dejected that he could not have sons, and one day expressed his sorrow to his wife Kunthi. Kunthi informed him that she had a solution for this dilemma, since Durvasa had blessed her with a mantra to obtain sons from anyone she desired. Pandu then convinced her to invite Yamadharmaraja, the lord of hell, through whom their first son, Dharma, was born. She then had Bhima from Vayu (god of the wind) and Arjuna through Indra (king of the gods). Pandu convinced Kunthi to impart the mantra to Madri, his second wife, so she could also have children. Madri then obtained the twins, Nakula and Sahadeva, by invoking the twin gods, the Asvins. However, Pandu died soon after, as he desired union with Madri one day, and Madri committed the ritual of *sati* (suicide on the funeral pyre of the husband). Kunthi raised the five children in the household of the Kauravas in Hastinapur.

Pandu's wife Kunthi is the sister of Vasudeva, father of Krishna. Krishna has a close relationship with the Pandavas. Arjuna and Bhima, the second and third Pandavas, are close associates of Krishna. Krishna shares a friendly and soulful (*sakhya*) relationship with Arjuna. Krishna also imparted the *Bhagavadgita* to Arjuna, and they are represented as the *Naranarayana* pair, representing the relationship between the human and divine. Bhima was instrumental in eliminating Jarasandha, the archenemy of Krishna and the Yadavas. Dharma, Nakula, and Sahadeva respected Krishna and paid homage to him. It was Sahadeva who proposed that Krishna must be propitiated first at their *Rajasuya* ceremony in Indraprastha. Dharma always consulted Krishna on all matters of importance. He nominated Krishna as the envoy of the Pandavas to negotiate peace with the Kauravas before the *Mahabharata* war.

Numerous temples are dedicated to the Pandavas across India, while the festival of Draupadi is celebrated with utmost respect and fanfare in southern India. The shore temple complex on the east coast of India near the city of Mahabalipuram contains shrines for the five Pandavas and their wife Draupadi, which are popularly known as *pancapandavarathas* and *Draupadiratha*. These shrines and shore temple were the earliest rock-cut temples, constructed during the late sixth century. The temples provide important evidence for the early worship of the Pandavas. They are also considered early examples of the evolution of temple architecture from cave temples to architectural structures.

See also: Arjuna; Bhima; Jarasandha; *Mahabharata*

Further Reading

Picard, B. 1968. *Story of the Pandavas*. London: Dobson Books.

PANDURANGA VITTHALA

The first reference to Panduranga occurs in an inscription dated to 516 CE, referring to Pandarpur as "the village of Panduranga," which might indicate the presence of the deity Panduranga in the village prior to the date of the inscription. It is not unusual for Krishna to assume the name of the village or town where he is established as the central deity. Krishna is known as Guruvayurappa (lord of

Vitthala in Popular Culture

Panduranga Mahatmyam, a Telugu film released in 1957, portrays the story of the arrival of Krishna in Pandarpur and Pundalika's devotion. Telugu poet Tenali Ramakrishna's *The Panduranga Mahathmyam* and Bahina Bai's *Pundalika Mahatmya* are well-known texts on the arrival of Vitthala in Pandarpur. Several Marathi and Hindi films depict Panduranga and the sacred history of Pandarpur. A 2008 Marathi film depicts the miracles of Panduranga Vitthala as he helped one of his devotees.

Guruvayur) in Guruvayur (Kerala), Venkatesvara (lord of Venkata) in Tirupathi (Andhra Pradesh), and Ranganatha in Srirangam (Tamilnadu). Hence, Krishna being referred to as Panduranga in Pandarpur (Maharashtra) is not unusual, but merely emblematic of this tradition. Panduranga Vitthala is a combination of three names, Pandu, Ranga and Vitthala, denoting Krishna in Pandarpur (the city of Pandar or Pandari), Maharashtra. Pandu is the shortened name of Pandari, which is the colloquial name for the city of Pandarpur. Ranga denotes play or playful, a ubiquitous quality of Krishna, noted in classical texts as well as the folk traditions of India. Vitthala, or Vittu (Vitthala is Vittu joined with "ala," the prefix or suffix denoting respect), is a Prakrit form of Vishnu, the Sanskrit name of the highest god, equated with Krishna. However, this name is interpreted differently in the popular bhakti tradition of Maharashtra, the *Varkari* tradition. The popular tradition narrates that Krishna visited the town looking for Rukmini, who had left him, as she was upset about his dalliances with the cowherd women, the *Gopis*. He got thirsty and, looking for information, stopped at the door of a householder, Pundalik, and asked for directions. Pundalik, who was serving his parents, told Krishna to wait and threw a brick for him to stand on, so he did not have to stand in mud. As Pundalik was eternally serving his parents, Krishna was held there waiting for Pundalik, standing on the brick, where a temple was built for him. Since brick is known as *vit* in Marathi, it is considered to have contributed to the origin of the name of Krishna as Vitthala, "Lord standing on the Brick." However, some scholars have variously explained the name of Panduranga as representing the color white, since the Sanskrit word *pandu* means white, connecting the temple to Saivism, which is too farfetched. Panduranga is praised as the beloved Krishna in the *abhangs* of the *Varkari* saints of Maharashtra beginning in the twelfth century. The *Varkari* saints of Maharashtra (Jnanadev, Namdev, Eknath, and Chokhamela) praise Vitthala, the lord of Pandarpur, as Krishna and Vishnu in their devotional poems. *Varkari* pilgrimages, arriving twice each year to Pandarpur, bring numerous devotees from all across Maharashtra to the temple of Vitthala to worship and venerate the central deity. There is no question about the identity of the god in Pandarpur in the minds of devotees. Panduranga Vitthala is Krishna, settled in Pandarpur with his wife, Rukmini, who connects with devotees directly, listening to their prayers, as noted in the biographies of the *Varkari* saints. Devotees of Vitthala may undertake pilgrimages to visit other holy places associated with Krishna, such as

Mathura, Brindavan, and Dvaraka. However, Vitthala, the Krishna of Maharashtra who has made Pandarpur his home, is none other than the Krishna who played in Gokula and Brindavan. Krishna is a family man in Pandarpur, living with his first wife, Rukmini; he is a householder who has left his childhood pranks in faraway Mathura. The Krishna of Pandarpur is unlike the Krishna of any other holy city, as Namdev said upon his return to Pandarpur from his long pilgrimages with Jnanadev in northern India.

See also: Brindavan; Chokhamela; Dvaraka; Eight Wives of Krishna; Eknath; *Gopas and Gopis;* Jnanadev; Mathura; Namdev; Pandarpur Temple; Radha; *Varkari* Tradition

Further Reading

Dealery, G. A. 1960. *The Cult of Vitthoba*. Pune: Deccan College.
Dhere, R. C. 1984. *Sri Vitthala Eka Mahasamanvaya*. Pune: Srividya Prakasan.
Vaudeville, C. 1996. *Myths, Saints and Legends in Medieval India*. Delhi: Oxford University Press.

PERFORMING ARTS AND KRISHNA

The performing arts of India, in addition to sculpture, painting, and literature, are tremendously influenced and inspired by numerous events of the life of Krishna narrated in the *Bhagavatapurana* and the *Mahabharata*. Dances are based on events such as the *Kaliyadamana*. The episode of *Kaliyadamana* prompted scholarly theories that the subjugation of the serpent Kaliya might not initially have involved Krishna's dancing on its hoods, an event that might have been a later embellishment as artistic tradition becomes commonly associated with almost all events of Krishna's life as part of his divine play (*lila*) in Vraj. The *Raasalila* (popularly known as *Maharas*) of Krishna in Brindavan provides recurring themes and inspiration for a number of dance styles and theater performances. Some traditions, such as the *Satriya* dance, *Ankiya Nat*, *Kuchipudi*, *Krishna Attam*, *Ghumar*, *Jatra*, *Kirthana*, and *Haridasu* originated within the Krishna devotional tradition and continue to thrive on religious performances held during festival days and regular ritual performances at Krishna temples.

The performing arts have always held a special place in Hindu religious life. Dance is a sacrifice in Vedic practice, which continued to influence Vedanta religious practice; in relation to Krishna, dance became a part of divine *lila* in the *puranas* and the *Mahabharata*. The performing arts (dance, drama, and music) fulfill the dual role of celebration and offering (*seva* or *upacara*). They celebrate the deity on the one hand, while on the other hand performances serve as offerings to the deity similar to the *seva/upacaras* (services) offered to the deity during *puja*. Devotees can pay for the service (*seva/upacaras*) to be performed by an artist as an offering to the deity on their behalf. *Pancaratra agamas* note that dance, music, and enacting (theater) for Krishna (Vishnu) are important forms of offerings (*upacaras*). *Krishna bhakti* contributed to the development of numerous performance traditions and a variety of regional styles in India. *Ankiya Nat* theater and the *Satriya* dance of Assam owe their origin to the Krishna devotional tradition founded by Sankaradeva in Assam, while *Jatra* in Orissa and Bengal owes much of its popularity to Caitanya. The Maharashtrian *sants* (*Varkari* tradition) contributed to the *kirtan* tradition; the *samaj gayan* tradition was developed by Haridasi *sampradaya* and Hit Harivams; *yakshagana* in Karnataka and Andhra Pradesh was developed by *Haridasas* and *Bhagavatakaras*; while a unique dance style of Andhra Pradesh, *Kuchipudi*, as well as the *Manipuri* dance style of Manipur originated in the Krishna devotional practices.

See also: Ankiya Nat; Baredi; Bhagavatamela; Bhakti; *Haveli Sangit; Jatra; Krishnattam; Kuchipudi; Lila; Manipuri* Dance; *Maya; Pancaratra; Samaj Gayan*

Further Reading

Gupta, R. K. 1984. *The Yoga of Indian Classical Dance: The Yogini's Mirror.* Rochester, VT: Inner Traditions/Bear.

Vastyayan, K. 1990. *Classical Dance of India.* New Delhi: Publications Division, Government of India.

Sobha Naidu, a popular, internationally renown dancer, performs Krishna Parijatham Kuchipudi dance during *Naatya Tarang* in April 2012 in Hyderabad, India. (B R Ramana Reddi/Dreamstime.com)

PERIYALVAR

The name Periyalvar could literally be translated as the Big *Alvar* or the Great *Alvar*, although he referred to himself by the name Vishnucitta, which means "He Whose Mind Is Full of Vishnu." Information about the life of Periyalvar is scant. Details about his service at the Villiputtur temple and his achievements in the theological and religious arena are common knowledge from his compositions, which were also supplemented by the compositions of his daughter. One could also learn important information from the compositions of another *alvar*, his adopted daughter, Andal, who calls him *Bhatta Piran*, meaning "Lord of the Learned," although

---

Srivilliputtur

The Srivilliputtur temple is associated with father and daughter *alvars* Periyalvar and Andal. The temple tower (*Rajagopuram*) of the Srivilliputtur temple is the official symbol of the state government of Tamilnadu. The temple tower is 192 feet high and is the second tallest temple tower in the state of Tamilnadu next only to the temple tower of the Srirangam temple. One of the special festivals of the Srivilliputtur temple is the procession of Periyalvar leading the five Garudas of the nearby temples, who visit him on the festival of *Panca Garuda Seva* on the occasion of the fifth day of the *Aadi Utsavam*. Periyalvar receives them at the eastern entrance of the temple. The procession takes place around the temple on Mada and Ratha streets. Periyalvar is seated at the head of the procession facing the five Garudas, who follow him in the procession.

Srivaishnava hagiographies depict him as a naïve gardener of absolute faith and simple life. There are two major aspects of the life of Periyalvar: one is winning a debate at the theological council organized by the Pandya emperor at Madurai, and the second is marrying his adopted daughter, Andal, to Krishna in his worshipful (*arcavatara*) form as Sriranganatha. Periyalvar was an erudite scholar of the classical Sanskrit literature including the Vedic and *purana* literature; he clearly envisaged his compositions in liturgical recitations since he is said to have set his compositions to music and danced in praise of Vishnu. As Periyalvar admitted in one of his poems, "singing and dancing these ten verses from the thousand Tamil songs sung by Catakopan" (*Tiruvaymoli* 9.10.11), he lost himself.

Although not much is known about Periyalvar's educational background, it can be understood from his own references in the *Tiruvaymoli* that he was well versed in Sanskrit and learned in Vedic scripture as he himself stated that he "reaped the fruits of the *Vedas*" (*Tiruvoymoli* 2.8.10) and that he "reveres the *Rig*, *Sama*, and *Yajurveda*" (*Tiruvoymoli* 5.1.6). Periyalvar's descriptions within the text of *Tirumoli* also indicate his thorough grasp of the knowledge of the Krishna legend as known from the earlier Sanskrit text, the *Harivamsa*.

The first major event in the life of Periyalvar was winning the debate at the theological council organized by the Pandya ruler in Madurai. Hagiographical literature notes that Periyalvar was a reluctant participant in the debate, nudged by none other than Vishnu himself, who had urged him to participate in the assembly of theologians. As the legend goes, Periyalvar had let his concerns about his lack of knowledge be known to Vishnu in his dream vision, which the Lord dispelled by promising to help him with all the knowledge he needed to win the debate at the assembly. Periyalvar susequently attended the assembly and won the debate with the help of Vishnu. Praising Vishnu as the supreme deity, Periyalvar composed the *Tirupallandu*, which forms the first twelve compositions of the *Nalayira Divya Prabandham*.

Another major event in the life of Periyalvar is related to his daughter Andal's marriage to Vishnu. It so happened that one day while clearing the garden of basil (*tulasi*) he found a child, whom he raised as his own daughter. As Andal grew up

 nu, not any ordinary mortal. Legends of Andal
3hudevi, Goddess of the Earth, who was finally
, after marriage.

Periyalvar lives on in the temple traditions of the
alvar is an important part of the festival celebra-
ne Srivilliputtur Andal temple.

Divya Prabandham; Ramanuja; Srirangam Temple;

Playful Son, Krishna: Periyalvar's 9th Century Tirumoli.
in Studies Association.
rious Tiruvallaval: An Exploration in the Methods and
ntary." Journal of African and Oriental Studies 111:

Early History of Krishna Devotion in South India. Delhi:

itten Comments on Tiruvaymoli." In Text in Context:
. Asia, edited by J. Timm, 85–109. Albany: SUNY Press.
ns: Andal's Wedding and Nammalvar's Moksa." Journal
90.
the Drowning: Poems for Vishnu by Nammalvar. Prince-

. places in the legend of Krishna. For the devotees
the only remaining landmark of what is left of the
city, which was submerged in the ocean according
y renowned as a pilgrimage city, which was de-
Prabhasatirtha (Mahabharata 118.15, 119.1–3).
ction with Krishna at least twice in the Bhagavata-
: associated with death.
vith death is narrated as Krishna launched a search
Krishna reached Prabhasa while searching for the
: looked everywhere but failed to find him. Reach-
na summoned the ocean (Sagara), demanding to
den the son of the sage Sandipani. The God of the
a that Pancajanya (a demon who assumes the form
iducted the boy. Krishna dove into the ocean and
nell with him, and from then on, Pancajanya the
adornments.
annihilation of the Yadavas on the beach of Prab-
hasa, which was followed by Krishna's death. The legend states that Samba, a son
of Krishna by Jambavati, angered the sages, who cursed the Yadavas with annihilation. Since Samba disguised himself as pregnant, the sages' curse stated that a

pestle would be born to Samba, which would cause the end of the race of Yadavas. Samba changed his disguise to find an iron pestle. Panicked, Samba and the other Yadava boys met the Yadava king, Ugrasena, who had the pestle finely ground and thrown into the ocean. However, the powder reached Prabhasa where it was absorbed by the reeds on the banks of the ocean. When the Yadavas reached the beach to have a picnic, they began hitting each other with the reeds in a drunken brawl and died instantly, thus bringing about their annihilation. Seeing this, Krishna and Balarama retreated. Balarama sat in meditation on the beach, later emerging as a snake out of his human body; he entered his abode, the world of *nagas* (serpents). Krishna entered the forest and sat in meditation under a tree. A hunter hit Krishna's big toe with an arrow, mistaking it for the ear of a deer, which caused Krishna's death. A temple marks the spot where Krishna died. This is one of the important pilgrimage spots devotees of Krishna visit on their pilgrimage circuit from Dvaraka.

The city of Prabhasa is an entry point into India from both the sea and land routes from the Gulf Coast and Pakistan respectively. Prabhasa is only two kilometers away from Somnath, another holy city, a major Saiva pilgrimage center, which was subjected to a number of Muslim raids from the sultans of Afghanistan, including Mohammad Ghori and Mohammad Ghazni. Prabasa is also a place of west-flowing rivers. The historical river Saraswathi is said to have flowed west from this city (*Bhagavatapurana* 30.6) toward the Indian Ocean. The *Bhagavatapurana* refers to it as *Sankhoddharatirtha*, a place of pilgrimage, in order to signify it as a place of mythological significance associated with Krishna. The *Bhagavatapurana* also mentions that Prabhasa is located on the Saraswati River and the coast of Gujarath. Prabhasa is located on the river Hiranya (or Hiran) where it joins the Indian Ocean. The Archaeological Survey of India has conducted undersea explorations and excavations in Prabhasa on the Somnath Coast area to establish the relative dating and historicity of Prabhasa along with Dvaraka. Numerous stone artifacts and pottery fragments recovered from the marine explorations reveal similarities and close affinities with Dvaraka, the submerged capital city of Krishna.

See also: Death of Krishna; Dvaraka; Samba

Further Reading

Rao, S. R., S. Tripathi, and A. S. Gaur. 1992. "A Preliminary Exploration of Prabhasa-Somnath." *Marine Arachaeology* 3: 13–17.

PRADYUMNA

Pradyumna is the son of Krishna and Rukmini. The demon Sambara took him away and threw him in the ocean, since he knew that the child would kill him if he were allowed to live. The child was swallowed by a large fish, which was subsequently caught by some fishermen, who gave it to Sambara as a gift. The fish was then sent to the kitchen for cooking. Upon cutting up the fish, the cooks discovered a male child and brought him to Mayavati, who was assigned to cook grains by Sambara. Incidentally, Mayavati is Rati in disguise, whose husband was Kama.

Shiva had annihilated Kama's body; hence, Mayavati was waiting for him to be reborn into another body. In fact, Narada informed her that the child in front of her was her husband, reborn as Pradyumna, the child of Krishna and Rukmini. Mayavati took care of the boy, and when he had grown up, she approached him with love. Pradyumna told her it was inappropriate, to which she responded by telling him about their relationship and his former life. She also urged him to kill Sambara, who had thrown Pradyumna into the ocean to kill him. Pradyumna subsequently killed the demon Sambara. They married. Pradyumna desired to meet his parents. Pradyumna and Rati reached Dvaraka and went to the women's quarters, where the women had mistaken Pradyumna for Krishna, since Pradyumna resembled Krishna closely. Rukmini saw Pradyumna and felt her motherly instincts, so she approached him. Learning that he was in fact her long-lost son, Rukmini felt elated and embraced him.

See also: Dvaraka; Eight Wives of Krishna

Further Reading

Brinkhaus, H., and Jagatprakasamalla. 1987. *The Pradyumna-Prabhavati Legend in Nepal: A Study of the Hindu Myth of the Draining of the Nepal Valley.* Stuttgart: F. Steiner Verlag Wiesbaden.

PRASADA

Prasada, translated as mercy, grace, or sacrament, has important theological significance for Hinduism, and especially for the followers of Krishna. *Prasada*, also referred to as *mahaprasada*, is any food preparation offered to the deity in a temple, which is then distributed among the attending devotees as *prasadam*. In the first sense of the word, *prasada* or *mahaprasada* is an offering to the deity, but in the second sense of the word, *prasada* is leftover food distributed to the devotees. *Prasada* therefore signifies the interconnectedness of deity and devotee, as well as the cyclical nature of life. In fact, as stated by Krishna in the *Bhagavadgita* (3.13), "those who eat food offered to the God are released from their sins while others who eat only for themselves without first offering it to the God are eating only sin." Krishna also specified what could be offered as a *prasada*: simple natural products such as "flower, fruit, leaf, and water," offered with love. Krishna said, "I will take it" (*Bhagavadgita*. 9.26). The *Bhagavadgita* also divides food into three categories (*Bhagavadgita*. 17.7–10): as *tamasika* (food in ignorance or darkness), *rajasika* (food of the middle way, which signifies attachment and desire), and *satvika* (food in goodness). *Satvika* food (*Bhagavadgita*. 17.8) is considered good for a person's health and well-being, in that it promotes balance of thought, leading one to happiness, calmness, and compassion, thus contributing to positive energy around the person. Hence, the ideal offering is thus considered to be vegetarian food. All the devotional traditions of Krishna follow these guidelines of *prasadam*, and only vegetarian food is offered to the god. *Pancamrita* is one of the most common offerings, made by mixing milk, curd, sugar, honey, and ghee. *Pancamrita* is very easy to prepare and also considered most auspicious, and hence it is the most commonly offered *prasada* in temples as well as in homes during *puja* (worship). However, an elaborate lunch preparation is offered to the god, called *mahabhog* or *mahaprasad* (*naivedya*), consisting of several varieties of food freshly prepared each day. Temples are equipped with large kitchens that cook *prasadam* to be offered to the deity, which is subsequently served to the devotees every day. The Jagannatha temple at Puri, the Ranganatha temple in Srirangam, and the Venkatesvara temple in Tirupathi are noted for distributing *prasadam* to thousands of visiting devotees every day, as well as for serving a free lunch (also considered *prasadam*) to thousands of devotees. The concept of *prasadam* also pervades the food practices of devotional traditions centered on Krishna. Vegetarianism, insistence on moderation in alcoholic drinks, and abstinence from hallucinatory substances are universal principles followed among all the Krishna devotional traditions.

See also: Bhagavadgita; Bhakti; Puri Temple; *Seva*; Srirangam Temple

Further Reading

Pinkney, A. M. 2013. "Prasada, the Gracious Gift, in Contemporary and Classical South Asia." *Journal of the American Academy of Religion* 81 (3): 734–756.

Schweig, G. 2010. *Bhagavadgita: The Beloved Lord's Secret Love Song*. New York: HarperOne.

PRIYAPRAVAS

The story of the *Priyapravas* depicts the love play of Radha and Krishna in Brindavan, which finally ends when Krishna leaves for Mathura, never to return. Although it is a story of Krishna and Radha, it can be considered a story of Radha for the ingenious changes it introduced into the depiction of Radha's character. Although the *Priyapravas*'s depiction of Radha is similar to earlier narratives in its broad outline, it differs significantly in the characterization of Radha from the other original stories written earlier about the love of Radha and Krishna by numerous devotional poets. In the earlier narratives Radha is completely passive, depending on Krishna and her friends for her every need to be provided. She is drawn by Krishna through his charms, searching relentlessly for him, helped by her friends. However, in the *Priyapravas*, she is initially indifferent to Krishna, and she only falls in love with him after he woos her through his constant efforts. Radha felt sad once Krishna had left for Mathura and never returned, but she recovered quickly from a penchant for Krishna. A complete reversal of Radha's role is seen in the episode of Uddhava's return to Braj with Krishna's message. When Uddhava delivered his message to the *Gopis* (cowherd maidens) in the other texts, they listened and cried in desperation, only to find temporary relief from Uddhava's words. However, Radha, in the *Priyapravas*, has her own message for Uddhava, which she delivers to him in a thoughtful and mature manner. In the *Priyapravas*, Radha is not the lovelorn desperate woman waiting for the return of her beloved, but a smart, educated, and independent woman who devotes herself to social work in the absence of her beloved instead of being driven into depression out of desolation without her beloved. Changes in Radha's depiction between texts are common.

The *Priyapravas*'s depiction of Radha is akin to that of modern twentieth-century women in India, its date of composition. The *Bhagavatapurana* does not even mention Radha by name, calling her a "special *Gopi*" of Krishna, while Radha is the central character of the *Gitagovinda*, noted as an epitome of love. It is in the *Priyapravas* that Radha finally speaks as an individual. Her resurrection as a modern, educated woman committed to social causes is completed by the *Priyapravas*.

See also: Bhagavatapurana; Brindavan; *Gitagovinda*; Radha; Uddhava

Further Reading

Ritter, V. 2004. "Epiphany in Radha's Arbor: Nature and the Reform of *Bhakti* in Hariaudh's *Priyapravas*." In *Alternate Krishnas*, edited by G. L. Beck, 177–208. Albany: SUNY Press.

PUJA

Puja, also referred to as *arcana* or *arati/harati*, is worship of the deity and varies depending on the location and occasion. *Puja* takes place in temples; there is a domestic *puja* by individuals, as well as *puja* at festivals (in temples, houses, and businesses), and personal *puja* or *vrata* on special occasions such as birth, marriage, and entering a new home or any new beginnings. For Vaishnavas in general and the devotees of Krishna in particular, the domestic rituals, festivals, and temple *pujas* are centered on Vishnu or Krishna, following the procedures depicted in the manuals connected to Vaishnavism: *Pancaratra* and *Vaikhanasa agamas*. Traditions of *puja* may also include special practices created by the Vaishnava *alvars, acaryas, sants*, and *gurus*, which are in a distinct style for each region of India. Hence, general differences can be noticed in the *pujas* offered in the temples of northern India and southern India.

The goal of *puja* in general is to involve the devotee or all the participants in a meditative mood, to dissolve oneself in mindful meditation, thereby assuming a temporary unity with the divine by the transfer of light from the deity. The concept of *puja* invokes the presence of the god as an honored guest who is to be pleased with services (*sevas* or *upacaras*, between twelve and sixteen different services). *Puja* (worship) also involves *darsana* (mutual vision), representing a mutual relation between the deity and devotee. The number of *pujas* offered in Krishna temples ranges from two to eight times per day, with two being the minimum (morning and evening) and eight being the maximum number of *pujas* offered, beginning with waking up in the morning to putting the deity to bed at night. Several of these *pujas* are accompanied by various *upacaras* and *darsan*. The daily *pujas* (*nitya*) differ from the *pujas* on festival days (*naimittika*)—for example, *Holi* differs from *Diwali*—from temple to temple as well as from region to region. The most important difference between the *pujas* in northern and southern Indian temples concerns the transfer of *tejas* (light) between the deity and the worshipper. In the temples in Orissa, Bengal, and other northern Indian temples, the transfer of light (*tejas*) between the main icon and worshipper is mediated through *puja*. However, in the southern Indian temples or the temples following the *Pancaratra* or *Vaikhanasa* tradition, the main icon (*mulabera*) is always considered endowed with *tejas*, which is transferred to the worshipper through offering *puja* to a *karmabera* (smaller metallic image of the deity) housed in the temple. The *mulabera* is offered only the services mandated by the *Pancaratra* or *Vaikhanasa agamas*. The *mulaberas* (main icons) of Krishna represented by Vishnu in southern India are never taken out in festival processions; *utsava vigrahas* (processional images) are used for this purpose. In northern India it is not uncommon for the central icons of the temple to be taken out in festival processions. However, in the unique tradition of the Jagannatha temple of Puri, the original images of Krishna, Balarama, and Subhadra are taken out during the *navakalevara* ritual (new icons replace the old icons) in the *ashadha* month every twelfth or nineteenth year when the *ashadha* occurs as the *adhikamasa* (extra month) of the year, and also for the *rathayatra* (chariot festival) each year.

The sixteen *upacaras* normally offered to the deity in a *puja* are invocation (*avahana*), fixing (*stapana*), water for washing the feet (*padya*), water for sipping (*acamana*), water for washing the hands (*arghya*), water for bathing (*abhisheka*), offering dress and perfume (*vastropavita*), offering flowers (*pushpa*), offering incense (*dhupa*), waving the lamp (*dipa*), offering food (*naivedya*), offering sacrifice (*bali*), offering fire oblation (*homa*), daily festival (*nityotsava*), offering music (*vadya*), offering dance (*nritya*), and finally dismissal (*udvasana*). In the temple *puja*, omission of eleven *upacaras* is allowed, but five *upacaras* are mandatory, including offerings of sandalwood paste (*chandana*), flowers (*pushpam*), incense (*dhupa*), lamp (*dipa*), and food (*naivedya*). Domestic *pujas* at the home shrine may include the bare minimum of services or elaborate rituals, based on one's time and interest. In addition to the above mentioned material, *upacaras* and *pujas* are also accompanied by recitation of mantras particular to the deity and the time of day.

Krishna temples include *nitya* (daily) and *naimittika* (calendrical or festival) *pujas* according to regional traditions, as well as the unique practices established by their founders, such as Ramanuja, Vallabha, and Caitanya.

See also: Arati; Bhakti; *Darsana*; Guruvayurappa and Guruvayur Temple; *Haveli Sangit*; Mantra; Puri Temple; *Seva*

Further Reading

McHugh, J. 2014."From Precious to Polluting: Tracing the History of Camphor in Hinduism." *Material Religion* 10 (1): 30–53.

McNeal, K. E. 2012. "Seeing the Eyes of God in Human Form: Iconography and Impersonation in African and Hindu Traditions of Trance Performance in the Southern Caribbean." *Material Religion* 8 (4): 490–519.

Padhy, S. 2008. "Ethnobiological Analysis from Myth to Science, IX: Pancha Yajnya (Five Sacrifices), the Composite Principle for Applied Human Ecological Environment." *Journal of Human Ecology* 23 (2): 151–158.

Prasad, L. 2006. "Text, Tradition, and Imagination: Evoking the Normative in Everyday Hindu Life." *Numen—International Review for the History of Religions* 53 (1): 1–47.

Srinivas, T. 2006. "Divine Enterprise: Hindu Priests and Ritual Change in Neighbourhood Hindu Temples in Bangalore." *South Asia—Journal of South Asian Studies* 29 (3): 321–343.

PURI TEMPLE
see Jagannatha

PURUSHA

Purusha is a Sanskrit word with various meanings: man, human, presiding deity, transcendent being, and so on. Unlike other terms associated with the divine, *purusha* is not abstract and is certainly corporeal, a term applied commonly to the body or embodied subjects. Vishnu and also Krishna is identified with the primeval *purusha*, whose disembodiment is described in the *Vedas* (*Rigveda* 10.90). Although the real meaning of the verse is not clear, it purports to be part of the cosmological origins of the universe and society. Following this Vedic verse, several Vedanta texts as well as the *Mahabharata* and the *puranas* explain the concept of *purusha*. Krishna is called *Purushottama,* the supreme man. Puri is the shortened name of *Purushottama Kshetram*, where the Jagannatha (Krishna) temple is established, as described in the *Purushottama Mahatmya* of *Skandapurana*. Krishna explains the concept of *purusha* in chapter 15 of the *Bhagavadgita*, known as the chapter on *Purushottama* yoga. In this chapter, Krishna describes the qualities of *kshara* (perishable) *purusha*, *akshara* (imperishable) *purusha*, and finally *purushottama* (the supreme *purusha*), the god Krishna himself. While the *kshara* and *akshara purusha* belong to this world (*Bhagavadgita* 15.16), *purushottama* is the eternal sovereign of the world (*avyaya isvara*), and Krishna also notes that he is praised as *purushottama* in this world (*Bhagavadgita* 15.19).

Two other principal concepts are also associated with *purusha*. The first concept is that *purusha* is an unchanging permanent being and male, while *prakriti,* his counterpart, is constantly changing and evolving feminine energy. Both *purusha* and *prakriti* contribute together to sustain creation. Krishna is understood as *purusha*, while Radha is understood as his energy (*sakti*) and the feminine counterpart of Krishna. The second concept is associated with geometry and architecture, with the view that any structure built in this world bears certain features of the supreme body. The *Vastupurusha* mandala especially is drawn before the construction of a sacred structure such as a temple takes place.

The concept of *purusha* is closely linked to Krishna, so one of his names came to be *Purushottama,* on an equal level with other names such as Narayana and *Bhagavan* that also represent Vishnu. This shows the status of Krishna as the ultimate divine within Hinduism.

See also: Avatara; Jagannatha; Krishna; Mandala; Mantra; Narayana; Radha; Vishnu; Yoga and Krishna

Further Reading

Kramerisch, S. 2007. *The Hindu Temple*. 2 vols. Delhi: Motilal Banarsidas.

Nilakantam, R. 1964. "*Prakriti* and *Purusha* in the *Bhagavadgita*." *Indian Archaeology* 3 (1): 254–264.

Tripathi, G. C. 1978. "On the Concept of '*Purushottama*' in the *Agamas*." In *The Cult of Jagannntha and the Regional Tradition of Orissa*, edited by A. Eschmann, H. Kulke, and G. C. Tripathi. New Delhi: Motilal Banarsidas.

R

RAASALILA

Lila is associated with Krishna in a number of meanings and also expresses a variety of complex concepts. However, the divine play of *Raasalila* (play of dance) is unmistakably associated with the divine play of the Lord with his devotees. The *lila* of God is always clouded in *maya* (illusion); only those devotees with true knowledge of the Supreme God can grasp its esoteric meaning. Hence, the *Raasalila* has a different esoteric meaning bereft of its sexual imagery. Only those souls that have passed beyond the materialistic understanding of life can grasp its true meaning. As the story is narrated in the *Bhagavatapurana*, one beautiful full-moon night during autumn, Krishna played his flute in Vraja, which attracted the *Gopis* (cowherd maidens) to leave their families and rush to the forest looking for him, but Krishna was nowhere to be found. When they got exhausted and were about to return to their homes, he reappeared, and the round dance of the *Raasalila* began in which each *Gopi* felt that Krishna danced with her only, but in reality Krishna danced with each one of them individually. As the dance ended the exhausted *Gopis* and Krishna bathed in the river and returned to their respective homes. At first reading, this may appear as a completely sexual, selfish, and unethical incident. However, it has a secondary and esoteric meaning, which is clouded under the illusion of *maya*. Those whose minds are under *maya* (illusion) may not see the symbolic secondary meaning and may accept only the first meaning as true. However, the second meaning becomes clear after rereading, the study of which was adopted by later teachers and followers of Krishna. The second meaning is that of understanding the *Gopis* as the enlightened souls, the only ones who can hear the divine call through Krishna's flute and who join him hastily, forgetting all their worldly connections and responsibilities. *Gopis* come to be regarded as the ultimate devotees, serving as a model for the other devotees to emulate. Even though this event is described as having happened in the forest of Vraja, the setting itself is also transformed to the divine setting as the *Vrajamandala* by the divine presence of Krishna and the *Gopis* experiencing his divine presence. Krishna introduced a number of ways for humanity to find unity with the divine; one of them is complete surrender, as seen in this *Raasalila* episode, which is elaborated further in the *Bhagavadgita* as part of bhakti yoga.

The *Raasalila* dance is a particularly round, swaying dance, almost like swooning; its legacy endures in several regional dance forms, such as *Hallisaka*, *Ghumar*, and *Jhumar*, mainly performed by women. In southern India, the *Raasalila* dance of Krishna, called the *Kuravai* dance, has been known from the early centuries of the first millennium (200–300 CE) from Tamil texts, the *Silappadikaram* and the

Manimekalai. Numerous other modern round dances, which commonly use *Raasalila* themes in their songs and music, exist in various regional formats, such as the *Bhojpuri Jhoomar* (Bihar), *Ghoomar* (Rajasthan), *Jhumar* (Punjab, northwestern India, and Pakistan), *Garbha* (Gujarath), *Ginder* (Rajasthan), *Panihari* (Rajasthan), *Dindi* and *Kala* (Maharashtra), *Madan Bramari* (Brindavan), *Manipuri Ras* (Manipur), *Natwari Nritya* (Kathak), and *Kolatam* (Andhra Pradesh). The *Charukula* dance of the Braj region is particularly notable: to songs about Krishna, women dance with a lamp stand containing 108 lighted oil lamps. This dance is performed in temples, particularly on the third day after *Holi* to mark the birthday of Radha, the beloved *Gopi* of Krishna. The *Sattriya* dance style of Assam, created by Sankaradeva, mainly uses Krishna-centered *lila* themes in its performances. A variety of musical instruments and classical music accompanies the dance. This dance is mainly performed in the *sattras* and was preserved as a classical religious dance tradition by the devotees of Krishna. In southern India, *Bharatanatyam* and *Kuchipudi* developed a style of dance known as *Tandava*, a set of vigorous dance moves mainly performed with brisk movements of the feet, which was once said to have been performed by the child Krishna while he defeated the serpent Kaliya in Kalindi Lake in Brindavan. Although *Raasa* symbolizes the divine dance of Krishna in *Raasalila*, the word *raasa* itself as well as its derivative, *raasaka,* came to denote a particular genre of narrative theater in India, including dialogue, music, and dance. Prakrit literature, especially Jain literature, contains a number of narratives named *raasa*, such as the *Neminatha raasa*, which describes a combat between Krishna and his cousin Neminatha, the twenty-second Jain *thirthankara*. The Rajasthani oral narratives such as the *Prithviraj raaso* also belong to this genre of *raasa* theater. Hence it can be seen that *Raasalila* is an important theological event in the legend of Krishna, one that has had a profound impact on the culture of India as shown in the numerous distinct dance styles, theater, and narrative traditions that drew inspiration from it. *Raasalila* is not only a theologically important event, but also a culturally prominent occurrence.

See also: Ankiya Nat; *Baredi*; *Bhagavadgita*; Bhakti; *Gopas* and *Gopis*; Jainism and Krishna; *Kuchipudi*; *Lila*; Mandala; *Manipuri* Dance; *Maya*; Performing Arts and Krishna; *Rasa* Theory

Further Reading

Mason, D. 2009. *Theater and Religion on Krishna Stage*. New York: Palgrave.
Nanddas. 1993. *The Round Dance of Krishna and Uddav's Message*. New York: Luzac.
Pauwels, M. 1996. *Krishna's Round Dance Reconsidered*. London: Curzon.
Schweig, G. 2005. *Dance of Divine Love: The Rasalila of Krishna from Bhagavatapurana*. Princeton: Princeton University Press.

RADHA

Radha is the soul mate of Krishna rather than his wife, although some texts refer to her as the wife of Krishna. Radha's position, equal to Krishna, is typical of Vaishnava traditions from 1000 CE onward. Jayadeva's *Gitagovinda* epitomizes the *sringara* of Radha and Krishna and brings it forward as one of the major concepts associated with Krishna. Radha's ascent as a central deity worshipped along with Krishna can be attributed to the devotional traditions located in Mathura such as the *Gaudiya* Vaishnava, Radhavallabha, Haridasi, and *Pushtimarga* (Vallabha) traditions. In fact, it is the *Gaudiya* Vaishnava tradition of Caitanya that can be credited with installing the images of Radha for worship on the temple altars alongside Krishna. However, her superior status could also be attributed to Radhavallabha *sampradaya*, whose temples are primarily Radha's temples, where she is regarded as the primary deity. Other Vaishnava *sampradayas* such as the Vallabha, Caitanya, and Haridasi traditions also affirm her superior position as the soul mate of Krishna.

Radha appears as an anonymous *Gopi*, the favorite of Krishna, in texts such as the *Bhagavatapurana* and the *Cilappadikaram*. Radha also appears alongside Krishna in early sculptures depicting the events of Krishna's life, such as *Danlila* (300 CE, from Suratgarh, Rajasthan), and several depictions of *Govardhandharana* (lifting Mount Govardhan) from across India, dated from 400 CE onward. However, Radha acquires utmost importance as the feminine counterpart of Krishna toward the last quarter of the first millennium (800–1100 CE), as evidenced by the composition of Andal's *Tiruppavai* and Jayadeva's *Gitagovinda*, as well as several miniature paintings from 1200 CE onward depicting her as the partner of Krishna.

Radha is idolized as the ideal *Gopi* by Andal, the female saint-poet (*alvar*) of southern India, in the *Tiruppavai*, and she also invoked the *Gopis* of Vraja who

Radha Rejecting Krishna, watercolor from Chamba, Himachal Pradesh, India, ca. 1760. (Los Angeles County Museum of Art)

performed a vow to Goddess Katyayani, so they might obtain Krishna as their husband. In the *Tiruppavai*, Andal imagines herself as the special *Gopi* of Krishna, praying to Krishna, so she may obtain him as her husband. In a further development of the legend, Andal is even identified as the reincarnation of the favorite *Gopi* of Krishna in Srikrishnadevaraya's *Amuktamalyada*. She figures as the prominent and favorite *Gopi* of Krishna during his autumnal *Raasalila*, the round dance in Braj.

Although Radha is regarded as the partner of Krishna, she was regarded later on as the wife of Krishna. However, there is also a poetical tradition that regards her as an adulterous lover of Krishna. This trend can be seen in several vernacular poetical traditions, such as that of the Bengali poet Baru Candidasa, according to whom Radha is married to another cowherd.

However, Radha's centrality in devotional traditions can be attributed to the *Haritray* (the three Haris: Hit Harivams, Hariram Vyas, and *Svami* Haridas), also known as the *rasikatrai* (the three connoisseurs of Radha-Krishna). All three of them openly proclaim their loyalty to Radha, referred to as *Svamini* in their poems. While Hariram Vyas signed off his poems with the signature stamp (*chap*) of Vyas's Lady (*Vyas ki Svamini*), Hit Harivams and *Svami* Haridas founded the Radhavallabha and Haridasi traditions, which accord a special place to Radha in their devotional practices.

Radha's rise to such a central position is also accompanied by theological developments within Vaishnava devotional traditions. Caitanya, founder of *Gaudiya* Vaishnavism (also known as Caitanya Vaishnavism), is considered an incarnation of Radha and Krishna together. Rupa *Gosvami* noted that Radha represents the highest *rasa*, the *mahabhava*. Hence, according to Caitanya Vaishnavism, she is the *hladinisakti* of Krishna, revered even by Krishna. This theory is taken a step further in the Vaishnava *Sahajiya* tradition of Bengal, which applies the Radha-Krishna concept to tantric practice. According to Vallabha tradition she is the *svamini* of Krishna, who is worthy of devotion. As noted above, the Haridasi and Radhavallabha *sampradayas* consider Radha as supreme, even above Krishna. The *Gitagovinda* represent the divine love of Radha and Krishna, although Radha's actual relationship to Krishna is ambiguous, while Baru Candidasa's *Srikrishnakirtana* represents Radha as another person's wife, thus making her *parakiya* and her love for Krishna forbidden.

The later *puranas* reflect these theological developments within the devotional traditions and describe her as the special partner of Krishna. According to the *Brahmavaivartaprana* (1500 CE), Radha is depicted as eternally sporting with Krishna in *Goloka*, the divine world of Krishna. The *Devibhagavatapurana* and the *Padmapurana* describe her cosmological role as *prakriti* and *sakti*. Radha's birthplace, Barsana, is a major pilgrimage center, and the festival of *Holi* is celebrated by imagining Radha among their midst there in Barsana every year.

See also: Barsana; Caitanya Vaishnavism; Childhood of Krishna in Brindavan; Haridasi *Sampradaya*; *Holi*; *Raasalila*; *Radhashtami*; Radhavallabha Tradition; Vallabha Tradition

Further Reading

Chakraborty, B. D. 1984. "Chandidas' Radha in Vaishnava Lyrics." *Indian Literature* 27 (1): 89–95.

Dimock, E. C., Jr. 1966. *The Place of the Hidden Moon*. Chicago: University of Chicago Press.

Golsan, K. 2011. "Desperately Seeking Radha: Renoir's *The River* and Its Reincarnation." *South Central Review* 28 (3): 103–125.

Simmons, C. 2010. "The Goddess as Role Model: Sita and Radha in Scripture and on Screen." *International Journal of Hindu Studies* 14 (2–3): 334–336.

RADHASHTAMI

Radhashtami is the birthday of Radha. *Radhashtami* is celebrated in Barsana (although she is considered to have been born in Rawal at her maternal grandparents' house) fifteen days after the birthday of Krishna. *Radhashtami* is also celebrated in all the temples of Krishna, since Radha is considered the foremost of the devotees of Krishna, who obtained soulful union with Krishna through her unwavering devotion to him. Hence, devotees worship her as the closest partner of Krishna, who could guide them in their pursuit of divine union with the ultimate reality, represented by Krishna. *Radhashtami* is also celebrated in temples associated with Radha in Braj such as the Radhavallabha temple in Brindavan and Sevakunj, and also the *Ashtasakhi* temples where she is the central deity. In the Radhavallabha temple, celebrations begin in the morning with the distribution of clothes, sweets, and fruits. In several temples across India, especially Srivaishnava temples, *Radhashtami* is a day of cleaning the golden jewelry of the temple. The Haridasi tradition also especially celebrates *Radhashtami*, since the birthday of the founder, Haridas, falls on the same day. Haridasi tradition celebrates the day with *samaj gayan* in Nidhivan, attended by a large number of devotees. The temple and the deities are decorated with flowers, and only on this day can Radha's feet be seen by devotees during their *darsan* (viewing). The Bankebihari temple is especially famous for their flower decorations known as *phul bangla* (flower house). Followers of Caitanya Vaishnavism perform a half-day fast, breaking it at midday after receiving the *darsan* (seeing) of Radha in the temple and receiving *prasad* (grace or mercy). *Radhashtami* is celebrated over nine days in the Radhavallabha temple. The Radhavallabha temple organizes a special procession of Radha and Krishna along with the eight friends of Radha. Music, dance, special decorations, and food preparations accompany the festivities.

See also: Braj *Parikrama*; Caitanya; *Haritray*; Mathura; Radha; Radhavallabha Tradition

Further Reading

Merchant, K. 2001. *Festival Tales: Hindu Festivals*. London: Wayland.

RADHAVALLABHA TRADITION

Hit Harivams, founder of the Radhavallabha *sampradaya* (tradition), did not try to link it with any of the earlier four Vaishnava *sampradayas* (*Catuh Vaishnava sampradayas*), but later followers claim affiliation with the Vishnusvami *sampradaya*. The Radhavallabha *sampradaya* places divine love at the center of its practice. This tradition even denounces common practices associated with Hinduism such as fasting and other rituals.

The Radhavallabha experience of bhakti is through *sringara rasa* (conjugal love), the *nitya vihara* (eternal play) of Radha and Krishna. At the same time, Radhavallabhas are also cautious to distance themselves from some tantric groups that use sex for ritual religious practice. For Radhavallabhas, Krishna is the only male participating in the love play, while the *Raasalila* between Radha and Krishna releases *sringara rasa* to the devotees for the world to achieve bhakti to obtain release from this world (*moksha*). As a *Rasika*, the Radhavallabhas understand Radha and Krishna as a married couple who engage in love play in the sacred grove, Nikunj.

The Radhavallabha tradition is known for its contributions to Braj culture, its music, and more importantly, for venerating Radha above Krishna. Radhavallabha tradition rests on a very simple premise: that obtaining nearness to Krishna (*moksha*) can be achieved through offering *seva* (service), with wholehearted devotion, in the form of attending to the deities Radha and Krishna, and participating in devotional *seva* in the temple as well as at home. The Radhavallabha temple has seven services spread throughout the day, beginning at 6 a.m. and ending at 10 p.m. Devotees can attend services at any of these times for *darsana* and participation in *seva*.

The main hymnal text of the Radhavallabha *sampradaya* is the *Sri Radhavallabhji ka Varsotsav*. Poems in this text include most of the verses from the *Caurasipada* of Hit Harivams, the *Sri Bayalis Lila* of *Dhruvadas*, some poems of Hariram Vyas's text, the *Vyasavani*, and several poems of Vrindavan Das. Radhavallabha *seva* and *samaj gayan* is performed only in seclusion for devotees who are appreciative of the aesthetic feelings and devotional nuances of the worship. There is a concern that a

---

Khichri Utsav

Khichri utsav is celebrated for a month during winter between the months of *Pushya* and *Magha* of the Hindu calendar. This festival is specific to the Radhavallabha tradition, and it is celebrated with sumptuous food (*bhog*) offered in the temple and Krishna dressed up in various disguises. During the *Khichri utsav* Radhavallabha is prepared in different disguises each morning immediately following the *Mangal arati*. After the first and main disguise is completed, the devotees are treated to a number of disguises throughout the morning. Radhavallabha is prepared in the different disguises behind a curtain, which opens and closes revealing the changing process. The curtain is opened once the process is completed, and the disguise is left on display for a little while before the curtain is closed again to prepare the next disguise. This process continues for the whole morning. The most favorite disguises include those of *Krishnalila* depicting scenes of Krishna's childhood, although scenes of contemporary life are also increasingly represented.

less-adept devotee may misinterpret the highly erotic *padas* of the tradition. *Samaj gayan* is the central *seva* of Radhavallabha tradition. The poetical repertoire of the Radhavallabha tradition is unique; so also its practice of placing Radha at the center of worship. The Radhavallabha tradition is unique in a number of ways that contribute to the multiple aspects of Krishna bhakti in India.

The Radhavallabha tradition now manages more than six temples in Brindavan. The most important temples are the famous Radhavallabha temple; the Jugalkishore temple, Ras Mandal, which houses memorials of Radhavallabha poets Sevakji and Dhruvadas, and the place where the annual *Raasalila* festival is held by Radhavallabhas in *Chaitra* to *Vaishakh* (March–April); and a walled garden called Sevakunj.

See also: Braj *Parikrama*; Brindavan; *Gaudiya* Vaishnavism; *Lila*; Mathura; *Raasalila*; Radha; *Radhashtami*; *Samaj Gayan*; Vallabha Tradition

Further Reading

Beck, G. L. 2011. *Sonic Liturgy: Ritual and Music in Hindu Tradition*. Columbia: University of South Carolina Press.

Beck, G. L. 2011. *Vaishnava Temple Music in Vrindavan: The Radhavallabha Songbook*. Kirksville, MO: Blazing Sapphire Press.

Goswami, L. 1978–1980. *Sri Radhavallabh ji ka Varshotsav*. 3 vols. Brindavan: Radhavallabh Sanstha.

Mukhopdhya, D. 1990. *In Praise of Krishna: Translation of Gita-Govinda of Jayadeva*. Delhi: Motilal Banarsidas.

Pauwels, H. R. M. 2002. *In Praise of Holy Men: Hagiographic Poems by and About Hariram Vyas*. Groningen: GMBH.

Thielemann, S. 1996. "Samaja, Haveli Samgita, and Dhrupada: The Musical Manifestation of Bhakti." *Journal of Vaishnava Studies* 4 (2): 157–177.

Thielemann, S. 2000. *Singing the Praises of Divine: Music in the Hindu Tradition*. New Delhi: Motilal Banarsidas.

White, C. S. J. 1996. "The Remaining Hindi Works of Sri Hit Harivams." *Journal of Vaishnava Studies* 4 (4): 87–104.

White, C. S. J. 1977. *The Caurasi Pad of Sri Hit Harivams*. Honolulu: University of Hawaii Press.

White, C. S. J. 2001. "Sri Radha and the Radhavallabha Sampraday." *Journal of Vaishnava Studies* 10 (1): 91–113.

RAGANURAGA

Raganuraga, also known as *raganuraga bhakti sadhana* (the devotional practice of *raganuraga*), is an important mode of spiritual practice in the Caitanya Vaishnava tradition. *Raganuraga bhakti sadhana* is the higher level of spiritual practice for one who has successfully passed the *vaidhibhakti sadhana*. Jiva *Gosvami* describes two types of devotees (*bhaktas*) who may start their spiritual practice of *raganuraga bhakti* in his text *Bhakti-sandarbha*. These two types of *bhaktas* are called *jata-ruci* (those who have a taste) and *ajata ruci* (those who do not have a taste). Both of these types of devotees can benefit from the practice of *raganuraga bhakti*. However, it is preferable for most devotees to start their spiritual practice with *vaidhi bhakti sadhana,* progressing quickly once they know they have been on an advanced path of self-realization. Once a devotee is on this advanced path, he or she may acquire the *siddha-form*, often known as *manjari-bhava* in Caitanya Vaishnava tradition, which could be either a male or female form. This is one's spiritual form in the higher realm. However, this practice does not involve dressing up (as a *Gopi,* etc.) as *Sahajiya* practitioners do, but only involves spiritual realization with clearly focused meditation. Hence, *lila-smaranam* (remembering the *lilas* of Krishna) forms one of the central practices. Rupa *Gosvami's* poem on *ashta-kaliya-lila* (divine play of eight periods) is a short, cryptic recollection of Krishna's play, which may be used to help one's meditation on the path of *raganuraga bhakti.* The eight-period *lilas* of Krishna also closely resemble the eight-period (*astayam*) *arati* services offered in temples of devotional tradition, such as the Caitanya Vaishnava and Vallabha traditions.

Gaudiya Vaishnavism consists of a unique devotional practice including spiritual practice (*raganuraga sadhana*), singing the names (*namasamkirtana*), and meditation with *mahamantra.* The *mahamantra* (great mantra) is a sixteen-name verse consisting of the three names Krishna, Rama, and Hare: *Hare Krishna Hare Krishna/ Krishna Krishna Hare Hare/Hare Rama Hare Rama/Rama Rama Hare Hare.* The repetition of this mantra is considered to be efficacious in bringing one in contact with Krishna. *Nama sankirtana* in the form of singing is another mode of achieving closeness to Krishna. *Kirtana* and meditation with *mahamantra* are central to Caitanya Vaishnava practice.

See also: Bhaktivedanta Swami Prabhupada; ISKCON; Jiva *Gosvami*; *Kirtana*; *Raasalila*; *Rasa* Theory; Rupa *Gosvami*

Further Reading

Case, M. H. 2000. *Seeing Krishna:The Religious World of a Brahman Family in Vrindaban.* Oxford: Oxford University Press.

Ghosh, P. 2005. *Temple to Love: Architecture and Devotion in Seventeenth-Century Bengal.* Bloomington: Indiana University Press.

Haberman, D. L. 1988. *Acting as a Way of Salvation: A Study of Raganuraga Bhakti Sadhana.* New York: Oxford University Press.

Kapoor, O. B. L. 1999. *The Saints of Vraja.* New Delhi: Aravali Books.

Nelson, L. E. 2004. "The Ontology of Bhakti: Devotion as Paramapurusartha in Gaudiya Vaisnavism and Madhusudana Sarasvati." *Journal of Indian Philosophy* 32 (4): 345–392.

RAMANUJA

Ramanuja (1017–1137), also known as Ramanujacarya, is one of the principal thinkers of Vedanta, a Hindu philosophical and theological perspective based on the Upanishads. Ramanuja is associated with Srivaishnava theology and temple ritual in southern India (see Srivaishnavism). His central philosophical concept, *visishtadvaita* (qualified monism/qualified nondualism), is one of the most popular understandings of Vedanta philosophy. Ramanuja contributed to the immense development of popular Vaishnavism, followed by the construction of numerous temples in southern India. At one stage his enthusiastic support of Vaishnavism drew contempt from Saiva groups of southern India, finally leading to the wrath of the Chola emperor, a known supporter of Saivism. Ramanuja then stayed for twelve years in exile in Andhra Pradesh and Karnataka, adjacent states to the north of Tamilnadu in southern India. This period is known as one of the most productive of his life, both theologically and also for his contribution to the ritualistic traditions of Vaishnava temples. It is also said that he converted King Vishnuvardhana to Vaishnavism from Jainism. Several temples in southern India owe their significant cultural heritage to Ramanuja.

Ramanuja was born near Chennai into a Brahman household committed to studying and teaching the *Vedas*, which ensured that as a young boy he acquired Sanskrit and knowledge of the *Vedas*. He was subsequently educated further under the eminent *acaryas* Yadavaprakasa and Yamunacarya. He was well versed in the Sanskrit grammatical and literary conventions, and also had a strong grasp of non-Sanskritic popular traditions prevalent in southern India at that time, as well as the non-Sanskritic Tamil traditions of the *alvars*. He became a *sanyasi* at a young age and traveled extensively across India visiting holy places including Dvaraka, Mathura, and Varanasi, finally settling in Srirangam.

Ramanuja's greatest contributions came from the time he assumed leadership of the Srivaishnava community in southern India as a teacher and general manager of the Vaishnava temple of Srirangam. Ramanuja authored the *Sribhashya* in Sanskrit, an authoritative commentary on the *Brahmasutras* of Badarayana. In addition, he also authored eight other texts. Ramanuja's *Vedarthasamgraha* (Compendium of the Meaning of the *Veda*) is a selected discussion of Vedic concepts. His other texts, including the *Vedantasara* (The Gist of Vedanta) and the *Vedantadipa* (The Lamp of/ for Vedanta), are commentaries on the *Brahmasutras* of Badarayana, one of the source texts of Vedanta philosophy and religious theology, similar to the *Sribhashya* noted above. The *Gitabhasya* is a commentary on the *Bhagavadgita*. His prose text, *Gadyatraya*, is a short composition of three prose hymns, and the *Nityagrantha* (A Treatise on Daily Worship) is an elaboration of worship of the divine on a daily basis. The central concept of Ramanuja's thought is the philosophical premise of *visishtadvaita* postulates that the Brahma (universal soul) and *atma* (individual soul) are nondifferentiated. The central concept of Ramanuja's thought is *cidacidavastu*, which states that all finite conscious and nonconscious entities are born out

Sribhashya

The *Sribhashya* is the most important text composed by *acarya* Ramanuja. The *Sribhashya* is a commentary on the *Brahmasutras*. Through his close analysis and examination of the *Brahmasutra* Ramanujacarya offers a critical commentary on the text, supporting his central theory on *visishtadvaita*. Therefore, for the followers of Ramanuja in particular and Srivaishnavas in general, the text of the *Sribhashya* provides basic theological and philosophical contextual background.

of the body of Brahma and during their existence appear in a threefold relationship with Brahma. This concept of the unity of body/embodied self (being and *atma*) is expressed by Ramanuja in the *Sribhashya* in detail. He explains this through the understanding of *sarirasariribhava* (concept of body, embodied).

See also: Advaita; Ranganatha; Srirangam Temple; Srivaishnavism; Vishnu

Further Reading

Bartley, C. J. 2002. *The Theology of Ramanuja: Realism and Religion.* London: Routledge.

Buitenen, J. A. B. van. 1956. *Ramanuja on the Bhagavadgita: A Condensed Rendering of His Gitabhashya with Copious Notes and an Introduction.* The Hague: H. L. Smits.

Lester, R. C. 1976. *Ramanuja on the Yoga.* Madras: Adayar Library and Research Center.

Lott, E. J. 1976. *God and the Universe in the Vedantic Theology of Ramanuja.* Madras: Ramanuja Research Society.

Raghavachar, S. S. 1956. *Vedarthasamgraha of Sri Ramanujacarya.* Mysore: Ramakrishna Asrama.

Ramakrishnanda, S. 1965. *Life of Sri Ramanuja.* 2nd ed. Madras: Sri Ramakrishna Math.

Raman, M. S. 2004. "Soteriology in the Writings of Ramanuja: Bhakti and/or Prapatti? (Regarding the formation and consolidation of Srivaisnava theology between the 10th and 14th centuries AD)." *Zeitschrift Der Deutschen Morgenlandischen Gesellschaft* 154 (1): 85–129.

Raman, S. 2007. *Self-surrender (prapatti) to God in Srivaishnavism: Tamil Cats and Sanskrit Monkeys.* London: Routledge.

RANGANATHA

Ranganatha, although understood as Vishnu, is also imagined as Krishna in the compositions of the *alvars*. Although there are numerous temples of Ranganatha in Tamilnadu, the most important are in Srirangam and in Srivilliputtur. Ranganatha in the Srirangam temple is in the reclining position as Anantapadmanabha. The Anantapadmanabha form represents Vishnu at the beginning of creation resting on the bed of coils of the divine snake Ananta, from whose navel appears a lotus, inside which Brahma appears. Brahma then performs meditation (*tapas*), following which the process of creation begins, marking the beginning of the universe, the Earth, and all life forms on the Earth. This marks the *lila*, the play of creation. The lord in "play" creates the universe. Hence, the Lord Vishnu, reclining in his primeval position, is also known here as Ranganatha, the lord of play also known as Krishna. This connects Ranganatha to Krishna, the central convention of Srivaishnavism, the central Vaishnava tradition associated with this temple in which Krishna is considered the Lord Vishnu himself.

Ranganatha is represented in two-armed form reclining on the bed with arms at rest and with adornments commonly associated with Vishnu, such as the *vaijayanti mala* (never-fading garland) and *kaustubha* (gem on the chest), and fully covered in a thin layer of gold. However, the *utsava vigraha* (festive form) is represented as the four-armed Lord Vishnu, standing along with both of his wives, Sridevi (Goddess Laxmi) and Bhudevi (Goddess Earth).

Marriage of Meenakshi

The sister of Ranganatha, the goddess Meenakshi is married to Shiva (Sundareshwara). Vishnu planned to attend her wedding and arrived on Earth from *Vaikuntam*. However, he missed Meenakshi's wedding as he reached Madurai. This angered Ranganatha, so he settled in a nearby place and vowed never to enter Madurai. However, he was pacified later. A festival, *Alagar Tiruvila*, is celebrated each year after the wedding of Meenakshi in the Madurai temple.

There is also another aspect to the name of Ranganatha that connects him directly to Krishna. Krishna is the playful God (*lilavatara*), and as Ranganatha, he is the lord of play, the name that identifies Ranganatha as Krishna. This connection is reflected in the hymns of the *alvars*, especially the hymns of Andal, who identified Krishna with Ranganatha. According to the Srivaishnava tradition, Ranganatha is the *arcavatara* (incarnation of ritual worship) of Krishna, the Lord Vishnu himself, who has taken the earthly form of *arcavatara* to bless his devotees with his *darsan* in *Kaliyuga*. Numerous temples across India are dedicated to Ranganatha, and one of the most popular forms of Krishna worship is of Ranganatha in southern India. Five auspicious temples of Ranganatha on the banks of the Kaveri River are known as *pancaranga* temples, which are visited as part of the pilgrimage circuit by Krishna devotees in Srirangapatnam (Karnataka), Srirangam (Tamilnadu), Kumbhakonam (Tamilnadu), Sirkazhi (Tamilnadu), and Indaluru in Mayiladuturai (Tamilnadu). Ranganatha temples are found across India, and recently some have been constructed outside of India. An important temple of Ranganatha called the Rangji temple, founded by the *Tengalai* (southern) Srivaishnava tradition, is found in Brindavan. The Rangji temple is the largest temple in Brindavan, closely resembling the temple of Ranganatha in Srirangam. The temple contains numerous cloisters, which are used by devotees to perform circumambulations (*pradakshina*) around the temple. Some of the gateways are in the simple north Indian style, while others are in the style of southern India and decorated with ornate sculptures and tall towers (*gopura*). Temple celebrations and festivals in the Rangji temple are organized in a similar calendar and style as the Ranganathaswamy temple in Srirangam. The deities are taken out in procession around the temple precincts for *Brahmotavam* and other major festivals. On the annual *Rath ka Mela* organized in the Rangji temple, the deity is brought out on a large ornamental chariot to the *Rang ji ka Bagica* (walled garden of the temple).

Andal, one of the *alvars*, considered herself a *Gopi* in her previous life and vowed to marry only Krishna (or Vishnu) in her present life. The legend of Andal describes how she married Ranganatha in the Srivilliputtur temple and was finally united with Krishna. This legend of the Srivaishnava tradition not only identifies Krishna with Ranganatha but also, through the marriage of Andal, establishes that Ranganatha is the worshipful form (*arcavatara*) of Krishna in *Kaliyuga*. Daily ritual worship of Ranganatha, as an accessible lord on Earth, includes Vedic verses as well as the hymns of *alvars*. The *Nalayira Divya Prabandham* is read as part of the daily ritual, as well as festival celebrations of Ranganatha, ever since Ramanuja instituted them in the traditional worship early in the eleventh century. Krishna is reborn as the worshipful form (*arcavatara*) of Ranganatha and becomes the center of a new devotional tradition utilizing regional language as an expression of devotion. Hence, Ranganatha epitomizes the bhakti movement in southern India, which spurred the use of regional languages in the worship of Krishna and inspired numerous devotional traditions.

See also: Advaita; Alvars; Andal; Avatara; Nalayira Divya Prabandham; Ramanuja; Rathayatra; Srivaishnavism

Further Reading

Padmaja, T. 2002. *Temples of Krishna in South India.* New Delhi: Abhinav.

RASA THEORY

Rasa acquires a special meaning and place with relation to Krishna. *Rasa* is used several times in the *Bhagavadgita* to denote taste, the meaning with which it is commonly used in relation to Krishna. *Rasa* is infused with theological significance in Krishna devotion. Although Bharata's *Natyasastra* lists only eight *rasas* (*sringara,* romance; *hasya,* comedy; *karuna,* compassion; *raudra,* fury; *vira,* heroism; *bhayanaka,* horror; *bibhatsa,* revulsion; *adbhuta,* amazement), Rupa *Gosvami* was instrumental in conceiving *bhakti rasas* as a *rasa*. According to Rupa *Gosvami,* the emotions experienced by Krishna and his associates are *alaukika* (otherworldy), although experienced as *rasa*. Hence, *rasa* through the *lilas* experienced by Krishna's associates and devotees is, in essence, the *rasa* of all *rasas* and a medium of experience between the deity and devotee. Rupa *Gosvami* wrote plays and poems of Krishna's *lilas* as a central devotional practice to help devotees cultivate *rasa*. *Raasalila* is the essence of all *lilas*, and the supreme expression of devotion of the *gopis* is found in this *lila*. Hence, listening, performing or participating in *Raasalila* is an important part of understanding Krishna for Krishna devotees.

See also: Gopas and *Gopis;* Jiva *Gosvami; Lila; Maya; Raasalila;* Rupa *Gosvami*

Further Reading

Raghavan, V. 1967. *The Number of Rasas.* Madras: Adyar Library and Research Center.
Schweig, G. M. 2005. *Dance of Divine Love: The Rasa Lila of Krishna from the Bhagavata Purana.* Princeton: Princeton University Press.

RATHAYATRA

Rathayatras are the most popular public ceremonies associated with Krishna. *Rathayatra* is celebrated as a visit by Krishna to one of his favorite places to visit friends or relatives. In Puri, Krishna (Jagannath) comes out of his temple to visit his aunt (at the Mausima temple) in the town; in Brindavan, Krishna visits his friend

Uddhava; and in Nathdvara, a public procession is held with dance and music, with Krishna traveling the town in his silver chariot, to mark the annual mango festival, when the festival culminates in offering 24,000 mangoes to Srinathji (Krishna). The chariot festival of Venkatesvara of Tirupati and Ranganatha of Srirangam are held for ten days during the annual temple festival known as *Brahmotsavams*. *Rathayatra* and *Brahmotsavams* are held after *Holi* in the Rangji temple in Mathura.

The largest chariot festival in India is the Jagannatha *Rathayatra* of Puri, attended by thousands of devotees from India as well as other parts of the world. The three central deities, Jagannatha, Subhadra, and Balabhadra, are taken out in three chariots of different sizes and colors. The largest chariot measures almost thirteen and a half meters in height and contains sixteen wheels covered by red and yellow cloth. Balabhadra's chariot measures slightly less than Jagannatha's, 13.2 meters high with fourteen wheels and covered by red and green cloth. Subhadra's chariot measures 12.9 meters in height, contains twelve wheels, and the chariot is covered by red and black cloth. The wheels are uniformly constructed and contain twelve spokes each. Traditional aboriginal priests called *Daityas* bring the images to the chariots in the afternoon at the start of the festival. The chariots are then approached by the traditional descendants of the royal family associated with the temple, who sweep the path of the chariots with a golden, jewel-encrusted broom and symbolically begin the pulling of the chariots. The traditional hereditary workers of the temple, called *kalabetiyas*, who may number in the thousands, pull the chariots. They are also assisted by a large number of devotees who come to participate in the *rathayatra*. The gods return to their temple after three days and are welcomed by Srilaxmi, accompanied by a number of traditional rituals held at the temple. The chariots are dismantled as soon as the chariot festival is completed, and some parts are saved for reuse in subsequent years. *Rathayatra* is celebrated in numerous Krishna temples across the world each year.

See also: Caitanya; Jagannatha; Puri Temple; Ranganatha; Srirangam Temple; Tirupathi; Vallabha Tradition; Venkatesvara

Further Reading

Mohapatra, G. 1979. *The Land of Vishnu: A Study of Jagannatha Cult.* Delhi: B. R. Publishing.

RAVIDAS

Ravidas (Raidas or Rohidas) was a poet-saint of the bhakti tradition from the low-caste (*Chamar*) community. Very scant details about his personal life are available, although a lot of information is available about his religious life, teachings, and compositions. He must have lived in northern India in the 1500s. He was a contemporary of Kabir and also was noted as one among the five non-Brahman disciples of Ramananda, along with Kabir, Pipa, Dhana, and Sen. It is impossible to ascertain the authenticity of the claim, however, Ravidas's biographies claim that *sant* Mirabai came to meet him and was converted to Krishna bhakti. Ravidas traveled widely across India and composed poems, which form part of a number of collections.

Several biographies of Ravidas are well known; the earliest is Ananta Das's book, the *Ravidas Paricai* (1590). Another early religious biography of Ravidas is found in *Pothi Prem Ambodh*, which consists of biographies of 15 *bhagats* (saints) whose poems are included in the Sikh holy text *Gurugranth Sahib* (1693). A number of special events routinely form part of the biography of Ravidas based on this early template. Events of Ravidas's life such as his birth as a *Chamar*, receiving a golden bracelet from the goddess Ganga, the story of the *saligram*, and the story of a queen of Rajasthan becoming his disciple form the standard repertoire of his biographies. Although his birth as a *Chamar* is well known, the veracity of the miraculous occurrences narrated cannot be established. In the golden bracelet story, it is mentioned that the goddess Ganga gave him a bracelet, and in the *saligram* story the Brahmans complained to the king that Ravidas was worshipping a *saligram*, which he was not supposed to do. When the king invited the Brahmans and Ravidas to prove their innocence by undergoing a floating test, Ravidas's stone *saligram* floated while the Brahmans' *saligram* sank, even though it was made of wood. These incidents prove his popularity and his acceptance as a respected saint by the sixteenth century. Ravidas's legacy endures in his centrality as a bhakti saint of the lower castes.

See also: Bhakti; Mirabai; *Nirguna/Saguna*; *Sants*

Further Reading

Agrawal, B. P. 1908. *Raidasji ki Bani*. Allahabad: Belvedere Press.
Singh, D. 1977. *Sant Ravidas and His Life*. Delhi: Kalyani.

RAVIDASI TRADITION

The Ravidasi tradition was established by the poet-saint Ravidas, a devotee of Krishna and also Rama, two major incarnations of the god Vishnu. Ravidas is a *sant* in the Nath *sampradaya* (tradition). A biography of Ravidas is found in the *Bhaktamal* of Nabhadas and in Ananta Das's book, *Ravidas Paricai*. In addition to urging low-caste devotees to adopt devotional traditions in their own way, Ravidas centered his devotion on Krishna. For Ravidas, Krishna is the personification of compassion, and several of his poems address Krishna as the most merciful and compassionate deity. Ravidas addressed Krishna under several names; the most commonly used names are Madhava, Murari, Kanha, Gopala, Govinda, Banvari, and Syama. Although Ravidas uses the name Ram frequently in his compositions, it is used as a reference to God rather than as the name of an individual deity. The most important aspect of the Ravidasi tradition is *nama jap* (chanting the names of God).

See also: Bhakti; *Kirtana*; Mantra; *Puja*; Ravidas; *Sants*

Further Reading

Callaewart, W. M., and P. G. Friedlander. 1992. *The Life and Works of Ravidas*. New Delhi: Manohar.

REVATHI

Balarama's wife Revathi is noted as the goddess of drink; she is also called Varuni or Madira, indicating her relation to drink. Revathi is depicted as holding a wine jug in her right hand in a number of sculptures. Balarama is referred to as a heavy drinker in the *Mahabharata* and the *Bhagavatapurana*. Therefore, both Revathi and her husband Balarama are closely linked to alcoholic drinks.

A number of temples of Balarama also contain the icons of the goddess Revathi. It is not unusual for Revathi to be depicted as larger than Balarama in some images. Legends also narrate that Revathi is much older than Balarama. Revathi was born in an earlier era than Kakudmi, who had visited Brahma with her to consult about her wedding prospects. It so happened that Brahma was busy when they visited, thus Revathi and Kakudmi had to wait for him for a few minutes. When they finally met Brahma, to their shock they found that many years had elapsed on Earth. Time cycles differ in different worlds. One day in the world of Brahma is equal to one *Kalpa* (four *yugas*). Since one day of Brahma is equal to a *Kalpa* on Earth, the period they waited translates to twenty-seven years on Earth, which is also alternatively mentioned as twenty-seven *yugas* in some texts. Kakudmi showed the list of prospective grooms he brought with him to Brahma, but Brahma informed him that times had changed on Earth, the *Dvaparayuga* was nearing its end, and none of the grooms on his list were still alive. Therefore, Brahma advised Kakudmi to return to Earth immediately and conduct the marriage of his daughter, Revathi, with Balarama. When they returned to Earth Kakudmi met Balarama and requested that he marry his daughter Revathi. Although Revathi was much older and was also larger in size, since the size of humans decreases with progressive eras in a *Kalpa*, Balarama agreed to marry her and tapped her on the head with his plow, which brought her size down to the normal human size common during the last phase of *Dvaparayuga*. Revathi and Balarama had two sons and a daughter. Their daughter, Shashirekha, was married to Abhimanyu, son of Arjuna and Subhadra. There are also other goddesses known by the name of Revathi in the classical texts of Hinduism, such as the serpent Revathi and the star constellation Revathi, although it is not clear if they are related to Revathi the wife of Balarama. Revathi is also revered along with Balarama.

See also: Balarama; Pandavas; Subhadra: Krishna's Sister

Further Reading

Vemsani, L. 2006. *Hindu and Jain Mythology of Balarama*. Kingston, ON, and Lewiston, NY: Edwin Mellen.

ROHINI

Rohini is the stepmother of Krishna. She was the first and favorite wife of Vasudeva, the biological father of Krishna and Balarama. Rohini lived in Vraja along with her son Balarama, who was transferred to her as an embryo from Devaki. While Krishna and Balarama played and grew up together in Vraja, Rohini, along with Yashoda, took care of them.

Rohini is described as the daughter of the king of Bahlika of the Puru lineage. Bahlika is variously identified as a tribe from the region of Bactrioi near Arachosia and with Baluchistan, between the Bolan and Quetta passes on the banks of the Nori and Gokh rivers in the present-day Baluchistan autonomous region in Pakistan.

Rohini and Vasudeva had eight other sons and a daughter in addition to Balarama, who are referred to as *Rohinikula*, the lineage of Rohini, while Balarama is described as *Rauhineya*, a Sanskrit epithet that means son of Rohini. Rohini's daughter Subhadra is an incarnation of the goddess Nidra, also venerated as Ekanamsa, a part of Krishna. Subhadra, in her form as Goddess Nidra and the sister of Balarama and Krishna, is one of the most commonly worshiped goddesses in the Mathura region.

Etymologically Rohini means "deer, red cow, or red color." She is also identified with the divine cow Surabhi, born on Earth, waiting in Vraja for the incarnation of Vishnu as Krishna. Rohini is also the name of a star constellation. The star constellations Rohini and Surabhi have similar origins in Hindu mythology. Both are described as the daughter of Daksha and red in color; while the star Rohini is the wife of the Moon, the divine cow Surabhi is the wife of Kasyapa. Rohini is also identified as Kadru, the mother of snakes (*sarpa mata*) in the later *puranas* (*Brahmavaivartapurana* Vol. II, 9.17.40), thus closely aligning her with the *nagas* (serpents), since Balarama is known as the incarnation of the divine serpent Sesha.

Jain stories of Balarama include a simple and straightforward story of Rohini. Jain texts narrate the marriage of Rohini in great detail, including the *svayamvara* and her life with Vasudeva in Sauryapura after her marriage. Rohini is described as the princess of Kosala, a state in the Gangetic valley not far from Mathura, unlike the Hindu texts, which describe her as a princess of lands beyond the commonly travelled Khyber Pass in India, a well-known borderland.

In the Jain stories, as the mother of the divine son, Balarama, Rohini envisions four dreams, and she conceived Balarama directly, unlike the typical Hindu stories of the birth of Balarama, which describe the transfer of Balarama as an embryo from Devaki to Rohini. The four dreams of Rohini contain a lion, a white elephant, the moon, and the ocean, which are common symbols associated with Balarama in Hindu and Jain mythology. Rohini raised Balarama while living in Sauryapura. She did not stay in Vraja, and in the Jain stories Balarama was sent to Vraja as an adult to take care of Krishna, as Vasudeva was concerned that Kamsa might discover Krishna's location.

It is clear from the Hindu and Jain stories, which note her as the first and favorite wife of Vasudeva, that Rohini is an important goddess in the mythology of Krishna. Rohini, along with Balarama, played a major role in Balarama's childhood in the Hindu texts, while she performs no direct role in Krishna's life in the Jain texts. This change of role accorded to Rohini in the Jain texts might be due to the changed character of Krishna in the Jain tradition, rather than to any changes in her own divine status. Rohini is presented as a divine mother and an important wife of Vasudeva in both the Hindu and Jain traditions.

See also: Balarama; Devaki; *Gopas* and *Gopis*; Kamsa; *Maya*; Nidra; Subhadra: Krishna's Sister; Vasudeva; Vrishnis; Yashoda

Further Reading

Joshi, N. P. 1986. *Mother in Kushana Art.* New Delhi: Kanak.

RUPA *GOSVAMI* (1493–1564)

Rupa *Gosvami* along with his brother Sanatana *Gosvami* were two of the principal and most important disciples of Caitanya, and they were instrumental in developing the Caitanya Vaishnava tradition, also known as the *Gaudiya* Vaishnava tradition. Rupa *Gosvami* spent most of his life in Braj, where he supervised the construction of temples, contributing to the redevelopment of Braj as the most important center of pilgrimage, based on the wishes of his teacher Caitanya, who expressed distress at the desolation of Braj when he visited. Rupa *Gosvami* was a prolific writer, writing poetry, theology, literary theory, and religious practice that contributed significantly to establishing the basis for Caitanya Vaishnava practice and philosophy. Rupa was born in Fatepur in the 1500s. Rupa and Sanatana are the names given by Caitanya for the brothers; their original names are unknown, although they were sometimes known by their Muslim job titles as Dabir Khas and Sakar Mallik respectively. Rupa and Sanatana kept in touch with Caitanya through letters while working for the Muslim ruler of Bengal, Sultan Shah. Caitanya encouraged them to keep their positions with the ruler while continuing their worship of Krishna. However, after meeting with Caitanya they decided to renounce their positions and join Caitanya in their quest for spiritual enlightenment. The brothers were taught personally by Caitanya and charged with reviving Braj, which occupied them for the rest of their lives. Rupa and Sanatana settled in Braj while trying to revive the Krishna pilgrimage center. They were natural leaders and well liked by the Vaishnavas in Braj such as *Haritray* (the three Haris) and others. After Caitanya's passing, Rupa's younger brother, Anupama, along with his son Jiva, also

---

Bhaktirasamritasindhu

The *Bhaktirasamritasindhu* (Ocean of the Nectar of Devotional *Rasa*) is one of the main books written by Rupa *Gosvami* while living in Brindavan. Cultivating and experiencing the taste of devotional worship (*Bhaktirasa*) forms the central theme of the *Bhaktirasamritasindhu*. Rupa *Gosvami* describes the various modes of *Bhaktirasa* for a devotee to perfect his practice. Varieties of devotional service including *Sadhanabhakti* (service of devotional practice), *Raganuragabhakti* (spontaneous devotional service), and *Madhurabhakti* (devotional service of love) are clearly expounded utilizing the related evidence from classical texts including the *Bhagavatapurana*. Rupa also describes the principles and purity of devotional service, qualities of a devotee, qualities of Krishna, and the performance of devotional service in detail.

settled in Braj. Raghunatha Bhatta from Banaras and Gopala Bhatta from Srirangam also joined them. Together these six teachers of Caitanya Vaishnavism are known as the "six *Gosvamis*," who functioned as the base of the movement. Rupa lived for some time in the village of Nandgaon, while he spent the last part of his life in Sevakunj, where he worshipped Krishna in a small hut, which is still visited by devotees wishing to revere him. In Brindavan, Rupa discovered a *murti* (icon) of Govindadeva and constructed a small temple to house the deity in the center of Brindavan. Rupa's modest temple has been transformed into a magnificent temple, known as the largest temple in Brindavan, built with financial support from Raja Man Singh. However, for fear of Muslim raids the *murti* (icon) of Krishna was moved to Jaipur in the seventeenth century. Rupa passed away in 1568, and his tomb is located in the Radha Damodara Mandir in Brindavan. Rupa *Gosvami* was a prolific author and composed a number of texts. His principal works are the *Caitanya Caritamrita* and the *Bhakti Ratnakara*. His *Laghubhagavatamrita* and *Samkshepabhagavata* analyze the various manifestations of Krishna and the different types of devotees. The most important work of Rupa *Gosvami* is *Bhaktirasamritasindhu*, which analyzes the primary and secondary emotions of bhakti. His *Upadesamrita* explicates the six ways of practicing devotion, such as chanting the name of Krishna, honoring and serving other devotees, and practicing *raganuraga bhakti*. Rupa also wrote the *Krishnajanmatithividhi*, which outlines the observances for the birth anniversary of Krishna (*Krishnajanmashtami*). Rupa also composed plays and linguistic texts. Taking his theological basis from the *Bhagavatapurana*, Rupa wrote theological texts for his followers. He established the basic ritual practices for Krishna worship. Rupa defined devotion as "continuous service to Krishna" and outlined three different stages of devotion: *sadhanabhakti* (devotion in practice), *bhavabhakti* (devotion in emotion), and *premabhakti* (devotion in love). He also outlined two types of devotional and spiritual practices based on levels of spiritual attainment to reach Krishna: *vaidhi bhakti* (following the rules of scripture) and *raganuraga bhakti* (following passion). Rupa was unquestionably instrumental in the revival of Braj and the establishment of the Caitanya Vaishnava tradition in Brindavan. His texts still serve as the basis for *Gaudiya* Vaishnava philosophy and tradition.

See also: Bhakti; Braj: Classical History; Braj *Parikrama*; Brindavan; *Haritray*; Jiva *Gosvami*; Mathura; *Rasa* Theory; Six *Gosvamis*

Further Reading

Brzezinski, J. 1999. *Mystic Poetry: Rupa Gosvami's Uddhava Sandesha and Hamsaduta*. San Francisco: University of California Press.

Case, M., ed. 1996. *Govidadeva: A Dialogue in Stone*. New Delhi: Aryan Books International.

Haberman, D. 1988. *Acting as a Way of Salvation: A Study of Raganuraga Bhakti Sadhana*. New Delhi: Motilal Banarsidas.

Rosen, S. 2002. *The Gosvamis of Vrindavana*. New Delhi: Rasbihari Lal and Sons.

S

SAHAJIYA TRADITION

The *Sahajiya* tradition, composed of a Vaishnava tantric group from Bengal, derives its devotional views from Caitanya, but diverges drastically from Caitanya Vaishnava tradition in practice. *Sahaja* is a Sanskrit word usually translated as "spontaneous," "innate," "easy," or "natural." Like child's play, *Sahajiya* practice is supposed to arise from one's innate nature. The dominant theoretical precept of the practitioners of the *Sahajiya* tradition is based on the nature of Caitanya, who represented an incarnation of Radha and Krishna, the personification of eternal happiness of the divine union. This Caitanya precedent was refashioned by emerging devotional schools in Bengal in various ways often influenced by Tantra. The practices of almost all the bhakti traditions of Krishna such as Haridasi *sampradaya*, Radhavallabha *sampradaya*, and *Gaudiya* Vaishnavism also consist of *raganuraga bhaktisadhana* (following the way of passion) or *manjarisadhana* (practices as a young maiden), but limit it only to mental and meditative practice (*sadhana*). While these other devotional schools are cautious in their practice, seeing the difference between divine and human manifestation, *Sahajiyas*, through their esoteric practices, blur this line. For the *Sahajiyas*, *manjarisadhana* is not merely a meditative practice, but also a complete physical assumption of the personality of the young maiden in oneself, including living one's life as a maiden. Although the origin of the *Sahajiya* tradition remains obscure, there are four important poetical texts that contain its basic tenets. These are the *Amritaratnavali* of Mukundadasa, the *Anandabhairava* of Premadasa, the *Agamasara* of Yugaleradasa, and the *Amritarasavali* of Mathuradasa. The *Samkhyayoga*, *Hathayoga* practices, and mantras provide the crucial cosmological and philosophical background of the *Sahajiya* tradition. The concept of *Krishnatatva* of Caitanya is blended with the esoteric yogic practices, which require sustained long-term practice and unique selfless involvement of the disciples. Beginners practice only singing and dancing, which are considered *bahya* (external) and ritualistic (*vaidhi*) practices by the *Sahajiya* tradition. However, an advanced devotee may be permitted advanced practice with a second initiation under the guidance of a teacher (*sikshaguru*). The third and final stage involves a disciple's final initiation, which leads to individual practice toward perfecting the devotee's *prema* (spiritual love) of Krishna and Radha. *Sahajiyas* place emphasis on the bhakti in accomplishing the spiritual love of Radha and Krishna within one's body. According to the *Sahajiya* tradition, the body is an important tool for accomplishing "a bond of Radha and Krishna" within oneself. The divine bond of love, once established in the heart of a devotee, leads to immense joy and ecstasy as exemplified by Caitanya. *Sahajiya* tradition considers Caitanya as incarnation of both Radha and Krishna together, exemplifying the joy and ecstasy of such a union. *Sahajiya* tradition is a less widespread subsidiary school of the Krishna bhakti movement in India because of its innovative and unusual blending of disparate systems of thought.

See also: Bhakti Movement; Caitanya Vaishnavism; Haridasi *Sampradaya*; Radhavallabha Tradition

Further Reading

Bose, M. M. 1986. *The Post-Caitanya Sahajiya Cult of Bengal*. Delhi: Manohar.

Dimock, E. C. 1989. *The Place of Hidden Moon: Erotic Mysticism in the Vaishnava-Sahajiya Cult of Bengal*. Chicago: University of Chicago Press.

Hayes, G. A. 2011. "Eroticism and Cosmic Transformation as *Yoga*: The *Atmatattva* of Vaishnava Sahajiyas of Bengal." In *Tantra in Practice*, edited by D. G. White. Princeton: Princeton University Press.

SAMAJ GAYAN

Samaj gayan, kirtana, and *bhajan* are similar in their nature and ritualistic sense of performance, while *bhajan* differs slightly in performance, but is similar in concept to the other two traditions of musical practices associated with devotion. *Samaj gayan, kirtana,* and *bhajan* are generally performed in the temple or at private ceremonies and also at public festivals and rallies associated with temples. These performances, generally with musical instruments and singers, may sometimes also involve dancers. Although *samaj gayan* shares features with *pada kirtan* and *nama kirtan*, it is less widely known than the latter two because its highly ritualized nature requires years of training. *Samaj gayan* is practiced within the three Krishna bhakti traditions: Nimbarka *sampradaya*, Radhavallabha *sampradaya,* and Haridasi *sampradaya*; while *kirtana* is practiced in the *Varkari* tradition of Maharashtra and the Caitanya Vaishnava tradition. The Nimbarka tradition attributes ancient origins to *samaj gayan,* connecting it to Narada, the eternal singer of Hari. Nimbarka tradition has neither a daily practice of *samaj gayan* as does the Radhavallabha tradition nor calendrical ritual singing as does the Haridasi tradition, but organizes multiday singing in a location for festivals such as *Holi* or other special occasions such as birthdays of its *acaryas*. South Indian *Burrakatha* and *Harikatha* traditions are similar, but not as ritualistic, and they are performed in an informal manner.

The traditional performance of *samaj gayan* involves one principal singer (*mukhiya*) and two subordinate singers (*jhelas*). The principal sings lines, while the other two respond with exclamations, questions, or another line, as is appropriate. This highly ritualized tradition places interaction at the center of singing, since it is established that the relationship of Radha and Krishna could only be brought forward through such interactivity. Instruments used in these performances may be similar to those in the other Krishna singing traditions such as *haveli sangit*. A drum (*tabla* or *pakhavaj*), hand cymbals (*kartal* or *jhanjh*), and a harmonium are also used as musical accompaniments. More elaborate performances may utilize a *tanpura* (lute), *sarangi* (Indian chordophone), *israj* (Indian stringed instrument), and so on. The Radhavallabha tradition claims to have been the first to use *samaj gayan* in its temples. *Samaj gayan* is a daily practice in the Radhavallabha tradition. The singers of the Radhavallabha tradition are known as *samajis*. In fact, the founder of the Radhavallabha tradition, Hit Harivams, is the author of *Hitcaurasi* (so called after his name), which contains eighty-four songs in Brajbhasha, commonly used in *samaj gayan*. Among other popular song compilations of the Radhavallabha tradition are *Sri Radhavallabha ji ka Varshotsav*, a large anthology of three volumes with numerous *kirtans*.

The Haridasi tradition has the most ritualistic *samaj gayan* tradition. Haridasi *sampradaya* has a strict calendrical tradition of *samaj gayan*. Each calendrical event is characterized by a particular style of *samaj gayan*. Swami Haridas, the founder of Haridasi *sampradaya,* was a well-known and accomplished musician of his time who is regarded as the teacher of Tansen, a musician in the court of the Mughal emperor Akbar. Haridas's poetical text, the *Kelimal,* is the central text of the Haridasi tradition. This text contains several *dhrupads* (lyrical verses) with accompanying musical notes of *raga*, which describe the intimate romantic play of Radha and Krishna in Brindavan. Styles of *samaj gayan* vary based on the occasion of the calendrical ritual marking its singing tradition. A particular *pada* is assigned to each day of the calendar year. A special type of *samaj gayan* is performed on festival days and special occasions such as the birthday of an *acarya*, where all participants will be divided into two groups singing in response to each other, rather than the three singers that traditionally sing it.

See also: Caitanya Vaishnavism; Haridasi *Sampradaya*; *Haritray*; *Radhashtami*; Radhavallabha Tradition

Further Reading

Salomon, C. 1995. "Baul Songs." In *Religions of India in Practice,* edited by D. S. Lopez, 186–208. Princeton: Princeton University Press.

SAMBA

Samba is the son of Krishna from his wife Jambavati. Samba is also one of the *Pancaviras* (the five heroes) of the Vrishni clan, along with Vaasudeva (Krishna), Samkarsana (Balarama), Padyumna, and Aniruddha. Although Samba is known as a great hero, he is also famous for his pranks and lackadaisical nature. However, one of his pranks did not go as planned and caused the annihilation of the Yadava clan. One day Samba and his brothers and friends saw the sage Durvasa visiting Dvaraka. Aware of the short-tempered nature of the sage, they decided to play a trick on him and see what he would do. They dressed Samba as a pregnant woman by hiding a large pestle in the dress and took him to Durvasa, pretending they wanted to receive his blessings. However, Durvasa was aware of their disrespectful stunt and placed a curse on them: the pestle concealed in the dress would cause the end of the Yadava clan. This scared Samba and the other Yadava boys. They thoroughly ground up the pestle and threw the powder in the Yamuna River so that no one would be able to use it to cause the end of the Yadava clan. However, the reeds that grew on the banks of the river absorbed the powder of the pestle from the water. Later when the Yadavas were in a drunken rage at Prabhasa, they picked the reeds and hit one another with them. In this way, the sage's curse did in fact cause the destruction of the Yadava clan.

Ancient temples dedicated to the *Pancaviras* in India have been dated to as early as 200 BCE. Archaeological excavations at the Besnagar temple complex (200 BCE) revealed a Garuda capital (the emblem of Vaasudeva), palm leaf capital (the emblem of Balarama), and deer capital (the emblem of Pradyumna), and inscriptions found there mention the followers of Bhagavata. Based on these three capitals and two inscriptions found at the site, archaeologists proposed that a *Pancavira* temple complex containing shrines dedicated to the five heroes might have existed there. A fifth-century temple in Mahabalipuram currently known as the Parthasarathy temple is said to have been an ancient temple dedicated to the *Pancaviras* containing their icons dated to 600 CE.

See also: Eight Wives of Krishna; *Pancaratra*; Prabhasa; *Vyuhas*

Further Reading

Bakker, H., and A. Entwistle. 1981. *Vaishnavism: The History of the Rama and Krishna Cults and Their Contribution to Indian Pilgrimage.* Groningen: Institute of Indian Studies.

SANDIPANI

The sage Sandipani is the teacher (guru) of Krishna and his brother Balarama, and also of other friends of Krishna such as Sridama. After killing Kamsa in Mathura, Krishna and Balarama were sent by his family to obtain a proper education. The sage Sandipani's ashram was located in a town near Ujjain in Madhya Pradesh. The modern town of Ankapata, near Ujjain, has been identified as the site of the legendary ashram of Sandipani. After completing his education, Krishna offered his *gurudakshina* (preceptor's fee). Guru Sandipani initially refused any fee, but upon Krishna's insistence, he requested that his son, who disappeared in the ocean near Prabhasa, might be rescued and returned to him in lieu of the preceptor's fee. Krishna reached Prabhasa and summoned the Ocean (Sagara) to find the guru's son. Sagara confirmed that there was in fact a mighty demon, known as Pancajana, who took the form of a conch and traveled, but noted that he had not seen the guru's son in the ocean or with the demon. Krishna quickly entered the ocean and killed that demon. However, he did not find the boy on the inside of the conch shell. Krishna took the conch shell, known as *Pancajanya* from the name of the demon it once housed. This conch shell is one of Krishna's attributes commonly depicted in images. Krishna returned to the surface of the ocean, confirming that the sage's son had been killed. Krishna then went to Samyamani, the city of the god of death, Yama, since the dead go to the world of Yama. Yama received Krishna courteously and returned the boy to Krishna, obliging him. Krishna then brought the boy back to his guru.

The city of Prabhasa on the ocean, where the son of the sage Sandipani disappeared, is also the site of the annihilation of the Yadavas and the death of Krishna.

Prabhasa is one of the important centers of pilgrimage for Krishna devotees. The town of Ankapata, near Ujjain, is another important pilgrimage site for devotees of Krishna. It is marked with temples denoting the sage's ashram and a stepped tank (*Gomti kund*).

See also: Balarama; Kamsa; Prabhasa; Uddhava; Vasudeva

Further Reading

Entwistle, A. 1987. *Braj: Center of Krishna Pilgrimage*. Groningen: Egbert Forsten.
Lal, B. B. 1997. *The Earliest Civilization of South Asia*. New Delhi: Aryan Books.

SANJAYA

Sanjaya is the legendary narrator of the Bharata war, which also includes the *Bhagavadgita*. His name is ubiquitous in the verses of the *Bhagavadgita*. Sanjaya is the confidante, personal adviser, and charioteer of Dhritarashtra, the blind king of the Kauravas.

Sanjaya's narration of the Bharata war, including the *Bhagavadgita,* was recorded by Vyasa in the *Mahabharata*. As the most important text of Hinduism, its distinct narrative position is apparent. As a result of this special narration, the *Bhagavadgita*, as it is received in its current form, underwent three individual receptions before it finally became part of the *Mahabharata*. The *Bhagavadgita* was directly transmitted to Arjuna, the first receiver, an event that was indirectly envisioned by Sanjaya, the second receiver. Both Dhritarashtra and Vyasa, the third receivers of the message, in turn received it from Sanjaya. Sanjaya, the true preceptor, transmitted the *Bhagavadgita* directly to Dhritarashtra, an event that was indirectly envisioned by the sage Vyasa, who recorded the entire text of the *Mahabharata*. Therefore, the narration of the Bharata war, including the *Bhagavadgita,* stands out from the rest of the *Mahabharata* for its unique transmission.

It is unclear in the narration of the text of the *Mahabharata* how the text of the *Bhagavadgita* was transmitted between Sanjaya and the sage Vyasa. However, Vyasa endowed Sanjaya with the power of distance vision, which permitted him to observe events happening in a distant place. Vyasa, the direct perceiver and narrator of all the events of the *Mahabharata*, could have easily narrated the Bharata war, including the *Bhagavadgita*. Even then an all-perceiving omniscient narrator, Vyasa chose not to narrate the war directly, but render it through the voice of Sanjaya. Hence, in this episode the primary narrator, Vyasa, takes a secondary position, allowing Sanjaya to take the primary position. Divine vision, or special vision to see the proceedings of the god's dialogue, is central to this episode in the *Mahabharata*. Krishna provided divine vision to Arjuna at the beginning of the narration of the *Bhagavadgita*, while Vyasa gave the power of distance vision to Sanjaya. These two were the only primary spectators and receivers of the divine knowledge Krishna had brought forth at the beginning of the war. Therefore, the narration of the *Bhagavadgita* as attributed to Sanjaya places the *Bhagavadgita* in a distinct narrative status, setting it apart from the rest of the *Mahabharata*. This indicates the primary position of the *Bhagavadgita*. Sanjaya performs a central role in the transmission of the divine wisdom, acquiring a special place as an important preceptor of true knowledge in India.

See also: Arjuna; *Bhagavadgita*; *Mahabharata*; *Pandavas*

Further Reading
Swcheig, G. 2007. *Bhagavadgita: The Beloved Lord's Secret Song.* New York: HarperOne.

SANJHI

Sanjhi (Sanjhikala), which is also known by a variety of names across India, such as *kolam* (Kerala and Tamilnadu), *rangoli* (Karnataka), *muggu* (Andhra Pradesh), *madana* (Rajasthan), *alpana* or *aripan* (Bengal), *sathaya* (Gujarat), and *cita* (Orissa), is an informal temporary art drawn by women on the front yards of their houses or on walls. These are line drawings of natural images such as animals, birds, and fish, which are always drawn freshly every morning. The *sanjhi* is drawn with elaborate designs to celebrate festivals or other special occasions. *Sanjhi* is a ritual art associated with the purification of the Earth in the morning. Women draw *sanjhi* in their front yards with white or colored powders. On special occasions rice flour or flower petals could be employed to draw the special designs. In the Braj area *sanjhikala* is said to have originated with Radha. *Sanjhi* is used as floor decorations in the temples of Krishna, and on special festivals it is drawn in elaborate colors in the temple courtyards. Although *sanjhikala* is the purview of women,

Women drawing ornate floral designs as part of traditional festival celebrations. (Vjrithwik /Dreamstime.com)

men can also be seen taking part in drawing *sanjhi* in temples. It is a skillful art, but stencils for numerous designs are available to make drawing *sanjhi* easier. Devotional traditions of Krishna such as the Radhavallabha tradition encourage the drawing of *sanjhi* as a *seva* offering in the temple of Radhavallabha in Brindavan.

Threshold designs sometimes utilize the geometrical designs employed in a mandala. Symbols of infinity, planets, stars, natural themes, as well as religious themes such as the symbols of Vishnu and Shiva are popular designs. At the beginning of construction, the ground is sanctified with *bhumipuja*, which involves sprinkling water followed by drawing *rangoli* (*sanjhi*). Therefore, the *sanjhikala* (*rangoli*) is understood to have extensive religious and ritual importance.

See also: Mandala; *Seva*

Further Reading

Archana, S. 1985. *The Language of Symbols: A Project on South Indian Ritual Decorations of Semi-Permanent Nature.* Madras: Crafts Council of India.

Kilambi, J. 1986. "*Muggu*: Threshold Arts of India." *Res: Anthropology and Aesthetics* 10: 71–102.

Layard, J. 1937, 1986. "Labyrinth Ritual in South India: Threshold and Tattoo Designs." *Folk Lore* 48: 115–182.

Nagarajan, V. 1993. "Hosting the Divine: The Kolam in Tamilnadu." In *Mud, Mirror, and Thread: Folk Traditions in Rural India,* edited by N. Fisher. Albuquerque, NM: Museum of New Mexico.

SANKARADEVA

Sankaradeva (1449–1569) was a religious contemporary of Caitanya who lived in the same geographical region (eastern India) as Caitanya, although it is not known if they ever met. Sankaradeva was the key contributor in establishing the bhakti movement leading to the revival of Vaishnavism in Assam. His influence on Assam is not limited to the religion, but notable in all fields of Assamese culture and society. Assam was a very politically and religiously complex territory governed by four different dynasties during the fifteenth and sixteenth centuries: the Koch, Ahom, Chutiya, and Kachari dynasties. However, in the sixteenth century the Ahoms took over the Chutiya and Kachari kingdoms, while the Koch tribe became stronger within the older Kachari state, leaving only two states in Assam in the sixteenth century: Ahom and Koch. Assamese kingdoms consisted of loosely organized tribes and chieftaincies. Such political instability also affected the foundation of Sankaradeva's devotional tradition of Krishna, contributing to its unique features. Sankaradeva was born into a *Bara Bhuyan* (independent landholding) family of the *Kayastha* caste in the region of Nagaon in central Assam. He married in his teens and took over the chieftainship. However, after the death of his wife, he renounced everything and went on a twelve-year pilgrimage. Upon his return to the village he built his first *namghar* and began practicing the bhakti mode of worship. Sankaradeva attracted a large following immediately, which made the

Ahom king grow suspicious of him and his religious gathering, resulting in the arrests and executions of his chief disciples. Sankaradeva went to the neighboring Koch kingdom, where suspicion continued to follow him, and the new king, Naranarayana, forced Sankaradeva into hiding once again. However, King Naranarayana's brother Chilaraya had become a follower of Sankaradeva. A meeting between Sankaradeva and the king cleared the suspicions, while Sankaradeva eventually succeeded in changing the mind of the king and the religious landscape of Assam. Sankaradeva was a prolific writer with proficiency in several languages. He translated the *Bhagavatapurana* into Assamese. He also wrote song compositions on Krishna, including the *Krishnaghosha* and the *Gunamala*, explaining the qualities of Krishna. Sankaradeva's *Bhaktiratnakara* is his theoretical exposition of the bhakti centered on Krishna. Sankaradeva also wrote several *Ankiya Nat* dramas and *Satriya nritya* (dances), which were performed in the *namghars* during festivals. In fact, he was the progenitor of the *Ankiya Nat* dance-drama theater in Assam. As explained in his texts, Sankaradeva's bhakti tradition is based on two principles. The first concept is the *Ekasarana Nama* dharma, which lays down the basic rule of Krishna bhakti as taking refuge in Krishna by chanting the name of Krishna. The second concept is *Mahapurushiya* dharma, which is acceptance of Vishnu as the supreme deity and worshipping Krishna as Vishnu. Sankaradeva's bhakti tradition differs from the other bhakti traditions of this period in not worshipping Radha, but focusing only on Krishna. Sankaradeva did make accommodations for the caste hierarchy in his *satra* but initiated anyone with discipline and commitment into his Vaishnava tradition. Sankaradeva was also ahead of his time in initiating women and also allowing women to become chief of a *satra*. The establishment of *satras* and *namghars* in villages completely changed the life of the Assamese countryside.

See also: Ankiya Nat; *Bhagavatapurana*; Bhakti; Caitanya; Childhood of Krishna in Brindavan; *Lila*; Performing Arts and Krishna; *Raasalila*; *Rasa Theory*; Satra

Further Reading

Barman, S. 1999. *An Unsung Colossus: An Introduction to the Life and Works of Sankaradeva*. Guwahati: Forum for Sankaradeva Studies.

Barua, B. K. 1965. *Temples and Legends of Assam*. Guwahati: Bharatiya Vidya Bhavan.

Cantlie, A. 1984. *The Assamese Religion, Caste and Sect in an Indian Village*. London: Curzon Press.

Goswami, K. D. 1982. *Life and Teachings of Mahapurusha Sankaradeva*. Patiala: Punjabi University.

Kakati, B. K., ed. 1959. *Aspects of Early Assamese Literature*. Guwahati: Guwahati University.

Murthy, H. V. S. 1973. *Vaishnavism of Sankaradeva and Ramanuja*. Delhi: Motilal Banarsidas.

SANTS

Sants (saints; derived from Nath *sampradaya*) are found across India, but the term is also used to denote poet-saints of Maharashtra associated with the Krishna devotional tradition commonly known as the *Varkari* tradition. The *sants* of

Maharashtra sang *abhangs*, simple poetical compositions similar to the *padas* or *sakhis* seen in the Krishna devotional traditions across India. *Sants* of Maharashtra, including Jnanadev, Namdev, and Eknath, composed and sang *abhangs*, made pilgrimages, and often lived in Pandarpur, a central pilgrimage site of Krishna devotion in Maharashtra. Their compositions were initially passed on in the oral tradition, rarely written down. Maharashtrian saints come from varied social backgrounds including high- as well as low-caste devotees of Krishna. Several *sant* traditions are known from north India, including Ravidasis (Punjab and north India), Radhasaomi *satsang* (Punjab), Kabir *panthis,* and so on. However, followers of the Ravidasi tradition have only recently started taking part in the biennial *vari* to Pandarpur.

See also: Bhakti Movement; Eknath; Jnanadev; Namdev; *Varkari* Tradition

Further Reading

Schomer, K., and W. H. McLeod. 1987. *The Sants*: *Studies in a Devotional Tradition of India.* Berkeley: University of California Press.

SATNAMI TRADITION

Satnami sampradaya is one of the oldest schools of Vaishnavism, following the practice of worshiping the divine in its *nirguna* (formless/without attributes) aspect. Hence, according to the *Satnami* tradition the central god is understood only in the name, but not in the form. Hence the tradition itself is called the *Satnami* (true name) tradition. The *Satnamis* do not worship personal idols but express devotion through singing and meditating on the names of God. The *Bhagavadgita* serves as the central text of the *Satnami* tradition, but several other texts and oral tales are also part of its central repository of religious knowledge. Although known to have been popular in the northwestern and central territories of India since the fifteenth century, the origins of the *Satnami* tradition are not clear. However, *Satnamis* were known as an active political force in central India for their rebellions during the Mughal Empire (1769–1771) and the period of British rule (1850–1880). It appears that initially the *Satnami sampradaya* may have followed the normal practices of Vaishnava bhakti movements in its ritual practices and pilgrimage traditions. The *Satnami* tradition is spread over several regions of India, including the northwestern provinces (Rajasthan, Gujarat, Punjab, and Sindh), northern India (Himachal Pradesh and Kashmir), and central India (Chattisgarh, Madhya Pradesh, and Orissa). Regional differences, changes, and adaptations in practices over time can be observed among the various *Satnami* groups. Like the Vaishnava bhakti traditions, *Satnami sampradaya* also rejects caste and expects a strict food regimen from its followers. Followers of the *Satnami* tradition of Punjab rose up in a rebellion against the Mughal Empire over a tax dispute. Although their rebellion was initially successful, the Mughal forces crushed it gradually by ruthlessly killing a large number of *Satnamis*. This forced some *Satnamis* to migrate to other states of India, including Rajasthan, Gujarat, and the central provinces. The *Satnami* tradition of Rajasthan is said to have been founded by

Jagjivandas of Barabanki in Rajasthan. A smaller group of *Satnamis* in northern India, called *sadhs*, follow distinct ritual practices and vegetarianism. It is said that the founder of the *Satnami* tradition of Chattisgarh (in the 1820s), Ghasi Das, and his son Balak Das embarked on a pilgrimage to one of the most popular Vaishnava pilgrimage centers in Puri (the Jagannatha temple), but returned without completing the journey. Upon his return, Ghasi Das gave up his familial responsibilities, adopted asceticism, and left his village to live in the forest, appearing only periodically to speak to his followers. After his death, leadership of the group continued in his family through his son, grandsons, and so on. Basic rules of practice involve abstaining from meat and alcohol. Due to its rejection of caste, the *Satnami* tradition of Chattisgarh attracted a considerable following from the lower castes of central India, especially the Chamars. This lower-class membership of the group led some to connect the *Satnami* tradition of Chattisgarh with the Ravidasi tradition of northern India, which is also a devotional tradition with a large following among the lower castes.

See also: Bhagavadgita; Bhagavatas; Narayana; *Nirguna/Saguna*; Sankaradeva; *Varkari* Tradition

Further Reading

McGovran, D. A. 1990. *The Satnami Story: A Thrilling Drama of Religious Change*. New Delhi: W. Carey Library.

Publications Division. *Census of India 1891 Vol. 16. Part I,* 140–144. New Delhi: Government of India.

SATRA

Construction of Krishna temples or centers of worship known as *satras* began in the fifteenth century in Assam, although Vishnu temples have been known to exist in Assam since the ninth century (Suryapahar and Goalpara). Architecturally, the *satras* differ from the existing temple styles of Assam, which may consist of two (*garbhagriha, mandapa*) or three parts (*garbhagriha, antarala,* and *mandapa*) in the usual style of temple building common in northern India.

A *satra* is a cultural center associated with Krishna in Assam, although a temple in Assam is generally referred to as *mandap*. The concept of the *satra* came from Sankaradeva, the Vaishnava saint of Assam. A *satra* is a religious complex rather than a single building and is dedicated to cultural, educational, spiritual, and artistic aspects of life. A *satra* contains a monastery, *namghar*, and cultural center for music, dance, and handicrafts as well as a cultural repository of crafts including mask making. In its most simple form, the *satra* consists of a large prayer hall facing a simple shrine, where Krishna is worshipped through dance, drama, music, and poetry. The complex is surrounded by modest residential facilities for monks. Details of the following *satras* help elucidate the nature of the *satra* in Assam. Since *Raasalila* is an essential feature of Assamese devotional Vaishnavism, a dance school is a common feature of the *satra*. *Auniati Satra*, founded by Niranjan Pathakdeva, is known for a typical style of dance known as *Paalnaam* (*Apsara* dances). It also

Women devotees at a daily prayer meeting in a *Satra* for women on Majuli Island, Assam State, India. (Daniel J. Rao/Alamy Stock Photo)

holds an extensive collection of ancient artifacts, specimens of Assamese utensils, jewelry, and handicrafts. *Dakhinpat Satra* was founded by Banamalidev, an exponent of *Raasalila*. During *Rasotsava*, several thousand devotees visit these holy *satras* every year. *Garamurh Satra*, founded by Lakshmikantadeva, is known for *Raasalila*, and also for preserving ancient weapons called *bortop* (cannons). *Kamalabari Satra*, founded by Bedulapadma Ata, is a center of art, culture, literature, and classical studies. Majoli Island's best boats are manufactured here. Its branch, *Uttar Kamalabari Satra*, has showcased *satra* art in several states of India and abroad. *Bengenati Satra* is a cultural repository of antiquities of cultural importance and an advanced center of performing art. Its display includes the royal robes of Ahom king Swargadeo Gadadhar Singha and the royal golden umbrella of the Ahom rulers. *Shamaguri Satra* is noted for its mask-making tradition. A *mandap* is also known colloquially in Assam as *dol* (a derivation from *deol* or *deval*, meaning temple in eastern and southern India).

See also: Ankiya Nat; Caitanya; Ramanuja; Sankaradeva

Further Reading

Barua, B. K. 1965. *Temples and Legends of Assam*. Gauhati: Gauhati University.

Cantlie, A. 1984. *The Assamese Religion, Caste and Sect in an Indian Village*. London: Curzon Press.

Choudhury, R. D. 1985. *Archaeology of the Brahmaputra Valley of Assam*. Delhi: Abhinav Prakasan.

Goswami, K. D. 1982. *Life and Teachings of Mahapurusha Sankaradeva*. Patiala: Punjabi University.

Sarma, P. C. 1982. *Architecture of Assam*. Gauhati: Gauhati University.

SEVA

Seva (service) to the deity is an expression of love for the deity, which delights both Krishna and the devotee. *Seva* involves serving a personal icon of the deity known as *murti*, *svarupa*, *vigraha*, or *salagrama*, which represents Krishna as though the deity were present in person. Overcoming this physical aspect to establish a spiritual connection with the deity through performing simple services is the goal of *seva*. *Seva* is an important instrument of devotion for the devotees of Krishna for establishing mindful meditation, seeking a spiritual connection, and bridging the human soul and divine soul. Waiting on Krishna and performing services for Krishna such as offering food, singing, performing music or dance, wearing adornments, creating paintings, and decorating floors are considered intimate acts of relationship with the deity. Worship of Krishna centered on bhakti primarily utilizes *seva*. *Seva* involves serving the deity as if he were present among the devotees. The home shrines as well as temple services are organized with *seva* as the central motive. *Seva* offered by the devotees at home takes the form of bathing, dressing, and putting adornments on the deity, and offering food lovingly and carefully in a timely fashion. While these types of *sevas* are performed by the priests in temples, devotees participate by attending services in close proximity (*darshan*). Devotional services in the temple may also involve *kirtana* or *samkirtana* (singing the holy names) along with other devotees, or listening to others chanting the names of the deity. *Seva* is an important aspect of the bhakti traditions since bhakti traditions emphasize the establishment of a spiritual connection between the devotee and the deity as the most important aspect of god realization.

See also: Arati; Bhakti; *Prasada*; *Puja*

Further Reading

Haberman. D. 1988. *Acting as a Way of Salvation*. New York: Oxford University Press.

SIX *GOSVAMIS*

The first two of the Six *Gosvamis* to settle in Brindavan were Rupa *Gosvami* and his brother Sanatana *Gosvami*. Jiva *Gosvami*, their nephew, the son of their younger brother Anupama, later joined them. Rupa *Gosvami* initiated Jiva *Gosvami* upon his arrival in Mathura. Gopalbhatta *Gosvami* from southern India, Raghunathbhatt *Gosvami* from Varanasi, and Raghunathdas *Gosvami* from Bengal also joined these three *Gosvamis* (Rupa, Sanatana, and Jiva) in their efforts to revive Braj and bring the teachings and devotion of Krishna close to the common people. Their efforts at reviving the sacred centers of Braj were remarkable, and their devotional literary works are well known and have served as inspirational literature for later devotees of Krishna. Rupa *Gosvami* was the first to arrive at Brindavan in 1517; he was joined by his brother Sanatana two years later in 1519. Both were about thirty years of age when they arrived in Brindavan. Initially they stayed in Dhruv Ghat, but later settled in Brindavan, spending the rest of their lives in Brindavan. Their *samadhis* (memorials) and a *bhajankuti* (prayer hall) were constructed near the Madanmohan and Radhadamodar *mandirs*. Another *bhajankuti* was also constructed under the name of Sanatana near Radhakund and Manasi Ganga, and another was constructed in the memory of both the brothers, Rupa and Sanatana, at Nandgaon beside the Pan Sarovar. Rupa and Sanatana discovered their respective deities, Govind Dev and Madanmohan, in Brindavan. Although initially housed in small shrines, the deities were later moved to the larger temples of Govind Dev and Madanmohan in Brindavan. Gopalbhatta *Gosvami*'s text *Haribhaktivilasa* is a comprehensive work on ritual. It is said that Gopalabhatta *Gosvami*'s family belonged to the traditional Brahmans associated with the Ranganatha temple in Srirangam. Gopalbhatta brought a *salagram* from Gandak, which manifested as the icon of Radharaman. It so happened that one day he read the story of *Prahladavijayam*, and wondered how lucky the young boy Prahlada was to obtain the direct incarnation of Vishnu through his prayers. While wondering he felt sleepy and took a nap under a tree, hanging his basket of *salagramas* on a branch. When he woke up a little while later he noticed that the lid of the basket was slightly open. Gopalbhatta thought that a snake might have entered the basket and tried to shake the basket. However, the lid fell off and he was enchanted to find an image of Radharaman in the basket. He constructed a temple for Radharaman later. Gopalbhatta initiated a lineage of priests with the permission of Caitanya. Caitanya also sent him him his *japmala* (prayer beads), *kaupina* (cloth), and *asana* (seat). Raghunathdas *Gosvami*, son of a wealthy zamindar, lived in the company of Caitanya for many years at Puri. He composed several poems on Radha and Krishna, and hymns for the Govardhan hill and the ponds in Govardhan. Raghunathdas's book *Vrajavilasastava* contains descriptions of the places in Vraja along with the narration of the adventures of Krishna. Raghunathdas bought lands around the Radhakund and also developed and enlarged the pond. He could be considered pivotal in establishing the Radhakund as an important center of *Gaudiya* Vaishnava tradition. His *samadhi* and *bhajankuti* are constructed on the banks of the Radhakund and continue to be visited by devotees. Raghunathbhatt *Gosvami* is noted for his daily sermons at the Govind Dev temple, although he did not write any texts. Jiva *Gosvami*, the youngest of the six *gosvamis*, was the most prolific writer of theological texts and commentaries, which enrich the Caitanya Vaishnava tradition and practice.

The greatest credit for the revival of Braj goes to the Six *Gosvamis*. Each of them contributed by constructing temples, organizing devotional rituals and prayers, and composing devotional literature to guide the next generation of their followers. *Gaudiya* Vaishnavism multiplied in India as well as abroad based on these early foundations laid by the Six *Gosvamis*.

See also: Braj *Parikrama*; Brindavan; Caitanya; *Gaudiya* Vaishnavism; Jiva *Gosvami*; Mathura; Rupa *Gosvami*

Further Reading

Chakravarti, S. C. 1969. *Philosophical Foundation of Bengal Vaishnava Tradition.* Calcutta: Academic Publishers.

SKANDAPURANA

Skandapurana is an important *purana* that contains not only the mythology of Krishna, but also descriptions of sacred places associated with Krishna. *Skandapurana* is important for understanding the sacred geography of Mathura. The Vaishnavakhanda of *Skandapurana* contains chapters describing the sacred cities of Mathura, Kashi (Varanasi), Puri, and Ayodhya. Although the *Vaishnavakhanda* of *Skandapurana* is generally dated to 1300 CE, scholars lack consensus on the precise dating of the text. The *Mathuramahatmya* chapter of *Skandapurana* opens with an invocation praising the sacredness of Mathura, followed by narration of the benefits of visiting and bathing at Mathura on the *paurnami* (full moon) during the month of *Margashira*, which normally occurs between December and January. The *Mathuramahatmya* section of *Skandapurana* can be compared to the *Mathuramahatmya* sections in the other *puranas* such as the *Varahapurana*, the *Padmapurana,* and the *Vayupurana*. It can also be compared to the *Mathuramahatmya* text composed by Rupa *Gosvami*. The *Skandapurana* version of the *Mathuramahatmya* shows similarities and differences with these other versions of the *Mathuramahatmya*, which leads one to consider that a lost source text may have been used as the base text of the original verses that occur in all of these *Mathuramahatmya* texts, although each text improvised and added its own material, which contributes to the uniqueness of each text. Thus one can argue that the existing *Mathuramahatmya* texts may not have borrowed from one another, but they may have borrowed material from the now extinct original *Mathuramahatmya* source text, which may have existed prior to the thirteenth century.

However, the *Mathuramahatmya* section of the *Skandapurana* also contains material that is not found in any of the other *puranas* noted above. Hence, the *Bhagavatamahatmya* section of the *Skandapurana* can be considered an original text not derived from other texts by its similar name. The *Bhagavatamahatmya*, true to its name, contains chapters that extol the sacredness of the *Bhagavatapurana* as a sacred text capable of leading one to salvation in the *Kaliyuga*, the present age. The first three chapters of the *Bhagavatamahatmya*, known as the *Vrajabhumimahatmya*, describe the process of Vajranabha's return to Mathura, his meeting with Uddhava, identification of the places associated with Krishna, as well as Vajranabha's efforts to repopulate Braj by reviving and constructing several temples in Brindavan, Govardhan, Barsana, and Dig. Vajranabha's meeting with Uddhava is described in great detail, naming the places in Mathura. When Vajranabha met Uddhava, he gave a sermon on the importance of the *Bhagavatapurana*. Although earlier versions of the *Mathuramahatmya* existed, the *Skandapurana*'s extensive descriptions of sacred places in Mathura and Braj serve as the background of the popular pilgrimage circuit of Mathura. The *Skandapurana* version of the text also served as an itinerary for later popular pilgrimage texts extolling the virtues of Mathura as a sacred center of Krishna. The *Skandapurana* pays special attention to *tirthas*, the merits of bathing in various tanks, and bathing *ghats* on the banks of the Yamuna. As a river connected to death (Yama) and noted for its importance for the performance of *sraddha* rituals, the Yamuna finds special mention in the *Mathuramahatmya* texts, including *Skandapurana*.

See also: Braj *Parikrama*; Brindavan; Eight Wives of Krishna; Mathura; Uddhava

Further Reading

Entwistle, A. 1990. "*Mahatmya* Sources on the Pilgrimage Circuit of Mathura." In *The History of the Sacred Places in India as Reflected in the Sacred Texts,* edited by H. Bakker, 5–29. Leiden: E. J. Brill.

SRILAXMI

Srilaxmi is Vishnu's consort, depicted as his wife in all his incarnations, and one of the major goddesses of Hinduism. Srilaxmi is the goddess of fortune, wealth, and good luck. As such, Srilaxmi is also worshipped independently for wealth and prosperity. Because she is worshipped and liked by everyone, it is surprising that her veneration has not evolved into a separate popular tradition, as seen in the case of Vishnu (Vaishnavism), Shiva (Saivism), Kali, or Durga (*Upasakas* and Tantra). She is worshipped as Vaishnavi, one of the forms of Devi (Shakti), and also she is venerated in her eight forms as Ashtalaxmis; there are special *pujas* offered to her on *Dipavali* (*Diwali*). However, in the mythology of Krishna, Laxmi is identified with more than one of his wives. In the *Mahabharata* and the *Harivamsa*, Srilaxmi is also identified with other feminine goddesses who were not Krishna's wives, which causes some confusion about her role within the Krishna cycle of narratives. The earliest textual resource on Laxmi, known by the name *Srisukta,* is an appendix of the *Rigveda* (500–1000 CE). Almost all the *puranas* include Laxmi's stories and praises (*stotras*). One of the most important praise poems of Laxmi, composed by Sankara, was known as the *Kanakadharastotram* (Shower of Gold Prayer), popularly recited in *Laxmipuja* (worship of Laxmi). Narratives about her appearance from the Ocean of Milk (*Kshirasagara*) when it was being churned by the gods and demons to extract *amrita* (ambrosia) is her standard origin story from the classical texts of India, although the texts may differ in minor details. She chose Vishnu as her husband. Laxmi is often depicted holding a lotus in her hand while sitting or standing on a lotus with two elephants at her side. Several early sculptures from Mathura (100–200 CE) bear a resemblance to her and are depicted with a lotus, a symbol associated with her. Srivaishnavism places Laxmi at the center of its textual sources and ritual practices. Sri, another name for Laxmi, is venerated along with Vishnu, hence giving the name Srivaishnavism to the tradition. South Indian temples have the most elaborate iconic representations of Laxmi; and the

The Hindu goddess Srilaxmi, Tamilnadu state, India, 9th century granite sculpture, with 12th-century recutting. (Los Angeles County Museum of Art)

Sthalapuranas of Tirupathi and others narrate miraculous stories of her appearance on Earth. However, her appearance from the Ocean of Milk, holding a pot of gold, presents her as a unique goddess who holds the key to happiness on Earth—material wealth (gold, money). As a consort of Vishnu, or representing one of the other partners of Krishna, she also carries out an important role in the cosmogony and cosmology of the universe.

See also: Radha; Srivaishnavism; Subhadra: Krishna's Sister; Venkatesvara; Vishnu

Further Reading

Benard, E. A., and B. A. Moon. 2000. *Goddesses Who Rule.* New York: Oxford University Press.
Couture, A., and C. Schmid. 2001. "The *Harivamsa,* the Goddess Ekanamsa, and the Iconography of the Vrsni Triads." *Journal of the American Oriental Society* 121 (2): 173–192.
Penumala, P. 1995. *Srilakshmi in Srivaishnava Tradition.* Atlanta: Scholars Press.

SRINATHJI *HAVELI* NATHDVARA

The term *haveli* is used to denote Krishna temples in the Vallabha (*Pushtimarga*) tradition, and in common practice these temples contain individual sections, such as Nandababa's *bhavan* (Father Nanda's house, indicating the house where Krishna lived as a child), where Krishna is worshipped as if he dwells there as a child, in accordance with the practices of living theology of devotional traditions. The term *haveli* also means "mansion." Wooden household shrines are also commonly known as *havelis.* However, the Krishna temple is organized structurally as a mansion, and the services (*sevas*) in the *haveli* are performed by volunteers called *sevaks* (servants). The architecture of the *haveli* closely aligns with the dominant theological perspectives of the Vallabha tradition of Vaishnavism. The Srinathji temple in Nathdvara contains several *havelis*: the shrine of Srinathji, Navnitpriyaji *Haveli,*

Dvarakadhishji *Haveli*, Banmaliji *Haveli*, Madanmohanji *Haveli*, Gopallalji *Haveli*, Vittalnathji *Haveli*, Kalyanrayji *Haveli*, Jamunaji *Haveli*, and Govindarayji *Haveli*. Architecturally, the Srinathji *Haveli* of Nathdvara is comprised of the following parts where most of the temple rituals and activities are conducted: *Nagarkhana* is at the entrance; the daily announcements of Krishna's public audiences (Prince of Nand Bhavan) are announced by a drummer and are held at this entrance. *Govardhan Chok* derives its name from the miniature Govardhan Hill created here during *Divali* and New Year celebrations. Usually this courtyard is occupied by vendors selling fruit and vegetables, and tailors preparing ceremonial garments. *Suraj Pole* is the eastern entrance of the *haveli*, guarded by Suraj (the sun), hence it is called *Suraj Pole*. It is also called the "ladies' gate," because only ladies are permitted to enter through this gate during busy festival days as a crowd control measure. *Hathi Pole* is the doorway flanked by silver doors leading into *Ratan Chok* to proceed with the Lord's *darshan*. It is also known as the "men's gate," as men enter from this gate during festival days. *Ratan Chok* is the first courtyard immediately outside of the Srinathji's inner chambers. This courtyard also has three other doorways, *Suraj Pole*, *Hathi Pole*, and another door opening into Srinathji's walled garden, in addition to the doors of the inner chambers. *Hatadi* (Market of Nandrani) is set up in this courtyard (*Ratan Chok*) with Srinathji on *Diwali*. *Mani Kot* is the antechamber of the Srinathji, which is normally occupied by the singers during *darshan* (audience). Only members of *Vallabhkula* (family of Vallabha) or special servants of the Srinathji *Haveli* may enter beyond this point. *Nija Mandir* (sanctum) is beyond the *Mani Kot* where Lord Shrinathji resides and the main center of the *haveli*. *Dolti Bari* is the main audience hall of the *haveli*. The chamber is often transformed for the numerous occasions celebrated in the temple depending on the festival celebrations of the calendar. *Dolti Bari* leads into *Anar Chok*, which links the kitchen and the *Kamal Chok* where food from the *haveli*, especially *prasad*, is distributed. *Kamal Chok* is the main courtyard decorated with a distinct lotus design in the middle. Devotees can sit here and wait for *darshan*, and also submit their gifts to Srinathji and receive *prasad*. The *haveli* is the most common temple form of Vallabha *sampradaya* of the Vaishnava tradition, which is characterized by a unique practice of bhakti. *Haveli* has also been associated with home shrines of individual devotees, which are used to house the idols and perform the daily *puja* (worship) in most Hindu homes. Although Nathdwara is the foremost of the *havelis*, there are several *Pushtimarga* temples constructed with similarly elaborate architectural arrangements with minor alterations, replicating the daily practice and ritual noted at Nathdwara. Notable among these are the *Pushtimarga Havelis* in Mathura (Dwarakadhishji temple and Govardhannathji ki *Haveli*), Mumbai (Shri Vallabh *Darshan* and Govardhannathji ni *Haveli*). *Haveli* temples of the Vallabha tradition are also constructed in the United States. The largest is the Nathdvara *Haveli* located in Houston; the most extensive one is located at Vraj in Pennsylvania. The Srinathji *Haveli* in the Vraj temple in Moundsville, Pennsylvania, recreates the sacred space of *Brajbhumi* on its large campus. Most of the Vallabha tradition's temples in the United States are developed through the efforts of wealthy benefactors and form a pilgrimage circuit undertaken by the followers of the Vallabha tradition. The

Vallabha tradition is one of the devotional traditions that has stayed close to its original practices even though it is transplanted into the United States.

See also: Bhakti, Braj *Parikrama*; *Diwali*; *Govardhan Puja*; Mathura; Vallabha; Vallabha Tradition; Vitthalnath

Further Reading

Bhatt, G. H. 1943. *Rasalila Chapters, Critically Edited and Translated into Gujarati with Introduction and Notes.* Bombay: Vadilal Nagindas Shah.

Gupta, R. M., and K. R. Valpey. 2013. *The Bhagavata Purana: Sacred Text and Living Tradition.* New York: Columbia University Press.

Sukhabala, R. 1980. *Vallabha sampradaya aura usake siddhanta.* Avara, Rajasthana: Pandita Ramapratapa Sastri Ceritebala Trasta.

SRIRANGAM TEMPLE

The Ranganathaswamy temple is located in Srirangam, a small island town formed by the Kaveri River on one side while one of its tributaries, the Coleroon River, joins it on the other side. The Srirangam Temple is the most important temple of Vaishnavism, and it is also included on the list of the 108 *divyadesams* (sacred sites) of Vaishnavism. Considered to be the largest temple in India, the Srirangam temple is spread over 156 acres of land. The temple is constructed in the imposing style of Dravidian architecture with highly embellished towers on the gateways (*gopura*), pillared halls (*mandapas*), and central sanctum (*garbhagriha*). The *vimana* (tower above the sanctum) on the central sanctum sanctorum (*garbhagriha*) is plated with gold. The *Rajagopuram* (tower on the main gate) is 237 feet high. Other towers and *mandapas* (pillared halls) are equally large and ornately decorated with beautiful sculptures. The temple consists of 21 tall towers in total. There are several *mandapas* (halls) within the temple complex. The thousand-pillared hall, decorated with 956 ornately carved pillars, is constructed with granite and organized as an open theater.

The Srirangam temple was attacked in 1326 by Malik Kafur, who destroyed several structures in the temples and killed a large number of Vaishnava devotees. However, expecting the impending danger from invading Muslim armies, the Vaishnava *acaryas* removed the central icon of Sriranganatha and replaced it with a fabricated image. Malik Kafur destroyed the fabricated image, assuming it to be the original icon of Ranganatha, during his attack. The original icon of Ranganatha was brought back to the temple in 1371. Except for this disturbance the temple of Ranganatha in Srirangam continued to enjoy the patronage of successive rulers of south India and the devotion of the common people.

Although it is considered by devotees to be an ancient temple, inscriptions in the Srirangam temple could only be dated to the tenth century, and the main idol of Ranganantha is said to have been found accidentally by a Chola emperor.

The Hindu Religious and Endowments Board of the government of Tamilnadu currently manages the temple. The *Vaikuntha Ekadasi*, also known as *Mukkoti Ekadasi*, and an annual temple festival (*Brahmotsavam*) are the most popular celebrations of the temple, attended by large numbers of devotees. The temple also remains busy with numerous devotees during the month of *Margali* (December–January), considered to be the holiest period of the year. During *Brahmotsavam* (an annual festival) Ranganathasvami processions take place for ten days, attended by large numbers of devotees. The annual chariot festival of the temple (*Rathothsavam*) is celebrated in the month of *Thai* (January–February), during which the deity is taken in a chariot procession around the temple.

As an earthly incarnation of Krishna in *Kaliyuga*, Ranganatha is the center of a new bhakti tradition of south India, which influenced numerous other bhakti traditions of India. The Srirangam temple as such is credited with a regional bhakti tradition that also served as inspiration for arts and culture, leading to several artistic compositions in regional languages of south India, including Tamil, Telugu, Kannada, and Malayalam.

Sri Ranganathaswamy Temple (Srirangam, Tamilnadu) is a UNESCO World Heritage site and the second largest religious complex in the world. The temple contains tall and ornate *gopurams* (gateway towers) and ornately decorated pillars and *mandapas* (halls). (Iuliia Kryzhevska/Dreamstime.com)

See also: Advaita; Alvars; Andal; Ramanuja; Srivaishnavism

Further Reading

Rao, V. N. H. 1967. *The Srirangam Temple Art and Architecture*. Tirupathi: Sri Venkatesvara University.

Srivathsan, A. 1995. "The Persecution of Ramanuja, a View from the Srirangam Temple Complex." *Indian Economic and Social History Review* 32 (4): 475–487.

SRIVAISHNAVISM

Srivaishnavism is the religion of the goddess Sri (Laxmi) and the god Vishnu together. According to Srivaishnavism, Krishna and Vishnu are the same, since Krishna is the *purna avatara* (full incarnation) of Vishnu. Consequently, it is Krishna who is worshipped as Vishnu and venerated in the hymns of *alvars* (*Nalayira Divya Prabandham*) and *stotras* of *acaryas*, since Krishna is the *purna avatara* (full manifestation) of Vishnu. Srivaishnavism draws its traditional philosophical system from Vedanta, *Bhagavata*, and *Pancaratra* traditions in combination with poetical revelations of the bhakti saints of Tamilnadu (*alvars*). This combination yields a rich treasury of textual, ritual, and devotional practices characteristically associated with Srivaishnavism. Traditionally compositions of twelve *alvars* (700–900 CE) form the most distinctive literature of Srivaishnavism, which was collected by the Srivaishnava *acaryas* Nathamuni (920–950 CE) and Yamunacarya, and which were later included in daily temple rituals by Ramanuja. However, early Srivaishnavas faced persecution by some Chola emperors of Tamilnadu, and later the raids of the Muslim armies of Malik Kafur. Those raids resulted in closing many Srivaishnava temples and moving the icons to other temples in Tirupathi (Andhra Pradesh) and Melkote (Karnataka) for safekeeping. Such movements led to theological differences, which split Srivaishnavism into two groups known as the *Vadakalai* (Kancipuram and Ahobilam) and the *Tenkalai* (Srirangam). The main theological difference between these two groups is known as "cat hold" and "monkey hold" in popular parlance. The "cat hold" signifies obtaining *moksha* without much effort, like kittens being carried by their mother, without any effort on the part of the kittens: this is widespread among *Tenkalai* Srivaishnavism. The second mode of obtaining *moksha*, known as the "monkey hold," points to the effort required on the part of the devotee, similar to the baby monkey that has to hold on to its mother while being carried. Srivaishnava tradition follows the *Pancaratra* tradition of accepting the appearance of Vishnu in five forms: *para* (supreme) form: Vishnu who resides in heaven eternally; *Vyuha* (emanation) form: four forms (Vaasudeva, Samkarshana, Padyumna, and Aniruddha) that emanate from Vishnu at the beginning of creation; *Vibhava* or *Avatara* (incarnation): ten descents of Vishnu to earth; *Antaryami* (Vishnu as present in the heart and soul); and *Arcavatara* (manifest icon), which can be worshipped in the temple. *Stotrapatha* (reading the *stotra*—praise poems) forms one of the main devotional rituals of veneration of the deity in Srivaishnavism. Krishna is the personified form of Vishnu worshipped in most of the Srivaishnava temples, epitomizing the play aspect of Krishna. The temples follow a set routine of service to the lord of the temple, following the *Pancaratra Agamas* generally, while some temples may also follow the *Vaikhanasa Agamas*. Srivaishnavism is the earliest bhakti movement of India that centers on popular devotion to a personal deity and is most often represented by Krishna. Srivaishnavism popularized the worship of the goddess and god as one, which is a popular mode of worship in the later Vaishnava traditions. Srivaishnavism remains one of the most important inspirational systems of the bhakti traditions, and it continues to grow in popularity, establishing itself beyond the borders of India.

See also: Alvars; Bhagavatas; Pancaratra; Ramanuja; Venkatesvara

Further Reading

Hopkins, S. P. 2002. *Singing the Body of God: The Hymns of Vedantadesika in Their South Indian Tradition.* New York: Oxford University Press.

Hopkins, S. P. 2007. *An Ornament for Jewels: Love Poems for the Lord of Gods.* New York: Oxford University Press.

Kalidos, R. 1999. "Dance of Visnu: The Spectacle of Tamil Alvars." *Journal of the Royal Asiatic Society* 9: 223–250.

Narayanan, V. 2003. "Two Processions: Andal's Wedding and Nammalvar's Moksa." *Journal of Vaishnava Studies* 12 (1): 122–137.

Venkatachari, K. K. A. 1978. *The Manipravala Literature of the Srivaishnava Acaryas*. Bombay: Anantacarya Research Institute.

SUBHADRA: KRISHNA'S SISTER

Subhadra is the sister of Krishna and Balarama, daughter of Rohini and Vasudeva. She is also considered the daughter of Yashoda and Nandagopa since Subhadra is identified as a reincarnation of Ekanamsa or Nidra, the goddess that was born to Yashoda and died when Kamsa smashed her, instead of Krishna, on the rocks as soon as she was handed to him as the newborn child of Devaki. Subhadra is praised as Laxmi, which sometimes leads to confusing identifications of her as both wife and sister of Krishna. However, it is common in Hindu classical parlance to praise a good-looking woman as a Laxmi, and it should not be confused with her identity as Srilaxmi, wife of Vishnu. Subhadra's marriage to Arjuna was arranged by Krishna, while Balarama, her other brother, tried to arrange her marriage with Duryodhana. It was achieved by a trick by Arjuna and Krishna. Arjuna reached Dvaraka while on a pilgrimage. Krishna had him disguised as a sage, and appointed Subhadra to serve the sage with the permission of Balarama. However, Subhadra fell in love with him, figuring out that it was indeed Arjuna, disguised

Subhadra tells Abhimanyu that his engagement to Vatsala has been annulled, scene from *The Story of the Marriage of Abhimanyu and Vatsala* folio from the manuscript of the *Epic Mahabharata*. (Los Angeles County Museum of Art)

as a sage. Balarama could not oppose his sister's wishes, and hence he agreed to have her married to Arjuna instead of Duryodhana as he had planned earlier. However, archaeological excavations brought to light images that show that Subhadra is memorialized and worshipped along with her brothers Krishna and Balarama. Several such images of Subhadra flanked by her brothers, which are called by the name of the goddess, the Ekanamsa triads, because of her being depicted larger than her brothers, have been discovered in archaeological excavations in the Mathura region. The one place where Subhadra is epitomized and still worshipped along with her brothers Balarama and Krishna is in the Jagannatha temple of Puri.

See also: Balarama; Devaki; Kamsa; Krishna; Nidra; Vasudeva; Yashoda

Further Reading

Ate, L. 2014. "Oṉṟaṉpakuti—a 'Single Part' of the Tamil Epic *Cilappatikāram* and Its Significance to the Study of South Indian Vaiṣṇavism." *Journal of Hindu Studies* 7 (3): 325–340.

Starza, O. M. 1993. *The Jagannatha Temple at Puri: Its Architecture, Art, and Cult.* Leiden: E. J. Brill.

SURDAS

Surdas (1478–1583) was the most prominent devotional poet of Krishna bhakti in the regional language, Brajbhasha, a dialect of Hindi spoken in the Braj region. Surdas was a blind poet who sang of Krishna and described his *lilas* (childhood playfulness) in Vraja, in Brindavan (*Gopilila*), as well as Krishna's divine roles in the *Mahabharata* including the *Bhagavadgita*. Surdas is epitomized by the popular legend that depicts the child Krishna coming to listen to Surdas sing his poems every night. Surdas's biography is narrated in the *Bhaktamal* of Nabhadas, and also *Chaurasi Vaishnavon ki Varta*. Vallabha tradition includes him as one of the *Ashtachap* (Eight Poets) whose poems are sung in the *Pushtimarga* temples. These two texts highlight the two most important qualities associated with Surdas's poems: they are so sweet and lyrical that Krishna himself comes to listen, and they are infused with the philosophical message of the Vedanta religion and sung as part of the temple rituals. This episode is illustrated in a mural in the Dwarakadhish temple in Mathura, which depicts Krishna listening to Surdas's singing. Paintings and prints of Krishna listening to Surdas's singing are one of the most popular depictions of any singer saint, and are widely sold in India. Beyond his blindness, not much is known about the personal life of Surdas, and it is not known whether he was born blind or developed blindness later. Surdas's book, the *Sursagar,* contains 125,000 poems. The poems include the essence of the *Bhagavatapurana* and hence are pleasing to Krishna, which is also beneficial to devotees as they are composed in the popular language of the region, Brajbhasha. The poems of Surdas were later organized thematically following the *Bhagavatapurana*, which is sung as the *Surdasi Bhagavatapurana* (Surdas's *Bhagavatapurana*). Numerous illustrated manuscripts of the *Sursagar* are available with accompanying illustrations, dated as early as 1562 CE, although containing only a small portion, about 241 verses, of Surdas's compositions. Some of these early illustrated copies of Surdas's compositions are preserved in the National Museum in New Delhi.

See also: Astachap; Braj: Classical History; Braj *Parikrama*; Brindavan; Vallabha Tradition

Further Reading

Hawley, J. S. 2009. *The Memory of Love: Surdas Sings to Krishna.* New York: SUNY Press.

Hawley, J. S. 2012. *Three Bhakti Voices: Mirabai, Surdas, and Kabir in Their Time and Ours.* Delhi: Oxford University Press.

Misra, N. 2010. *Krishna in Indian Art: Sursagar Paintings of Awadh School.* Gurgaon: Shubhi Publications.

SWAMINARAYAN TRADITION

The Swaminarayan tradition is a modern Krishna devotional tradition that draws its traditional lineage and inspiration from Uddhava *Sampradaya*, inspired by the teachings of Uddhava, friend and follower of Krishna. The Swaminarayan tradition was founded by Swami Sahajanandswami (1780–1830), who was considered an incarnation of Krishna in his highest form. Two of his followers established devotional traditions based on his teachings in Ahmedabad and Vadtal. Both devotional groups of the Swaminarayan tradition are widely represented in India and abroad. The Swaminarayan tradition of Ahmedabad established its International Swaminarayan Satsang Organization (ISSO) to oversee its activities in India and abroad. An offshoot of the Vadtal Swaminarayan *sanstha* (group) known as Bochasanvasi Sri Akshar Purushottam Swaminarayan Sanstha (BAPS) was developed from the teaching of Yagnapurushdas. The teachings of Yagnapurushdas derive inspiration from Gunitanand Swami (1785–1867), a disciple of the original founder, Sahajanandswami, who is recognized as a God-realized saint and hence known as *purushottam*. The highest reality is perceived as eternal (*akshar*). Gunitanand Swami is considered to be an incarnation of the eternal true form of the god. Both Swaminarayan organizations, the BAPS and the ISSO, have international outreach and are managed by boards of trustees involved in temple construction as well as social welfare activities. Although the *Bhagavatapurana* is considered the central text of the Swaminarayan traditions, other texts, such as the *Shikshapatri* written by Sahajanandswami and the *Vacanamrit* containing the discussions and dialogue of Sahajanandswami, composed by five of his disciples, also form the central canon of the tradition. The Swaminarayan tradition is one of the most important devotional traditions of Hinduism, well known for its large temples in India and across the world. The largest Hindu temple in India is the Askharadam temple in Delhi. Similar to other Krishna devotional traditions such as ISKCON and *Pushtimarga,* the Swaminarayan tradition has followers from various ethnic groups.

See also: Bhagavatapurana; Bhakti; ISKCON; Uddhava; Vallabha Tradition

Further Reading

Williams, R. B. 1984. *A New Face of Hinduism: The Swaminarayan Religion.* Cambridge: Cambridge University Press.

TEMPLES OF KRISHNA IN INDIA

Temples of Krishna in India are built in the traditional architectural style of the regions in which they are located. Temple architecture is broadly classified into three styles based on the style of the *shikhara* (temple tower) rising above the roof of the *garbhagriha* (sanctum sactorum): it is called *Nagara* (north Indian), *Dravida* (south Indian), or *Vesara* (middle or central Indian). The temple complexes may vary in size due to the shrines within their precincts, as well as the style of the temple. Krishna temples are found across India in a variety of regional and innovative styles, dating to various periods. Each regional style has further evolved into several variations, and there have been stylistic changes within each region. The sacredness of Hindu temples derives from two distinct features that are part of the sacred geography of Hinduism. First, temples are situated on spots that are considered to have been previously visited or touched by the divinity in some way. In the case of Krishna temples, the sacred places of the Mathura region are identified by the legend of Krishna as narrated in the *Bhagavatapurana*; or a deity may inhabit a sacred site in a new form in the current era (*Kaliyuga Pratyaksha daivam*), indirectly representing Krishna in another form (Srivenkatesvara and Sriranganatha). Temples of Krishna in other regions of India indicate a direct movement of Krishna or his images. For example, central icons that were moved from Braj already were imbued by the divinity of Krishna (Srinathji temple in Nathdvara and others) and may pick their own sacred location, or God's form appeared miraculously in an earthly image, indicating the sacredness of the place (Udupi Srikrishna temple, Guruvayur Srikrishna temple), and God expressed himself (*arcavatara*) as in the case of the Srirangam temple, Venkatesvara temple, and Guruvayurappa temple. Second, sometimes the temples can also be connected to the saints, who have a special connection with the divinity. Therefore the sacred spot indicates a direct connection to divinity and hence is called *devasthana, devalaya,* and so on, indicating the dwelling place of the god and illustrating the philosophical concept of heaven on earth. The heaven on earth concept found common expression in connection with Vishnu and Krishna in a number of sacred regions across India. As such a number of temples are called *Bhuloka Vaikuntam* (Vishnu's heaven on earth). Similarly, Brindavan is the earthly representation of the divine world of Krishna (*Goloka*). The sacredness of the ground on which the temple stands is additionally sanctified ritually by the presence of the *Vastupurusha* mandala (geographical body of the divine map). The rituals accompanying construction (*bhumi puja*) and consecration (*dhvajarohana*) are connected to these cosmological and cosmogonic connections of the temple with the god. Hence the devotees visiting the temples are

Sri Krishna Temple, in Udupi, Karnataka state in India. Established by Madhva Acarya, this is the most important temple in the Madhva tradition. The central image of the temple is thought to have been sculpted during the life of Krishna at the request of Rukmini. (Gaurav Masand/Dreamstime.com)

not simply visiting them to admire the structures, but to partake in the divine presence of the deity in the temple by offering *puja, seva, arcana,* and so on. The earliest temples in India are related to Krishna or Vishnu. Inscriptions from western India dated to as early as 200 BCE mention Narayanavatika, constructed for the deities Samkarsana and Vaasudeva. Numerous other inscriptions also mention erecting the Garuda pillar (*Garuda Stahmabham*) in the Bhagavata temple (Besnagar, Uttar Pradesh) as well as construction of the temple for the *Pancaviras* (Five Heroes: Krishna Vaasudeva, Samkarsana Balarama, Pradyumna, Aniruddha, and Samba) in Mathura. The earliest temple of Krishna (Vishnu) is found in the Nagarjunakonda valley in Andhra Pradesh and is dated to 200 BCE. It is an apsidal temple, but an inscription in the vicinity of the temple mentions it as a temple of the Ashtabhujasvami (eight-armed deity), identified as Vishnu. Vishnu is commonly venerated as *Bhagavan* and is habitually depicted with multiple hands, heads, and so on, also known as the *Vishvarupa*. Depiction of the image with eight arms is prevalent across India in connection with Vishnu. A number of small temples were built across India between 200 BCE and 200 CE. Well-preserved images of Krishna are found in the Dasavatara temple (325–450 CE) of Deogarh in Uttar Pradesh. Images of Krishna as Naranarayana (Krishna with Arjuna—this image is currently housed in the National Museum, Delhi) and the child Krishna being handed by Devaki to her husband Vasudeva are notable in this temple.

However, several temples in north India were destroyed in the numerous raids conducted by the Muslims between 950 CE and 1650 CE. It is not uncommon for broken statues or broken images to be discovered in archaeological excavations in northern India, which may have been the remains of such destruction. Mathura, a major pilgrimage center of Krishna, could serve as an example of such destruction over many centuries. Broken statues recovered from around Mathura are housed in the Mathura Museum, while the current temples of the Mathura region were only revived and rebuilt since the 16th century when the Mughal emperor permitted ritual bathing by pilgrims in the Yamuna River and allowed the construction and repair of temples. In fact, historians of Mahmud of Ghazni claim that several hundred temples in Mathura were destroyed. Therefore temples of Krishna dating from before the sixteenth century are only rarely found in northern India, although they are found in southern India including Orissa and remote areas of northeastern India. However, the most impressive temples of Krishna in India date from the ninth century onward, owing to the devotional movement centered on Krishna influenced by contributions of the *alvars* of south India. Devotional traditions are undertaking the construction of numerous temples of Krishna in India and across the world. Bochasanvasi Akshar Purushottam Swaminarayan Sanstha (BAPS) and the International Society for Krishna Consciousness (ISKCON) have constructed large modern temples in India and the United States.

See also: Guruvayurappa and Guruvayur Temple; Krishna; Narayana; Pandarpur Temple; Srirangam Temple; Srivaishnavism; Venkatesvara

Further Reading

Branfoot, C. 2008. "Imperial Frontiers: Building Sacred Space in Sixteenth-Century South India." *Art Bulletin* 90 (2): 171–193.

Craven, R. C. 1988. "The Realm of Jagannath—Hindu Temple Architecture in Orissa." *Arts of Asia* 18 (2): 80–94.

Datta, S. 2010. "Infinite Sequences in the Constructive Geometry of Tenth-Century Hindu Temple Superstructures." *Nexus Network Journal* 12 (3): 471–483.

Davidson, R. M. 2011. "The Archaeology of Hindu Ritual: Temples and the Establishment of the Gods." *Bulletin of the School of Oriental and African Studies—University of London* 74: 502–504.

Ghosh, P. 2002. "Tales, Tanks, and Temples—The Creation of a Sacred Center in Seventeenth-Century Bengal." *Asian Folklore Studies* 61 (2): 193–222.

Granoff, P. 1997. "Heaven on Earth: Temples and Temple Cities in Medieval India." In *India and Beyond: Aspects of Literature, Meaning, Ritual and Thought: Essays in Honor of Frits Staal,* edited by Dick Van Der Meiji, 170–193. London: Oxford.

Granoff, P. 2006. "Reading between Lines: Colliding Attitudes Towards Image Worship in Indian Religious Texts." In *Rites Hindous: Transfer et Transformations,* edited by G. Colas and G. Tarabout, 389–422. Paris: Ecole de Paris.

Indorf, P. 2004. "Interpreting the Hindu Temple Form: A Model Based on its Conceptualization as a Formal Expression of Measured Movement." *Artibus Asiae* 64 (2): 177–211.

Kaimal, P. 2005. "Learning to See the Goddess Once Again: Male and Female in Balance at the Kailasanath Temple in Kancipuram." *Journal of the American Academy of Religion* 73 (1): 45–87.

Meegama, Sujatha Arundathi. 2010. "South Indian or Sri Lankan? The Hindu Temples of Polonnaruva, Sri Lanka." *Artibus Asiae* 70 (1): 25–45.

Okada, A. 1996. "Vijayanagar—Medieval Hindu Temple Architecture." *Connaissance des Arts* (531): 108–115.

Presler, F. A. 1987. *Religion under Bureaucracy—Policy and Administration for Hindu Temples in South-India.* New York: Cambridge University Press.

Sadler, A. W. 1975. "3 Types of Monastic Temple in Hindu India." *Horizons* 2 (1): 1–23.

Sanford, A. W. 2002. "Painting Words, Tasting Sound: Visions of Krishna in Paramanand's Sixteenth-Century Devotional Poetry." *Journal of the American Academy of Religion* 70 (1): 55–81.

Schmiedchen, A. 2013. "Patronage of Saivism and Other Religious Groups in Western India under the Dynasties of the Kalachuris, Gurjaras and Sendrakas from the 5th to the 8th Centuries." *Indo-Iranian Journal* 56 (3–4): 349–363.

Sears, T. I. 2008. "Constructing the Guru: Ritual Authority and Architectural Space in Medieval India." *Art Bulletin* 90 (1): 7–68.

TIRUMALISALVAR AND TIRUPPANALVAR

Tirumalisalvar and Tiruppanalvar are the untouchable *alvars* among the *alvars*, noted for their devotion and sacred poetical compositions. Tirumalisalvar is considered the incarnation of Vishnu's weapon, the *cakra* (wheel), in Srivaishnava tradition, although he had been born in a *parayar* or untouchable caste. Tirumalisalvar's poems, *Nanmugan Tiruvantati* and *Tiruccandaviruttan,* are both included in the *Nalayira Divya Prabandham.*

Tiruppanalvar

Tiruppanalvar was found in a paddy field by an untouchable *panar* (untouchable singers) couple, who raised him as their own son, hence he is known as Tiruppanalvar. Tiruppanalavar is considered an incarnation of the *Srivatsa* mark on the chest of Vishnu. There is an important event narrated about the life of Tiruppanalavar and his poem *Amalanatipiran* (Pure Primordial Lord), commented upon by Vedantadesika in his *Munivahanabhogam.* Tiruppanalvar would always stand on the banks of the Kaveri facing the Srirangam temple where Lord Sriranganatha is housed, singing the praises of the lord. Being an untouchable, Tiruappanalvar was not allowed anywhere near the temple or the priests. One day the temple priest came to the Kaveri River to fetch water, and he warned Tiruppanalvar to move out of his path. Tiruppanalvar, deep in his ecstatic devotion to the Lord of Srirangam, did not hear the calls of the priest. Impatient, the priest threw a small stone at Tiruppanalvar to alert him, which hit Tiruppanalvar on his forehead. The priest then got water and returned to the temple. As the priest entered the temple, he noticed a small bump on the forehead of Lord Ranganatha in exactly the same spot

---

Munivahanabhogam

Vedantadesika's commentary, the *Munivahanabhogam*, is the greatest tribute to the poet-saint Tiruppanalvar. Vedantadesika praises the composition of Tiruppanalvar, *Amalanatipiran*, included in the *Nalayira Divya Prabandham,* as superior to the *Vedas.* The ten verses (*Amalanatipiran*) of Tiruppanalvar are elaborated and closely examined in the *Munivahanbhogam.* Vedantadesika explains the fifteen qualities of Sriranganatha outlined by Tiruppanalvar. Vedantadesika also comments on the *Srisukti* of Tiruppanalvar, which is central to understanding the divinity of Sriranganatha as envisioned by Tiruppanalvar. Finally, Vedantadesika concludes the *Munivahanabhogam* by comparing it with the divine world of *Vaikuntam* enjoyed by enlightened souls.

on the forehead where the stone he had recently thrown had hit Tiruppanalvar. This bewildered the priest. Lord Ranganatha then appeared to the priest in a dream vision in the night and commanded him to bring Tiruppanalvar to the temple. The next morning the priest carried Tiruppanalvar on his shoulders and brought him into the temple sanctum to the front of the lord. Facing Lord Sriranganatha, Tiruppanalvar, overcome with devotional emotion, composed a poem (*Amalatipiran*) for the lord, which was later included in the *Nalayira Divya Prabandham*, and as he finished the poem he disappeared into the lord. This event is celebrated by Vedantadesika in his composition, the *Munivahanabhoga*.

See also: Alvars; Ranganatha; Srirangam Temple; Srivaishnavism; Vedantadesika

Further Reading

Hopkins, S. P. 2007. *Singing the Body of God*. Oxford: Oxford University Press.

TIRUMANGAI *ALVAR* AND TONDARADIPODI *ALVAR*

Tirumangai composed the largest number of poems (1,361) included in the *Nalayira Divya Prabandham*. Tirumangai *alvar* is said to have written his *Periyatirumoli* soon after his accidental realization of Vishnu, ca. 800 CE. Legend has it that Tirumangai Mannan was a chieftain under the Cholas. He was married to Kumudavalli, who converted him to Vaishnavism and bound him with a vow to feed 1,008 Vaishnavas every day for a year. Unable to cover the expenses of feeding more than a thousand devotees each day, Tirumangai resorted to robbery. One day while robbing a wedding party, he could not remove the toe rings of the bride, who was revealed to him as Vishnu himself. Vishnu taught him the Narayana mantra, which completely transformed Tirumangai. He gave up robbery and went on to compose *Periyatirumoli* in praise of Krishna. Tirumangai also wrote *Tirunedunthandakam*, *Tirukurunthandakam*, and *Tiruvelukkutirukkai*, which are included in the *Nalayira Divya Prabandham*.

Tirumangai *alvar* also composed a variety of love poems in *pillai-tamil* (a common language in northern Tamilnadu), in a style known as *madal,* called *Periya Tirumadal* and *Siriya Tirumadal*. *Madal* is an old Tamil poetic style used to describe the separation of lovers. Typically, a rejected lover might give up food, bath, dress, and sleep and wander around singing about his lover. If his lover would not come around to accept his love, the singer might attempt suicide. As it happens, the *madal* tradition united many lovers. Women, however, were traditionally prohibited from performing *madal* under any circumstances. Thus Tirumangai's *madal* is startling in that he assumes the role of a *Gopi*, a woman desiring union with Krishna. Tirumangai explains that he is following northern Indian tradition in which a woman can freely express her love. Both *Periya Tirumadal* and *Siriya Tirumadal* express a *Gopi's* desire to unite with Krishna, her beloved.

Tondaradipodi *Alvar*

Tondaradipodi *alvar* is considered the *amsa* of *vanamala* (the garland of Vishnu). Tondaripodi *alvar* lived in Srirangam and prayed to the main deity, Ranganatha.

His original name was Vipranarayana, although he came to be known as Tondar-adipodi (dust of the feet of devotees) due to his obeisance to even the devotees of Vishnu because of his total reverence for Vishnu. It is recorded in his legends that he was accused of stealing by a court prostitute and was sent to jail. After this drastic event Tondaradipodi *alvar* had a change of mind and dedicated his life to worshipping Vishnu. Tondaradipodi *alvar* composed two poems, *Tirumalai* and *Tirupalli Elucci.*

See also: Alvars; Andal; Kulasekhara *Alvar*; *Mutatalvars*; *Nalayira Divya Praband-ham*; Ramanuja; Srirangam Temple; Tirupathi; *Visishtadvaita*; Yamunacarya

Further Reading

Aiyangar, K. 1906. "Tirumangai Alvar and His Date." *Indian Antiquary* 35: 228–233.
Raghavan, V. K. S. N. 1983. *The Tirupalliyelucchi of Tondaradippodiyalvar.* Mylapore, Madras: Sri Visishtadvaita Pracharini Sabha.

TIRUPATHI

Tirupathi is the sacred city of Venkatesvara (Lord of Venkata hills), considered a regional *avatara* of Krishna and Vishnu simultaneously. Tirupathi itself means Vishnu, the Auspicious Lord as well as Lord of Laxmi. The main temple of the presiding deity Venkatesvara is located on the Tirumala hill (also called Seshacha-lam hills), which also lends its name to the deity as Tirumalesa (Lord of Auspicious hills). The annual temple festival, *Brahmotsavam*, celebrated in fall (September–October), attracts a large number of pilgrims. *Brahmotsavam* is celebrated over nine days, during which the *utsava vigraha* of Venkatesvara is taken out in a chariot procession around the main temple in nine different forms, appearing in a special form each day. *Rathasaptami* is another well-attended special temple festival in Tirupati. *Rathasaptami,* a day-long festival celebrated in spring (March–April), re-sembles the annual *Brahmotsavam*, except that the chariot procession of the deity dressed in nine different forms is performed in a single day.

Tirupathi is located in the Chittore district of Andhra Pradesh, not far from the site of early temple activity in Guntur (Nagarjunakonda). Andhra Pradesh is known for the oldest temple (Ashtabhuajasvami temple in Nagarjunakonda); icons of dei-ties found here in excavations have been dated to 200 BCE. An early reference to Samkarsana, Vaasudeva is noted in an inscription issued by Satavahana queen Na-ganika (100 BCE) recovered from the Nasik caves. A large panel depicting the im-ages of *Pancaviras* along with Narasimha was also connected to the Satavahana Empire, which was excavated in the Guntur region. The Satavahana Empire (200 BCE–300 CE) included most of peninsular India touching the Indian Ocean coast on both sides of the country, providing evidence for the early worship of Krishna in south India.

The earliest reference to a temple of Ashtabhuajasvami (Eight-armed Lord) was recorded in an inscription from the Nagarjunakonda excavations in Andhra Pradesh dated to 200 BCE. Ashtabhujasvami noted in the inscription here is identified with Vishnu, and the temple is identified as a Vaishnava temple. Another sculptural slab containing an image of *Pancaviras* with Narasimha in the middle is also found in the same region, which might have formed part of a temple or another similar sacred structure. The above evidence indicates that a number of temples may have existed in the area. Several early temples in Karnataka built between the sixth and ninth centuries are found in Aihole and Badami. Cave temples in Aihole indicate a replication of timber construction. The largest Vaishnava temple, known as the Chennakesava temple (originally called the Vijayanarayana temple), was built between the eleventh and twelfth centuries, while the best-known Krishna temple in Karnataka is the Srikrishna temple in Udupi, founded by Madhvacarya.

The most important temple of Krishna in Andhra Pradesh is the Sri Venkatesvara temple in Tirupathi, a temple of a regional form of Krishna popular in Andhra Pradesh. This is considered an ancient temple of Govinda (also called Venkatesa, the Lord of Venkata) referred to in Tamil poetry and the *Cilappadikaram*. The earliest instance of the name Srivaishnava appears in an inscription from Tirupathi (966 CE). Tirupathi is one of the sacred centers among the 108 *Divyadesams* associated with Vaishnavism. Tirupathi is referred to as *Bhuloka Vaikuntam* (Vishnu's heaven on earth). Hence a visit to the temple is considered efficacious to purify a person of all sins (*papa vimocanam*). The main temple complex is located in the context of the seven hills (*edu kondalu* in Telugu) in Tirupathi, epitomizing the seven gates to heaven.

See also: Bhagavatas; Krishna; Narayana; *Pancaviras*; Srilaxmi; Srivaishnavism; Venkatesvara; Vishnu

Further Reading

Gerard, F. 1996. *A Complete Guide to Hoyasala Temples*. Delhi: Abhinav Publications.

Gundavarapu, L. 1975. *Tirupati Venkatiyam*. Visakhapatnam: Srinivasa Pablisars.

Hardy, A. 1995. *Indian Temple Architecture: Form and Transformation: The Karnata-Dravida Tradition 7–13 Centuries*. Delhi: Abhinav Publications.

Ray, H. P. 2004. "The Apsidal Shrine in Early Hinduism: Origins, Cultic Affiliation, Patronage." *World Archaeology: The Archaeology of Hinduism* 36 (3): 343–359.

Ray, H. P. 2010. *Archaeology and Text: The Temple in South Asia*. Delhi: Oxford University Press.

Sadhu, S. S. 1981. *Tirupati Sri Venkatesvara*. Tirupathi: Tirumala Tirupathi Devasthanams.

TUKARAM

Tukaram (1577–1650) is a renowned poet-saint of Maharashtra, a follower of the *Varkari* tradition, devoted to Vitthala at Pandarpur. The story of his life is included in the *Bhaktavijaya* of Mahipati. His life included a number of miraculous events. Tukaram was born in the town of Dehu near Pune in Maharashtra state, where he spent most of his life. Tukaram's poems depict his contempt for social issues such as the caste system. His death is recorded clearly as he voluntarily gave up his life in 1650. Tukaram wrote several poems (*abhangs*) praising Vitthala of Pandarpur. He regarded himself as the disciple of Namdev, although tradition places him as a disciple of Jnanesvar. His legacy endures in Maharashtra in the *Varkari* pilgrimage and literary culture.

Tukaram in Popular Memory and Modern Media

Sant Tukaram is epitomized in movies and his *abhangs* (poems) are the most commonly sung Marathi lyrics. In India, numerous films based on Tukaram's life have been released in the last sixty years, while the film *Sant Tukaram*, released in 1936, won the Venice film award. A southern Indian film was also produced on the life of Tukaram in Telugu in 1973. Numerous TV shows and theater performances based on the life of Tukaram are common, not only in Hindi and Marathi, but also in southern Indian languages such as Kannada and Telugu.

See also: Panduranga Vitthala; *Sants*; *Varkari* Tradition

Further Reading

Chitre, D. 1991. *"Says Tuka"—Selected Poetry of Tukaram*. New Delhi: Penguin Books.
Ranade, R. D. 1994. *Tukaram*. Albany: SUNY Press.

TWELVE FORESTS OF BRAJ

The geographical location of the Krishna legend is in the idyllic settings of Braj, a naturally beautiful area with numerous forests, ponds, and wells. Especially noted are the descriptions of forests where important events of Krishna's life occurred. The pilgrimage texts describe twelve major forests and twenty-four *upavanas* (minor forests) associated with the life of Krishna. These groves and woods are protected by religious groups, which also care for the special trees mentioned in the *Mahatmya* texts.

Mahavana

Mahavana, known as Mahavan in local usage, is identified as the legendary *Gokul*, where Krishna spent his infancy. Because the Vallabha tradition developed another township known as Gokul, this place is called "old *Gokul*." Activities of Krishna's infancy happened here.

Kumudavana (Forest of Lotus)

This is the third forest noted as the place where Krishna played with the *Gopis*. There is a pond in this forest known as Krishnakunda, said to be the pond where Krishna and the *Gopis* engaged in water play. The pond is also known by other names such as Padmakunda, Kumudakunda, and Viharakunda. There is a small shrine for Kapila near the pond.

Khandiravana (Forest of Acacia Trees)

Khandiravana is referred to as Khaira, a short form of the name. There is a pond named Krishnakund here, beside which is a temple of Dauji. Nearby is a *baithak* of

Lokanath containing the images of Caitanya and Nityanand. A little further to the west of Khandiravana is Brijwari, which is known for the pond Kishorikund from which Lokanath *Gosvami* discovered the icon of Radhavinod.

Bhandiravana (Forest of Banyan Trees)

Bhandiravana is the eleventh forest in the list of twelve in the pilgrimage texts of Mathura. Bhandiravana is the site where Balarama killed Pralambha. Hence this forest is closely tied to the worship of Balarama. Some identify the bhandira tree (Bhandiravat) and Bhandiravan as located on both sides of the Yamuna River, but the descriptions in the textual sources of the *Harivamsa* and the *Bhagavatapurana* leave little doubt that the Bhandiravana containing the bhandira tree is a single location where Balarama killed Pralamba. There is a well in the forest variously referred to as Dauji ka kup, Bhandirkup, Venukup, and so on. This forest is also identified as an important place for Krishna, since it is described as the location of Radha and Krishna's marriage, which according to the *Gargasamhita* took place right under the banyan tree (Bhandiravat).

Bilvavana (Wood Apple)

Bilvavana is currently known as Belban, a shortened modern form of the original name. There is a Laxmi temple here that is managed in the *Gaudiya* tradition. There is also a *baithak* of Vitthalnath in this forest.

Bahulavana (Forest of Cardamom Trees)

The village of Bahulavana is called Bati in current usage. Classical *puranas* provide various meanings for the name, although the cardamom tree is known as *bahula*. Bahula (Vakula) is identified as the name of a *sakhi*, and also as the name of a wife of Hari. Sources relate a story of the cow called Bahula. A tiger is said to have attacked the cow, but the cow begged to be given leave to meet its calf one last time, to give it her last message and a last feeding of milk. The tiger agreed, and the cow returned, keeping her word, at which the tiger was impressed and let her go free. This story is commemorated in a small shrine with the image of the cow Bahula. Near the cow shrine is a temple dedicated to Krishna called Bahulabihari. There are also tanks in this village called Balramkund, Man Saras (Man Sarovar), and Krishnakund. The temple of Krishna, referred to variously as Mohanray, Madanmohan, or Muralimanohar, is found on the banks of Krishnakund. There is also a Shrivaishnava temple dedicated to Laxminaryana or Laxmisakrishna.

Talavana (Forest of Palmyra Trees)

Talavana, also known as Talban in modern usage, is the second of the twelve forests listed in the *Mahatmya* texts. This forest is identified as the forest where

Balarama vanquished the demon Dhenuka. The nearby village is known as Tarsi, considered a short form of Talasthali (place of the Palmyra trees). In this village there is a pond called Samkarsanakund, named after another name of Balarama. On the northeast side of the pond is the temple of Balarama, known as the Dauji temple, managed by the priests of the Nimbarka tradition. Images of Balarama's wife Revathi and Krishna are also found in this temple. The *Gargasamhita* gives a different story for the origin of the pond of Samkarsanakund, naming it alternatively as Vetra (Bet) Ganga (Bent Ganga). The *Gargasamhita* states that Krishna and the *Gopis* got thirsty one day while dancing in the forest; Krishna stuck the ground with a stick, which brought the water up and created a pond, hence known as Bet Ganga. No temples of Krishna, however, are noted in this area, and the *Gargasamhita* story appears to be a modified version of the Balarama story from the *Bhagavatapurana*. In the *Bhagavatapurana*, it is said that Balarama changed the course of the Yamuna by pulling her with his plow, as he was angered that she did not oblige his request to come near him when he wanted to take a bath after his dance with the *Gopis* upon his return to Vraja from Mathura.

Shantanukund (Satoha) is mentioned in connection with Talavan, being located at about a *yojana* (about eight miles) away from it. The temple is located on a ridge in the middle of the lake, which is approached by a small causeway paved with red sandstone. The *Varahapurana* states that Shantanu performed worship of the Sun God (Surya) here, which resulted in his obtaining Bhishma as his son. Although it is not frequently recounted, in this context it is important to remember the mythological connection of Balarama to the seventh month of pregnancy. According to the legend of the birth of Balarama recounted in the *Harivamsa*, the embryo of Balarama was transferred to Rohini during the seventh month of Devaki's pregnancy. As a result of this miraculous transfer, Rohini became pregnant with Balarama, while Devaki is purported to have had a miscarriage. Hence this place is frequently visited by those desiring sons, who perform the *santan saptami* vow, observed on the seventh day of the bright half of the moon during the month of *Badon* (*Bhadrapada, Suklapaksha Saptami*), which normally occurs between the months of August and September, the rainy season in India. However, it is common for women desirous of obtaining offspring to visit the temple during the seventh day of any lunar month. The ritual of *santan saptami* normally includes bathing in the lake and *darsan* of Krishna in the Santanubihari temple, which is followed by women drawing *swastikas* on the back wall of the temple with cow dung or vermilion.

Madhuvana

Madhuvana, popularly known as Madhuvan, which can be translated as forest of honey, is listed as the first of the twelve forests in the *Mahatmya* texts in reference to the sacred centers of Braj. This forest is identified with the place where the demon Madhu resided, which also explains the name Madhuvana. The forest at Maholi is said to be the remainder of the ancient forest of Madhuvan. Near the forest is located a mound known as Dhruv Tila, and a temple of Vishnu belonging to the

Ramanandi ascetics is located in the Madhuvana. On the edge of the forest is a cave of Lavanasura with steps leading to a low-lying site. Madhuvan is listed in the itineraries of the Braj *parikrama* and is the second place visited right after the *parikrama* begins in Mathura.

Kamavana (Forest of Love or Desire)

Kamavana is the fifth forest mentioned in the pilgrimage texts of Mathura. It is identified with the town of Kaman in the modern Mathura, also referred to as Kamyavana, Kamban, and so on. Kaman is a low-lying town with several ponds, including Vimalkund, Dharamkund, and Shrikund. The town is surrounded by seven gateways, which are still intact, although the walls have been destroyed. There are two Krishna temples of the Vallabha tradition in Kaman for the deities named Gokulcandrama and Madanmohan.

Bhadravana (Auspicious)

Bhadravana is mentioned as the sixth forest in the pilgrimage texts of Mathura. Bhadravan might have been named due to the number of auspicious trees found here, or alternatively it might have been named after the wife of Krishna called Bhadra, or his sister called Subhadra. As noted earlier, Krishna's sister Subhadra, who was also identified with Ekanamsa, was also an important deity in ancient India. An important event from the legend of Krishna is associated with this forest. It is identified as the place where Krishna swallowed the forest fires identified as Munjban or Munjatavi (forest of reed/rushes). The *Bhagavatapurana* (*Bhagavatapurana* 10.19) narrates that one day while the *Gopa* boys were at play, their cows wandered off into the forest, only to be found by them later being led by Krishna. When they found the cows, the cows were terrified and trapped in the forest fire, which was burning the reeds quickly and was about to consume the cows. Krishna commanded the *Gopa* boys to close their eyes and consumed the forest fire through his mouth. When the *Gopa* boys opened their eyes, they were surprised to find that the fire was gone and everything looked calm as usual. Seeing that, the *Gopa* boys thought that Krishna might not be a common human being, but an immortal. Therefore, the Bhadravana is visited by devotees on their Braj *parikrama* as a sacred forest associated with the life of Krishna.

Lohavana (Lohajanghavana)

Lohban or Lohavana (also known as Lohajanghavana) is the ninth of the twelve forests of Mathura mentioned in the classical pilgrimage texts of Mathura. Lohban is said to be named after Lohajangha, a demon popularly said to have been killed by Krishna, although the *puranas* do not mention this incident. The *Mahatmya* texts mention an alternative account in which Lohajangha is the guardian of the forest, giving it his name. Other stories mention Lohajangha as a sage who performed austerities in the forest. There is a Krishnakund on the southeastern side of the village containing *ghats* (stairs on the river bank). Near it is Krishnakup, also known by another name, Gopikund. Near this is an open hall (*tivari*) where offerings are made in iron bowls. There is a cave dedicated to the seven sages (Saptarishi Kandara) and a temple of Gopinath belonging to the Vallabha tradition.

Brindavan

Brindavan is the most important location connected with the Krishna *lilas* (plays). Brindavan (also known as Vrindavan) is the twelfth forest mentioned in the *Mahatmya* texts of Mathura. The forest is named after the goddess Vrinda (Brinda), who is said to have performed her austerities in this forest. There are several *ghats* and important temples in Brindavan. Circumambulation of Brindavan is performed independently of the Braj *parikrama*, although the Braj *parikrama* also includes Brindavan in its itinerary. Brindavan contains significant temples of Krishna. Throughout the town much use is made of the several *ghats* and temples celebrating festivals and the legendary presence of Krishna. Brindavan is the most important sacred place for the Krishna pilgrimage. Brindavan is equated with *Goloka* (the eternal residence of Krishna), and the mandala images depict Brindavan with its sacred groves and ponds (appropriately marked with temples and *tirthas*).

See also: Birth and Early Childhood of Krishna; Braj *Parikrama*; Brindavan; Childhood of Krishna in Brindavan; *Goloka*; Mandala; Mathura; Nandgaon

Further Reading

Entwistle, A. 1987. *Braj: Center of Krishna Pilgrimage*. Groningen: Egbert Forsten.

Growse, F. S. Reprint 1979. *Mathura: A District Memoire*. New Delhi: Asian Educational Service.

Haberman, D. 1994. *Journey Through the Twelve Forests*. New York: Oxford University Press.

U

UDDHAVA

Uddhava is the best friend of Krishna and appears as a messenger of Krishna on more than one occasion in the *Bhagavatapurana*. Uddhava therefore remains as an eternal messenger in the minds of devotees through the legends of the *Mathuramahatmya* that locate him as an unknown small green plant, identified as the vine in Sakhisthala near Govardhan.

Uddhava Brought Krishna's Message to the *Gopis*

The *Bhagavatapurana* describes Uddhava as a minister, a distinguished member of the Vrishni clan, a beloved friend of Krishna, a disciple of Brihaspathi, and extremely clever (*Bhagavatapurana* 10.46.1). When he returned to Vraja with messages from Krishna, the *Gopis* (cowherd maidens) mistook him for Krishna because he was dressed like Krishna in yellow robes. The *Gopis* treated him with the deference due to Krishna. They attentively listened to the message Uddhava delivered on Krishna's behalf. It was appropriate for Uddhava to deliver Krishna's message while dressed as Krishna because of the impact it would have on the *Gopis*. The message makes it clear to the *Gopis*, who were anticipating Krishna's return, that he would never return to Braj. This distressed the *Gopis* greatly, and one of the *Gopis* (devotional traditions, such as the Caitanya Vaishnava tradition of Mathura, identify her as Radha), due to her extreme distress, drifted unknowingly into meditating on her association with Krishna. In her meditative mode she saw a bee, but mistaking it for Krishna, she asked it numerous questions intended for Krishna. Uddhava heard these questions and responded appropriately from Krishna's messages. The *Gopis* were consoled by his explanations, and they realized that Krishna was their soul mate even though he was not present among them. The *Gopis* paid reverence to Uddhava, thanking him for the message. Uddhava stayed in Vraja,

---

Uddhava Temple

The temple of Uddhava is located near Kusum Sarovar in Brindavan. Uddhava is credited with bringing messages from Krishna for the *Gopis* and also for receiving Krishna's last message when Krishna was on his deathbed. Uddhava is said to be living somewhere in *Brajbhumi* as a creeper (*lata*). Hence the temple is symbolic of his presence in Vraja as an eternal messenger of Krishna.

singing the stories of Krishna and visiting the places associated with Krishna, which helped alleviate the pain of separation for the people of Vraja, and especially the *Gopis*.

Uddhava Received the Last Message of Krishna

During the annihilation of the Yadavas in a drunken brawl, Uddhava went into the forest searching for Krishna. When Uddhava met Krishna privately and learned that Krishna had informed his kinsmen of the impending danger of the drowning of Dvaraka, and that he had instructed them to proceed to Prabhasa with their families, Uddhava was alarmed that this might be the end of time. Uddhava understood that Krishna had not taken any measures to counteract the curse of the Brahmans, and that Krishna was withdrawing from this world, leaving his family, friends, and others. Uddhava told Krishna that he could not bear the thought of not being able to see (*darsan*) his Lord. Uddhava subsequently beseeched Krishna to be allowed to go with him as he could not bear to live apart from Krishna. Thus addressed, Krishna spoke his divine message to Uddhava to console him and also to help him realize the true knowledge, generally known among the followers of Krishna as the *Uddhavagita*. This is also sometimes referred to as the second *Bhagavadgita*, for it also contains the message of the Lord (*Bhagavan*). The topics covered in this message relate to metaphysics as well as social duties. It contains a discussion on types of yoga, liberation, the nature of samsara (the cycle of life), reflections on devotion, and a number of other subjects. The *Uddavagita* is extensive and is narrated in thirteen chapters in the eleventh book of the *Bhagavatapurana*.

Uddhava Helped Vajranabha Revive the Mathura Mandala

When Vajranabha returned to Mathura in order to identify places associated with Krishna, his main source for Krishna's life was Uddhava. Uddhava appeared as a small vine in Sakhisthala, near Govardhan, a lowly life when compared to his former life as a friend of Krishna. However, Uddhava explained to Vajranabha that to be born in Mathura and to live in Mathura was the best life one could have on Earth; therefore, he decided to live in Mathura in an inconspicuous form so he could continue his meditation and serve the devotees of Krishna. Sakhisthala, where Uddhava appeared, has its own special legend in connection with Krishna. It is known as a place where Krishna met Radha and her friends. It is also said to be the village of Radha's friend Chandravali, which is currently known as the village Sakarwa near Govardhan, and the tank near it is called Uddhavakund to commemorate the appearance of Uddhava at this place. It is normally included in the circumambulation of Govardhan. Once a messenger of Krishna to the *Gopis*, Uddhava therefore remains an eternal messenger of Krishna in Braj, even though in an inconspicuous form as a plant. It is said that Uddhava remains in the same place where he once conveyed the message of Krishna to the *Gopis*, but inconspicuously. However, devotees visit Uddhavakund with hopes of feeling his presence and getting enlightenment even though they cannot see him.

See also: Braj *Parikrama*; Brindavan; Dvaraka; *Gopas* and *Gopis*; Mandala; Mathura; Prabhasa; Radha; Vajranabha; Vrishnis

Further Reading

Rosen, S. 2007. *Krishna's Other Song: A New Look at the Uddhava Gita.* Santa Barbara, CA: Greenwood.

V

VAJRANABHA

Vajranabha (son of Aniruddha), the great-grandson of Krishna, is the lone survivor of Krishna's progeny. After the death of Krishna and the annihilation of the Yadavas, Arjuna brought the surviving Yadavas to Mathura and coronated Vajranabha as the king of the Yadava dynasty in Mathura. The Pandavas also enthroned their grandson Parikshit as the king of the Kuru dynasty in Hastinapur, and they left on their *mahaprathana* (great journey). Vajranabha was astonished by the deserted conditions of Mathura. Vajranabha met Parikshit and expressed his concern that the kingdom he inherited was in a desolate condition. Parikshit then invited the sage Sandilya for a consultation. Sandilya informed Vajranabha of the divine life and pastimes of Krishna in Vraja, and then took him to visit the places associated with Krishna. He identified the places connected with the life of Krishna and advised Vajranabha to construct temples in those places, and since they were the sacred places associated with Krishna, they should be given good care and not left without guardians. Sandilya advised Vajranabha to establish villages near the temples to denote the *lilas* of Krishna, so that Mathura could be returned to the previous idyllic state that it experienced during Krishna's life on Earth. Heeding the advice of Sandilya, Vajranabha visited Mathura and met Uddhava, a friend of Krishna, and Kalindi (a form of Yamuna), wife of Krishna. He constructed temples in Dirghapura (Dig), Mathura (Mahaban), Nandagrama (Nandgaon), and Brihatsanu (Barsana). Vajranabha also revived the towns of Gokul, Govardhan, Baladeva (Baldeo), and Brindavan, where he also constructed temples establishing settlements in the vicinity. The *Mathuramahatmya* text included in the *Skandapurana*, the *Gargasamhita*, the *Varahapurana*, and the *Padmapurana* attribute the most important role in the revival of Mathura as the sacred center of Krishna devotion to Vajranabha. Tradition describes Vajranabha as the first person to undertake the *parikrama* (circumambulation) of sacred places associated with Krishna, accompanied by the sage Sandilya. Vajranabha is the legendary founder of the sacred center of Braj.

See also: Aniruddha; Braj *Parikrama*; Brindavan; Eight Wives of Krishna; *Gargasamhita*; Krishna; *Lila*; Mandala; Mathura; Prabhasa; Pradyumna; *Skandapurana*; Vrishnis; Yamuna

Further Reading

Gupta, A., ed. *The Varahapurana*. Varanasi: All India Kashiraj Trust.
Vaudeville, C. 1976. "Braj Lost and Found." *Indo-Iranian Journal* 18: 195–213.

VALLABHA

Vallabha *acarya* (1479–1530) is the founder of the Vaishnava devotional tradition, Vallabha *sampradaya* (tradition), also known as *Pushtimarga* (way of nourishing grace). Vallabha received the *Brahmasambandha* mantra due to Krishna's grace, which he began imparting to his followers soon after. Numerous biographical narratives of Vallabha were written within the Vallabha tradition by a number of his followers. However, three early texts contain the biography of Vallabha in detail, and they served as a template for the later biographies on Vallabha: the *Caurasi Vaishnavon ka Varta* (Bulletin of the Eighty-four Vaishnavas) by Gokulnatha (1552–1641), a grandson of Vallabha; the *Nathaji Prakat ki Varta* (Bulletin of the Appearance of the Auspicious Lord) by Hariraya; and the *Caurasi Baithak Caritra* (History of the Eighty-four Seats) by Gokulnatha, which was later reworked. Another text, the *Srivallabhadigvijaya*, was written by Yadunatha (1615–1660), a grandson of Vallabha.

The *Bhaktamala* of Nabhadas mentions that Vallabha was a disciple of Vishnusvami, founder of *Rudra sampradaya*. Vishnusvami understands Krishna as *Balagopala* (child cowherd) as the most approachable and adorable manifestation of the supreme God. This theory finds central expression in the Vallabha tradition, which places the child-god Krishna as Srinathji at the center of its practice. The *Bhaktamala* also mentions Jnanadev and Namdev, *sants* of the *Varkari* tradition, as disciples of Vishnusvami.

Vallabha traveled widely across India while writing several treatises on religion, including the *Subodhini* (Commentary on the *Bhagavatapurana*); the *Anubhasya,* also known as the *Brahmasutranubhashya*, a commentary on the Vedanta text, the *Brahmasutras* (Subtle Exposition); the *Tattvarthadipanibandha* (Fundamental Principles of Reality); and the *Sodasagrantha* (Sixteen Books on Devotion). Vallabha noted that he described basic doctrines in the *Siddhantamuktavali* (Theoretical Compendium) and stated that anyone following those basic doctrines would be freed from all skepticism.

The basic principle of his *suddhadvaita* (pure monism) doctrine outlines that Krishna is both the cause and the substance of the universe. According to the *suddhadvaita* Krishna is expressed in three dimensions simultaneously: as the highest Brahma (supreme soul), *nirguna* (impersonal) Brahma, and also the universe in which all life forms exist (*srishti*). These three existences of the Lord are known as the *adhidaivika*, *adhyatmika,* and *adhibhautika* dimensions in the philosophy of Vallabha. The *adhidaivika* refers to the supreme soul (Brahma) represented by Krishna from which everything arises; the *adhyathmika* refers to the spiritual, the *atma* that pervades all creation; and the *adhibhautika* represents everything that is physical in this material world. The *adhibuatika* dimension of Krishna is the material world that Krishna himself creates as if in play (*lila*). Therefore, Krishna is both the substance and the cause of the world. Vallabha states that *seva* (service) is the principal way of receiving the grace of Krishna, since the devotee forgets the ego in the intense service of Krishna, being entirely focused on Krishna. Vallabha's *suddhadvaita* does not fully oppose the *advaita*, but regards the creation (*srishti*) and creator (*srishtikarta*) as true but different dimensions of the divine.

Vallabhacarya was born in a south Indian Telugu Brahman family. His biographies narrate that three divine incidents proclaim his divine birth and describe him as an incarnation of Krishna's mouth. Tradition narrates that Krishna himself appeared to Vallabha's father, Lakshmana Bhatta, and informed him that he would have a divine son. Soon after this incident his parents, Lakshmana Bhatta and Illammagaru, settled in Varanasi, which was under siege due to the political struggles and Muslim upheavals in north India at that time. They fled the city in the night, arriving in Camparanya (the modern Chattisgarh region), where Illammagaru gave birth to a boy prematurely, who seemed dead and was left under a *sami* tree. However, Krishna informed them in a dream that he had recently been born in their family, after which they went out and found the baby healthy and playing, surrounded by a protective ring of fire. Filled with happiness, they picked up the child and heard a voice informing them that their child was the mouth of Krishna. Within a few years after his birth the political turmoil passed in Varanasi, and his parents returned with Vallabha to Varanasi. A precocious child, Vallabha quickly acquired knowledge of the *Vedas*, the Upanishads, and other philosophical texts, and the religious treatises he produced later attest to his mastery of Hindu philosophy and theology.

It is mentioned that Vallabha accepted *diksha* (initiation) in the Vishnuswami tradition (*Rudra sampradaya*), but not much is known about his connection with the Vishnuswami tradition. When he was ten years of age he went along on a pilgrimage with his parents, and his father passed away in Tirupathi. He then went to Hampi, the capital of the Vijayanagara Empire, with his mother; leaving her with his uncle's family, he reembarked on the pilgrimage because he received a vision from Krishna urging him to go immediately to Govardhan Hill. He reached the town of Gokul on the eleventh day of *Sravana* (July–August), where he received another vision from Krishna giving him the *brahmasambandhamantra*, which is the central mantra of the Vallabha tradition. Vallabha discusses this in his treatise *Sodasagrantha* and explains in detail devotional aspects such as *seva* and bhakti for Krishna.

Vallabha subsequently initiated his companion, Damodaradasa Harsani, thereby founding the Vallabha tradition based on the vision he received from Krishna. Srinathji was already revealed to Saddu Pande in Govardhan, whose cow was dropping milk on the Govardhan Hill, where Srinathji's image had gradually emerged. Upon his arrival at Govardhan, Vallabha met Saddu Pande, who showed him the image of Srinathji. Vallabha immediately had a shrine constructed there and initiated a local ascetic, Ramadas Cauhan, who lived in a cave near Apsarakund, with the *Brahmasambandhamantra*, and entrusted him with performing daily *seva* to Srinathji. Vallabha also instructed locals on the proper worship of Srinathji. A number of local people were initiated by Vallabha. Kumbhandas Gorva, who sang devotional compositions in the Srinathji temple, was also initiated here. Srinathji was later shifted to the larger temple when the construction was completed. A wealthy merchant of Ambala, Puranmal (Purnamall) Khatri, was said to have been commanded in a dream by Srinathji to construct the temple. He met Vallabha and offered to financially support the construction of the temple. However, it took a long time to complete the construction. Although the foundations were laid for the Srinathji temple in 1499, the completion and shifting of Srinathji's icon didn't take place until almost twenty years later. A number of changes occurred in the devotional and ritual services of Srinathji during this period. For some time Srinathji was hidden in the nearby village of Gantholi for fear of the Delhi sultanate, which had already issued *firmans* (royal decrees) banning several rituals in Mathura. It was in Gantholi that Madhavendra Puri worshipped Srinathji, and Caitanya visited Gantholi to have a *darsan* of the deity. This tradition of shared worship of Srinathji continued between the *Gaudiyas* and followers of Vallabha until Vitthalnath assumed the leadership of the Vallabha tradition around 1530 when Vitthalnath and the manager of the temple, Krishnadas, expelled the *Gaudiyas* from the Srinathji temple.

Although Vallabha did not make Brindavan his permanent residence, he is said to have visited regularly, staying for at least three to four months each year. Vallabha is said to have performed two Braj *parikramas* (circumambulation of Braj). *Baithak* shrines on the path of the Braj *parikrama* mark places of Vallabha's rest where he meditated and explained the meaning of the *lilas* (plays) of Krishna narrated in the *Bhagavatapurana*, while conducting his *parikrama*.

Unlike other founders of the bhakti traditions in Brindavan, Vallabha was a householder with two sons. Vallabha gave up his life by wading into the river Ganges in Varanasi a month after taking *sanyasa* in 1530. He appointed his eldest son Gopinath as his successor and took care of other succession issues of the tradition before his death. Vallabha laid down the rule of male succession: since he was the *adhibhautika* dimension of Krishna, his sons, who shared his *adhibhautika* flesh, also shared the *adhibhautika* dimension of his mouth. Hence every male heir of Vallabha was capable of administering the *Brahmasambandhamantra*. Although the line of his first son, Gopinath, died out, his second son, Vitthalnath (Gosainji), had seven sons, and *havelis* and the Vallabha tradition spread through India, reaching the West through their descendants.

See also: Advaita; Bhakti; Braj *Parikrama*; Brindavan; *Darsana*; *Gaudiya* Vaishnavism; Jnanadev; *Lila*; Mantra; Mathura; Namdev; *Puja*; *Sants*; *Seva*; Vallabha Tradition; *Varkari* Tradition; *Visishtadvaita*; Yashoda

Further Reading

Barz, R. 1992. *The Bhakti Sect of Vallabhacarya*. New Delhi: Munshiram Manoharlal.

Smith, F. M. 2009. "Dark Matter in the *Vartaland*: On the Enterprise History in Early Pushtimarga Discourse." *Journal of Hindu Studies* 2: 27–47.

Smith, F. M. 2011. "Predestination and Hierarchy: Vallabhacarya's Discourse on the Distinctions Between Blessed, Rule-Bound, Worldly, and Wayward Souls (the *pustipravahamaryadabheda*)." *Journal of Indian Philosophy* 39 (2): 173–227.

Timm, J. R. 1988. "Prolegomenon to Vallabha Theology of Revelation." *Philosophy East & West* 38 (2): 107–126.

Timm, J. R. 2007. "Biography, Hagiography, Sacred Story: Vallabha, Vitthalanatha and the Vallabha Sampradaya." *Journal of Vaishnava Studies* 15 (2): 3–17.

Yadav, B. S. 1994. "Vallabha Positive Response to Buddhism." *Journal of Dharma* 19 (2): 113–137.

VALLABHA TRADITION

The Vallabha tradition is also known as *Pushtimarga* (way of grace), a devotional tradition centered on Krishna as its major deity. The basic tenets of the Vallabha tradition follow the Vedanta tradition based on the *suddhadvaita* philosophy. Accordingly Krishna is the supreme god; *jivas* (individuals/souls) depend on him for grace (*pushti*), which is based on the relationship of love between the god and the *jiva*. Another unique feature of this tradition is that its leadership is passed down only through the male descendants of the founder, Vallabha.

According to Vallabha's *Suddhadvaita*, Krishna is not different from the universe and the *jivas*. Although they are the same, ego-dominated *jivas* cannot realize the truth of their existence and need the support of the grace of Krishna. Krishna himself revealed the *brahmasambhandha* mantra while Vallabha's friend and companion, Damodaradas Harsani, was also present. Damodaradas Harsani, while able to visualize the presence of Krishna, could not deduce anything Krishna said to Vallabha. Damodaradas was the first to be initiated by Vallabha, who gave him the mantra and thereby founded the Vallabha tradition. The form of worship in Vallabha *sampradaya* is based on *seva* (service), one of the nine practices of bhakti. Adornment of Srinathji (Krishna), called *sringar*, is as important as offering *seva* to the icon. Srinathji is considered a young boy of eight to ten years of age. Hence, the services and schedule are organized around this concept. The *svarupa* of Srinathji is Krishna himself, and he is taken care of as he was when he lived in Nandagopa's palace as a child. The eight services offered to Krishna every day are at set times, and *darsan* (vision of the deity) is also permitted on a daily schedule. Arts are an important aspect of Vallabha *sampradaya*. Singing *kirtans*, making paintings (*pichvai*) and floor and wall drawings, and writing poems or texts on Krishna form a major part of the aesthetic presence. The simultaneous experience of *bhava* by a large group of devotees is encouraged in the Vallabha tradition.

Vallabha *sampradaya* was passed on by Vallabha to his sons before his death. The tradition multiplied gradually within India and spread to several countries

Vraj Temple, Pennsylvania

Vraj is an old resort that was purchased in 1987 and was gradually developed into the headquarters of the Vallabha tradition in the United States. It soon evolved to represent authentic Vallabha tradition practice and rituals. The central building has been transformed into a *haveli* housing the central icons, and the rest of the campus was also developed accordingly to replicate the landscape of Braj. For example, the buildings are given traditional *Pushtimarga* names; there are constructions such as a pond named Candrasarovar and there is a mountain of rocks called Govardhan to enhance a devotee's experience of visiting sacred sites associated with the life of Krishna. Although Vraj is in America, because of the replication of structures and the adoption of the names commonly used in Braj mandala in India, while following authentic ritual practices, it could be said that the Vraj temple is partially successful in recreating the sacred geography.

beyond India. The individual leaders (known as *maharaja*) have their separate *havelis* (temples), which function as independent units.

During the early eighteenth century the main images of the god Krishna belonging to the temples of the Vallabha tradition were moved to Gujarath and Rajasthan for fear of destruction by Aurangzeb and his generals. The Krishna *janmasthan* temple under the maintainance of the Vallabha tradition was destroyed in the attacks, along with several other temples in Brindavan. However, Purushottam, one of the successors of the second *gaddi* (second son of Vittalnath), returned to Braj in the late eighteenth century and began the revival of the Vallabha tradition in Braj, undertaking the reconstruction of the destroyed temples. Purushottam is known for organizing large groups of devotees to undertake the Braj *parikrama* (circumambulation), which looks like a mass procession. Brajnath, a great-grandson of Vallabha, wrote the first authoritative and descriptive itinerary of the Braj *parikrama*. The Vallabha tradition has a number of temples in Mathura, the Madanmohan Dauji, and another known as Chote Madanmohan, and also acquired the Govardhannath temple on Svami Ghat. However, the most important temple of the Vallabha tradition in Mathura is the Dwarakadhish temple in the center of Mathura.

Vallabha *sampradaya* was established in order to impart teachings on the correct relationship of Krishna and human beings. Through its six hundred years of existence, the *sampradaya* has carried out its mission successfully, despite several setbacks it faced over the years.

See also: Arati; *Ashtachap*; Bhakti; Brindavan; *Haveli Sangit*; *Janmasthan* Temple; *Kirtana*; Kumbhandas Gorva; *Lila*; *Seva*; Surdas; Vallabha; Vitthalnath

Further Reading

Barz, R. 1976. *The Bhakti Sect of Vallabhacarya*. Faridabad: Thomson Press.
Graheli, A. 2010. "The Happening of Tradition: Vallabha on *Anumana* in *Nyayalilavati*." *Indo-Iranian Journal* 53 (1): 50–56.

VARKARI TRADITION

Although the *Varkari* tradition is not organized as a unified *sampradaya* (tradition) as are the other bhakti *sampradayas* (devotional traditions) it is still known as a tradition due to several unifying observances noted in its practice by the followers. Its unifying features are veneration of Vitthala (Krishna) at Pandarpur, a rich poetical (*padas*) *kirtan* tradition, a number of *sants* (poet-saints), and two annual pilgrimages (*vari*) to Pandarpur. The most important feature of the *Varkari* tradition is *vari*, the walking pilgrimage.

These unique features more than compensate for the absence of a central leadership overseeing the rules, regulations, and practices of the tradition. The importance of the tradition lies in the identification of Pandarpur with Krishna.

The *Varkari sampradaya* consists of devotees in groups of varying sizes (*phads* or *sampradays*) under a male leader known as the *maharaj*. Initiation as a follower of the *Varkari* tradition is simple, but years of training are required to become a *maharaj* of a *Varkari* group. The training takes place under one's guru, or in the Varkari Sikshan Sanstha (Varkari Training Institute) in Alandi.

Vitthal is a Marathi derivative of Vishnu, the Sanskrit name of the supreme God in Vaishnavism. Vitthal is referred to as *Vitthoba* (father Vitthal) or *Vittai* (mother Vitthal) to signify the central notion that Vitthal takes care of his devotees as parents would normally take care of their children, without even asking for help. The story of Krishna's (Vitthal's) visit is interesting as an event leading to the establishment of the temple in Pandarpur. It is said that Krishna came to Pandarpur looking for his wife Rukmini, who left him since she was upset about his dalliances with Radha in Brindavan. Krishna was tired from searching for his wife and wished to rest as he reached Pandarpur. He stopped at a house to seek water and some leads for his search. He called in from the door. Pundalik, whose house it was, was serving his parents, but he heard Krishna and told him to wait while he served his parents. Pundalik threw a brick outside for Krishna to stand on above the mud. As it happened, Pundalik never stopped serving his parents and Krishna is still waiting there. A temple was built for him at that spot. Hence the temple and the icon of Vitthala in the temple are considered very sacred and represent Krishna himself.

Numerous *sants* of the *Varkari* tradition are widely known and memorialized through celebration of pilgrimages to the places of their residence, and also through the recollection of the stories of their life. The most important *sants* of this tradition are Jnanadev, Namdev, Ekanath, Janabai, Chokhamela, and Tukaram, whose biographies were preserved in the numerious hagiographic texts written in Marathi. Several texts of the *padas* (poems) composed by the *sants* are also popular, and the *padas* are commonly sung by the devotees. *Kirtan* (singing) is one of the typical features associated with the *Varkari* tradition. The *Kirtankars* (*kirtan* performers and musicians) sing in the temples of Vitthala, and also some take up an itinerant life and sing as they travel.

Varkari pilgrimages are organized to the Vitthala temple in Pandarpur twice a year and to the temples of important *sants* on festival days. Two annual pilgrimages take place in *Ashad* (June to July) and in *Kartik* (October to November) of the Hindu calendar. Since *vari* is a walking pilgrimage, devotees set out days ahead to reach the Vitthala temple during the auspicious times; some groups may set out as early as forty days in advance. Most groups travel regular routes organized by their local *maharaj*. Most of the pilgrimage groups join *palkis* (palanquins) carrying the sandals of a *sant*, which travel from the *sant's* temple to the Pandarpur temple. As the *palkis* pass through the villages and towns, people may come out to worship by touching and offering gifts, receiving *darshan* and *prasad* from the groups. The largest of these *palki* groups are Jnanadev and Tukaram, which attract thousands of pilgrims. The Jnanadev and Tukaram *palkis* have water tankers, medical vans, and food vans in their entourage.

The *kirtan* is another distinct feature of the *Varkari* tradition. It consists of singing the *padas* with physical gestures and interpretation. There is a set style and music for each *kirtan*. The *Kirtankars* could be a *maharaj*, or an independent performer. The main performer is accompanied by groups of performers to give chorus support, and some provide musical accompaniment by playing instruments such as the cymbals or *pakhavaj* (*mridangam*). The *Varkari* tradition is one of the most popular Krishna bhakti traditions in India.

See also: Arati; *Darsana*; Eknath; Jnanadev; *Kirtana*; Namdev; Pandarpur Temple; Panduranga Vitthala; *Prasada*; *Sants*

Further Reading

Chitre, D. 1996. *Sri Jnanadev's Anubhavamrit: The Immortal Experience of Being.* New Delhi: Manohar.

Karve, I. 1988. "On the Road." In *The Experience of Hinduism: Essay on Religion in Maharashtra,* edited by E. Selliot and M. Berntsen, 143–173. Albany: SUNY Press.

Prill, S. 2009. "Representing Sainthood in India: Sikh and Hindu Images of Namdev." *Material Religion* 5 (2): 156–179.

Vaudeville, C. 1996. "Pandarpur, City of Saints." In *Myths, Saints, Legends in Medieval India,* edited by V. Dalmia, 199–221. Delhi: Oxford University Press.

Vaudeville, C. 2003. "The *Varkaris*—Following the March of Tradition in Western India." *Critical Asian Studies* 35 (2): 287–300.

VASUDEVA

Vasudeva is the biological father of Krishna. Although popularly referred to by the name Vasudeva, he also has another name, Anakadundhubhi. However, in the *puranas* he is only rarely referred to as Anakadundhubhi and is commonly noted as Vasudeva, a name attributed to him from his famous son Vaasudeva Krishna. Scholars have noted that Anakadundhubhi might have been replaced by his popular name acquired from Krishna (rather than it being a patronymic of Krishna). Krishna was popularly worshipped as Vaasudeva (the second *vyuha* identified as Krishna), whose followers were called Vaasudevakas as early as 600 BCE, as noted in Panini's *Ashtadhyayi.* Vaasudeva as the name for the second *vyuha* has unique theological significance in early Vaishnavism. Vasudeva supported his wife and completed his role as a responsible husband and father under the most difficult circumstances. According to the *Harivamsa,* soon after Vasudeva's marriage to Devaki, he was getting ready to leave Mathura with his bride. Her brother, Kamsa, volunteered to drive their chariot to take them home. While they were on the road a voice from the sky proclaimed that the eighth son of Devaki would bring death to Kamsa. On hearing this Kamsa became enraged, pulled Devaki out of the chariot, and drew his sword to kill her. Vasudeva quickly came to her rescue. He promised Kamsa that he would hand over every child born to Devaki to Kamsa. Thus they arrived at a compromise, and Kamsa imprisoned them in his palace. Vasudeva took care of Devaki in the prison and continued to hand over their babies to Kamsa. Six of their newborn babies were thus handed over to Kamsa and killed. The goddess Nidra transferred the seventh child as an embryo to Rohini in Vraja during Devaki's seventh month of pregnancy. Krishna was born as Devaki's eighth child, showed his *visvarupa* (four-armed form of Vishnu) to his parents, and convinced Vasudeva to transfer him to Vraja for protection.

Sidh Sen (reigned 1684–1727) as Vasudeva carrying Krishna over the Yamuna river, Mandi, India, mid-18th-century watercolor. (Los Angeles County Museum)

The locks of the prison opened automatically, while the doorkeepers and the town of Mathura slept deeply under Yogamaya's watch. However, as Vasudeva came out, rain poured down heavily, but Vasudeva pressed forward to Vraja. The Yamuna was in flood due to the heavy rains, but gave him passage, while the divine serpent Sesha followed him and protected the child with its thousand hoods, spread as a cover. Vasudeva reached Nanda's home and exchanged Krishna for Nanda's girl child. He returned to Mathura, went back in his prison cell, and laid the child back on Devaki's bed. Vasudeva and Devaki then stayed in the prison until Krishna released them from the prison twelve years later, after he killed Kamsa. Vasudeva also has six other wives in addition to Devaki (mother of Krishna) and Rohini (mother of Balarama and Subhadra). Vasudeva's story aquired numerous accretions and became an extensive independent narrative in Jain tradition. The entire narrative of the *Vasudevahindi* (Travels of Vasudeva) describes the travels of Vasudeva to various regions and his marriages to numerous women he met during his travels.

See also: Avatara; Balarama; Brindavan; Devaki; Kamsa; Mathura; Nandagopa; Nidra; Rohini; Subhadra: Krishna's Sister; Vishnu; *Visvarupa*; *Vyuhas*; Yogamaya

Further Reading

Bryant, E. 2003. *Krishna: The Beautiful Legend of God*. London: Penguin Books.

VEDANTADESIKA

Vedantadesika (1268–1369) is also known as Venkatanatha or Venkatesa. Vedantadesika was a well-known philosopher of the *visishtadvaita* (qualified monism) philosophy founded by Ramanuja. Vedantadesika wrote prolifically in expounding the tenets of *visishtadvaita*. He is known as the *Kavitarkikasimha* (lion of poetry and logic) and *sarvatantrasvatantra* (master of all arts and sciences) for his prolific and scholastic commentaries and philosophic works. Vedantadesika's work, the *Yadavabhyudayam*, is one of the esteemed texts of India, receiving commentaries during his lifetime not only from his followers, but also from the followers of rival sects. Vedantadesika wrote in a variety of genres in the Sanskrit language such as *kavya* (poetical texts), *natya* (dance drama), *stotra,* and *prabhanda* (religious hymns). His legacy endures in the Vaishnava traditions of India.

The early life of Vedantadesika is shrouded in mystery. It is narrated in his biographies only that he was born at Tirupathi, and that his mother and the priest of the temple were informed in separate visions that the temple bell would be born as the boy. A precocious child, Vedantadesika acquired spiritual wisdom quickly and surpassed his rivals in philosophical and theological debates. Hence Vedantadesika is known as a victorious scholar and wonderworker. He is said to have traveled widely, making pilgrimages to the most important sacred sites of Hinduism such as Varanasi, Mathura, Vraja, Ayodhya, and Haridvar. Political and religious life in south India was in great turmoil during his lifetime. Due to Muslim invasions (1312 and 1323), the main idols of the Srirangam temple had to be shifted to Tirupathi by his friend and rival Pillai Lokacarya. Vedantadesika stayed back to protect the Srirangam temple, but unable to do this, he left for Melkote to live in exile. Eventually, he returned with the Brahman general Gopanarya to retake the city and revive the temple. However, this move left a permanent rift in the Srivaishnava tradition; it split into two branches, *Vatakalai* (northern) and *Tengalai* (southern), tracing their origin to Vedantadesika and Pillai Lokacarya.

Vedantadesika has left an indelible mark on the Vaishnava bhakti traditions. The Srivaishnava tradition and its practices follow the basic philosophical and theological conventions laid down by Vedantadesika.

Yadavabhyudayam

The *Yadavabhyudayam* is a text of compositions describing the life of Krishna. Written by Vedantadesika, the compositions of the *Yadavabhyudayam* found expression in musical and theatrical compositions across India. The legend of Krishna is described in detail beginning with his birth in Mathura, including his infancy in Braj, his childhood in Brindavan, his return to Mathura to kill Kamsa, and the subsequent founding of Dvaraka. Numerous sections of the *Yadvabhyudayam* are individually utilized for musical compositions and theatrical performances across south India due to the lyrical nature of the composition.

See also: Advaita; Ramanuja; Ranganatha; Srirangam Temple; Srivaishnavism; Tirumalisalvar and Tiruppanalvar; Tirupathi; Venkatesvara; *Visishtadvaita*

Further Reading

Granoff, P. 1985. "Scholars and Wonderworkers: Some Remarks on the Role of the Supernatural in Philosophical Contests in Vedanta Hagiographies." *Journal of the American Oriental Society* 105 (3): 459–467.

Hopkins, S. P. 2002. *Singing the Body of God: The Hymns of Vedantadesika in their South Indian Tradition.* Oxford: Oxford University Press.

Varadacari, V. 1983. *Two Great Acaryas: Vedantadesika and Manavala Mamuni.* Madras: M. Rangacarya Memorial Trust.

Venkatacari, K. K. A. 1978. *The Manipravala Literature of the Srivaishnava Acaryas, 12–15 Century A.D.* Bombay: Anantacarya Research Institute.

VEDIC KRISHNA

Due to the cryptic nature of Vedic texts, any references to popular deities of Hinduism are limited. Vedic texts refer only to cosmological manifestations of deities associated with *Kritayuga*, and they mention popular deities of the *Treta* and *Dvapara yugas* only cryptically. Popular deities of Hinduism and their associated divinities are noted in detail only in the Vedanta and *purana* literature.

The *Rigveda* verses 1.116–117 mention Krishna as a word, which is accepted variously and interpreted by some scholars as an indirect reference to Krishna. Other scholars do not think that it indicates Krishna.

In the *Rigveda* verses 1.22.16–21 the evidence is more explicit. Here, Vishnu is referred to as *Gopa*. Some may argue that while *Gopa* may simply mean "protector," it could also be a direct reference to Krishna, since there are other more likely words that could be used to indicate "protector," and that by choosing to use the word *Gopa*, the author of the text made a deliberate choice to indicate the connection between Vishnu and Krishna. *Gopa* stands for cowherd, a well-known epithet associated with Krishna due to his early life as a cowherd in Vraja. Thus, this Vedic reference indeed indicates Krishna, the cowherd god and the eighth incarnation of Vishnu.

In the *Chandogya* Upanishad (3.17) part of *Samaveda* (1500–1000 BCE), Krishna is mentioned as the son of Devaki (*Devakiputra*), which beyond doubt identifies Krishna as a Vedic god. Thus early Vedic texts dated between 2300 BCE and 1800 BCE provide the earliest, but cryptic textual evidence on Krishna followed by numerous textual and archaeological sources. Later Vedic texts (1800–1000 BCE) provide clear evidence of Krishna.

Although there are concerns about connecting the Vedic evidence to Krishna, it is also true that the *Vedas* only include cryptic information on later Vedic deities, of which Krishna is one. Krishna's full theology and devotional traditions are continuously referred to from an early period, which itself is notable in understanding the importance of Krishna in Indian religions.

See also: Bhagavatas; Biography of Krishna; Devaki; *Gopas* and *Gopis*; Historical Krishna; Krishna; *Pancaratra*; Vishnu

Further Reading

De, S. K. 1942. "The *Vedic* and Epic Krishna." *Indian Historical Quarterly* 18: 297–301.

Griffith, R. T. H. 1863. *The Hymns of the Rigveda*. 2 vols. Varanasi: Chowkamba Sanskrit Office.

Ray, H. C. 1924. "Allusions to Vasudeva Krishna Devakiputra in the *Vedic* Literature." *Journal of the Royal Asiatic Society of Bengal* (New Series) 19: 371–373.

VENKATESVARA

The *Sthalapurana* of Tirupathi connects Venkatesvara (Lord of Venkatahills) to Vishnu, popularly referred to as Govinda. Venkatesvara is one of the regional forms of Krishna, although he is identified with Vishnu in textual sources and popular literature. Venkatesvara is referred to by one or more of his local names including Tirumalesa (Lord of Tirumala), Venkatesa (Lord of Venkata), Edukondalu (Sevenhills), Srinivasa (Lord of Laxmi), and so on. As Vishnu, Venkatesa is worshipped with *stotras* and *bhajans* of Vishnu, while at the same time he is also epitomized in the *padas* (poems) of Annamayya, Tyagaraja, and others as Krishna. The first *arati* (*mangala arati*) of the day is performed by singing *Suprabhatam,* written by Prativadi Bhayamkaracarya (Bhayankara Annan) at 4 a.m. every day.

According to the *Sthalapurana* of Tirupathi, Srilaxmi left Vishnu when the sage Brigu kicked him. Vishnu paid obeisance instead of kicking the sage Brigu back. Vishnu then came to Earth searching for his wife Srilaxmi; instead he found Vedavathi, whom he had promised to marry earlier in his previous *avatara* as Rama. Unable to find his wife Srilaxmi, Vishnu began living with his adopted mother Vakula. Meanwhile Vedavathi was born as Padmavati, who was found as a child by Akasaraja and his wife while plowing the fields. She grew up to be a beautiful princess. One day she was visiting a garden near the Venkata hills where Venkatesa saw her and fell in love with her immediately. Venkatesa then went home afflicted with love and sat depressed without eating his food. Questioned by his mother Vakula, Venkatesa revealed his heart to her. Vakula then approached Akasaraja with the proposal of marriage to which the king gave his consent. However, to conduct the marriage Venkatesa had to borrow money from Kubera, since he did not have Srilaxmi (goddess of wealth) with him, hence he possessed no wealth. It is said that the money collected by Venkatesa every day is for interest payments to Kubera, and hence the Lord is also known as Vaddeekasulavadu (lord of interest money).

Bathing at the Papavinasanam, a spring near Tirupathi, is considered auspicious and purifying of one's sins. Another important ritual undertaken here by the devotees is head shaving (*shiromundana*) at the *kalyanakatta*, and leaving the hair as a donation to the Lord. Children's first haircuts are performed in Tirupathi. The temple is visited by sixty to seventy thousand pilgrims each day, a majority of whom return home with shaven heads.

See also: Avatara; Krishna; Srilaxmi; Srivaishnavism; Tirupathi; Vedantadesika; Vishnu

Further Reading

Krishna, N. 2007. *Balaji-Venkatesvara: Lord of Tirumala-Tirupati: An Introduction*. Bombay: Vakils, Feffer, and Simons.

Ramesan, N. 1981. *The Tirumal Temple, Tirupati*. Tirupati: S. V. University.

Rao, S. K. R. 1993. *The Hill-Shrine of Vengadam: Art, Architecture, and Agama of Tirumal Temple*. Bangalore: UBS Publishers.

Sitapati, P. 1977. *Sri Venkatesvara, the Lord of the Seven Hills*. Tirupati. Bombay.

Viraraghavacarya, T. K. T. 1979. *History of Tirupati (The Tiruvengadam Temple)*. 2 vols. Tirupathi: S. V. University.

VISHNU

Vishnu is one of the major gods of Hinduism. However, Krishna came to be equated with Vishnu, as *Goloka*, Krishna's divine realm, came to be equated with *Vaikuntha* or *Vishnuloka*. Cosmologically, Krishna is the originator of creation by this transformation. However, Vishnu, as noted in the earlier texts, is held responsible for the creation. Krishna assumed all of the qualities of Vishnu by the turn of the first millennium. While Krishna has historicity, it is important to understand that not much is known about Vishnu, Purushottama (Purusha), and Narayana, other than textual evidence. Of these three names associated with Krishna, Vishnu is most commonly referred to as the supreme deity in the *Vedas*, as well as the other classical texts of Hinduism: the *puranas* and epics. Vishnu is referred to in the *Vedas* as *vis*, a Sanskrit word meaning "to spread." Vishnu is a cosmological deity in the *Vedas*, similar to the other Vedic deities. The *Vedas* contain short, crisp accounts of the qualitative representation of the major deities and their achievements with a connection to the creation. Hence, the references to Vishnu in the *Vedas* are short, but capture the most essential features connected with him. Only six verses of the *Rigveda* depict Vishnu (*Rigveda* 1.154–156; 6.69; 7.99–100). Vishnu appears as *Vritrahan* (killer of Vritra), the one who took three strides (*Rigveda* 1.154.1,4), and as *Gopa*, a cowherd (*Rigveda* 1.22.18; 3.55.10; 1.155.4), which connects him to Krishna, a cowherd in Vraja, described in the *Harivamsa* and the other *puranas*. Vishnu is therefore connected to three of the *avataras*: Narasimha (*Vritrahan*), Vamana (dwarf with three strides), and Krishna Gopala (cowherd). These references from the *Vedas* connect Krishna to several cosmological concepts connected with Vishnu. Three strides connect him to the cosmologic spread encompassing the three worlds (*vikrama*), the cosmic pillar (*skamba*) as axis of the world, and further spread (*vis, viraj*) to pervade the entire creation. Other epithets of Vishnu such as *vyapin* and *sarvavyapin* connect him to the all-pervasive nature of Vishnu, while *vibhu* signifies his all pervading might and sovereignty. Although cryptic, the Vedic Vishnu is closely connected to the later narrative that provides extensive details about Vishnu, his *avataras*, and his role within creation. Hence, to perform his role as maintainer of the balance between good and evil, Vishnu assumes numerous forms (*murti, rupa, vapu*), first as part of *caturvyuha* (quadruple form) before creation begins, then as *trimurti* (triple form) during creation, *dasavataras* (ten incarnations) within creation, and *Vaikuntha rupa* (Vishnu with three heads—Boar and

Vishnu (the central god of devotional Hinduism) sculpture in copper alloy from Tamilnadu, dated to ca. 1300 C.E. (Los Angeles County Museum of Art)

Narasimha on each side of his head) as the cosmogonic form. Vishnu's connection with creation is important to note at every stage of its propagation, not limited to his role within creation. As such, Vishnu came to be known by different numbers of names, sometimes 108, or 1,008, which only indicates the forms and concepts associated with Vishnu rather than several independent individual deities. Vaishnavism takes note of this multifold and pervasive nature of Vishnu, as its foremost ritual of devotion consists of reciting the names of Vishnu. Repeating the names of Vishnu is a noted feature in the *Mahabharata* (13.135.14–120), and it is considered the most efficacious way of reaching Vishnu according to several Vaishnava traditions, such as Caitanya Vaishnavism and the *Varkari* tradition. Vishnu is worshipped across India in numerous temples, depicted as standing, sitting, or reclining, and as one of the ten *avataras*. Standing and reclining images of Vishnu are most common, in addition to the depiction as Krishna. Vishnu is seen with *caturbhuja* (four hands) and sometimes with eight hands (*ashtabhuja*). Vishnu holds the wheel (*cakra,* known as Sudarsana) and the conch (*sankha,* known as Pancajanya), while one hand is depicted in *abhayamudra* (gesture of protection) and another hand rests on his waist. It is also not unusual to find Vishnu depicted with a club (*gada,* known as *kaumodaki*), a sword (*khadga,* known as Nandaka), a bow (*dhanus,* known as *saranga*), and a lotus flower (*Padma*). When Vishnu is depicted in eight-handed form (*ashtabhuja*), all of the above weapons and attributes are placed in his arms. As a symbol of prosperity and lord of Laxmi (Goddess of Wealth), Vishnu is always depicted with fine jewelry made of gold and precious stones, and wearing silk garments along with other adornments.

Although numerous temples of Vishnu are found all across India, the most impressive temple of Vishnu (the Chennakesava temple) is in Somanatha, near Mysore, Karnataka, which contains four major shrines on the four sides of the temple. While the image of Kesava in the main shrine is missing, the north and south shrines host Venugopala (Krishna playing a flute), with Janardhana in the eastern shrine. The most important temple of Vishnu (Sri Venkatesvara) is in Tirupathi, Andhra Pradesh, which receives visits from approximately sixty to eighty thousand devotees daily. Other important temples of Vishnu include the Sri Ranganatha temple (Srirangam, Tamilnadu), which is the largest temple complex in India; the Jagannatha temple (Puri, Orissa); and the Anantapadmanabha temple (Trivandruam, Kerala). Many of the Vishnu temples are also identified as Krishna temples. For example, Venkatesha in Tirupathi is also called Govinda, a name for cowherd Krishna; Jagannatha of Puri is also Krishna; while Ranganatha (master of play) is an epithet of Krishna indicating his *lila* (play) in Vraja. The densest concentration of Krishna temples is found in Vraja and its surrounding cities, Brindavan and Mathura.

See also: Avatara; Jagannatha; Krishna; Panduranga Vitthala; Ranganatha; Srilaxmi; Srinathji *Haveli* Nathdvara; Vasudeva; Venkatesvara; *Vyuhas*

Further Reading

Biardeau, M. 1994. *Etudes de Mythologie Hindouoe II: Bhakti et avatara*. Paris: Ecole de Paris.

Cheuse, Alan. 2013. "Vishnu Sleeping on the Cosmic Ocean." *Antioch Review* 71 (3): 440–453.

Saindon, M. 2003. "The Buddha as the Ninth *Avatara* of the Hindu God Vishnu." *Studies in Religion—Sciences Religieuses* 32 (3): 299–309.

Slusser, M. S. 1996. "Lord Vishnu and the Kings of Nepal." *Asian Art & Culture* 9 (3): 9–29.

Soifer, D. A. 1992. *The Myths of Narasimha and Vamana: Two Avatars in Cosmological Perspective*. Delhi: Motilal Banarsidas.

Whitaker, J. L. "Divine Weapons and Tejas in the Two Indian Epics." *Indo-Iranian Journal* 43: 87–113.

VISHRAMGHAT

Vishramghat is one of the most important bathing *ghats* of the riverside in Mathura. It is covered with large ornate arches and nicely laid stairs approaching the river. Vishramghat is noted for the Yamuna *arati* performed every day early in the morning and evening in honor of the Yamuna River. It is also the focal point for the celebration of *Yamuna Chhat* and *Yam Dvitiya*. Vishramghat is referred to as Vishrantitirtha in most *Mahatmya* texts, which note it as the foremost of the *tirthas*. The Jain *purana*, *Adipurana*, by Jinaprabha Suri, written in the fourteenth century, mentions it as the most popular Hindu *tirtha*. Therefore, at least since the thirteenth century, the significance of Vishramghat has been widely acknowledged. It is said to have acquired the name of Vishramghat or Vishrantitirtha (the Sanskrit word *vishranti* as well as the Hindi word *vishram* means rest) because Krishna and Balarama rested here after killing Kamsa. The *Varahapurana* narrates another story, however, mentioning that it is so named because Krishna rested there. Early *Mahatmya* texts mention temples of deities such as Dirghavishnu, Vishrantideva, Padmanabha, Swayambhu, Keshava, Govinda, and Hari, none of which survived. The area consists of temples built from the sixteenth century onward replacing the well-known older temple ruins, which were destroyed by numerous Muslim raids; also, Hindus were not allowed to undertake repairs to their temples or build any new ones under the Muslim rule of the Delhi sultanate (1200–1556 CE). The older temples were only recovered based on the accounts of the *Mahatmya* texts, since many temples were destroyed beyond recovery. Broken images of *vyuhas* and other images, dated to as early as 200 BCE, were recovered in archeological excavations, and they are currently housed in the Government Museum of Mathura. The temples on the *ghat* that are currently visited regularly by devotees are the Krishna and Balarama temple, Muralimanohar temple, Radhadamodar temple, Yamuna temple, Languli Hanuman temple (in the alley leading to the *ghat* from *Chhata Bazar*), Narasimha temple, and a *baithak* of Vallabha. Apart from the *Mahatmya* texts and the hagiographies of *acaryas*, gurus also mention the significance of Vishramghat. Caitanya and Vallabha are said to have visited the Vishramghat first upon their arrival in Mathura.

The Vishramghat has a special significance for devotees performing Mathura *parikrama* (circumambulation), as it is the traditional starting point of the *parikrama* in Mathura. Starting from the Vishramghat, devotees proceed along the southern *ghats* on the banks of the Yamuna and walk the periphery of the old town, reaching the northern end of the Yamuna, then returning on the northern side of the river to the Vishramghat on the other side. The Yamuna River forms a nice half-circle around the old town and is marked by six *ghats* on either side. The first and last *tirthas* in this twelve-*tirtha* circle are known as the northern Kotitirtha and the southern Kotitirtha.

See also: Braj *Parikrama*; *Diwali*; Govardhan; *Janmasthan* Temple; Mathura; Yamuna

Further Reading
Entwistle, A. 1987. *Braj: Center of Krishna Pilgrimage*. Groningen: Egbert Forsten.

VISISHTADVAITA

Visishtadvaita is the principal philosophy developed by Ramanuja. Although it is similar in concept to the *advaita* of Shankara, Ramanuja goes steps ahead to establish complete nondualism between the creation and the creator (the universe and the divine). At the core of *visishtadvaita* are the concepts of *cidacidavastu* (all finite conscious and nonconscious entities) and *sarirasariribhava* (body and embodied). These two concepts offer a concrete explanation of how the created universe is one within the body of Brahma (the universal self/divine), the fundamental philosophy on which the *visishtadvaita* is based. Understanding the definition of body (*sarira*), according to Ramanuja, is important in understanding the concept of *visishtad-vaita*. In the *Sribhasya*, Ramanuja defines the body as "any substance (*dravya*) which is conscious (*cetana*), being entirely capable of controlling and supporting its own ends, and whose nature is to be solely subordinate to the being (*cetana*) and is the body (*sarira*) of that conscious being (*cetana*)" (*Sribhasya* 2.1.9). Important conclusions can be drawn from this definition of the relationship of the body and soul. According to the definition of Ramanuja noted above, the body is a substance (*dravya*), while the individual self (*jivatma*) is the controller. Thus nature (*prakriti*) constantly gives rise to material, some of which can be animated by the individual self (*jivatma*) within the cosmos. Ramanuja's commentaries explain the Vedanta religion in a theistic concept: Vishnu is both the material as well as the cause of the universe, thus the material world is within the body of God. Ramanuja, therefore, states that the relation between the divine and the individual self is like that of whole and part (*amsa-amsi-bhava*). Ramanuja's work on Vedanta firmly established theistic primacy by declaring that by following God's will the individual soul can obtain the grace of God and obtain salvation, thus leading the way for bhakti (devotion) as *prapatti* (total surrender). Ramanuja has served as an inspiration to several Vaishnava schools of thought in India as well as abroad. The Srivaishnava community is theologically, philosophically, and institutionally strengthened by the service of Ramanuja. Ramanuja developed and structuralized the daily rituals of the Srivaishnava community, as well as those of individual devotees. The Srirangam temple continues to draw from his inspiration, while the Sri Venkatesvara temple in Tirupathi, which was taken over and developed by Ramanuja, continues to grow and attract millions of visitors each year. Numerous temples for Sri Venkatesvara have been built in India and abroad.

See also: Advaita; *Alvars*; Ramanuja; Srilaxmi; Srivaishnavism

Further Reading

Barua, A. 2010. "God's Body at Work: Ramanuja and Panentheism." *International Journal of Hindu Studies* 14 (1): 1–30.

Buck, H. M., and Philip Clayton. 2010. "Pantheisms East and West." *Sophia* 49 (2): 183–191.

Lott, E. J. 1976. *God and the Universe in the Vedantic Theology of Ramanuja*. Madras: Ramanuja Research Society.

Van Buitenen, J. A. B. 1956. *Ramanuja's Vedartha Samgraha: Introduction, Critical Edition and Annotated Translation*. Pune: Deccan College Post Graduate Research Institute.

VISVARUPA

The revelation of *visvarupa* (universal form), commonly associated with Vishnu, is one of the reasons Krishna is called *Svayam Bhagavan* (*Bhagavan* himself). *Visvarupa*, the most expansive form of *Bhagavan* Vishnu, spreading beyond the Earth and the sky, has its earliest reference in the *Vedas* in the form of *Vamana* (Dwarf). This concept is most expressively associated with Krishna in the *Mahabharata* and the *Bhagavadgita*. Vishnu appears in three forms in this world, *rupa, murti,* and *avatara. Rupa* is the actual reflection of the deity that can be visualized by humans, but not an incarnation or appearance of the deity on Earth. *Rupa* is also used loosely to refer to the icons of the god in the temple or any representation. It was also used in nonreligious instances in ancient India. The modern denomination for Indian currency, the *rupee*, comes from *Rupyaka,* a denotation used to refer to coins since they are stamped with an image of the deity or a symbol of the deity. *Rupakam* denotes a dance-drama, so called because it involves the representation of divinities. *Visvarupa* is the form of Vishnu shown by Krishna, with the universe forming part of his divine body. Krishna showed his *visvarupa* to Duryodhana and Arjuna, while he showed his *caturbhuja* (with four arms) divine form to his parents, Devaki and Vasudeva, soon after his birth. Yashoda only partly saw the *visvarupa* when she asked baby Krishna to open his mouth in order to see whether he was indeed eating dirt as his brother Balarama had complained—instead of finding dirt, she found the universe along with the planet Earth in his mouth. Yashoda was shocked by this vision, but due to Krishna's *lila,* she forgot it immediately and behaved as his doting mother. Krishna revealed the *visvarupa* two times before the *Mahabharata* war. Krishna revealed his *visvarupa* to Duryodhana in the full court of Dhritarashtra in Hastinapura. Krishna was sent to the court by the Pandavas as their envoy to negotiate peace with the Kaurava side, headed by Duryodhana, Dhritarashtra's son. However, Duryodhana was not ready to negotiate peace. Instead he tried to capture Krishna, intending to imprison him. At that precise time, Krishna declared to Dhritarashtra that Duryodhana's attempt to capture an envoy was not good, and asked Dhritarashtra to restrain Duryodhana. Dhritarashtra could not stop Duryodhana. Duryodhana tried to restrain Krishna with ropes, but Krishna assumed his *visvarupa,* which shocked everyone, who did not realize the true meaning of the events, and Krishna left the court of the Kauravas unharmed. The *visvarupa* form of Krishna appeared as lightning to the people assembled in the court of the Kauravas. Krishna showed his most elaborate form of *visvarupa* (the *viratsvarupa*) to Arjuna on the battlefield of Kurukshetra. The *viratsvarupa* form could not be seen by normal human eyes; hence, even though this form was revealed in the middle of the battlefield with numerous heroes assembled for battle, no one could see it. Krishna gave Arjuna *divyacakshus* (divine eyes) to envision the *virata* form of *visvarupa.* The only other person who could visualize this form was Sanjaya, who was already endowed with *divya drishti* (divine vision), and sitting with Dhritarashtra, reported to him what was happening on the battlefield.

See also: Arjuna; *Avatara; Bhagavadgita; Mahabharata;* Pandavas; Sanjaya; Vishnu

Further Reading

Craven, R. C. 1992. "A Unique Vaikunta-Style Visnu (Narasimha-Varaha) Hindu Art and Iconography—Sculpture from the Mathura Area in the Collection of the Harn Museum of Art, University of Florida, Gainesville." *Oriental Art* 38 (3): 145–153.

Maxwell, T. S. 1983. "The Evidence for a *Visvarupa* Iconographic Tradition in Western India, 6th-Century-A.D. to 9th-Century-A.D. The Sculptural Depiction of Mahavisnu and Visnu *Visvarupa* at Samalaji." *Artibus Asiae* 44 (2–3): 213–234.

VITTHALNATH (VALLABHA SECT, 1516–1586)

Vitthalnath was the second son of Vallabha, the successor who received the seven auspicious images (*svarups*) of Krishna, which Vallabhacarya had found during his lifetime. He also inherited the right to initiate disciples with the *Brahmasambandhamantra*. Why Vitthalnath took precedence over his elder brother, Gopinath, is shrouded in mystery. Vallabha died in 1530. The records of the mysterious deaths of Vitthalnath's elder brother Gopinath and of Purushottam, his brother's son, are not clear, but traditional accounts place their deaths in the same year, either 1533 or thirty years later in 1563. Of these the date 1533 seems plausible. However, it is Vitthalnath who emerged as the sole successor of Vallabha by the middle of the sixteenth century.

Vitthalnath also had faced troubles initially from members of his own group. Krishnadas Patel, a manager in the Srinathji temple, banned Vitthalnath from the temple because of personal disputes, which were mediated later by the priest of the temple, Ramdas Cauhan, who would bring *prasad* from the temple for Vitthalnath. Krishnadas consulted the elder brother, Purushottam and told Vitthalnath that he would be allowed back into the temple only with Purushottam's permission. However, Purushottam died mysteriously, and his son Gopaldas left for Puri and disappeared mysteriously. Again Vitthalnath was the sole successor. Krishnadas and Vitthaldas reconciled later, and they both were crucial in eliminating the participation of *Gaudiya* devotees in the worship of Srinathji. The *Gaudiyas* then expanded their settlement at Radhakund in the 1540s and focused their efforts on developing their temples. Vitthalnath settled in Braj only in 1543, when he is said to have completed the circumambulation (*parikrama*) of Braj. Vitthalnath was very influential and secured followers from royalty and wealthy traders alike. He was granted six *firmans* (official grants) by Akbar for lands at Jatipura, tax-free land for such things as temple expenses. Vitthalnath is also said to have converted Durgavathi, the queen of Gondvana, and Biharmal, the king of Marwar.

Vitthalnath focused on ritual in the temples. He reformed the daily and festival rituals to include a variety of garments and adornments for the deity. He also formalized the food offerings made at different times of the day as well as for festivals. Vitthalnath organized the first *Annakut* festival (*Chappanbhog*, the fifty-four varieties of food) in 1588.

Vitthalnath had seven sons to whom he distributed the seven images. An additional image of their home deity, considered to be the most powerful image of Krishna by the followers of Vallabha, was given to his adopted son, Sri Lalji, who was told to take it to Sindh to serve the members of the Vallabha tradition there, but, since he was not a son of Vitthalanath, and therefore not a direct agnate descendant of Vallabha, his successors would have to be initiated by the direct descendants of Vallabha to obtain the authority to initiate devotees. In this way, Vitthalnath ensured the tradition of *gaddi*, a continued inheritance in the line of his sons, which continued to multiply and spread in popularity.

Vitthalnath left Braj with icons of Srinathji, worried about the impending attacks of Aurangzeb. As they were crossing the river Banas, the cart carrying the *svarups* got stuck and, taking this as the sign, they built a temple there. The place was named Nathdvara (gateway of the Lord) and became a famous pilgrimage site for followers of the Vallabha tradition, as well as Vaishnavas in general. Through this move to Nathdvara, construction of the *haveli* to establish a sacred center in Rajasthan, and through distribution of the eight auspicious images of Krishna to his successors, Vitthalnath contributed to the success and spread of the Vallabha tradition.

See also: Balarama; Braj *Parikrama*; Brindavan; *Haveli Sangit*; Vallabha; Vallabha Tradition; Vishramghat; Yashoda

Further Reading

Pal, M. K. 1978. *Temples of Rajasthan*. Alwar, Jaipur: Prakash.

Spink, W. M. 1971. *Krishna Mandala*. Ann Arbor: University of Michigan, Center for South and South East Asian Studies.

VRISHNIS

Vrishnis are considered to be a family of Yadavas, descendants of Yadu, historically connected to northwestern India. Krishna was born into the Vrishni clan, and hence he was known as Vrishneya. Historical evidence in the form of coins and inscriptions reading Varshni has been found in the Punjab, Sindh, and Rajasthan regions of western India. Early Indian texts, such as Panini's *Astadhyayi* (600 BCE) and Kautilya's *Arthasastra* (300 BCE), mention *Vrishni Ganarajya* (Vrishni Republic) as one of the tribal republics of northwestern India. Vrishni coinage depicts a composite symbol of a lion and an elephant on one side of the coins, which is recognized as a symbol of Balarama. Although there are questions about the authenticity of the connection between the clan of Krishna and the historical tribe of northwestern India, it is clear that the rulers of the tribe believed themselves to be descendants of Krishna's clan of Yadavas, as indicated by the symbols displayed on their coinage.

Krishna is also referred to as Satvata, another clan often mentioned in the *Bhagavatapurana* as one of the clans of the Yadavas.

See also: Bhagavatas; Bhakti; Devaki; Kamsa; *Pancaratra*; Vasudeva; *Vyuhas*

Further Reading

Lahiri, B. 1974. *Indigenous States of Northern India (Circa 200 B.C. to 320 A.D.)*. Calcutta: University of Calcutta.

VYUHAS

Vyuhas (emanations), also known as *Caturvyuhas* (four *vyuhas*) as the four *vyuhas* are commonly described in the classical Hindu sources, is an alternative theory of incarnation (*avatara*) known in Vaishnavism. *Vyuha* is also an incarnation, but it supports multiple incarnations of equal or similar importance existing at the same time. Any number of *vyuhas* may originate from a single ultimate divine principle, although the most well-known *vyuhas* are the four *vyuhas* Samkarsana, Vaasudeva, Aniruddha, and Pradyumna. Vaasudeva is the second *vyuha* that emanates from the primeval nothingness at the time of the origin of a new *kalpa* (age). Vaasudeva is used as an alternative name of Krishna based on his name of the *vyuha,* although the name Vaasudeva has been interpreted as a patronymic derived from the name of his father Vasudeva. However, current theories rule out the possibility of a patronymic since Vasudeva's original name was Anakadundubhi. Therefore, the name Vaasudeva may have been used as another name of Krishna to indicate his *vyuha* emanation.

As can be seen from the deities included in this list of *Caturvyuhas*, it is a family group of Krishna, with his elder brother Balarama preceding him as Samkarsana, and his son and grandson succeeding him as third and fourth emanations. Except for the first two *vyuhas,* Samkarsana Balarama and Krishna Vaasudeva, other *vyuhas* are only described in nominal cosmological roles. However, *Pancaratra* texts consistently describe the *vyuhas* as having important roles in the created world. A sculptural depiction of *vyuhas* dated to 200 BCE was found and is currently preserved by the Government of Mathura in the town of Mathura. It is a literal representation of the *vyuhas* emanating one after the other, beginning with Samkarsana Balarama. All four *vyuhas* are considered to be forms of Vishnu because of the names of the *vyuhas,* and hence they are depicted with four arms, and Vishnu is referred to by these names simultaneously (*Vishnupurana* V. 18.58). Identification of the four *vyuhas* with Vishnu here denotes only the prevalence of the *avatara* concept, according to which Vishnu incarnates in single or multiple form, as necessary, to end evil in the world. The *puranas* continue this trend of equating *vyuhas* with *avataras,* leading to the composite concept of *vyuhavataras.* The *Pancaratra* texts continue to depict *vyuhas* as individual emanations of primeval Vishnu, adding various other *vyuha* emanations such as *vibhavas.* The *Mastyapurana* describes the cosmic roles of the four *vyuhas* (*Mastyapurana* 247.46–49): Vaasudeva lives in all, Samkarsana pulls all, Pradyumna makes all dharmas exist in the world, and Aniruddha is the powerful energy that cannot be restrained.

See also: Avatara; Balarama; *Hiranyagarbha*; Krishna; Subhadra: Krishna's Sister; Vishnu

Further Reading

Couture, A. 2006. "The Emergence of a Group of Four Characters (Vasudeva, Samkarsana, Pradyumna, and Aniruddha) in the 'Harivamsa': Points for Consideration." *Journal of Indian Philosophy* 34 (6): 571–585.

Osto, D.2009. "The Supreme Array Scripture: A New Interpretation of the Title *Gandavyuha-sutra.*" *Journal of Indian Philosophy* 37 (3): 273–290.

Srinivasan, D. 1979. "Early Vaishnava Imagery: *Caturvyuha* and Variant Forms." *Archives of Asian Art* 32: 39–54.

W

WAYANG

Wayang is a form of storytelling with large shadow puppets. It is a traditional art form in the southeast Asian islands of Java, Bali, and Indonesia. Originating in south India as *Tholubommalata* (leather-puppet play), the art form was introduced into Java with the spread of Hinduism. Audiences may view shadow plays from both sides of a lighted screen: on one side of the screen one sees the actual puppets, and on the other side, their shadows. The stories generally have religious themes (Krishna is often seen in the performances related to the *Mahabharata*) but are evolving to adopt some secular and romantic stories. UNESCO (United Nations Educational, Scientific, and Cultural Organization) has recognized the Indonesian shadow play known as *Wayang Kuli* as one of the art forms representing the Masterpieces of Oral and Intangible Heritage of Humanity (MOIHH).

See also: Bhagavatapurana; *Mahabharata*; Music and Krishna; Performing Arts and Krishna

Further Reading

Becker, A. L. 1979. "Text-Building, Epistemology, and Aesthetics in the Javanese Shadow Theatre." In *The Imagination of Reality: Essays in Southeast Asian Coherence Systems*, edited by Aram Yengoyan and Alton L. Becker. Norwood, NJ: ABLEX.

Brandon, J. 1970. *On Thrones of Gold—Three Javanese Shadow Plays*. Cambridge: Harvard University Press.

Long, R. 1982. *Javanese Shadow Theatre: Movement and Characterization in Ngayogyakarta Wayang Kulit*. Ann Arbor: University of Michigan Research Press.

Ness, E. V., and S. Pawirohardjo. 1981. *Javanese Wayang Kulit*. Oxford: Oxford University Press.

Ward, K. 1987. *Javanese Shadow Plays, Javanese Selves*. Princeton: Princeton University Press.

Ward, K. 1992. *Javanese Shadow Puppets*. Oxford: Oxford University Press.

WOMEN AND KRISHNA

With the centrality of women noted in Krishna narratives, it is surprising that a specialized women's group taking inspiration from Radha or the *Gopis* has not been formed, although female saints and traditions of women's songs, *bhajans*, and arts form a major part of Krishna bhakti practice. Several female saints are revered within the Vaishnava tradition: Andal, Mirabai, Janabai, and Bahinabai; and feminine-centered devotional traditions such as the Radhavallabha, Haridasi, and

Sahajiya traditions form an important part of current devotional practice. In all the devotional traditions centered on Krishna the feminine aspect of devotion dominates as the *Gopis* are considered the model devotees of Krishna; even male devotees assume the mood of the *Gopis* to come nearer to Krishna. This nondistinction of gender, whether male or female, that dominates Krishna bhakti traditions may preclude the necessity of forming distinct, female-centered groups.

See also: Bhakti; *Gopas* and *Gopis*; Mirabai

Further Reading

Malhotra, A. 2012. "*Bhakti* and the Gendered Self: A Courtesan and a Consort in Mid Nineteenth Century Punjab." *Modern Asian Studies* 46: 1506–1539.

Y

YAKSHAGANA

Yakshagana, a mixed storytelling tradition with a narrator and several performers, originated in the twelfth century in the devotional atmosphere of the southern Andhra region of Rayalaseema. *Haridasus* and *Bhagavatakaras* contributed to the development of *Yakshagana,* a popular outdoor opera-style art form, which is similar to the *Ankiya Nat* (Assam), *Jatra* (Bengal, Orissa, and Bihar), and *Bhagavatamela* (Tamilnadu). The caste of performers known as *Jakkulu,* which is derived from the Telugu word *Yakshulu* meaning *Yakshas,* the legendary custodians of music and dance, are associated with *Yakshagana* performances in southern India.

Elaborate costumes, headgear, and musical instruments accompany the performance to create special effects. Another specialty of this art form is the innovative use of puppets in addition to the performers. Traditionally Krishna stories from the *Bhagavatapurana* and the stories from the epics *Mahabharata* and *Ramayana* form the popular subjects of the *Yakshaganas.* Folk myths and the *Sthalapuranas* are also attempted sometimes. The staging of *Yakshagana* currently extends to national and international subjects, and secular theater including Shakespeare's plays.

Krishnalila Tarangini

The *Krishnalila Tarangini* (Ocean of Krishna's Play) is a *Yakshagana* composed by Narayana Tirtha (1700s). It is considered to be the longest *Yakshagana* (dance-drama) composed in Sanskrit. Narayana Tirtha, who is associated with the Telugu Krishna devotional tradition, lived in the towns of Kuchipudi (Andhra Pradesh) and Melattur (Tamilnadu) connected with the performance traditions of the *Bhagavata.* Narayana Tirtha also taught the performance of the *Tarangams* of *Krishnalila Tarangini* to the Krishna devotees in about sixty villages in the Addanki division of Andhra Pradesh. The *Krishnalila Tarangini* contains twelve sections called *Tarangas* (waves) depicting the *lilas* of Krishna. It contains 155 *kirtanas* marked with clearly assigned *ragas* (musical notes in the Karnataka musical tradition), depending on the occasion of the *lilas* (wondrous deeds) of Krishna. Most of the *kirtanas* form the repertoire of the *Kuchipudi* dance tradition, although the entire dance-drama is also performed as a *Yakshagana.* The *Krishnalila Tarangini* is still part of performances and represents the living performance traditions of *Yakshagana* and *Kuchipudi* in southern India.

See also: Ankiya Nat; Bhagavatamela; Bhagavatapurana; Jatra; Mahabharata

Further Reading

Ashton, M. B. 2003. *Yakshagana*. New Delhi: Abhinav Publications.
Gowda, K. C. 2013. *Yaksha Siri*. Mangalore: Mangalore University Press.
Karanth, K. S. 1997. *Yakshagana*. New Delhi: Abhinav Publications.
Mandekolu, C. 2011. *Yakshagana Bhandary*. Mangalore: Mangalore University Press.
Nagaveni. 2013. *Yakshasthree*. Mangalore: Mangalore University Press.
Uppura, S. 1998. *Yakshagana and Nataka*. Mangalore: Digantha Publications.

YAMUNA

Yamuna is a goddess mentioned in the *Vedas*, but in the *puranas* she acquires importance as the sacred river in which Krishna played with the *Gopa* (cowherd) boys and frolicked with the *Gopis* (cowherd maidens). The sacred status of the river Yamuna could be understood from the traditional custom of devotees performing Braj *parikrama* (circumambulation of Braj) to first take a holy bath in the Yamuna River before embarking on their circumambulation. The Yamuna water is considered auspicious and used to anoint the main icons in the temples of the Mathura region. Water is also transported to Nathdvara for use in the service of Dvarakadhish in the *haveli* of Nathdvara.

The Yamuna River, along with the Ganga River, is the most venerated river of India, and Yamuna is the most often represented iconographical river goddess of India. The land between the Ganga and the Yamuna rivers is considered the most fertile. The river basin is known in India as the *Ganga-Yamuna doab* (the two rivers region) and is considered to be the most spiritual and sacred place on Earth. In the Hindu classical texts it is known as the *Aryavarta*. The Yamuna *arati* is performed at the *ghats* in Brindavan. Several *tirthas* (fords) and *punyaksetras* (sacred sites) are marked with temples and *ghats* (stairs) on the banks of the Yamuna River.

According to the *Vedas*, the river's name, Yamuna, derives from Yami, a twin sister of Yama, the first humans to be born to the Sun God (Surya or Vivasvat) and his wife, Samjna. However, Yamuna desired sexual union with her brother Yama, and for desiring this incestuous relationship she was cursed to be born as a river on Earth. As her brother became the lord of *Yamaloka* (hell), Yami fell to Earth and

---

Yamuna *Arati*

Yamuna *arati* is performed every day in the late evenings at Kesighat with the *Yamunashtaka* composed by Vallabha. Although Yamuna *arati* is a popular ritual, originally performed and attended by followers of the Vallabha tradition, it is now commonly performed and attended by devotees of all traditions. Yamuna *arati* is also performed at other places on the banks of the Yamuna. In a recent new phenomenon, Yamuna *arati* was performed in Agra on the banks of the Yamuna to spread awareness about water pollution.

became the river of love in the Braj region. The local tradition holds that her waters can lead one to realize Krishna.

Several stories connect the river Yamuna to Krishna and his brother Balarama. The river Yamuna appears as Kalindi Lake, and finally as Krishna's wife, Kalindi, in the Krishna narratives. When Krishna was born, Vasudeva crossed the river Yamuna to leave him with Nandagopa at Govraja. As a child, Krishna subdued and banished the serpent Kaliya, making the lake water safe for the cows and the cowherds of Brindavan. Krishna played with the *Gopis* and stole their clothes while they were taking an early morning bath in Kalindi Lake. They were performing the vow of the goddess Katyayani to obtain Krishna as their husband. He performed the round dance (*Raasalila*) with the *Gopis* on autumn nights on the banks of the Yamuna River, after which they all bathed in the Yamuna. In another very important story, Yamuna appeared as a beautiful woman one day while Krishna and Arjuna were hunting in the forest. Krishna sent Arjuna to find out more about her. When Arjuna approached her he learned that she was Kalindi, a personified form of the river Yamuna. She told Arjuna that she was born as a woman desiring marriage with Krishna. After hearing this from Arjuna, Krishna agreed to marry her and she became one of his eight principal wives. All these stories of the goddess Yamuna's connection make the riverbanks in Vraja, Brindavan, and Mathura sacred for Krishna devotees. While she had pleasant relations with Krishna, the goddess Yamuna is said to have been dragged and violated by Balarama, brother of Krishna, in a drunken rage when he returned to Vraja.

Kalindi, the personified form of the river Yamuna and the wife of Krishna, appears in a crucial role in establishing Braj as a sacred center associated with Krishna in the *Mathuramahatmya* texts of the *Varahapurana*, the *Gargasamhita*, and others after the death of Krishna. Classical texts mention that Arjuna coronated Vajranabha, great-grandson of Krishna, as the king of Mathura. Vajranabha came to meet Kalindi, one of Krishna's wives, who assisted him in identifying the locations of Krishna's *lilas* (divine play) in the Mathura mandala. With her help Vajranabha also founded temples memorializing the sacred activities of Krishna in Brindavan, Govardhan, and other towns of Mathura.

The goddess Yamuna is praised for her purifying qualities and also for helping devotees reach Krishna. As wife and lover of Krishna, Yamuna shares her divine love with devotees and helps them reach Krishna. The bluish-grey waters of the Yamuna become darker as the river reaches Braj, which is considered as a symbol of her union with Krishna. It is said that the river Yamuna acquired the dark color from Krishna. The Yamuna is also considered particularly efficacious for brothers and sisters. Brothers and sisters visit the river and take a bath in it on the fifth day after *Diwali*, which is called *Yamadvitiya* (*bhaiduj* in Hindi), an especially auspicious day for brothers and sisters to be together. It is celebrated on the next day of the Govardhan *puja/Annakut* and concludes the five-day *Diwali* festival. It is said that Yama visited his sister Yamuna on that day. Yamuna felt happy and entertained him with food and offerings, and Yama gave her presents. For this reason bathing in the Yamuna river is considered purifying and helps alleviate any fear of Yama, the lord of death. Due to the river Yamuna's connection with Yama, *tirthas* (sacred places) on the banks of the Yamuna River are considered efficacious for performing *shraddha* (death rituals) upon the death of loved ones. Yamuna's birthday (*Yamuna Jayanti*) is celebrated on the sixth day of *Caitra* (March–April). The goddess Yamuna is offered *arati* every evening on the *ghats* of the river, and she is worshipped with the devotional hymn *Yamunashtaka*, written by Vallabha.

The Yamuna River is the second most sacred river of India after the river Ganga. The goddess Yamuna's life had interesting twists and turns, finally ending with her happy marriage with Krishna. Hence she represents a more accessible goddess for devotees. Therefore devotees attend the Yamuna *arati* and celebrate the festivals of Yamuna with great enthusiasm.

See also: Balarama; *Gopas* and *Gopis*; Krishna; *Raasalila*

Further Reading

Ghosh, P. 2002. "Tales, Tanks, and Temples—The Creation of a Sacred Center in Seventeenth-Century Bengal." *Asian Folklore Studies* 61 (2): 193–222.
Stietencron, H. V. 2010 reprint. *Ganga and Yamuna: River Godesses and Their Symbolism in Indian Temples.* New Delhi: Blackswan.

YAMUNACARYA (EARLY TENTH CENTURY)

Yamunacarya, second *acarya* of the Srivaishnava tradition, is the grandson of Nathamuni, the first *acarya* of the Srivaishnava tradition. He is said to have organized *alvar* poems, setting them to music. He was the preceptor of Ramanuja, recognized as the most eminent *acarya* of Srivaishnavism. In the role of *acarya*, Yamunacarya's contribution to Srivaishnavism endures in two important areas: first, setting the ritual practice of Srivaishnavism, and second, contributing to the philosophy of Srivaishnavism through his work and that of his disciple Ramanuja.

Scant information about his childhood and early life is preserved in the tradition. Nathamuni assigned the responsibility of raising Yamunacarya to Ramamisra, to carry the responsibility of developing the Srivaishnava tradition, which was nascent at that time. A true turning point for Yamuna was visiting the temple in Srirangam with Ramamisra: he then renounced the world and took over leadership of the Srirangam temple. Yamunacarya set out to reform the temple rituals in Srivaishnava temples by having *alvar* poems sung at regular temple rituals. Yamunacarya is also credited with collecting the poems of Satakopan *alvar* (Nammalvar) and including them in temple rituals. Yamunacarya appointed his sister's son Ramanuja to succeed him as *acarya* of the Srivaishnava tradition—one of his best contributions to Srivaishnavism. Yamunacarya's philosophical contribution includes the *Siddhitraya* (the three treatises). Yamuna proposed his most important theory in *Siddhitraya*, contributing to the foundation of *visishtadvaita*, by putting the supreme Lord, Vishnu, at the center of the tradition. However, it could only be understood in relation with Srilaxmi, a feature that places *visishtadvaita* in *Pancaratra* philosophy. In his other philosophical text, the *Agamapramanya*, Yamunacarya defended the *Pancaratra* system of philosophy and ritual and connected it firmly to Srivaishnava rituals. His texts, the *Catuhsloki* and the *Stotraratna*, are important for understanding the Srivaishnava ritual and practice. Yamunacarya's commentary on the *Bhagavadgita*, the *Gitarthasangraha*, served as background for Ramanuja's text, the *Gitabhashya*, which he aptly dedicated to Yamunacarya.

Yamunacarya's legacy in the philosophy and contribution of Ramanuja is of immense significance for the Srivaishnava tradition. His ritual reform in the Srirangam temple, which is also followed in other temples of south India, is unique in synthesizing *Pancaratra*, *alvar* poems, and Vedanta. Overall, it can be said that the imprint of Yamunacarya is distinct and has had long-lasting effects on the cultural and philosophical traditions of Srivaishnavism.

See also: Alvars; Nammalvar and Madhurakavialvar; Ramanuja; Srirangam Temple; Srivashnavism

Further Reading

Dutta, R. 2007. "Texts, Tradition and Community Identity: The Srivaishnavas of South India." *Social Scientist* 35 (9–10): 22–43.

Kumar, P. P. 1997. *The Goddess Lakshmi: The Divine Consort in the South Indian Vaishnava Tradition*. Atlanta: Scholars Press.

Mesquita, R. 1988. *Y mun c rya's Samvitsiddhi: Kritische Edition. Übersetzung und Anmerkungen. Mit einem Rekonstruktionsversuch der verlorenen Abschnitte*. Vienna: Österreichischen Akademie der Wissenschaften (Veröffentlichungen der Kommission für Sprachen und Kulturen Südasiens, Heft 21).

YASHODA

Yashoda was a cowherd maiden and wife of Nandagopa, and the adopted mother of Krishna. As soon as Krishna was born, Vasudeva brought him to Govraja and exchanged him with the newly born daughter of Nandagopa and Yashoda, without Yashoda's knowledge. Hence, Yashoda raised Krishna as her own biological son with the utmost attention and care. The whole of Govraja delighted in the pranks and simple mishaps of the child Krishna. Yashoda innocently contributed to more danger than help whenever she tried to control Krishna. Once she tied Krishna to a mortar to stop him from getting in trouble, but Krishna dragged it along with him and knocked down two ashoka trees, Yamala and Arjuna, which surprised the village elders and everyone else. Yashoda regretted her action. Once, informed by Balarama that Krishna was eating dirt, Yashoda asked Krishna to open his mouth, but instead of dirt she saw the universe in his mouth. She and Arjuna were the sole mortals able to see the divine nature of Krishna. Krishna, however, made her forget what she had seen in his mouth, so, unlike Arjuna, whose description of his *visvarupa darsan* (vision of *visvarupa*) is preserved in the *Bhagavadgita*, Yashoda's vision was lost. Nevertheless, she is remembered and cherished as a loving mother by the devotees of Krishna. The bhakti traditions base their *seva* on Krishna and imagine a personal relationship with him. While most of the bhakti traditions such

Yashoda swinging baby Krishna, Madurai, India, 17th–18th-century ivory sculpture. (Los Angeles County Museum of Art)

as the Radhavallabha and Caitanya Vaishnava traditions are based on the *Brajlila* and Krishna's relationship with Radha and the *Gopis* (cowherd maidens), centered on *Madhuryabhava* (emotion of love), the Vallabha tradition places Yashoda's motherly love (*vatsalyabhava*) at the center of its practices. The principal deity of the Vallabha tradition, Srinathji (Krishna), is imagined as a nine- or ten-year-old boy living with Nanda and Yashoda. Accordingly, all the services (*sevas*) are organized around this concept. Devotees imagine and replicate the *vastalyabhava* (motherly love) of Yashoda. Therefore, Yashoda has a special place in the devotional practices of Krishna, similar to the companions of Krishna, the *Gopis*.

See also: Braj *Parikrama*; Childhood of Krishna in Brindavan; Vallabha Tradition

Further Reading

Bryant, E. 2003. *The Beautiful Legend of God.* London: Penguin.
White, C. 1970. "Krishna as Divine Child." *History of Religions* 10 (2): 156–177.

YOGAMAYA
see Maya

YOGA AND KRISHNA

Yoga has an important connection to Krishna, as intimate a connection as *lila*. Krishna redefined yoga as a mindful action, instead of mere yogic meditation or renunciation. In fact, for Krishna any type of mindful action is yoga, and he refers to every action described in the *Bhagavadgita* as yoga, and in turn the name of each chapter in the *Bhagavadgita* has *yoga* in it.

The yoga of Krishna is not singular, but multifocused, sacral, and at the same time utilitarian. As a supporter of the universe that depends on action (karma), Krishna condemned renunciation of, and complete withdrawal from, the world (*sanyasayoga*) as inferior yoga. For Krishna, the best yoga is the *karmayoga* that is performed according to one's class and status (dharma), with a view to contributing positively to the world. The only requirement of this yoga (*karmayoga*) is that the performer should not desire its fruit, but perform it without any desire (*nishkama karma*) and stay untouched by it. Krishna equates *karmayoga* with *samkhyayoga* and declares that any or all yield the same result. Performance of one is not different from the other. Several modern traditions of yoga, including the meditative and physical yoga schools of thought, are influenced by the thought and life of Krishna. Events from the life of Krishna from the *Bhagavatapurana*, and also his thoughts noted from the *Bhagavadgita* provide the source for a number of yoga traditions.

See also: Bhagavadgita; Bhagavatapurana; Mahabharata

Further Reading

Woodham, E. 2000. *Bhagavadgita: The Song Divine.* Badger, CA: Torchlight.

Glossary

Acyuta: Means "one who does not fall down," a name for Krishna or Vishnu.

Adhokshaja: Means "beyond sense of perception," one of the names of Krishna or Vishnu.

Aditi: A Sanskrit term meaning "infinity," "unending," etc. Name of a goddess, noted as the wife of Kasyapa and mother of Indra and other gods, also mentioned as the mother of the Adityas, the solar gods.

Advaita: Hindu philosophical tradition of nondualism, one of the most dominant philosophical schools of Vedanta Hinduism, founded by Sankara.

Agha: Serpent demon, a deputy of Kamsa killed by Krishna.

Ahimsa: Nonviolence.

Ajita: Means "the unconquered one." A name of Krishna.

Akam: Tamil word describing the interior world of poetry, the world of love. *Akam* poetry is common in devotional poetry.

Akbar: Mughal emperor, 1556–1605.

Akrura: An uncle and devotee of Krishna.

Alvars: Vaishnava saints of south India.

Amsa: Incarnation of a deity embodying a portion or aspect.

Andal: Female saint of south India (ninth century), believed to be an incarnation of the goddess Earth (Bhudevi).

Aniruddha: Pradyumna's son, Krishna's grandson.

Aravinda: Means lotus, a name of Krishna.

Arishta: Bull demon killed by Krishna.

Arjuna: Middle Pandava, a close cousin of Krishna.

Asrama: Denotes stages of life in Hinduism (*Brahmacarya, Grihasta, Vanaprasta,* and *Sanyasa*) as well as a hermitage. It is commonly used in modern practice to denote a monastery.

Asura: Antigods, demons. The term *asura* is added to the names of demons such as Narakasura.

Atma: Individual soul, often translated as the self.

Aurangzeb: Mughal emperor, 1658–1707. Noted for his religious intolerance and persecution of non-Muslim religions.

Avatara: An incarnation of the god Vishnu who periodically descends into the world to protect dharma according to the needs of the time and place.

Baka: Crane demon killed by Krishna.

Balarama: Brother of Krishna.

Banyan tree: Sacred tree in Hinduism.

Bhagavadgita: Central text of Hinduism, containing core concepts and philosophy of Hinduism. It was spoken by Krishna to Arjuna.

Bhagavan: Meaning one possessing *bhaga*, namely prosperity, dignity, distinction, excellence, majesty, etc. A name for God, used to represent Krishna.

Bhagavata: Worshipper of *Bhagavan* represented by Krishna or Vishnu.

Bhakta: A devotee.

Bhakti: Devotion.

Bhaktiyoga:: The yoga of devotion.

Bhima: The second Pandava, notable for killing Jarasandha, sworn enemy of Krishna.

Brahma: The universal soul, and also the name of the god of creation in Hinduism.

Brahmans: Class of the learned, associated with the priestly class.

Caitanya: Vaishnava saint, 1486–1533, also known as the founder of the Caitanya Vaishnava tradition.

Cakra: The wheel, Krishna's weapon translated as a wheel or discus.

Candidasa: A fourteenth-century poet credited with composing devotional poems for Krishna.

Canura: Wrestler who fought with Krishna.

Caturvyuhas: The four divine forms representing the ultimate deity that emerged at the beginning of creation, represented by Samkarsana (Balarama), Vaasudeva (Krishna), Pradyumna, and Aniruddha.

Damodara: Meaning one whose belly is tied, a name for Krishna.

Darsan: Seeing, indicating soulful connection between the god and the worshipper.

Daruka: Krishna's charioteer.

Dasarha: A name of Krishna, meaning "descendant of Dasarha," legendary king of the Yadava clan.

Devaki: Birth mother of Krishna.

Dharma: One of the four goals (dharma, *artha, kama, moksha*) of life according to Hinduism.

Draupadi: Wife of the five Pandavas.

Dvaita: Hindu philosophical tradition of dualism founded by Madhva; philosophical thought in Vedanta Hinduism, which influenced numerous devotional schools of Krishna.

Dvaparayuga: The third age of a *mahayuga* containing four *yugas*. Krishna lived during the last century of *Dvaparayuga*.

Dvaraka: Krishna's capital city, submerged in the ocean after his death.

Ganga: Sacred river of Hinduism, personified as the goddess Ganga.

Garuda: Mount of Vishnu.

Ghanasyama: Meaning dark as a cloud, a name of Krishna.

Ghasidas: Founder of the *Satnami* tradition, which regards singing or praying to the names of God is more central to devotional practice than worshipping the icons.

Gita: Short name for *Bhagavadgita*.

Gokula: A place near Brindavan.

Goloka: A divine realm exclusive to Krishna, especially within the theology of the Vallabha and Caitanya traditions.

Gopa: A male cowherd.

Gopi: A female cowherd.

Govardhan: Sacred hill range in Brindavan, which was lifted by the child Krishna and held up with his little finger to protect the people of Brindavan from the rains.

Govinda: "Tender of cows," one of the most popular epithets of Krishna.

Guna: Qualities.

Guru: Teacher, preceptor.

Hari: Means "one who takes away (evil or sin)." A name of Krishna.

Harivamsa: A Sanskrit text narrating the life of Krishna, also known as a supplement of the *Mahabharata*.

Itihasa: History, a term used to refer to the epic of India, the *Mahabharata* and the *Ramayana*.

Jagannatha: Literally translates as "the lord of the universe," a name associated with Krishna as the central god in the temple of Puri, Orissa.

Jambavan: Bear follower of Rama, the seventh incarnation of Vishnu, who fought Krishna, the ninth incarnation of Vishnu, when he went into Jambavan's cave in search of the *syamantaka* jewel. Realizing his error, he gave the jewel to Krishna and married his daughter Jambavati to Krishna.

Jara: Means old age in Sanskrit. Name of the hunter who shot Krishna with a poisoned arrow in his foot.

Jarasandha: King and father-in-law of Kamsa, who fought Krishna eighteen times.

Kaliya: Multiheaded snake who polluted the Kalindi lake, banished by Krishna from the lake.

Kaliyuga: The fourth and last age in a *mahayuga*, identified with the current age.

Kamsa: King of Mathura, who devoted most of his life to attempting to kill Krishna since before Krishna's birth.

Karma: Action, the second goal of life in Hinduism. Karma yoga (the yoga of action) is mentioned as equaling any other yoga by Krishna in the *Bhagavadgita*.

Kaumodaki: A divine mace presented to Krishna by Agni after the burning of the Khandava forest.

Kaustubha: A red jewel that adorns the chest of Vishnu and also Krishna; one of the fourteen jewels obtained from the milk ocean.

Kesava: Means "having beautiful hair," a name of Krishna.

Khandava: A forest given to the Pandavas as their share of the kingdom, which Krishna together with Arjuna burned as an offering to Agni.

Kritayuga: The first age of a *mahayuga*, also known as *satyayuga* and Golden Age.

Kshatriya: Class of warriors, associated with the ruling class.

Kumaras: Also known as *Sanakadi* sages. The four boy sages, and sons of Brahma, known as Sanaka, Sanandana, Sanatana, and Sanat. Legendary founders of the Nimbarka tradition.

Lakshmi: Goddess of fortune, wife of Vishnu.

Lila: Sports and pastimes of Krishna.

Madhva: Lived in Karnataka, 1238–1317; founder of *dvaita* (dualism) school of Vedanta Hinduism.

Mahabharata: Longest epic in the world; also contains the *Bhagavadgita* and narration of the legend of Krishna.

Mathura: Krishna's birthplace near Brindavan.

Maya: Illusion, personified as the goddess Maya, sister of Krishna.

Mirabai: Female saint and devotee of Krishna who lived in north India, 1498–1597.

Moksha: Liberation from worldly existence.

Mucukunda: Legendary king who incinerated Kalayavana.

Nammalvar: The last of the *alvars* of the ninth century.

Nandagopa: Cowherd and adopted father of Krishna.

Nandaka: The divine sword of Vishnu.

Naraka: Demon enemy of Krishna.

Narayana: Another name for Vishnu.

Nirguna: Without qualities, a word used to represent pure divinity without any attributes.

Padmanabha: Means lotus navel, an epithet of Vishnu.

Pancajanya: A white conch of Krishna, fashioned from the remains of the demon Pancajanya killed by Krishna.

Pandavas: Five sons of Pandu and close associates of Krishna.

Papa: Evil, also referred to as sin.

Parijata: Celestial tree with never-fading scented flowers.

Pitha: Sacred base or spot associated with a deity.

Pradyumna: Krishna's eldest son from Rukmini, one the *caturvyuhas*.

Prakriti: Nature, also representing the material world and creation.

Pralaya: Final dissolution of the world.

Prasada: "God's grace," anything that has been offered to the deity and then returned to the devotee.

Puja: Worship. Nine types of *puja* are commonly used to worship one's favorite deity.

Puranas: Classical texts of Hinduism containing history, religion, ritual, law, and traditional social life.

Purusha: The primeval man of the *Vedas*. Purushottama is used as one of the names of Krishna and also Vishnu. *Purusha* is also used to refer to *atma*, denoting self/soul or pure consciousness.

Putana: Demoness appointed by Kamsa to kill Krishna.

Raasalila: Krishna's dance with the *Gopis*.

Radha: Krishna's soul mate, an eternal consort.

Ramanuja: Philosopher and founder of the *visishtadvaita* (qualified monism) school of Vedanta Hinduism.

Rigveda: The most ancient sacred text of Hinduism. Its oldest parts are dated to 4500 BCE, while its latest parts are dated to 2000 BCE.

Rukmini: Krishna's principal wife.

Saguna: With attributes, the visualized aspect of the divinity as opposed to the abstract.

Sakhya: Friendship, one of the bhakti modes of the devotees of Krishna.

Samkarsana: Name of Balarama, and also the first *vyuha* of the *caturvyuhas*.

Samkhya: A Upanishadic philosophical thought.

Samsara: Cycle of life.

Sanskrit: The perfected language, also called the language of gods. Language of the texts, rituals, and practices of Hinduism.

Sanyasa: Renunciation, last stage of life in Hinduism.

Saraswati River: Once a large river in Punjab supporting an early civilization of India called the Indus Valley civilization, now also referred to as the Sindhu-Saraswati civilization.

Sesha: Thousand-headed serpent upon which Vishnu reclines on the milk ocean, incarnated as Balarama.

Srivatsa: A white birthmark (or a curl of fine white hair) on the chest of Vishnu, depicted as a sacred symbol resembling a cruciform flower.

Tirumal: Tamil name for Vishnu, also the name of one of the sacred centers in Andhra Pradesh, Tirumala.

Tretayuga: The second age of a *mahayuga*.

Upanishads: Vedic philosophical texts of Hinduism dated between 1500 and 1000 CE.

Vaasudeva: Patronymic of Krishna, also the name of the second *vyuha*.

Vaijayanti: A type of never-fading flower used in Krishna's garland.

Vaishnava: Related to Vishnu, commonly used to refer to the followers of Vishnu in the form of one or many of the ten incarnations. The most popular Vaishnava deities are Krishna and Rama.

Vallabha: Founder of the Vallabha tradition, also known for the revival of several sacred centers of Krishna in Braj.

Varanasi: Sacred city of Hinduism, which every Hindu is said to visit at least once in a lifetime. Also known as Kashi and Banaras.

Vasudeva: Birth father of Krishna, and a Yadava king.

Veda: Knowledge; includes the four *Vedas, Aranyakas, Brahmanas,* and Upanishads.

Vedanta: Refers to the Upanishads, the last parts of the Veda, and also serves as the philosophical basis for later Hindu philosophy and modern Hinduism.

Venkatesvara: An Andhra god, form of Vishnu, identified with Krishna.

Viraha: Separation, particularly the separation of lovers, or from one's god. *Viraha* is a central concept in numerous bhakti traditions of Krishna.

Vishnu: Vis-, the most spread divinity. He is connected with creation and also maintenance of the balance of the world.

Vitthala/Vitthoba: A Maharashtrian god, a form of Krishna.

Vraja: Also known as Braj; the greater Brindavan region.

Vrishnis: A name synonymously used with Yadavas to refer to the dynasty of Krishna, after the legendary Yadava king, Vrishni.

Yadavas: Descendants of Yadu, one of the five sons of Yayati; refers to the clan of Krishna.

Yamuna: Sacred river of Hinduism, personified as the goddess Yamuna and worshipped along with the river goddess Ganga. Kalindi, a form of Yamuna, is one of the principal wives of Krishna.

Yashoda: Cowherd woman, adopted mother of Krishna.

Yuga: Age, part of a *mahayuga*. Each *mahayuga* contains four ages.

Further Reading

Ambalal, A. 1987. *Krishna as Shrinathji: Rajasthani Paintings from Nathdvara*. Ahmedabad: Mapin.

Amodio, B. A. 1992. "The World Made of Sound, Whitehead and Pythagorean Harmonics in the Context of Veda and the Science of Mantra." *Journal of Dharma* 17 (3; Jul–Sep): 233–266.

Anderson, Joshua. 2012. "An Investigation of *Moksha* in the *Advaita Vedanta* of Shankara and Gaudapada." *Asian Philosophy* 22 (3): 275–287.

Archer, W. G. 1959. *Indian Painting in Bundi*. London: Her Majesty's Stationery Office.

Barua, Ankur. 2010. "God's Body at Work: Ramanuja and Panentheism." *International Journal of Hindu Studies* 14 (1; Apr): 1–30.

Beck, G. L. 2005. *Alternative Krishnas: Regional and Vernacular Variations on a Hindu Deity*. Albany: State University of New York Press.

Bennet, P. 1993. *The Path of Grace: Social Organization and Temple Worship in a Vaishnava Sect*. Delhi: Hindustan Publishing.

Borden, C. 1989. *Contemporary Indian Tradition: Voices on Culture, Nature, and the Challenge of Change*. Washington, DC: Smithsonian Institution.

Bryant, K. E. 1978. *Krishna: A Source Book*. Oxford: Oxford University Press.

Bryant, K. E., and Suradasa. 1978. *Poems for the Child God: Structures and Strategies in the Poetry of Surdas*. Berkeley: University of California Press.

Case, M. H. 1996. *Govindadeva: A Dialogue in Stone*. New Delhi: Indira Gandhi National Centre for the Arts.

Case, M. H. 2000. *Seeing Krishna: The Religious World of a Brahman Family in Vrindavan*. New York: Oxford University Press.

Chaple, C., and M. Tucker. 2000. *Hinduism and Ecology: The Interaction of Earth, Sky and Water*. Cambridge, MA: Harvard University Press.

Clooney, F. X., SJ. 2001. *Hindu God, Christian God: How Reason Helps Break Down the Boundaries Between Religions*. Oxford: Oxford University Press.

Dasa, A. 1996. *Evening Blossoms: The Temple Tradition of Sanjhi in Vrindavana*. New Delhi: Indira Gandhi National Centre for the Arts.

Dasa, S. N., and Bruce Martin. 2005. *Sri Bhakti Sandarbha by Jiva Gosvami*. Vol. 1–3. Vrindavana: Jiva Institute Press.

Davis, R. 1997. *Lives of Indian Images*. Princeton, NJ: Princeton University Press.

De, S. K. 1961. *The Early History of the Vaishnava Faith and Movement in Bengal*. Calcutta: Firma K. L. Mukhopadhyaya.

Dehejia, V. 2009. *The Body Adorned: Dissolving Boundaries Between Sacred and Profane in India's Art*. New York: Columbia University Press.

Desai, L. B. C. 1923. *Svarupa Darsana*. Ahmedabad: Bombay Printers.

Dimock, E. C., and K. S. Tony. 1999. *Caitanya Caritamrita of Krishnadasa Kaviraja: A Translation and Commentary*. Cambridge, MA: Cambridge University Press.

Eck, D. 1998. *Darsan: Seeing the Divine Image in India*. New York: Columbia University Press.

Entwistle, A. W. 1987. *Braj: Center of Krishna Pilgrimage*. Groningen: Egbert Forsten.

Freed, S. A., and R. S. Freed. 1998. *Hindu Festivals in a North Indian Village*. Seattle: University of Washington Press.

Ghosh, P. 2005. *Temple to Love: Architecture and Devotion in Seventeenth Century Bengal*. Bloomington: Indiana University Press.

Gokulnatha, Hariraya, Shyam Das, and Vallabha Das. 2009. *Krishna's Inner Circle: The Ashta Chap Poets*. Kota: Pratham Peeth.

Gold, A. G. 2000. *Fruitful Journeys: The Ways of Rajasthani Pilgrims*. Prospect Heights, IL: Waveland.

Gopal, L. 1989. *The Economic Life of Northern India c. AD 700–1200*. Delhi: Motilal Banarsi Dass.

Gosvami, S., and Robyne Beeche. 2001. *Celebrating Krishna*. Brindvan: Sri Caitanya Prem Sansthana.

Gray, B. 1951. *Treasures of Indian Miniatures from the Bikaner Palace Collection*. Oxford: B. Cassierer.

Growse, F. S. 1883. *Mathura: A District Memoir*. Oudh: Oudh Government Press.

Gupta, D. D. 1948. *Ashtachap aur Vallabha Sampradaya*. Allahabad: Hindi Sammelan.

Haberman, D. L. 1988. *Acting as a Way of Salvation: A Study of Raganuraga Bhakti Sadhana*. New York: Oxford University Press.

Haberman, D. L. 1994. *Journey through the Twelve Forests of Vraja: An Encounter with Krishna*. New York: Oxford University Press.

Hardy, F. 1983. *Viraha Bakti: The Early History of Krishna Devotion in South India*. Delhi: Oxford University Press.

Hardy, F. 2005. *The Religious Culture of India: Power, Love and Wisdom*. New York: Cambridge University Press.

Hawley, J. S., and Shrivatsa Gosvami. 1981. *Pilgrimage Dramas from Brindavan*. Princeton, NJ: Princeton University Press.

Horstman, M., ed. 2002. *In Favor of Govindadevji: Historical Documents Relating to a Deity of Vrindavan and Eastern Rajasthan*. New Delhi: Manohar.

Huyler, S. P. *Meeting God: Elements of Hindu Devotion*. New Haven, CT: Yale University Press.

Kapoor, O. B. L. 1977. *The Philosophy and Religion of Sri Caitanya: The Philosophical Background of the Hare Krishna Movement*. New Delhi: Munshiram Manoharlal.

Lyons, T. 2004. *The Artists of Nathdwara: The Practice of Painting in Rajasthan*. Bloomington: Indiana University Press.

Mishra, V. *Devotional Poetics of the Indian Sublime*. Albany: State University of New York Press.

Pechilis, K. *Embodiment of Bhakti*. New York: Oxford University Press.

Prasad, S. S. *The Bhagavatapurana: A Literary Study*. New Delhi: Capitol Publishing House.

Rosen, S. 2000. *The Six Gosvamis of Vrindavan*. Vrindavan: Ras Biharilal and Sons.

Rukmini, T. S. 1970. *A Critical Study of the Bhagavatapurana*. Varanasi: Chowkamba Sanskrit Series.

Sanford, A. W. *Singing Krishna: Sound Becomes Sight in Paramanand's Poetry*. Albany: State University of New York Press.

Sanyal, R., and Richard Widdess. 2004. *Dhrupad: Tradition and Performance in Indian Music Tradition*. England: Ashgate.

Sastry, A. M. 1977. *The Bhagavadgita with Commentary of Sankaracarya*. Translation. Madras: Samata Books.

Schweig, G. M. 2005. *Dance of Divine Love. India's Classic Sacred Love Story: The Rasalila of Krishna*. Princeton, NJ: Princeton University Press.

Sheridan, D. P. 1986. *The Advaitic Theism of the Bhagavatapurana*. Delhi: Motilal Banarsidass.

Shukavak, D. N. 1999. *Hindu Encounter with Modernity. Kedarnatha Datta Bhaktivinoda, Vaishnava Theologian*. Los Angeles: Sri Press.

Singer, M. *Krishna: Myths, Rites and Attitudes*. Chicago: University of Chicago Press.

Snell, R. 1991. *The Eighty-Four Hymns of Hit Harivams*. Delhi: Motilal Banarsidass.

Spink, W. *Krishna Mandala: A Devotional Theme in Indian Art*. Ann Arbor: University of Michigan.

Tagare, G. S. 1976. Trans. *The Bhagavatapurana*. Delhi: Motilal Banarsidass.

Toomey, P. M. 1994. *Food from the Mouth of Krishna: Feasts and Festivals in a North Indian Pilgrimage Centre*. Delhi: Hindustan.

Valpey, K. 2006. *Attending Krishna's Image: Caitanya Murti-Seva as Devotional Truth*. London: Routledge.

Vemsani, L. 2006. *Hindu and Jain Mythology of Balarama*. Lewiston, NY: Kingston, ON: Edwin Mellen.

Williams, R. B. 1984. *A New Face of Hinduism: The Swaminarayan Religion*. Cambridge: Cambridge University Press.

Index

Boldface page numbers indicate main entries in the encyclopedia.

About the Author

Lavanya Vemsani, award-winning scholar and professor of History specializing in Indian History and Religions, is Distinguished University Professor of History in the department of Social Sciences at Shawnee State University, Portsmouth, Ohio. She holds two doctorates in the subjects of Religious Studies from McMaster University (Hamilton, Canada) as well as in History from the University of Hyderabad (Hyderabad, India), respectively. Dr. Vemsani's research and teaching interests are varied and multifold. She researches, teaches, and publishes on subjects of ancient Indian history and religions as well as current history and religious practices of India and the Indian diaspora across the world. She is the author of *Hindu and Jain Mythology of Balarama* and a number of articles on early history and religions of India. She is currently working on two book projects, *India in World History* and *Ancient Settlement Patterns of South India*. She is the editor of *International Journal of Dharma and Hindu Studies* and associate editor of *Journal of South Asian Religious History*.